JAIL BLAZERS

JAIL BLAZERS

HOW THE PORTLAND TRAIL BLAZERS BECAME THE BAD BOYS OF BASKETBALL

KERRY EGGERS

SPORTS
PUBLISHING

Sports Publishing books may be purchased in bulk at special discounts for sales promotion, corporate gifts, fund-raising, or educational purposes. Special editions can also be created to specifications. For details, contact the Special Sales Department, Sports Publishing, 307 West 36th Street, 11th Floor, New York, NY 10018 or sportspubbooks@skyhorsepublishing.com.

Sports Publishing® is a registered trademark of Skyhorse Publishing, Inc.®, a Delaware corporation.

Visit our website at www.sportspubbooks.com.

10 9 8 7 6 5 4 3 2

Library of Congress Cataloging-in-Publication Data is available on file.

Cover design by Tom Lau
Cover photos credit: AP Images

Print ISBN: 978-1-68358-260-1
Ebook ISBN: 978-1-68358-261-8

Printed in the United States of America

To Stephanie, who held my hand, both literally and figuratively, through the entire process of writing this book. Love you, girl.

"We had nobody going to jail when I was there.
But Trail Blazer, Jail Blazer—that's a good sound."
—Bob Whitsitt

INTRODUCTION: THE COLLAPSE

"I am still stunned. . . . It was like, 'Where did the lead go?' We were up by 16 points, and it should have been over."

—Damon Stoudamire

Outside Staples Center, the weather was seasonally warm for Los Angeles in late spring.

Inside the arena, the Los Angeles Lakers were feeling the heat.

The date was June 4, 2000, and the Portland Trail Blazers were attempting to become the seventh team in NBA history to come back from a 3–1 deficit to win a playoff series.

It was Game 7 of the Western Conference Finals, a duel between what many experts believed were the best two teams in the NBA.

The Blazers were on the precipice of facilitating the Lakers' first three-game losing streak of the season. More important, they were about to write a ticket to their first NBA Finals appearance in eight years.

Portland led 71–55 late in the third quarter, with Rasheed Wallace running rampant at the offensive end, Steve Smith outplaying 21-year-old Kobe Bryant at shooting guard, and Arvydas Sabonis doing a serviceable job keeping Shaquille O'Neal in check.

In New York, broadcaster Peter Vecsey was watching in the NBC studio.

"I got on the phone and made my reservations at the RiverPlace Hotel in Portland," Vecsey says today. "Done deal."

On the visitors' bench, Brian Grant was salivating.

"I'm thinking, 'Man, we're going to the NBA Finals, and we're going to win a championship,'" the Blazers' forward says today.

Teammate Jermaine O'Neal looked into the stands, "and I noticed some of the Laker fans were leaving the building," he says today.

Another Blazer, Antonio Harvey, was sitting behind the bench.

"I'm looking at my hand, and I'm thinking there is a 100 percent possibility I'll be putting a ring on this finger on opening night next year," he says today. "We're all thinking it. You could tell by the swagger of the team at that moment. We all felt like we were heading to the Finals and that we were going to win."

In the broadcast booth in the middle echelons of Staples Center, TV analyst Mike Rice reached for his cell phone and pulled out the antenna.

"At the end of the third quarter, I was calling a friend in Indiana to make tee times," Rice says. "That's how sure I was that that team wouldn't fall apart and lose."

The final seconds ticked down in the third quarter, and the ball wound up in the hands of Lakers guard Brian Shaw at the 3-point line near the top of the circle.

"Shaw overshot it and banked it in from 3," said Bob Costas, on the TV call for NBC along with Steve Jones and Bill Walton that day.

Even with the basket, the Blazers took a 71–58 lead into the fourth quarter. After outscoring the Lakers 29–19 in the third, they were in terrific shape to win the game and the series against a Laker team that had gone 65–17 during the regular season, the best record in the league.

Behind the Portland bench, though, Joe Kleine was shaking his head.

"When Shaw hit that shot, it made me feel very uncomfortable," the Blazers' reserve center says today. "It was lucky, and we didn't need the Lakers to get lucky."

Smith restored some order by scoring on a runner on Portland's first possession of the final period for a 73–58 advantage. The Blazers' edge was 75–60 with just over 10 minutes to go. The Men in Black were still very much in charge.

But suddenly, the worm turned for the Blazers. Sabonis got his fifth foul and departed with 8:35 left. Wallace's shooting touch vanished, and it was contagious. Portland missed 13 shots in a row from the field—six by Rasheed. The Lakers used a 15–0 run to knot the score at 75–75 with four minutes to go. Staples Center was a house of pandemonium.

Wallace finally broke the drought with a drop-over layup. But the 7-foot-3 Sabonis, who had returned to the Portland lineup, drew his sixth foul and was gone with 2:44 to play. Shaq made two free throws (he had hit 8-of-12 from the charity stripe), then scored on a bank shot to give the Lakers a 79–77 lead.

At the other end, O'Neal goaltended a Wallace jumper, and it was 79–79 with 1:50 left. Bryant made a pair at the line, and Wallace missed two gifters at the other end. Kobe knocked down a long jumper, and Scottie Pippen missed a 3-pointer. Bryant drove past Pippen and tossed a lob pass to Shaq, whose one-hand flush gave the Lakers an 85–79 lead with 41.9 seconds to go.

After a timeout, Wallace bombed in a long 3 to give the Blazers life with 34.1 seconds left; when the Lakers' Ron Harper splits a pair at the line to make it 86–82, Portland was still in it. Smith drove for a layup and picked up his sixth foul on Kobe, who helped out by clanking two free throws—the Lakers missed 17 for the game. But Smith was short on a jumper at the other end. When Robert Horry sank a pair at the line for an 88–82 lead with 17.8 seconds to go, it was all but over.

The Collapse was complete. The Blazers had blown a 16-point lead over the final quarter plus four seconds, getting outscored 31–13 in the fourth quarter while missing 18 of 23 shots from the field. It was the biggest fourth-quarter comeback ever in a Game 7 in NBA playoff history.

"I have never seen one quite like that," Jackson told the media afterward. "My condolences to Portland. Also, my congratulations on a great season and a well-fought series."

In the Blazers' locker room, heads were hung. Pippen, hunting his seventh NBA title—and his first away from the Chicago Bulls stable—was inconsolable.

"It's tough to swallow," he told reporters, beginning a harsh self-appraisal.

"I'm sure it will be all summer. We can't bring that fourth quarter back. Wish we could."

Headline in *The Oregonian* the next day: "In This Macabre Horror Film, the Choke is on the Blazers."

Years later, Portland coach Mike Dunleavy would take issue with the "choke" label.

For now, he said, "I believe if we had another game, we'd win."

Unfortunately for the Blazers, it wasn't a best-of-nine series.

After exhausting his time with the media, Dunleavy said, "I'm going to go home, have a cold beer, and relax. There is no sense talking about would've, could've, and should've."

Wallace, who scored 30 points in the final game of a "could've" season, was as big a competitor as any of his teammates. But he was not about to let anyone in on his feelings.

"It's upsetting," he said, "but hey, you've got to live another day. We've got next year."

Point guard Damon Stoudamire was writing a game-by-game diary through the playoffs with me for *The Oregonian*. He observed, "It hurts. I am blown away. We all sat in that locker room in disbelief. There wasn't much anyone could say. I am searching for the right words to describe the feeling. Maybe there aren't any. We gave up a big lead, and we paid the ultimate price. I am still stunned at what happened in the fourth quarter. It was like, where did the lead go? We were up by 16 points, and it should have been over."

The Lakers advanced to the NBA Finals, where they disposed of the Indiana Pacers in six games to claim their first championship since 1991.

The Blazers headed for Portland and then, the following day, were off to an earlier-than-hoped-for summer break. The team with the NBA's largest payroll ($73,898,705) was off on a soul-searching mission. What went wrong?

It was a metaphor for an exasperating period of history in the Trail Blazers franchise. The resources made available by owner Paul Allen created an opportunity for unbridled success, and the on-court talent that swept through the city provided the possibility for multiple championships.

There are many theories on why the promise was never fulfilled.

Chapter 1

PREAMBLE TO THE RAMBLE

(1990–1996)

"I actually liked Gary. He was a nice guy, but a scary guy, too. It was the law of the jungle with him. If somebody told me, 'Gary's looking for you,' I'd hide for a month."

—Broadcaster Mike Rice, on Gary Trent

Paul Allen's first years as owner of the Portland Trail Blazers after buying the club from Los Angeles real estate developer Larry Weinberg in June 1988 for $70 million were a success.

In 1989–90, with Rick Adelman in his first full season as head coach, Portland finished the regular season 59–23 and reached the NBA Finals, losing to the Detroit Pistons in five games.

The next season, the Blazers went a league-best 63–19 and drew a bead on an NBA championship before falling in six games to the Los Angeles Lakers in the Western Conference Finals.

In 1991–92, with Hall-of-Famer Clyde Drexler enjoying the greatest season of his career, Portland was back in the NBA Finals but were vanquished again, this time in six games by Michael Jordan and the Chicago Bulls.

Those Blazers were outstanding on the court but respected off it as well. Blazermania, born during the Bill Walton championship season of 1976–77, rose to perhaps its greatest heights. Portland's home sellout streak, which began in April 1977 and wouldn't end until November 1995 after the opening of the Rose Garden, reached an NBA-record 814 games.

Drexler, Terry Porter, Jerome Kersey, Buck Williams, and Kevin Duckworth attained folk-hero status in the community and region. They were great players and good citizens, which reflected the morality of a city that valued the latter traits almost as much as the former.

In NBA cities in which there was only one of the Big Four pro sports (NFL, NBA, NHL, and MLB), there was a special connection between the team and its fans. It was especially true in the Western Conference, with cities such as San Antonio, Sacramento, Salt Lake City, and Oklahoma City.

Portland may have been unique among them. Fans from all throughout the state of Oregon and southwest Washington lived and died with the Blazers—especially when they were good, as they were in the early '90s.

After three seasons averaging nearly 60 victories, though, the Blazers went 51–31 and lost in the first round of the playoffs to San Antonio in 1992–93. Following a first-round ouster by Houston the next season, change was in the air. Geoff Petrie resigned as general manager and, a few days later, Adelman was fired as coach.

Soon, P. J. Carlesimo was in place as the new head coach. Shortly thereafter, Bob Whitsitt became Petrie's replacement, with the title of president and GM.

Carlesimo interviewed with Allen and his right-hand man, Bert Kolde, a former roommate of Allen at Washington State, who carried the title of vice chairman. In the short period between Petrie's resignation and Whitsitt's hiring, Brad Greenberg—the director of player personnel—was running the front office.

"He was the one there for management," Carlesimo says now. "Bob was still under contract in Seattle, so there would have been some tampering [if he had been involved]. Once his contract was up in Seattle, he was the GM. I never felt like Bob was not a part of the process, even though I wasn't hired by him. He reassured me from Day One that he knew what was going on and totally supported my hiring."

* * *

Allen, who made his fortune as a Microsoft co-founder, lived in the Seattle suburb of Mercer Island. As a fan and eventual season ticket-holder of the SuperSonics, Allen became familiar with Whitsitt when he served as the club's GM from 1986–1994.

As a youngster, "sports was always the No. 1 thing for me," said Bob, whether it be football, basketball, hockey, or baseball.

Basketball was his first love, and he played the sport as a freshman at Wisconsin-Stevens Point. But he was also a three-year starter as an outfielder in baseball and went out for football as a senior, winding up as a starting receiver for the NAIA school.

An anecdote illustrates Whitsitt's commitment to his passion. The wedding of his older brother, Scott, coincided with a football game that season.

"Scott tells me before the season he wants me to be in the wedding," Whitsitt said. "I tell him, 'We have a game at Oshkosh that day.' He breaks out laughing, because he doesn't think I'm even going to make the team. We make a deal—I'll miss the game unless I'm starting."

Whitsitt missed the wedding.

Whitsitt wound up in a two-year sports administration master's program at Ohio State, fulfilling the final six months as an intern with the Indiana Pacers. For Bob, it was about getting a foot in the door and learning the business from the ground up.

"I did a lot of gofer work," said Whitsitt, listing such duties as "promotions and public relations . . . eventually writing the newsletter that went to season ticket-holders."

There's an irony to that. Few who knew Whitsitt during his time with Portland years later would have guessed he'd have a background in anything dealing with how a team was viewed in the public eye. Fans and the media were way down the list of priorities.

Whitsitt eventually worked his way into doing some volunteer scouting for head coach Jack McKinney, the same man who served as assistant coach to Jack Ramsay for the 1977 NBA champion Trail Blazers. Whitsitt said he watched Larry Bird play at Indiana State and recommended him to the Pacer brass.

"A few years later, after Bird was a star with the Celtics, I'm sitting around some big-name general managers and they're all saying, 'I knew Bird would be a great one,'" Whitsitt said. "The ego was incredible. If you won't acknowledge the fact that you miss once in a while, you're not as likely to hit on the next one."

Again, an irony there. Few who believed Whitsitt was a smart executive—and there were many in that camp—felt that humility was one of his virtues.

Whitsitt called it a valuable lesson, not to get caught up in the "herd mentality."

"That's the one thing that stuck in my mind—go with what you believe," he said. "And if you lose your job, don't feel bad if you lost it, because you've made your own mistakes rather than going with the flow."

During the last of his four years with Indiana, Whitsitt moved up the rung to assistant GM, a wunderkind of sorts at age twenty-four. In 1982, he left for Kansas City to work with the Kings, first as vice president of marketing and then as assistant GM. When the franchise moved to Sacramento, he was placed in charge of setting up the entire operation on the basketball and business sides and was promised the chance to become GM once Joe Axelson retired.

But the Seattle SuperSonics beckoned, and he became a GM at age twenty-nine in 1986. In 1992, he hired George Karl as coach, and that season the Sonics won 55 games and took Phoenix to seven games in the Western Conference Finals. Seattle went a league-best 63–19 the following season, and Whitsitt was named Executive of the Year. But the Sonics were upset by No. 8 seed Denver in the first round.

Even before that shocking development, Whitsitt was clashing with owner Barry Ackerley on a number of issues. On May 25, 1994, the Sonics released Whitsitt from a contract that had three years remaining. By that time, he had already agreed to join Allen in Portland, though the deal couldn't be announced until July 1.

Soon after he accepted the Portland job, Whitsitt revealed his philosophy: "I try to be flexible. I try to stay ahead of the game in terms of never having absolutes. I tend to be more on the aggressive side. You will have more success if you're aggressive with thought and have a plan as opposed to shooting from the hip.

"I think it's important to get as many good people with you and give them as much responsibility as possible and allow them input on what's going on. You need to communicate with people around you, and with fans, too. They deserve to know why. And as long as you tell them this is why we did it, even if it didn't work out, most fans will forgive you. They'd rather you take a few rips at the plate than to never swing the bat. But they do expect you to get a few hits, too."

Soon after Whitsitt took over, Clyde Drexler decided he wanted out. The greatest player in Trail Blazer history liked Carlesimo but didn't agree with the direction the franchise was headed, and he didn't like Whitsitt. At the February 1995 trade deadline, Whitsitt sent Drexler to Houston with Tracy Murray for Otis Thorpe, the draft rights to Marcelo Nicola, and a first-round draft pick (Randolph Childress was later selected).

Before the 1995 NBA Finals, as Drexler joined with Hakeem Olajuwon to lead the Houston Rockets to the championship, Clyde the Glide spoke about what led him to want to leave Portland. "I wanted to finish my career in Portland," Drexler said then.

Drexler said his distaste was about a lack of loyalty to a number of his fellow employees. Slowly, he watched them go: Adelman, assistants John Wetzel and Jack Schalow, Geoff Petrie, assistant GM Wayne Cooper, trainer Mike Shimensky, team doctor Bob Cook, equipment manager Roger Sabrowski, and media relations director John Lashway.

"Sometimes change is good; sometimes it's bad," Drexler said. "In this case, it was bad. I saw all my friends leave, and I felt like it was time for me to leave also. I felt very uncomfortable with the organization that had treated badly my friends who had been loyal to them for so many years."

Drexler put the onus on Allen and Kolde.

"They dumped on a lot of people," Drexler said. "I go back to when Paul first bought the team [in 1988], and he told me about how quickly they made changes at Asymetrix [Allen's computer software company]. I remember him saying, 'If somebody doesn't do the job, we fire them right on the spot. Bert is the hatchet man.' They were bragging about it. And sure enough, they brought out that same mentality to the Blazers organization the moment we didn't have a very successful season. It tells you a lot about them. They get away with murder, they really do."

It also bothered Clyde that Allen, Kolde, and Whitsitt all lived in the Seattle area.

"They're running the club from Seattle," Drexler said. "I don't know how much time they're spending in Portland, but it's not the ideal situation."

Once he had asked for a trade, Clyde admittedly preferred going to Houston, his hometown. "But I wanted change so bad, I wouldn't have thought twice about going anywhere," he said. "The Nets, the Clippers—I don't care where, I'd still say yes, get me out. I have a few principles I try to adhere to. I'm not going to compromise my happiness to be part of an organization I don't agree with anymore. We were family during Rick's regime. The players were genuinely good friends with the whole staff. It's more of a business with that team now."

Drexler predicted further changes: "Terry is looking to do something. Jerome wants to get out. Buck isn't very happy."

Porter departed as a free agent after the 1994–95 season. Kersey was left exposed and was taken by Toronto in the 1995 expansion draft. Williams was the last of the old guard to go, leaving as a free agent after the 1995–96 campaign.

* * *

Carlesimo was disappointed when the Blazers traded Drexler.

"When I got there, we still had four guys who were the lynchpins of their two runs to the NBA Finals: Terry, Buck, Jerome, and Clyde," Carlesimo says now. "I remember vividly when we moved C. D. We were in Dallas for the first game after the All-Star break. Bob called me in between the first and second bus [headed for the arena]. He told me about the deal.

"I remember going to knock on Clyde's door. My first trade as the Blazers coach, and we just traded the best player in the history of the franchise. But Clyde had wanted a trade. He was pleased where he was going.

I almost have tears in my eyes, and Clyde's saying, 'Coach, I'm fine.' But I wasn't."

Carlesimo was hired on the basis of a strong 12-year run as head coach at Seton Hall, which included a berth in the NCAA finals in 1999. He had also served as an assistant on Chuck Daly's staff with the "Dream Team" that won gold in the 1992 Olympic Games at Barcelona.

P. J. had grown up in Scranton, Pennsylvania, the eldest of ten children of Pete Carlesimo, a long-time coach and administrator at the University of Scranton and later athletic director at Fordham in New York City. P. J. had never coached in the NBA before he arrived in Portland, but he hired an outstanding staff of assistants—which included the late Dick Harter, who had been a head coach with the Charlotte Hornets, and Rick Carlisle and Johnny Davis, who would later become NBA head coaches.

Today, Carlesimo describes his time in Portland as "three of the favorite years of my life."

"It was my first NBA job. That was a big change," Carlesimo says. "Other than a short spell in Europe in the '70s, it was the first time I lived away from the East Coast. Portland was really special to me for a lot of reasons, even before I came. It was a city I knew very well because of my relationship with Nike. I had good friends in the city, including [pro golfer] Peter Jacobsen. [Blazer forward] Mark Bryant had played for me [at Seton Hall], so I was coming to a city where I was really comfortable. We had an exceptional staff with Rick, Dick, and Johnny, and later Elston Turner, and Dan Burke was our video coordinator.

"The organization was incredible. Paul was a great owner. He didn't interfere. He put the money out. A lot of owners don't invest in the team. I don't recall Paul saying no too many times in my three years. He loved the draft. We would always buy a second-round pick and end up with an extra pick. He never did anything other than show up and cheer for the team. He never questioned, 'Why do we do this; why do we play this way?' He let Bob be the GM, and he let me coach."

Carlesimo was a gregarious sort, with a quick smile and a penchant for greeting people—everyone—by name.

"P. J. was awesome," says Jay Jensen, who worked 19 seasons as a trainer for the Blazers (1994–2013). "He was an unbelievably caring person. He knew everybody's name when you got into an arena. After my kids were born, he sent them US Savings bonds every birthday. He'd send me a Christmas card every year. When he got on the court, between the lines, he was extremely intense. As soon as he got done with practice, he was back to his easy-going nature. I never had any kind of issues with him.

"Our first trip was to training camp at the Olympic Training Center in Colorado Springs. It was the first time I ever had a coach stand outside and watch the bags go onto the plane to make sure they got on. He was very involved in every detail, including the food catered on the plane. He'd go over the menus and see if it was to his liking. He had his favorite restaurants he wanted to cater from when we were in a particular city. He was very involved in every part."

* * *

It became clear early during the Whitsitt regime that the character of the players was not a critical virtue. He valued talent and was willing to take chances. "I didn't major in chemistry in college," was one of his famous sayings.

"Bob was straightforward," Carlesimo says now. "We were not on the same page enough in terms of type of player. Bob always liked to take advantage of a talented player who maybe had some baggage. He'd err on the side of talent and say to me, 'That's your challenge as coach. I'm going to get you more talent, but you're going to have to handle some personalities others have had trouble with.' If he could get great talent with great attitude, sure, he loved that, too. But the emphasis was more on talent than personality or character."

* * *

Whitsitt and Carlesimo inherited one player who had some behavioral issues. Before the 1992–93 season, Geoff Petrie had signed point guard Rod Strickland as a free agent.

Strickland had two stints as a Blazer, from 1992–1996 and then, at age thirty-four, for 21 games as an ill-fated late-season addition in 2001.

"Portland was great," he says today. "I had my ups and downs, and I could have handled some things differently. I had some great times there, some good battles. Some of the best years of my career in Portland."

Jim Paxson was with the Blazers during the Carlesimo era, first as an advance scout, then as assistant general manager under Whitsitt.

"P. J. was very organized, had a certain way of doing things," Paxson says. "The Rod Stricklands of the world had trouble dealing with the regimen of that. Once P. J. stepped into that head coaching role, he changed a little bit, had certain expectations and became more rigid in how he saw the game.

"But everybody around him loved him as a person. He was one of the most generous people I've ever been around."

Strickland was an immense talent but a troubled player during his two seasons with San Antonio in 1990–91 and 1991–92. He missed 24 games his first season after breaking his hand in a fight outside a San Antonio nightclub. The next season, he sat out the first 24 games because of a contract dispute. He feuded with Coach Larry Brown and was let go into free agency after that season despite averaging 13.8 points and 8.6 assists as a 25-year-old.

"I enjoyed playing with Rod," said Sean Elliott, a sweet-shooting small forward with the Spurs during those years. "He was one of my favorite guys to play with. Rod was a great offensive player, one of the best finishers around the rim I ever saw.

"It wasn't just Rod. Everybody had issues with Larry. He was the first coach I ever talked back to. We clashed. I was his whipping boy when I was a rookie. He was constantly on me. He'd yell at me for shooting a wide-open 10-footer. But when Larry left after my third season, I was heartbroken—devastated. He taught me a lot about the game. What a great X's and O's coach."

Strickland's first two seasons in Portland were under Adelman, where he thrived. The first season (1992–93), he wound up starting with Porter in the backcourt after Drexler was injured, averaging 13.7 points and 7.2 assists.

"We had a great team, with Clyde, Terry, Buck, Cliff Robinson, Kevin Duckworth, and Mario Elie," Strickland says today. "But Clyde got hurt, and we weren't the same. We lost in the first round of the playoffs."

Strickland started the next season, and Porter moved to a bench role. Drexler was traded at midseason, and Strickland finished the season averaging 17.2 points and 9 assists, the latter figure fifth in the league.

Strickland enjoyed a great relationship with Adelman.

"Rick was the guy who got me over the top in my career," Strickland says. "He made me a well-rounded player. I remember him pulling me aside and telling me, 'I don't care how much you shoot; you just keep doing what you're doing.' That encouragement from a coach. . . . I'll never forget that."

Adelman was dismissed after the 1993–94 season.

"When Rick told me he was fired, I cried," Strickland recalls. "I got choked up. That hurt. Rick was the guy who believed in me. Even when I had my ups and downs, my incidents, he never looked at me in any different way."

Carlesimo took over, and Strickland had the two most productive seasons of his 16-year NBA career, averaging a career-high 18.9 points and 8.8 assists in 1994–95 and 18.7 points and 9.6 assists in 1995–96. Their relationship, however, was much different than it had been for Rod under Adelman.

More than twenty years later, Strickland assesses his relationship with Carlesimo in a different light than he did at the time.

"It was strained," he says today. "I want to be fair when I talk about this. Now that I've been away from this for some years, I think I have a better handle on how it was then. When P. J. and I see each other now, we are great. If me and P. J. would have been able to talk then, if both of us could have got outside our BS, we could have gotten something done. That's why Rick was so great. He just worked with me, through my faults.

"P. J. may have come in thinking he had to deal with me in a certain way. That's just my interpretation. We could have sat down and figured it out. We never did. I took a lot of things personally. He came in as a college coach. They're so used to dealing with players in a certain way in college. Pros don't want to hear that. He couldn't separate that. I was a guy who, if I thought you were BS, there's no coming back. That's a quality I wish I didn't have, but that was one of my ways. P. J. could never get past that.

"I'm one of those people, I can hold a grudge. I remember how people treat you. P. J. came in with his rah-rah college BS, screaming and cussing. But it's water under the bridge. I'm glad we're good now."

Carlesimo sees it much the same way.

"Rod and I had a stormy relationship, for sure," he says. "I'm not Rod's favorite coach, no question about that. I see him now. We've had some great sit-downs. I'm glad about that. I harbor no ill feelings. Since he has been in coaching himself, I think he gets it more now than he did then.

"Rod was not a good player, he was an excellent player. He wasn't a great practice player. Cliff Robinson was the opposite. He might go out and party at night, but he was a practice animal. I don't ever recall Cliff missing a practice or not playing 100 percent.

"Our best offense was when the shot clock would get down to five seconds and Rod had the ball. It was, 'Get out of his way.' That was our most effective play."

Strickland had begun forming an opinion on Carlesimo several years earlier when he assisted John Thompson in the 1988 Olympic trials in Denver, in which Rod competed. Strickland, who had just finished an All-America junior season at DePaul, felt slighted in some of the scrimmages and drills that Carlesimo put on.

That was exacerbated during Carlesimo's first training camp with the Blazers in 1994, ironically, at the US Olympic training center in Colorado Springs.

"The second or third day, P. J. decided he was going to ride Rod's butt," said a team official, who asked to remain anonymous. "He chewed out Rod in front of the whole team, and he never really let up. He said Rod wasn't working hard, wasn't giving his best effort. A few minutes later, he singled Rod out and chewed him out for not doing a shooting drills the way he wanted. He told Rod: 'Go sit down. We don't want you.' A few minutes later, Rod got up and went over to rebound for Terry Porter, and P. J. yelled at him again, saying, 'I don't want you rebounding for Terry. Go over there and stand by yourself.'"

Burke, then the team's video coordinator, was at the training camp.

"P. J. went off on Rod," says Burke, who has gone on to more than 20 years as an assistant coach at Indiana. "He said, 'We're going to run those sprints again. Our starting point guard isn't running hard.' I think he got advice to be tough on those guys following Rick, who was a players' coach.

"P. J. got after the guys hard. After practice, I was a driver of one of the team vans. Terry, Buck, and Clyde piled in with me. They said, 'We're going with you. There's a friendly face in here.' It all started because of Rod. Rod was one of those rebels. P. J. had that voice that sounded like he might be yelling, but he wasn't really yelling, and some guys didn't know how to handle it."

Chris Dudley played for the Blazers from 1993–1997 and again from 2001–2003. The 6-foot-11 center was with the club for all three seasons of the Carlesimo regime.

"He [Carlesimo] was Jekyll and Hyde, on and off the court," Dudley says. "Off the court, he was the nicest guy you've ever met. On the court, he started off as a yeller. For me, I just took the yelling as part of it. It was nothing personal. I was able to laugh it off and go. That got him off on the wrong foot with Rod. But P. J. knew the game very well. I have a ton of respect for him."

But there were other players who thought Carlesimo overdid it with the discipline aspect. At times, his assistants agreed.

"The first training camp, we were running suicide sprints in Colorado Springs, and Dick was raising his eyebrows and saying, 'They don't do this,'" Carlesimo says today. "But I was thinking, 'They do it some places.' We'd be on a trip, and I'd think maybe we should practice, and Dick or Johnny would say, 'Nah, they need a day off. It's more important for them to rest today.' Those guys brought a perspective to me, Rick and Johnny and later Elston, from guys who had played in the league.

"If it were another NBA coach doing the same things, a lot of that wouldn't have caused any comment [from the players]. But because I was a college coach, the players questioned it. I had a label."

Was Carlesimo too much of a disciplinarian for the NBA?

"I thought no, but there were certain things," he says now. "Dick was great. He had coached college and pro. He had the perspective of having done both. He would talk to me a lot. Looking back now, that was about as good a staff as you could get, including Rick and Johnny, who were great with players and had played in the league.

"I coached with a whistle. I'd blow the whistle a lot. Dick would say, 'Most NBA coaches don't do that.' I knew that I had to adjust, but I also knew I had to be myself."

In Portland and later at Golden State, Carlesimo felt he suffered because he succeeded Adelman as coach.

"Rick has a reputation as a players' coach," he says. "I've probably been stereotyped as too hard or pick your words. But Rick was demanding. He had discipline. They typecast coaches. You see it a lot."

Davis, a soft-spoken assistant who had been a rookie guard on the Blazers' championship team of 1977, defends Carlesimo in the issue of discipline with Strickland.

"There was a disconnect in terms of the conditioning aspect of the game that got those two sideways with one another," Davis says now. "I thought P. J. was a good coach, I really did. He was one of the most giving guys I've been around. He would give you the shirt off his back.

"That was a veteran team, and they didn't need to be prodded quite as much. They had to be told things and disciplined—all of that is necessary—but the disconnect came with the way the players were receiving the message. They got a little sideways with how P. J. delivered it to them.

"But that wasn't right. The coach has to be who he is, true to himself. The players have to understand it's not a personal thing, it's a professional thing, that allows for you to grow. P. J. was the leader of the team in terms of setting the direction and the parameters. The players have to accept the leadership. You don't have to agree with it, but you have to do what is mandated by the coach. There was some resistance to how he delivered it as opposed to the message itself."

Davis, though, was captivated by "the creativity of Rod Strickland." Nobody was better with a mid-range game attacking the basket, scoring on a floater, or setting up teammates.

"He was a natural player in the sense that he played the game with a rhythm, a cadence on the floor that was his own," says Davis, who would coach 25 years in the NBA, including head-coaching stints in Philadelphia and Orlando. "He was like a jazz maestro. He was making things happen on the floor in a creative sense. His ability to penetrate and create and his imagination in terms of finishing around the basket impressed me. He was as talented as any guard in the league, and probably should have made the All-Star Game a couple of times."

A couple of years before he arrived in Portland, Strickland had been arrested in New York and, eventually, was found guilty of battery on a former girlfriend, the mother of their child, a couple of years earlier. During his NBA career, he had multiple arrests for assault, three DUIs, an indecent exposure charge, a disorderly conduct charge, and an indictment for punching a waitress in a restaurant parking lot in Bowie, Maryland.

During his first season with Portland, Strickland also had his share of dust-ups. He and Cliff Robinson were charged with battery after an altercation with a truck driver in the parking lot of a fast-food restaurant in Chicago (they were later acquitted).

On March 31, 1995, Carlesimo kept Strickland out of the starting lineup in a game at Philadelphia because he had not flown with the team from New Jersey to Philly. Rod had spent the night in New York and had believed that was OK with P. J. He played only four minutes in the first half, got into a shouting match with the coach at halftime, and did not play in the second half of an 86–85 loss to the lowly 76ers. After the game, Strickland let his feelings out to a reporter: "I don't like him—and you can write that. I didn't like him in the beginning, and I don't like him now."

The 1994–95 Blazers were still a formidable team after the Drexler trade, with Otis Thorpe added to a nucleus that included Strickland, Cliff, James "Hollywood" Robinson, Buck Williams, Porter, Jerome Kersey, Chris Dudley, and Harvey Grant. They struggled down the stretch of the regular season, though, going 8–10 over the final 18 games to finish 44–38. They were then swept by Phoenix in the first round of the playoffs.

* * *

The Blazers went into the 1995–96 season with Porter and Kersey gone but with a talented group led by Cliff Robinson, Strickland, and Arvydas Sabonis, who had finally been signed seven years after being drafted by Portland in 1988. Strickland and Carlesimo had patched up their differences—on the surface, anyway.

Meanwhile, Carlesimo was working his way into a relationship with Whitsitt.

"He was a better GM than not," Carlesimo says. "Bob was more upfront and more direct than most people. I respect that about Bob. You knew where you stood with him. Some guys will not tell you what they're thinking. If he didn't like something or the way you were doing it, Bob would tell you."

Eleven players made starts for the 1995–96 Blazers, including 21-year-old small forward Dontonio Wingfield, who had played as a rookie for the Seattle SuperSonics the previous year and had been acquired as a free agent by Whitsitt, as well as forward Gary Trent, a bruising rookie from Ohio University.

Wingfield, who would later be convicted of assaulting two suburban Cincinnati police officers after a dispute with a girlfriend and sentenced to a year in prison, spent two seasons plus three games with Portland, then was gone at age twenty-three, never to play another NBA game.

The 6-foot-6, 250-pound Trent lasted nine seasons in the NBA but never became a full-time starter at any of his stops, including Portland, Toronto, Dallas, and Minnesota. He spent the first two and a half seasons of his career with the Blazers.

Trent survived a disturbing childhood growing up in Columbus, Ohio.

His father, Dexter, who had been a drug dealer since age fourteen, received a life sentence at age thirty-one for dealing crack. He served 6½ years. His mother, Cheryl Gunnell Trent, became addicted to drugs and did three months for aggravated drug trafficking. His grandmother was convicted of killing one of her sons. His grandfather drank himself to death. Five uncles served time. Some were mobsters and gangsters, "but they were my family, and I loved every one of them," Trent said in 1995.

At one point, Cheryl fired a .357 Magnum at Dexter while he was in the shower. She missed.

Trent briefly dropped out of high school as a freshman and began selling crack.

"My life was drugs, murder, bank robbery, kidnapping, the whole nine [yards]," Trent said then. "It was generational dysfunction. That's when you get sucked into the pitfalls and the negativity of what came before you."

For years, the Trent family lived in a middle-class Columbus suburb, living off Dexter's lucrative business. At eleven or twelve, Gary recalls his father bundling up $100 bills: "He'd stack 'em so high, the pile was taller than me or my sister. Then he'd take all his ones, wad them up in his hands, and throw them at us. Anything we caught in the air, we could keep."

Until he was caught, Dexter was piling up big money, as much as $5,000 a day. He paid cash for his house, and it wasn't unusual for the parents to spent $10,000 on their kids for Christmas. They had a nice home, cars, jewelry, and more than $100,000 tucked away in a safety deposit box. Then Dexter was arrested and sentenced to life in prison. Gary was thirteen.

After his father's arrest, the Trents went from "having everything to having nothing," his mother said in a newspaper interview. "It was hard on all of us."

They moved to a small brick apartment on notorious East Livington Street. "It was a war zone. It was terrible," said Gary.

Trent started dealing drugs at fourteen, as a ninth grader. He missed so many days at Briggs High, he was eventually kicked out. "At that point, I didn't have anything, and I figured I had to do what I had to do to live," he said in 1995. "My dad had taken care of everything. Now I had to do it for myself."

Trent started dealing on Studer Avenue.

"You find a spot where the traffic and business are flowing, and you stay there until it gets hot, until the cops start coming through," he said. "I was big for my age, and I could stand up for myself. Plus, you have $5,000 or $6,000 on you all the time—you feel like you're the man. Hey, it felt good. You felt like you were somebody. I figured if I go to jail, I've got three meals [a day] and nothing to worry about. If I get killed, well, I don't have any more problems."

Trent said he never served time nor used drugs himself. His mother said she worried about him when he was on the streets. "I prayed more than anything," she said. "I was afraid I'd lose him."

Gary visited his father in jail, "and I told him to take a long look around the visitor's room," his father said. He said, "You see all this? You see us fools in here? This is where you're going to be, if you don't get killed first."

In desperation, when Gary was fifteen, his mother sent his sister to live with a great-grandmother and shipped him to the suburbs to live with a disciplinarian aunt, Rosalyn Terrell. She pushed and prodded him to get to class on time at Hamilton Township High and gave him household chores. He was also away from the city and had no access to the drugs he'd had. "That's when I started playing basketball," he said.

Trent became a starter as a sophomore; as a senior, he averaged 32 points and 16 rebounds and shot 81 percent from the field, the latter said to be a national prep record. Major colleges recruited him, but he had only a 2.3 grade point average, and it took him several cracks at the SAT before gaining an acceptable score. With the big schools looking elsewhere by then, Trent signed with Ohio U, where he became a sensation known as the "Shaq of the MAC," a two-time Mid-American Conference Player of the Year. In the 1995 draft, Trent was taken by Milwaukee with the 11th pick and traded that night to Portland.

During his rookie season with the Blazers, Trent appraised his family situation as "a horror story that turned into a good story."

"I don't walk around like some hardcore dude who's big and tough," he said. "People think everyone who comes from a messed-up situation is a troubled child, screwed up mentally. But the situation didn't mess me up mentally. It made me stronger."

Trent's role models in his early time with Blazers would be Rasheed Wallace and J. R. Rider. That's what he said at the time, at least. Today, he strikes a different chord.

"The best thing was being able to learn from a Buck Williams, a Cliff Robinson," Trent says now. "Aaron McKie mentored me and taught me everything. I learned most of my NBA life lessons from him. Just being around him, him teaching me about doing things on the road . . . he played an instrumental role in my life."

When Trent came in, he predicted he would someday be as great as Charles Barkley or Karl Malone.

"I stand by that," he said in January of his rookie year. "But maybe I should change that to Scottie Pippen. I'm not 6-foot-9. I'm 6-foot-6 with a lot of power."

Trent was a rough-and-tumble type of player who didn't back down from anybody. Johnny Davis saw that firsthand during a "brawl" after practice one day that season at Lewis & Clark College.

"Gary and Dontonio [Wingfield] got into it," the former assistant coach says. "They were doing some construction down there, and there was a bucket full of drywall mud. I forget who threw it, but it hit one of the reporters and got him drenched with drywall mud. It was a pretty heated go-to between two really strong guys.

"But they were buddies. They went out to dinner the next night. It was just a little flare-up of ego and testosterone. Those things happened sometimes."

Longtime television analyst Mike Rice tried to keep a bit of a wide berth from Trent.

"I actually liked Gary," Rice says today. "He was a nice guy but a scary guy, too. It was the law of the jungle with him. If somebody told me, 'Gary's looking for you,' I'd hide for a month."

Trent made a good impression as a rookie after coming to camp at 260, then losing about 10 pounds. At one point, he moved into the starting lineup for 10 games, beating out Harvey Grant. But Trent suffered a non-displaced fracture of the ring finger on his right hand on March 5, missing 22 games. By the time he returned to duty, he was out of the rotation.

* * *

Arvydas Sabonis was thirty when he arrived in Portland, regarded as one of the great big men in history but beyond his prime after a pair of surgeries on his Achilles. Portland had chosen him at age twenty-one with the 24th pick in the 1986 draft, the European Player of the Year who would lead the Soviet Union to a semifinal win over the US and a gold medal at the 1988 Olympic Games in Seoul.

Bucky Buckwalter, then the Blazers' VP/basketball operations, tried to use his connections to get Sabonis past the Soviet political red tape that would bring him from the Iron Curtain to the NBA but to no avail.

Sabonis could run like a deer during the '80s, when he weighed in the 250-pound range. His predecessor as a great Portland center, Bill Walton, first laid eyes on Sabonis during the European Championships at age nineteen in 1984.

"He probably had a quadruple-double at halftime, and his coach, Alexander Gomelsky, didn't even start him in the second half," Walton told Grantland.com. "You might as well just rewrite the rules of basketball after watching him play in the first half. He could do everything. He had the skills of Larry Bird and Pete Maravich. He had the athleticism of Kareem [Abdul-Jabbar], and he could shoot the 3-point shot. He could pass, run the floor, dribble. We should have carried out a plan in the early 1980s to kidnap him and bring him back right then."

Finally, in 1995, Sabonis met with Whitsitt for dinner in Spain, where he had been playing professionally for three seasons.

"[Whitsitt] said if I didn't come now, I wouldn't get to come ever, that I wouldn't get to feel what is the NBA," Sabonis told Grantland. "It was the last bullet, you know?"

Whitsitt asked team doctor Bob Cook to take a look at X-rays of Sabonis's injury-ravaged feet/ankles before he arrived.

"He said Arvydas could qualify for a handicapped parking spot based on the X-rays alone," Whitsitt told Grantland.

By the time he got to Portland, Sabonis had weighed about 295. He played seven seasons with the Blazers, sitting out the 2001–02 campaign and returning for a final season in 2002–03. By that time, he was about 310 pounds and still a force to be reckoned with.

Jim Paxson, the Blazers' assistant GM from 1995–1998, had "a unique relationship" with Sabonis.

"When we were bringing him over [from Europe], Bob put me in charge of getting Arvydas and his family settled in Portland, in every aspect," Paxson says today. "We developed a close relationship. He would invite me to dinner when he had family in from out of town.

"As a player, even though he was limited physically by the time he got to America, I believe he's a Top-20 player in the history of the game. His ability to pass, to shoot, to do all the things big men in today's game—he was doing all those things in the late '80s and '90s. When we had him [from 1995–2003], he didn't have the athleticism anymore, but he had a great feel for the game, and he really cared about winning.

"I have a high opinion of Arvydas. He was a really valuable player, a great guy, very generous. He was funny. He enjoyed his teammates, and they really liked him. He was smart. When Domantas [now with the Indiana Pacers] was born in Portland, he said, 'Now I have an American son.' He was really proud his son was born in America."

Carlesimo had Sabonis for the coach's final two seasons in Portland.

"The first time I met Arvydas was in his room when he and Sarunas [Marciulionis] were roommates at the European Championships in about 1989," says Carlesimo, who was then the head coach at Seton Hall. "I was scouting them, but mostly Sarunas. In his twenties, Arvydas was the best player outside the NBA in the world by far. He'd have been Top-10 even with the guys in the NBA. People have no idea how well he ran and jumped and how much less he weighed when he was in his prime.

"I loved coaching Arvydas. He was nowhere near physically what he had been before his leg problems. But with us, the skill level was still very good, the way he shot and passed. He didn't stop [Shaquille O'Neal], but we more than anybody could play him one-on-one. Shaq couldn't move [Sabonis] like he could the other guys. Nobody could play Shaq physically the way Arvydas could. He was an unbelievable passer. It was hard for him to do 82 games, but he was one of my favorite players I ever coached."

Mike Dunleavy had Sabonis for all four of his seasons as the Blazers' head coach.

"He was a pleasure to coach," Dunleavy says. "A real winner. The nights he had a favorable matchup, you knew he would come through. He'd get 30 that night. If a guy couldn't guard him, we'd get him the ball, and he'd deliver. He virtually won you the games you're supposed to win on those nights."

Sean Elliott had played against Sabonis in the 1986 World Championships in Spain.

"I saw him in his prime," says the former San Antonio forward. "If Sabonis had come over when he first got drafted and NBA fans had seen him, he'd be considered one of the greatest big men of all time. He was David Robinson with a 3-point shot and a better passer. Sabonis went over Charles Smith and David for one of the best dunks I've ever seen. He threw it down, and our jaws collectively dropped.

"When he was in the NBA, he was 300 pounds. I saw him at 250. He could run and jump as high as anybody. He shot the three like Jack Sikma and passed the ball like Bill Walton. Had he come to Portland earlier, [the Blazers] would have had a great shot at winning multiple titles."

Johnny Davis is the only person to have played with Bill Walton and coached Arvydas Sabonis. Davis was a rookie guard on the 1977 NBA champion Blazers and an assistant coach for Sabonis' first two seasons in Portland two decades later.

"Arvydas was no longer in his prime, but you could clearly see this guy was a very special talent," Davis says. "He was still very effective, even though his athleticism had diminished. I liked his intellectual approach to playing, the way he saw the game. His vision of the game was so much keener than what you normally find. That stood out to me. I referenced it to the way Bill Walton played. He had a different way of looking at the game as well.

"With both of them, you had to understand how the game should be played. If you couldn't get to where they were at in that regard, you couldn't play with them. They made good players better because they had a different way of looking at the game. Guys who didn't understand how to play with others on the floor would have a hard time playing with them. They didn't play isolation basketball; they played team basketball, inclusive basketball.

"It was interesting to see how closely matched Arvydas was from an intellectual standpoint with Bill. They could dominate a game without just scoring. They're two of the best passing big men in the history of basketball. I can't think of anybody who passed the ball from the center position as well as Bill or Arvydas. Portland had perhaps the two best passing centers of all time."

Brian Grant, who was with the Blazers from 1997–2000, had seen film of Sabonis in his prime.

"Because of his injury, by the time he got to us, he had to adapt his game," Grant says. "That's the real talent. Now his whole thing was making crazy passes, shooting threes. It was whatever he could make his body do at that point in the career, with his foot killing him. He'd come out of the shower after a game limping. I'm glad I got a chance to play with that Sabonis. The young one was really good, but he was something special when he was here."

Bob Medina, who would come on as the Blazers' strength and conditioning coach in 1997, taught Sabonis how to play cribbage.

"It was an interesting dynamic with Arvydas," Medina says now. "He was such a different guy from all the other players. When you go to a team meal, there are six or seven tables with eight or nine chairs at each table. Coaches usually sit at one table and the players at another one. I noticed early on that Sabonis would always sit by himself. I thought that was strange. He always sat by himself on the plane, too. It hurt my heart a little bit.

"One day at breakfast, I sat down with him. He looked surprised. We started talking. I knew I had to invest in him. I learned some words in his

[Lithuanian] language. I would sit on the plane with him, and we'd played cards. We played cribbage on all of our flights. He picked it up pretty quick. I learned a lot from him, too."

Sabonis hadn't spent much time in the weight room until he joined the Blazers.

"My biggest thing was to try to keep him healthy," Medina says. "There were things I couldn't do with him that I could do with younger players, but I tried to plug into him as much as I could."

Grant laughs at the memories of his time with the Lithuanian lug.

"People don't know how funny Sabonis was," Grant says. "He had his act down pat. 'I don't know English that well.' I started talking to him, and he started talking to me, like, 'That guy is an asshole.' And I'm thinking, 'So the guy *does* know some English.'

"If he liked you, he'd talk to you behind the scenes. Once we were on a trip to New Jersey, and he goes, 'You go to dinner with me tonight.' I went out with him. Applebees or something. Sarunas Marciulonis was there, too. We're going to drink. He pulls the vodka out and sets up shots. He slaps me across the face. I say, 'What's wrong with you?' He says, 'Always look me in the eye [during a toast]—always.' I started laughing. It was quite a night. All I remember is his buddies carrying me out of there."

* * *

Sabonis wound up coming off the bench most of that season. The usual starting lineup was Strickland and Aaron McKie at guard, Dudley at center, and Cliff Robinson and Harvey Grant at forward. The rookie Trent, the veteran Buck Williams, and James "Hollywood" Robinson were the others in the normal rotation.

It was not a good mix. Strickland's feud with Carlesimo continued to simmer, though the point guard played well. The Blazers had a six-game losing streak prior to Christmas. During that stretch, Cliff Robinson failed to show up for shootaround and sat out the first quarter of a 112–100 home-court loss to Washington. That was Carlesimo's routine for any insubordinate act.

Strickland showed up 45 minutes late for a Christmas Eve practice and 30 minutes late for a New Year's Day practice. P. J. benched him for the first quarter of the ensuing game both times. The second time, Strickland still had 22 points and eight assists in a 101–92 victory over the Knicks.

Then it happened again a week later, Strickland sitting for the first quarter of a 90–89 win over the Heat at the Rose Garden. The next day, Strickland was late for practice *again*, but Carlesimo told the media he wouldn't sit him this time because Rod said he had a flat tire. Later, team officials said Strickland didn't participate in the workout because he had a swollen knuckle on his left hand. No explanation was offered for how that might have happened.

Bob Whitsitt let Carlesimo handle any sanctions on his own. To the media, Whitsitt wouldn't even acknowledge them.

"Nobody plays the whole game," he said one time. "There were times [in Seattle] when Shawn Kemp and Gary Payton didn't start, and they're All-Stars. Who said it was a punishment?"

In February, the Robinsons had a post-practice brawl. Nobody was seriously hurt, and the players were fined but not suspended.

"You have two emotional people," Cliff told reporters. "It just escalated past what we even could have expected. We're fine. We talked about it, and we apologized to each other."

The day before the trade deadline, Strickland was smacked with $3,100 in fines for missing mandatory weight-lifting sessions during the season.

That night, he asked a reporter, "Any trade rumors? Me for J. R. Rider? Whatever. They'd better get rid of me," he said, or his relationship with P. J. could get "very ugly."

As the trade deadline passed and he remained with the Blazers, Strickland, angered that they hadn't honored his request to be traded, went AWOL. The Blazers responded by suspending him indefinitely without pay. At the time, Strickland was Portland's No. 2 scorer (19.3) and ranked third in the league in assists (9.5).

During his absence, Carlesimo was asked about not having his point guard.

"I'd hoped Rod would be here," he said, "but I'm not doing a play-by-play on what we're trying to do to work this out. I think I can get along with anybody. Why? Because that's my job."

During this time, Whitsitt was nowhere to be seen, evidently staying at his Seattle home. Some felt the GM was letting the coach twist in the wind, including *Oregonian* columnist Dwight Jaynes, who wrote about Whitsitt, "He's an admiral trying to lead a fleet from his bathtub."

The suspension cost Strickland $166,830 since he missed six games before returning. He finally showed up to practice and pledged to play the rest of the season, telling the media, "I don't regret anything I've done."

Carlesimo always seemed baffled by Rod's attitude toward him and didn't seem to understand its extent.

"Until these last few weeks, I thought we had a more productive relationship over the past year," P. J. said at the time. "Was there a huge difference? No. But we had talked about the need to work together as efficiently as we could. This is not to say that he doesn't have some reasons that are very valid in his mind, but at this point, I can't say I have a clear sense of what those reasons are."

* * *

With Strickland back in the fold, the Blazers began to win—and win big.

After a March 5 loss at home to the Rockets, Portland held a 26–34 record and was reeling. For the final six weeks of the regular season, they were the hottest team in the NBA, going 18–4 to finish at 44–38. Sabonis and Dudley were an outstanding tag team in the pivot, Sabonis at the offensive end and Dudley rebounding and playing defense. Strickland and Robinson had big nights. (Strickland finished the season averaging 18.7 points and ranked fourth in the NBA with 9.6 assists, while Robinson averaged 21.1 points.) It seemed to be all coming together.

Portland finished as the No. 6 seed in the West, earning a first-round playoff date with No. 3 seed Utah, which finished 55–27. Even with Karl Malone and John Stockton leading the Jazz, many national pundits felt the Blazers would win the series in an upset.

Utah won the first two games at home. Portland came back to win two highly contested games at the Rose Garden, including a 94–91 overtime thriller in Game 3.

The Blazers flew to Salt Lake City for the decider in a best-of-five series. It turned out to be a debacle as the Jazz rolled, 102–64. The Blazers set an NBA playoff record for fewest points in a half (24) and for a game and established a franchise low for shooting percentage in a playoff game (.329). They were outrebounded 54–33. They scored 12 points in the first quarter, 12 in the second, and 14 in the third. With nine minutes left, Utah led 74–41.

"If you'd told me this morning this game was going to end up like this, I'd have had a heart attack," Utah coach Jerry Sloan said. "I'm not going to say our defense was that great. They missed a lot of shots. If they make some of them, it's a different game."

More than two decades later, Carlesimo calls it "the worst Game 5 (in a five-game series) in history. From Jump Street, it was a massacre."

Sabonis had 14 points and 8 rebounds, but none of the other Blazers played well. Strickland shot 5-for-16 from the field, didn't get to the foul line, and couldn't stop Stockton, who scored 21 on 7-for-11 shooting.

"The most embarrassing moment of my career," Strickland said afterward. "After this game, we deserve any criticism we get."

It may be that some of the Portland players—including Strickland— didn't even want to get to a Game 5.

There were four days before Games 4 and 5. The night before they left for Salt Lake City, several of the players had partied late. Strickland was more than a half-hour late for the flight. Whitsitt wouldn't let the plane leave without the point guard. Strickland finally got there but was still hung over and couldn't take part in a shootaround that afternoon.

When they departed Portland, the Blazers had been ordered to pack for several days. If they were to win Game 5, they would head straight to San Antonio for the opener of the Western Conference Finals. Several of the players had purchased plane tickets to tropical sites such as the Bahamas the day after Game 4 and were pissed off they had to go to Salt Lake City instead.

After Game 5, Strickland reiterated his desire to be traded.

"I've got one foot out the door and one foot on a banana peel," he quipped. "I just think it's time for a change. I doubt if I'll be back. I think I'm pretty much out."

Strickland was correct. Big changes were in the offing. Soon, the leadership of the team would be held by such players as J. R. Rider and Rasheed Wallace.

Chapter 2

SO LONG, P. J.

(1996–1997)

"Some guys are calm, cool, and collected. Other guys are full of rage. It's just competitiveness, and I'm a competitive person."

—Rasheed Wallace

The last of the nucleus of the great teams of the early '90s departed in the summer of 1996 when the Blazers opted not to exercise a $3.4-million option and let veteran Buck Williams become a free agent. The veteran power forward, 36, signed with the New York Knicks for three years and $4.1 million. It left only Cliff Robinson, who had been the sixth man on those teams, on the Portland roster.

On July 15, Portland sent Rod Strickland and Harvey Grant to Washington for Rasheed Wallace and Mitchell Butler.

Today, Williams is a real estate investor in Maryland and has a wistful feeling as he looks back on his seven seasons in a Blazer uniform.

"When I left, I could sense the direction the organization was heading, with the players Whitsitt started bringing in," Williams says. "I knew at some point the whole complexion of the team would change from the original way. If you look just at talent, you miss the whole picture. You have to have a [general manager] who has a feel for people, a feel for the history of the team. When you get too far into the talent, that's when you find yourself in a position of decline.

"My last couple of years there, Portland put talent above character, and it was win at all costs. It was a learning experience for Paul and his management team. Especially in the playoffs, you win games with character and chemistry."

The 6-foot-11 Wallace was an immense talent who was ahead of his time, as a big man with shooting range that extended to the 3-point line, along with the requisite post-up skills. He was also all scowl and howl on the court, a raving maniac at times, ranting at officials. Fans were wise to stay on volcanic-ash alert; Mount Sheed could erupt at any time.

Rasheed grew up in Philadelphia, the youngest of three sons of Jackie Wallace, a social services employee of the state of Pennsylvania. He hardly knew his father.

"My dad wasn't around much," Wallace said in an interview not long after he arrived in Portland. "It was a hard fight for my mom."

Jackie had help from her father, James Williams, the family patriarch and the primary male role model for Rasheed, his brothers, and cousins.

"Our grandfather raised us all," said Rasheed's cousin, Joe Watson, who followed Rasheed to Portland in 1996 to become the player's business manager and director of his foundation. "Our mother was both a mother and a father figure, and our grandfather was the overseer. When it came to discipline, he was there."

Wallace started playing basketball at age twelve, tagging along with older brothers Muhammad and Malcolm. The two oldest boys were given Muslim names because their father was of that faith. Rasheed's father, a different man, was not Muslim, "but I couldn't have a Muhammad, a Malcolm, and a Fred," his mother quipped.

As a 6-foot-7 freshman, Wallace started on a Simon Gratz team—with future Trail Blazer guard Aaron McKie—that won the Public League city championship. By his senior year, he was hailed by many as one of the city's best NBA prospects ever.

"It took 35 years to find a Wilt Chamberlain and 35 more to find a Rasheed Wallace," Simon Gratz coach Bill Ellerbee said.

Wallace's temper often got the best of him, though at one point he thought he had the problem licked.

"Last year, if I made a mistake or my team made a mistake, I would get mad and start yelling," he said during a newspaper interview before his senior season. "I have calmed down. Now I say to my teammates, 'Let's get back on D.'"

Wallace had two successful seasons at North Carolina under Dean Smith before leaving to be taken by Washington with the fourth pick in the 1995 draft. The Bullets' general manager was John Nash, who would reunite years later with Wallace in Portland.

By now 6-foot-10 but a skinny 225 pounds, Wallace ranked 12th in scoring (11.7) and 8th in rebounds (4.7) among NBA rookies before breaking his left thumb and missing the season's final 15 games. He also picked up 22 technical fouls, good enough for 5th in the league. That was after a tumultuous preseason in which he was whistled for eight Ts in eight games, was fined for being late for practice, and threw a ball at Chicago's Luc Longley after Longley and teammate Chris Webber exchanged words.

In his regular-season debut in his hometown of Philadelphia, he sulked on the bench after sustaining a T. When assistant coach Derek Smith tried to approach him, he said, "Get the fuck out of here, Derek."

But Wallace didn't consider it a problem.

"Emotion is part of my game," he said during his rookie season. "I'm not out there to impress nobody."

Wallace had also been having domestic issues.

In April 1996, he was charged with misdemeanor assault after being accused of choking Chiquita Bryant, his former girlfriend and the mother of his child, while visiting her and his baby boy on Easter weekend. Prosecution was deferred when Wallace apologized in court and agreed to perform 50 hours of community service and seek counseling.

In June 1996, he was sued by a North Carolina daycare center after he was accused of cursing at Bryant, blocking her car, and not allowing other parents to enter or exit. Charges of criminal assault were eventually dropped.

Agent Bill Strickland said it was simply a case of the ex-girlfriend being jealous of his current one, Fatima Sanders, and Rasheed trying to be a responsible father.

At the press conference announcing the trade, Wallace said he would benefit from the change of scenery.

"I see it as a positive thing," he said. "I can't come in here with the attitude that I don't want to be here; I can't dog Portland. Right now, I'm trying to impress my bosses, and come training camp, I want to impress them some more."

Wallace was asked about his problem with referees as a rookie.

"That was mainly from determination and the will to win," he said. "Some guys are calm, cool, and collected. Other guys are full of rage. It's just competitiveness, and I'm a competitive person. Every once in a while, I will admit I'm wrong. On some occasions when I got the technicals, I wasn't wrong. It was just the competitive nature coming out in me."

But his behavior, he said, "is definitely under control. I'm just going to sit back and play."

Whitsitt said he hoped it wouldn't be a problem.

"There's nothing wrong with being an emotional player," Whitsitt said. "He just needs to learn to control those things better."

By the time he came to the Blazers, Wallace had two sons of his own, plus a third belonging to his fiancée, Fatima.

"I am just trying to be there for them so they won't have to go through what I went through, missing my dad when I was younger," Wallace said at the time.

But, Wallace added, "I can't complain about my childhood. I had my friends, my family, my mom. I don't wish I could change things."

During his time in Portland, he and Fatima would sponsor a drive that reaped Christmas ornaments for needy families, and he also continued a coat drive to help clothe Philadelphians during the cold winters. He would host free summer basketball camps for youths in both Philadelphia and Portland as well.

After the trade to Portland was announced, his mother told the *Philadelphia Daily News*, "I guess I'm going to have to move to Portland. I don't want my child all the way out there by himself. Portland? Doggone, give me a break. I'd rather live in California or Miami."

Rasheed, of course, had his soon-to-be wife and children with him in Portland. His mother never moved out, though she visited often.

* * *

The day after the Strickland-Wallace trade, the Blazers came to terms on a seven-year, $46.7-million contract with free-agent point guard Kenny Anderson. The 6 foot, 170-pound Anderson, 26, had been traded by New Jersey to Charlotte in January after turning down a six-year, $42-million extension offer from the Nets. He had become a star with New Jersey in his 4½ seasons there, making the All-Star Game during his third season in 1993–94, a season in which he averaged 18.8 points and 9.6 assists.

Anderson was one of four children raised by Joan Anderson in the New York City projects. She worked as a barmaid to pay the bills.

Anderson had been a high school legend at Archbishop Molloy High in Queens and was named Gatorade National Player of the Year as a senior. Carlesimo first learned of Anderson when he was in eighth grade and later tried to recruit him while at Seton Hall. Anderson wound up at Georgia Tech, where he spent two seasons and teamed with Dennis Scott to lead the Yellow Jackets to the Final Four as a freshman, then averaged 26 points as a sophomore.

"This is a great opportunity for him, a chance to start all over and make it go whichever way he wants it to go," Carlesimo said at the time of the signing. "I don't think his last year in New Jersey or his time in Charlotte are the happiest years for him. I'm not saying it was terrible or embarrassing, but it wasn't the way he wanted it to be."

Portland assistant coach Rick Carlisle had been an assistant in New Jersey during Anderson's first three years in the league.

"We always felt as a staff that as good as he was in the East, he'd be even better in the West because it's a faster-paced game," Carlisle said. "The East is more grind-it-out. The style out here is tailor-made for him."

There was one major difference between Anderson and Strickland: the former got along well with Carlesimo.

Today, Anderson speaks fondly of playing for Carlesimo in Portland.

"My high school coach was a disciplinarian, too," he says. "The way P. J. communicated was a lot different than players were used to after they got to the NBA, but I had no problems with it. Certain players react to things differently. I thought he was a good coach. I had a lot of respect for him."

A week later, Whitsitt made another move, sending James "Hollywood" Robinson, Bill Curley, and a future first-round pick to Minnesota for Isaiah "J. R." Rider. The Blazers absorbed the $17 million in salary owed to Rider over the next four years.

Rider, a 6-foot-5, 225-pound shooting guard who had played at Nevada-Las Vegas, was a talented but controversial and troubled player during his first three NBA seasons, all with the Timberwolves. He averaged 16.6 points while making the NBA All-Rookie team in 1993–94, also winning the slam-dunk contest during All-Star Weekend with what he billed as the "East Bay Funk Dunk." Rider averaged 20.4 points in 1994–95 and 19.6 in 1995–96, leading the Timberwolves in scoring in each of his three seasons.

Rider grew up in a large housing complex in Alameda, California, a suburb of Oakland and one of the roughest parts of town. His mother, Donna, was a domestic violence victim who sought a restraining order in 1976 against her husband, Isaiah Rider Sr. They divorced in 1987.

J. R. was Encinal High's top scorer as a junior but was ruled academically ineligible to play as a senior. He failed to graduate from Encinal but got his GED and then received a scholarship to play at Allen County JC in Iola, Kansas. During his six months there, he was charged with felony burglary for stealing a gold ring owned by another athlete at the school, Anthony Shaw.

According to reports in the *Minneapolis Star-Tribune*, Shaw said he saw Rider wearing the ring and confronted him. "J. R. smiled at me, took the ring off his finger, put it in his pocket, and said, 'I don't have no ring on me,'" Shaw told the *Star-Tribune*. "I never got it back."

Another person who saw Rider wearing the ring confronted him, too. According to reports, Rider punched him in the face and pleaded no contest to a battery charge. He was given a $201 fine, a 30-day stayed jail sentence, and six months' probation.

The next fall, Rider enrolled at Antelope Valley JC, located north of Los Angeles. The coach was Newton Chelette, a former assistant to UNLV's Jerry Tarkanian. Tarkanian's son, George, was an assistant coach. Rider averaged 33 points a game that season before signing with the senior Tarkanian and the Rebels.

In his first season at UNLV, Rider led the Rebels to a 26–2 record and a No. 7 ranking in the final AP poll. However, they were barred from appearing on national television and the NCAA Tournament because of recruiting infractions that season.

During his senior year, Rider averaged 29.1 points and was named Big West Conference Player of the Year, but the Rebels failed to make the NCAA Tournament. They played in the NIT, but Rider was prohibited from participating due to academic issues surrounding allegations that a tutor had done some of his classwork. A teacher at Southern Nevada JC also came forward and said that two years earlier, UNLV officials pressured her into giving Rider a passing grade in a correspondence course. His first name was spelled incorrectly on at least three papers he turned in. The passing grade gave him the minimum course units required by NCAA rules.

During his time at UNLV, Rider was charged with obstructing a police officer during a dispute at a fast-food drive-through window.

Even so, Minnesota took him with the fifth pick of the 1993 draft. At the time, Rider decided he wanted to go by "Isaiah," explaining, "now that I'm more business-like, more professional-like, I like Isaiah." But for most of his NBA career, coaches and teammates would refer to him as "J. R."

That summer, California police stopped him twice in two days and issued him a ticket for driving with a suspended license. A few weeks later, he was stopped again. In case of emergency, police asked, who should be called? "Ghostbusters," he cracked. He was arrested and released after posting $5,000 bail.

Rider signed a seven-year, $26.5-million contract with the Timberwolves in October 1993, then showed up late for his first practice. He missed several practices that first season. In an interview with the *Star-Tribune*, he explained, "I'm a pretty smart guy. I know right from wrong. It's just that, sometimes, I'm late. Or I'm lazy."

As a rookie with Minnesota, Rider kicked a woman employee in the back during an appearance at the Mall of America and pleaded guilty to fifth-degree assault. He later settled with the woman for more than $100,000 after she filed a civil suit. He received a sentence of two years' probation, community service, and anger counseling. He spent four days in the Hennepin County workhouse for failing to complete the counseling program.

In his second season with the Wolves, Rider piled up almost $100,000 in fines and lost salary for missing flights and practices while feuding with coach Bill Blair. Once, when a *Star-Tribune* reporter asked him about a missed flight, he allegedly told the writer, "I know people who can take you out."

During his last season in Minneapolis, Rider was ejected from a game after a run-in with referee Ken Mauer. He was finally shooed off the Target Center floor by his mother. He also missed a team flight to Washington.

During the offseason after the 1995–96 season, before he was traded to Portland, Rider had three arrests in less than two months in his hometown.

In May, a 20-year-old Nevada woman accused Rider and a friend of drugging and raping her in an Oakland hotel. Oakland police tried for some time to contact Rider, who ignored the requests. After officers finally reached him, he wound up spending a night in jail. The charges were eventually dropped because of inconsistencies in the alleged victim's statement.

In June, Rider was arrested in Oakland when police stopped his Mercedes-Benz because it had illegally tinted windows. They found marijuana and an illegal cell phone and arrested passenger and friend Donnie Davis on an outstanding warrant. Davis was a convicted rapist and crack dealer. During the traffic stop, several of his friends arrived and harassed police officers, according to the police report.

The last episode came on July 20 when he was arrested on a misdemeanor charge of gambling (a dice game) in public on an Oakland street corner. Two of the people in the dice game allegedly had several bags of marijuana.

At the time of the misdemeanor arrest, the Blazers and Timberwolves had been in serious discussions about a trade.

Three days later, Whitsitt pulled the trigger on the deal. Rider was now the property of the Blazers.

"We're not condoning any of the things that have happened, but we have confidence in him as a person and a player," Whitsitt said during the press conference announcing Rider's acquisition.

Asked about Rider's latest incident before the trade was consummated, Minnesota VP/basketball operations Kevin McHale said, "Just another situation where J. R. was involved with people he shouldn't be associated with.

"You're talking about a young, very talented athlete who, in the scheme of things, has probably been coddled and pampered," McHale said. "J. R. is burning so many bridges. He's on very thin ice with a lot of people. My tolerance level is below zero."

Rider was peeved at McHale after the deal was announced.

"A week before I got traded, he was my buddy," Rider said. "I was at his house and around his kids. And when I leave, he tears my head off."

At the press conference in Portland, Rider said it was a "new beginning."

"I'm pumped up," he said. "It's a winning organization with veteran leadership. They've been in the playoffs the last 14 years. I'm anxious to prove to the fans, the players, and the people of Portland it wasn't a bad decision.

"I've made mistakes. I'm one to realize those mistakes, learn from them, and move on. There are people in my circle who don't like the way I'm written about and perceived. They know the real me. A lot of people don't."

Mark Cashman did. Cashman, who would serve as the Blazers' equipment manager from 1994–1999, had worked with the Timberwolves as a locker room attendant during Rider's rookie season in 1993–94.

Cashman has a favorite Rider story.

"He had a well-documented habit of being late," says Cashman, now working as equipment manager and travel coordinator with the Cleveland Cavaliers. "One year, he didn't get the memo of daylight savings in the fall.

The day the clock changed, he thought he was 20 minutes late to practice at Lewis & Clark. He pulled into the locker room, only to find he was 40 minutes early. So he got in his car, left, and came back late. Practice starts, and he's nowhere to be found. It's like, 'He was just here. Where is J. R.? You kidding me?' I don't know why he did some of the things he did."

Cashman would get to know the players well during the early Jail Blazers years.

"There were a lot of unique personalities—that's a polite way of putting it," he says. "Having seen those teams and then having a chance to be a part of a championship in Cleveland, you learn a lot about talent and teams and chemistry and coming together. In the end, talent will prevail, but having the five most talented guys doesn't necessarily mean they're going to come together. It's still a team."

* * *

Carlesimo had strongly objected to the trade for Rider but was overruled by Whitsitt. Even so, P. J. played the good soldier at the press conference.

"It's a new beginning for both of us," he said. "J. R. is going to be great. And I like what I'm hearing from him. I just hope everybody can judge him from this point onward. How do you know that people aren't going to change?"

Today, Carlesimo looks back at his one season with Rider in Portland with mixed feelings.

"J. R. was an intelligent guy," Carlesimo says. "He had a great sense of humor. We had our moments, and in some ways, he was challenging, but in a lot of ways, he was great to coach. He played hard and was a talented player.

"Most of his problems were off the floor—being on time and things of that nature. I was always bothered by anybody who didn't do things the same as everybody else. If 12 guys could be on time, it bothered me if one guy couldn't. J. R. would test you—not intentionally. Things were always a challenge for J. R. But I enjoyed him. Same thing with Strick. But did we have our moments? Without question."

San Antonio GM Gregg Popovich—who would begin his NBA coaching career 18 games into the season after firing Bob Hill—was asked what advice he might have for the Blazers on how to handle Rider. Popovich had taken on notorious guard Vernon Maxwell with the Spurs.

"You tell [Rider] that it starts now," Popovich said. "If he messes up, you hammer him. If he doesn't, you love him, and you go from there.

"[The Blazers] could be tougher than hell this season. It's a tough, gritty team. They have talent, athleticism, and a great coaching staff. But they need Sabonis to stay healthy, and I don't think any questions have been answered yet about their inside/outside game. Are they going to be able to consistently knock it down from the outside? If they have that element, they could be really good."

The culture of the Trail Blazer locker room had changed considerably in the course of two years, from the time that Clyde Drexler, Terry Porter, Jerome Kersey, and Buck Williams controlled the premises. Now the leaders were Rider, Wallace, Anderson, and Cliff Robinson. Also on the roster during the 1996–97 season were Gary Trent, Stacey Augmon, and Dontonio Wingfield.

Dan Burke was still with the Blazers as video coordinator.

"The group we had by that time, it was an eye-opener," Burke says today. "Wingfield. Trent. Rider. Wallace. With that group, you kept your distance. Gary was a good, fun guy, but there was an edge to him. You were a bit leery."

Carlisle was coaching Portland's entry to the Salt Lake City Summer League. Wallace arrived and decided he was going to play. In the first game, he got two technicals and was ejected.

"We were in the locker room afterward, and Rasheed stood up and said, 'Fellas, I'm trying to get better at that,'" Burke says. "He got emotional. You could see his passion for his teammates and the game. He said, 'I'm never going to do this again.' We know the rest of the story. What a competitor. But he just couldn't handle his emotions during games."

Rider, Burke says, "was such a talent. But I never saw him work at anything. He was never on time."

Burke, now an assistant at Indiana for 22 years, says he has learned that culture matters.

"You can pile up all talent you want, but are they good teammates? Are they winners?" he says. "Some of those guys competed, but it was always on their terms and usually just in games, not in practice.

"I never understood the type of players they were looking at during those years. Some of the guys wouldn't even be in the league if management would have the guts to not sign them, to look past the talent and realize they're going to hurt you, not help you."

Mark Cashman came to Portland at the end of the Clyde Drexler/Terry Porter era.

"They had such a great group of players and people for a long time," Cashman says. "The city was very prideful about that. Those guys lived there year-round. That was their home. They were a part of the fabric of the community. As that group aged and it broke apart, it was no longer a family team.

"It was a transition time. It was hard for the fans to go from that to a team that, at least from the outside, looked like they didn't get along or were dysfunctional. It was such a divergence from what they had seen for the better part of a decade. Part of the transition was figuring out who were going to be the next core guys to build around."

Cashman is careful not to impugn the character of the players during his time with the Blazers.

"Character is a broad word," he says today. "It can mean so many things. It's good to have one, maybe two guys who have a little bit of edge to them. I've thought at times we could have used that more in Cleveland. But if everybody is like that, you don't get those elements you need to be a really good team. If you have too many guys like that, it can be combustible."

Cashman was a fan, mostly, of Wallace.

"He did some good things in the community, liked kids, and he was a great teammate," Cashman says. "But he had his troubles with the officials. Rasheed was wonderful to me. But my position is easier. I'm not asking people to do anything they might inherently want to. I don't control their money or their minutes or have to ask them to lift weights or to be there at 9 the next morning for an MRI, or to get back on defense. I'm handing them gear."

The seeds for the "Jail Blazers" had been planted the previous season. But the 1996–97 season, with Rider and Wallace coming into the fold, signaled the true beginning of the "Jail Blazers" era.

* * *

Portland added an additionally important new face for the 1996–97 campaign—6-foot-11 rookie Jermaine O'Neal, taken with the 17th pick in the '96 draft, four spots behind Kobe Bryant. The 17-year-old O'Neal, out of Columbia, South Carolina, became the youngest player in the NBA ever to appear in a game when he first stepped onto the court in the regular season.

"We took Jermaine at a time in the NBA when you didn't take high school guys," Mark Warkentien, the Blazers' scouting director, says today. O'Neal and Kobe Bryant were the only two high schoolers taken in the 1996 draft. In 1995, only Kevin Garnett was chosen. In 1997, only Tracy McGrady.

O'Neal and his older brother, Clifford, were raised in a single-parent household by his mother, Angela Ocean (Jermaine never knew his father). As a 6-foot-4 freshman, O'Neal made a negative impression on the Eau Claire High coach, George Glymph, a 53-year-old geometry teacher.

"I thought he was arrogant," Glymph said in an interview during O'Neal's time in Portland. "He couldn't really play that well. He had a lot of playground moves. We had to get that out of him."

By the end of the freshman year, O'Neal had grown to 6-foot-9 and helped Eau Claire win a state title. By the time he was a junior, O'Neal averaged 18.2 points, 12.8 rebounds, and 7.1 blocked shots. He averaged 22.4 points, 12.4 boards, and 5.2 blocks as a senior. During his four years, the Shamrocks went 97–16 and won three state 3A titles. O'Neal was voted most popular by his graduating class and, by that time, had won over his coach.

"He's one of the best kids I've ever coached," said Glymph, who had coached the likes of future NBA players Alex English, Tyrone Corbin, and Stanley Roberts. "He never put himself on a pedestal, which would have been easy to do. He took it all in stride and gave credit to his teammates."

Unlike his future teammates, O'Neal faced a legal issue while in high school. In November of his senior year, just after he turned 17, Jermaine was caught in bed with his 15-year-old girlfriend by the girl's father and charged with having sex with a minor. He entered a pre-trial intervention program that expunged his record after community service.

Jermaine signed a letter-of-intent with Kentucky, but poor grades would have made him ineligible as a freshman. It didn't matter because after going in the first round of the draft, he was headed to the NBA. After the draft, 20-year-old Clifford moved to Portland with him. They rented a five-bedroom house in Forest Heights.

* * *

Wallace, Rider, and Anderson entered training camp intent on making a good impression on Carlesimo and his staff.

However, there was controversy before things even got started.

Sabonis, who had been runner-up in voting for both the Rookie of the Year and Sixth Man of the Year the previous season, was featured on the cover of the annual press guide. Robinson, who had led the team in scoring the previous season, was asked if he considered it a slight.

"Not at all," he said. "I mean, I'm sure they're trying to trade me. So why promote somebody who might be traded?"

In reality, Robinson was offended. So was his agent, Brad Marshall. Their disgruntlement actually began after the previous season, when Marshall claimed Whitsitt reneged on a promise to renegotiate Cliff's contract. Heading into the 1996–97 campaign, Robinson was set to make $3.2 million in the final year of his contract. Uncle Cliffy and his agent were seeking a seven-year, $84-million extension.

"If the message [that Portland doesn't want him] hasn't been clear, it should be now," Marshall said after the media guide was released. "Isn't that a statement of what they think of him? They're giving him no respect at all. But Cliff is taking the high road. Cliff doesn't dwell on the negatives. He just wants to play basketball."

During the offseason, Marshall had tried to force a trade.

"Cliff would love to play in Miami," the agent told the media. "He wouldn't have a problem with Phoenix. But Bob [Whitsitt] wants to play hardball. He is making unreasonable demands. He created this mess he's in. Now he wants someone to bail him out. He said he would try to move him if we wanted, but he also made it clear he felt the best thing to do would be to stay in Portland and play out his option.

"It's like he thinks we're stupid or something. Cliff does not want to be [in Portland]. His position is, he trusted ownership, he trusted management, and they breached that trust. There's no reason for him to stay. If he is forced to stay, he won't be the same Cliff Robinson in spirit, mind, or heart. He just wouldn't be the same person."

Whitsitt struck back.

"We've made no promises, no commitments to anything," he said. "Every day, [Marshall] just keeps making up stories."

Asked why Marshall would lie about the promise, Whitsitt said, "Why don't you go look at his record in the state bar in Washington? He has a lot of ethics violations as a lawyer, OK?"

Once Whitsitt made it personal, Marshall stooped to the same level.

"Whitsitt has a reputation in the league, and it's not a good one," Marshall countered. "He has no conscience. He has a reprobate mind when it comes to the truth, and frankly, he can't be trusted."

As training camp neared, Marshall altered his stance.

"Cliff wants desperately to continue his career in Portland," Marshall said, "but he told me he will not play under Bob Whitsitt. That's a real issue."

Robinson would hold out for 11 days before reporting to training camp. He came back, Marshall said, with Whitsitt's assurance that the matter would be taken care of with an extension after the season.

The Blazers went to camp with a young group, with only Sabonis (31), Chris Dudley (31), and Robinson (29) older than 26. The starting five was penciled in as Sabonis at center, flanked by Wallace and Robinson at forward and Anderson and Rider at guard.

Portland assistant coach Dick Harter was more concerned about the players meshing together.

"Good chemistry isn't that important to an average or a poor team," Harter said. "But it is very important if you want to be an elite team. I don't think you can be in the top four without it."

During the preseason, Wallace admitted, "Up to now, [being emotional] has been a minus in my career, but I can't change the way I play. I'm an emotional, fiery player. You have someone like that on every team in the NBA."

It appeared that Dudley, Gary Trent, and guard Aaron McKie would get the most minutes off the bench. O'Neal, blessed with a $2.38 million rookie contract and a multi-year endorsement deal with Adidas, showed his potential, too. His teammates called him "The Kid," which Carlesimo—who had a nickname for everybody—shortened to "T. K."

"He reminds me of Kevin Garnett," Rider said. "You get the ball to Jermaine in a good position, he'll take one dribble and try to slam-dunk on whoever's there. And he has heart. If you have that and you're not afraid of guys 25 or 26, you'll do fine."

But Jermaine strained a knee in the preseason and started the regular season on the injured list, missing the first two months of his rookie year.

"My time will come," O'Neal said. "A couple of years from now, I'm going to be an NBA All-Star."

Today, Carlesimo looks back on his season with the rookie with fondness.

"I loved him, but he's the epitome of why I'm against the young guys coming out so early," Carlesimo says. "He comes to us at 17 years old, his first time away from home. It was such a hard thing. He was so talented and a really good kid, but it was a tough transition for him.

"You could see then he was going to be a great player. He was playing with men, and it was challenging, but Jermaine survived it. A lot of guys don't. He turned out to be one of the best players in the league. But we had older guys, and he wasn't getting the minutes he felt he deserved. His heart was in the right place, though, and he tried to work hard."

The irrepressible Trent, beginning his second season, had started 10 games as a rookie before an injury ended his season prematurely.

"I should start," Trent, who had just turned 22, told reporters. "I believe in paying your dues, but Bob Whitsitt drafted me to bring wins to this team. You should never lose your position because of an injury."

During camp, Rider had to return to Minneapolis to appear in court to settle a lawsuit filed by a card-show company, causing him to miss the Blazers' first public scrimmage.

But that was only the beginning. Rider made the team flight to Sacramento for Portland's first exhibition game but spent time that night with friends in Oakland. When he rushed back for the game-day shoota-round the next morning, he arrived at the wrong venue. There was no fine issued, and Rider was allowed to play in the game. Team officials tried to cover for him until word got out to the media a couple of days later.

It was about this time that the first recorded reference to "Jail Blazers" was published in a Portland alternative weekly. "I got a good laugh out of it," Wallace would say later. "It was funny. Some people want to label us. They say we are a team with problems. But there ain't no problems on this squad. We don't have any problems with one another. We just came in here and ignored all that. We're just going out there hoopin'."

Anderson put some of the blame on the media.

"They are always looking for negative things to write about," the point guard said. "I had turmoil in New Jersey. J. R. had some problems in Minnesota. There were questions about Rasheed. People don't look at the simple fact that we're here to play basketball."

As luck would have it, Washington had an exhibition against the Blazers in Portland. The Bullets' point guard was Rod Strickland.

"When I looked at the preseason schedule and saw we had a game there, I thought, 'Why do I have to go back there?'" the sometimes too candid Strickland told a reporter. "I would love to erase this game off the schedule."

The game highlighted his acrimonious relationship with Carlesimo, causing a flurry of questions from media.

On seeing Carlesimo again, Rod joked, "There's nothing for me and P. J. to talk about, unless we're going to get into the ring with some gloves on."

Things were a little more serious when Rider sat out Friday's season opener at Vancouver while serving a one-game suspension for missing Portland's final preseason game against Seattle in Corvallis. He said his "disappearance" on that day came about because he went to the wrong place to catch the team bus.

"There were circumstances both times, but still, you have rules," Carlesimo said. "Missing a game is serious, and it's not the first thing [Rider had done wrong]."

"It's just bad luck," Rider said. "It's an unacceptable thing, but at the same time, it was unintentional."

Whitsitt told the media, "I'm sure he just got lost."

Whitsitt and Rider met on the day of the regular-season opener.

"I was definitely listening," Rider said of the powwow. "Mainly, what he wants me to do is play hard, be on time, and let my basketball skill speak for itself because he feels I'm a great player."

Carlesimo had pushed Whitsitt for a suspension.

"We like J. R.'s work ethic," the coach said, "but we can't ignore punctuality and attendance."

The Oregonian's Dwight Jaynes wrote a column about the Rider situation.

"You're actually surprised by this?" Jaynes wrote. "When Rider told this town he'd be turning over a new leaf, you expected it to be something other than cannabis? . . . Acquiring Rider was a move that will dog Whitsitt for a long time and do serious damage to his credibility, if he has any left."

Jaynes consulted with Los Angeles–based sports psychologist Steve Berkowitz, who asked, "What was that general manager up there thinking? There were no secrets about Isaiah Rider. His record is pretty clear. I've seen people change, but they don't do it until they see a need to change, and he's probably having a very good time. You're talking about a lifestyle."

* * *

Two days before the opener at Vancouver, and three days after being suspended for the game against the Grizzlies, Rider was cited for possession of marijuana in the suburban Portland community of Lake Oswego. He was in the back seat of a parked car, using a soda can that had been converted into a pipe, when police came upon him. Deputies said Rider refused to take the citation, then crumpled it up and threw it on the ground.

When word got out about the arrest the following day, Rider was asked about it by the media.

"I happened to be a backseat passenger in someone's car," he said. "The cops didn't find a damn thing on me, but I'm a big name. It's kind of messed up."

The next day, after Rider's explanation was published, Damon Coates, public information officer for the sheriff's office, had his say after reading the player's comments in the newspaper.

"Not to slam a guy who already has sufficient problems, but I can't imagine a bigger contrast from the truth," Coates said. "This is about as clear of a possession case as you can get. When he looked up, it was the look of someone with his hand caught in the cookie jar.

"The officer could have searched the car for weapons, and for reasons of officer safety, he could have taken Mr. Rider to jail when he threw the citation to the ground [on an offensive littering charge]. The deputy took a conservative, calm approach."

The officer wasn't aware of Rider's identity, Coates said.

"He doesn't follow basketball, and the name Isaiah Rider meant absolutely nothing to him," he said.

Whitsitt said the Blazers could have fined Rider up to $2,500 but would not say whether he levied a fine. The GM chose not to issue an additional suspension.

"The kind of conduct we read in the police report, we don't condone," the Portland GM said.

With Rider sitting it out, the Blazers pummeled the Grizzlies, 114–85, in the regular-season opener at General Motors Place.

"The way we played tonight," Carlesimo gushed, "we could beat almost anybody."

The Blazers lost their next two games, the first one at Seattle (104–93), and two nights later, they were embarrassed in their home opener against the Hawks, 94–76. When Rider was pulled in the second half, he shot an angry look at Carlesimo, mumbled something under his breath that sounded like, "Don't pull this on me," then sat on the baseline. He covered his head with a towel, took one shoe off, and didn't get up when the coach called a 20-second timeout.

After a win over the Warriors, the Blazers improved to 3–2 when Anderson's falling-down 14-footer just before the buzzer in overtime beat Minnesota 95–94 at the Rose Garden. The Blazers had blown a 16-point fourth-quarter lead and failed to score in the final 3:38 of regulation.

Wallace scored 25 points while Sabonis had 17 and a career-high 17 boards. Cliff Robinson was ejected with 8:09 left in the fourth quarter after arguing a call and receiving his second technical foul.

"[Referee Derek Stafford] was telling me I had to learn something," Robinson said afterward, "and I told him he wasn't my teacher."

An anticipated matchup between Rider and his old team fizzled quickly. Carlesimo benched Rider—who finished with nine points on 2-for-8 shooting—at 5:02 of the third quarter and left him there.

"He was struggling," Carlesimo said. "I knew this was an important game for him against his old team, but Aaron [McKie] did a good job for us. Then it's hard to go away from a guy and bring him back cold."

"I'm as puzzled as you are," Rider told a reporter after the game. "I don't know what was going on. But I don't care if I'm out the whole game as long as we win. We'll work it out."

He was singing in the showers: "We won! I'm happy. Can't you see that? This is not a front. We're 3–2, baby. Usually for me, it's 0–5 or 1–4. I'm happy."

On November 12, Rider was booed in his return to the Target Center. In an interview during the preseason, he had called his former teammates "losers." *Star-Tribune* columnist Dan Barreiro referred to the Blazers as a "holding cell for petulant personalities, underachievers, and knuckleheads."

Barreiro quoted an unidentified agent as saying, "Either [the Blazers] are trying to blow up the franchise, or they are doing something no one else has figured out. Look at that team. It's full of hoodlums. I would not send a client of mine there unless I had no choice."

Despite 22 points by Rider, the Blazers lost to Minnesota, 100–97, falling to 4–4. After dropping their next game to Cleveland, they would win four in a row, the last a 105–65 pounding of Denver in which the woeful Nuggets missed their first 14 shots and set a franchise low for first-half points (25), total points, and shooting percentage (.274).

Two weeks later, in a rematch of the teams at Denver, O'Neal—who had spent 33 days on the injured list with his knee injury—became the youngest player ever to play in an NBA regular-season game in a 115–104 win.

On December 10, after missing a pregame shootaround, Rider was benched for the first quarter of Portland's 99–93 loss to the Magic. Later, he would explain that he actually went to the Rose Garden for the shootaround before departing after a confrontation with Carlesimo.

"Once I came in, me and P. J. just rubbed each other the wrong way," Rider said. "Maybe he was sick. Maybe I was sleepy. Whatever it was, we just rubbed each other the wrong way. . . . We both had a bad morning."

The next day, Rider said he drove to practice, then headed home, claiming he had too much on his mind to participate in the workout.

"It just stemmed from things that went on from training camp until yesterday's game," Rider would explain. "Me and P. J., we're not seeing eye to eye. Rather than go out there and be sluggish or have some things on my mind and be short-tempered, I felt like I wanted to talk."

With whom, he didn't say.

Rider felt unfairly badgered by the Portland media.

"You guys pump it up that I'm bad, so why fight you guys?" he said. "I do my own thing. I can look myself in the mirror. That's what it's all about. It's not about pleasing you, or about you pleasing me."

After Carlesimo and Whitsitt sat down for a meeting that lasted nearly four hours, Rider was handed his second one-game suspension of the young season.

"We knew there was a chance that this would happen, and the fact that it's happening is something we have to deal with," Carlesimo said.

* * *

Wallace was off to an excellent start to his first season with the Blazers. Through 27 games, the second-year forward was averaging 15.6 points and 7 rebounds while leading the NBA in field-goal percentage (.585).

On December 21, Wallace came through with a career-high 38-point performance in a 101–99 overtime loss to Sacramento.

"The thing I like about Rasheed is he's been a good guy in the locker room, on the court, off the court," Whitsitt said.

Two nights later, Wallace suffered a broken thumb in a 106–84 blowout loss at home to his old team, the Bullets, as Portland fell to 14–14 for the season. He would miss 17 games, returning on February 4.

During the game against Washington, Rose Garden fans jeered a totally disinterested Rider behind the Portland bench while booing at the sight of Rider, Trent, and Dontonio Wingfield laughing and joking during the loss. Some season-ticket holders left their seats early in disgust. Rider took a seat midway through the third quarter and did not return, taking just four shots in 18 minutes. His reaction? "If you know basketball, you'll be able to tell what's happening."

Said Carlesimo afterward: "It was the poorest we've played all year."

Anderson said something no Blazer fan wanted to hear: "I think everybody was looking forward to the holidays. Our heads were not in it."

Was Rider a distraction?

"I'd rather not comment," Anderson said. "Right now, we have more problems than playing basketball. We're getting along all right, but it's a thin line. You put this uniform on, you have to want to compete."

The Blazers took a 16–15 record into the New Year. Anderson was averaging 18 points and 6.3 assists and shooting well, but some of his teammates though he wasn't dishing the ball often enough.

"Guys used to think Rod shot too much, too," Carlesimo said. "Scorers don't like it when a point guard scores, which is wrong. I don't mind the point guard scoring as long as his other numbers are good."

On January 2, Rider was pulled by Carlesimo for loafing back on defense early in a 112–96 win at Houston. Rider openly cursed the coach in front of the bench, and Carlesimo ignored it. None of the Blazer players tried to calm Rider down, but he regrouped and finished with a game-high 31 points.

"There are going to be times when guys don't want to come out of games," Robinson said afterward. "The important thing is, J. R. was able to put that aside and keep playing."

Veteran Mitchell Butler, a character guy off the bench, was asked about the difference in players from an earlier era.

"Ten or 15 years ago, players played for the love of the game," Butler said. "Now, there are so many distractions. The players have the big money now. It doesn't seem like there's a big concern."

Over losing? Over deportment?

"We have guys who could step up and [lead]," he said. "But whether or not they want to do it, I don't know. I don't know if it's in their character."

On January 8, Robinson was suspended for one game for cursing Carlesimo and assistant coach Elston Turner during an 85–81 home loss to Miami. The veteran forward also directed a profanity-laced outburst at the media after the game. Cliff had exchanged words with teammate Aaron McKie before Carlesimo took him out late in the third quarter. As he left, he said in a loud voice, "What are you taking me out of the game for, you stupid motherfucker?"

Turner tried to calm him down, and Robinson started yelling at him.

"I don't take things personally," Carlesimo said afterward. "Players can say things emotionally to coaches or assistant coaches, but sometimes you can go too far with it, that's all. We have an emotional team. We're probably going to have other outbursts. It's going to happen. You can be emotional and say something, but there's a right way to say it, and there's a point where you go too far."

The suspension cost Robinson $39,000 in salary.

"It wasn't just for during the game," the coach said. "It was during timeouts, after the game. It was not one thing; it was a number of things."

Before the incident, Carlesimo said, "Cliff hasn't been just good this year, he has been exceptional in terms of attitude and leadership."

Before the Blazers beat Detroit at the Rose Garden in the next game, Pistons coach Doug Collins—one of the few coaches in the league willing to address the game's issues—mentioned the acidic effect of several players of questionable deportment on Whitsitt's chemistry experiment. He also stood up for his coaching cohort, Carlesimo, who was under fire.

"You have a GM who says, 'To get to the next level, we have to take a chance on these guys,'" Collins said. "You're expected to coach them and win more games when, in essence, you have such a bad blend, you can't do as well.

"I know P. J. loves the game. Every coach would like to make everybody happy, but it doesn't work that way. The coach puts himself out there on the firing line. If things go a little badly, he has to be the one to step up and say, 'I'm driving the car. I'll take the responsibility.' P. J. has had his highs and lows in Portland. I pull for him. I hate to see a coach suffer."

On January 16, Rider swaggered onto the Lakers' home court at the Fabulous Forum and scored 30 points in a 102–98 win. The Blazer guard was trash-talking, at one point telling the Lakers' Eddie Jones, "You can't guard me!"

Rider also got into it with Laker guard Nick Van Exel in the second quarter, who got a technical.

"I could just tell how confident they were at the start of the game," Rider said. "If I had [Shaquille O'Neal] on the floor with me, I'd be confident, too. They were thinking, 'This is going to be no problem.' I definitely got into Eddie's head. I got into Nick's head, too. But in the second half, they got into my head."

51

The Lakers, trailing by 16 at the half, rallied to within two points in the third quarter. Shaq was ejected after throwing an elbow in Sabonis's face with 1:18 left, which all but sealed the game for Portland.

The next day, before Toronto's 94–92 win at the Rose Garden, Raptors point guard Damon Stoudamire was asked for a comparison between the Blazers' current point guard, Kenny Anderson, and his predecessor, Rod Strickland. Stoudamire, a Wilson High grad and Portland native, was direct in his response.

"You don't know what [Portland's] coaches are asking Kenny to do," says Stoudamire, who would score 24 points to lead the Raptors past the Blazers. "Maybe they're asking him to shoot 21 times a game. But I think Rod brought a lot more to that team than Kenny does.

"[Strickland] was able to get a lot more players involved. He brought a lot to that team that they don't have now. I don't think they have the same kind of chemistry they had last year. Kenny is having a good year, but I look at everybody around him as suffering. The guy who has taken the biggest hit is Sabonis. He and Rod used to run the heck out of the pick-and-roll. Now it seems like all he does is shoot the 3."

On January 24, Portland traded the team's third guard, Aaron McKie, and little-used guards Randolph Childress and Reggie Jordan, to Detroit for swing man Stacey Augmon, who hadn't played for the Pistons since cursing Collins two weeks earlier (though they'd been at odds long before that). He was late to several practices and, according to some Pistons insiders, typically was the last to arrive and the first to leave.

"We butted heads," Augmon said of his relationship with Collins. "Neither one of us gave any ground. Maybe I should have; maybe I shouldn't have."

* * *

After a 17-point victory against the Wolves, the Blazers went on a five-game losing streak and fell to 25–23. Their fifth straight loss was an 88–84 setback to the Bulls at the Rose Garden. Michael Jordan scored 22 of the defending NBA champion's 28 fourth-quarter points in a rally that toppled the Blazers, including 18 in a 5½-minute span, which gave the Bulls their eighth straight win.

On February 11, in his second game back after returning from injury, Wallace was sensational off the bench in a 111–108 win over Phoenix at home, the first game after the All-Star break.[1] Wallace scored 30 points on 10-for-14 shooting to go with five rebounds in 31 minutes. It appeared to be only a matter of time before he reclaimed his spot in the starting lineup over Trent.

"I know Gary wants to start—it's natural—and he's done a good job when Rasheed was out," Carlesimo said. "But if Rasheed is back and playing better . . . we'll put the best five guys on the floor. Gary's feathers will be ruffled for a while, but he'll get over it."

Anderson was terrific, too, with 33 points and six assists, but his backcourt mate's behavior was erratic. Rider appeared to take issue with Anderson's ball distribution early in the game. Rider—who came into the game averaging 15.8 points and 13 shots a game—was open a few times, didn't get the ball, and started to pout. He did not take a shot after the first quarter, finishing with four points on 2-for-4 shooting. At times, as Carlesimo did a slow burn near the bench, Rider practically walked up and down the court. When fans or teammates tried to pump him up, he ignored them, or shot them a glare as if to say, "Don't push it."

The next day, Rider begged off halfway through practice when he tweaked an ankle.

Afterward, Carlesimo said, "Do I think he was passing up shots [in the previous game]? Do I think he could have practiced today? No matter what I say, it would just be opinion."

After two hot games for the Blazers, with Rider scoring 40 in a win against the Celtics and Wallace leading the way with 25 over the Heat, halting their 11-game winning streak, Rider sat on the sidelines during shootaround before the Heat game, telling coaches he couldn't participate because of stomach trouble. That night, he was spotted 45 minutes before

---

1   No Blazer was named an All-Star for the season.

game time wandering the parking lot of Miami Arena, talking on a cell phone and carrying a large bag of shoes. He entered the locker room 48 minutes late.

Rider, who finished with 16 points in 26 minutes, still began the game in the starting lineup, though was so ineffective that Carlesimo benched him for the final 15 minutes. Rider cursed at the coach as he left the game, then pulled himself into a cocoon away from teammates until the final buzzer. Rider later said he had the flu. Did it bother him during the game? "Sometimes," he said.

The next game at Philadelphia, Rider started again but sat out the final 18 minutes of a 97–80 loss to the 76ers, who were 25 games under .500. After being benched, he sat apart from his teammates, 10 feet down the baseline, leaning against a courtside sign, with a scowl his face and a towel over his head. He did not join team huddles.

"We have to take more pride in what we're doing out there," Robinson said. "Everything's rah-rah when we get ahead. But when things get tougher, it isn't like that. We're a front-running team. I hate to see anyone let the little things that go on during a game bother him. I used to be that way, and I still am once in a while. But you just can't be that way."

Trent, now in a reserve role after Wallace reclaimed his starting spot, snapped at Carlesimo during the second half, later saying he felt picked on.

"Did I finally have enough? I've had enough of it for a long time," Trent said. "He's always yelling at me. I know that's his style, but a guy can only take so much. I'm a man, too. Some of the things he has been saying to me disrespect me as a man. When a man talks to another man like that, there comes a time when you stand up for yourself."

Trent said he didn't like giving the starting job back to Wallace, but that he didn't intend to create waves over it.

"I started my career coming off the bench," Trent said. "I guess it isn't any big thing coming off the bench now. I'm not going to cuss and argue with P. J. That shit isn't going to do me any good. I knew it was going to happen. I knew it [his starting] was just a stunt to let people heal. You take it in stride and keep on moving. That's what I'm going to do."

Trent later apologized: "I know P. J. doesn't mean anything personal by what he says. I'm not taking it like that. I know I'll be around longer than some of these coaches will."

More than 20 years later, Trent has softened in his feelings for Carlesimo.

"He was a young coach," Trent says now. "He was still learning. He knew basketball. I don't know if he knew the culture of the program coming in, but who does when you're new? As a basketball guy, he was solid. He always had good preparation as a coach."

Was Carlesimo too much of a yeller and screamer?

"I didn't see it that way," Trent says. "He wanted to hold guys accountable, but he had not won the guys over yet for them to buy in. He wanted what any coach wants—accountability, leadership, guys doing the right thing and coming on time."

* * *

On February 24, with neither Rider or Wallace in the starting lineup, the Blazers were rolled 116–89 by Chicago at the United Center, with Michael Jordan scoring 30 of his 37 points in the first half. Rider had flown to Oakland because of the death of his cousin, while Wallace was held out of the first quarter because he missed the morning shootaround. Wallace, who said he overslept, wound up playing 12 minutes. Asked afterward for a reaction, Wallace shrugged, "Doesn't matter."

While his players didn't seem bothered, Carlesimo was extremely upset afterward.

"We don't even resemble the same team from earlier [in the season]," he said. "It isn't any one area—it's everything. There has been so much slippage. When we can't control the other team defensively, we can't play."

With Rider back with the team, he scored 11 points on 3-for-10 shooting in a 96–95 overtime loss to the Knicks. He said he was feeling less than 100 percent but that he "toughed it out" for 41 minutes.

"I felt decent enough," he said. "My stomach hurt once or twice. I was focused and into the game." Whether the stomach ache was from a physical or mental ailment, Rider was definitely hurting after the loss of his cousin.

"It wasn't good, seeing a lot of people you haven't seen for the wrong reasons," he said. "But I'm trying to put this out of my head and just move on. Maybe use it as a positive. I can't sit here and bring him back."

Speaking to the media the next day, Rider said he felt he had been unfairly criticized despite sacrificing his individual game for the good of the team.

"If you really look at the way I've played for much of the season, you have to say, 'He definitely has made a compromise in his game,'" Rider said. "But yet I'm a scapegoat, the one people point a lot of fingers at. But I know the facts; people who know basketball know the facts. Even people on this team know facts."

When people see him angry or with a towel over his head, Rider said, "It's because it's a shame we're not on the same page. Not because I didn't get 30 points. If I really wanted to score, I'd put my head down and score. I just want to play the right way."

The Blazers took a 29–28 record into the last game in February against Utah—four games ahead of the previous season's pace, but much less than the restocked Blazers were expecting. Additions had included Rider, Wallace, Anderson, and O'Neal, and Sabonis was in the starting lineup for the opener instead of Game 61, as had been the case the previous season.

Whitsitt denied a *New York Daily News* report of something that had been rumored for weeks—that Carlesimo was about to be fired.

"There is nobody in the organization saying that," the Portland GM said. "If and when I do a P. J. Carlesimo evaluation, the first person I'll sit down with is P. J., and we haven't sat down and had a conversation. P. J. has two years left on a five-year contract. I think that says a lot."

Whitsitt was also asked about Rider's up-and-down season.

"I don't know what up and down is," he said. "He has had a solid year for us."

Whitsitt had been spending much of his time in Seattle wearing another hat, fronting Paul Allen's drive to convince Washingtonians that the NFL's Seahawks were deserving of public support for a new stadium. That didn't seem right to *The Oregonian*'s Dwight Jaynes.

"I want a man running the Blazers who thinks of nothing but the NBA," Jaynes wrote. "I want someone in that seat who puts in countless hours running a basketball team, not a football team. And perhaps if Whitsitt spent a little more time on basketball, he would be able to educate himself about the team in this little hick town that was never quite good enough for him to live in. Whitsitt has always been one of those big-ego guys who figured he could run a team with his eyes closed. It seems that is exactly what he is doing."

* * *

And then, if by magic, the Blazers' season turned around.

It started with a 115–105 home win over the Jazz and turned into an 11-game streak that lasted for more than three weeks. There was a speed bump in Game No. 2, a 112–95 rout of Philadelphia on March 2, with Rider again sitting out the first quarter after missing the game-day shootaround. Rider said he had been under the weather.

"No big deal," said Rider, who needed only three quarters to register 19 points, five rebounds, and four assists. "Unless you're dying, they want you to come down and try to make it, even if it's just to pick up a couple of aspirin."

On March 5, Rider missed the team's charter flight to Phoenix by about 15 minutes. Blaming Flightcraft officials, he badgered them to supply him with another plane. When they refused, according to police reports, he became angry and abusive and challenged four employees. They said he screamed obscenities at them, got in their faces, behaved in a threatening manner, and spit in one man's face from a distance of four to six inches away. He also spat at another employee, who turned to avoid being hit. Rider then grabbed a third employee's cell phone and smashed it to bits on the pavement.

"I'll drop you, you motherfucker," he allegedly told one employee. Rider also damaged Flightcraft's main gate as he left. The employees said they had said nothing to upset Rider. "I thought he was going to come over and start punching me," one of them said.

Rider ended up taking a commercial flight and arrived later in the day.

Then the next day, he missed the team bus to the arena. Carlesimo sat him for the first quarter. "He had excuses," P. J. said, "but it didn't matter. He was late."

Rider was to be charged with misdemeanor criminal mischief and harassment from the incident. Three weeks later, he avoided criminal prosecution by reaching financial settlements with Flightcraft Inc. and three of the workers.

He still scored 24 points, to go with 26 from Anderson and 24 from Robinson, and the Blazers knocked down a franchise-record 16 3-pointers in a 121–99 burial of the Suns.

Two days later, Rider started in an 80–69 win over Dallas in Portland but had one of his most ineffective performances. He had 10 points, five personal fouls, and four turnovers in 21 minutes. After he was removed from the game early in the third quarter, Rider put a towel on his head and walked toward the locker room before returning to the bench.

Afterward, he explained, "It's not directed toward anyone. Go around the league and you'll see how many towels are over people's heads, whether it's from frustration, whether it's just their style, or whatever."

The next day, reserve forward Dontonio Wingfield was kicked out of practice after a dispute with Carlesimo and given a one-game suspension. Wingfield refused to comment.

"He said some things he shouldn't have said," Carlesimo said. "I don't think he would disagree with that. He's fine now."

Even with that, the Blazers' win streak had reached five games.

"We're not in turmoil here," Carlesimo claimed. "There is no turmoil."

That week, a story on the fussin' and feudin' Blazers in *The Sporting News* was entitled "Rift City."

* * *

Before a 103–93 win over Seattle on March 9, Rider observed of the Pacific Division–leading Sonics, "They're scared of us. The only thing they can hope for is we play bad because man-to-man, we have more talent and we have a better team."

Even as the Blazers mounted the streak, reports of Carlesimo's demise were being printed.

"The players like P. J., and none of them have anything negative to say about him," Whitsitt had told *The Sporting News*.

Local writers again asked Carlesimo about his job security, and he gave a surprisingly honest appraisal. "Any evaluation of the job I am doing has to come at the end of the season," he said. "If we continue to improve and do well in the playoffs, all this stuff will be forgotten. Right now, the jury's out. To a large degree, the whole thing rides on what happens the rest of the way."

Radio analyst Mike Rice was honest, too. "It really does affect P. J. and the team," Rice said. "It can't be positive. Those things are distracting. It doesn't go away. Everywhere we go on the road, [reporters] won't be asking about the players, they'll be writing about the coach."

Rider wasn't the only Portland player getting into trouble. On March 12, Trent pleaded guilty to harassment of his pregnant girlfriend, Roxanne Holt. She had told police Trent hit her in the face and kicked her in the ribs on January 7. Trent was put on probation and ordered to fulfill community service.

Whitsitt had John Christensen, the team's media relations director, release a statement on the situation. "We're disappointed and saddened by this behavior and fully support the court-mandated program and expect Gary to complete it satisfactorily," the statement read.

Three days later, Trent was involved in a late-night brawl at the Metropolis Restaurant and Bar in downtown Portland, where Trent allegedly hit another patron on the head with a pool cue. Trent's father, Dexter, was accused of biting the patron's ear during the fracas.

When word got out about the incident, reporters asked Trent for comment.

"Man, are you guys still running that story?" he said. "What's it been, six days? You guys put my story on top of Dean Smith [setting an NCAA coaching win record]. To me, it's a non-issue."

Weeks later, Trent missed a practice because he had to appear in front of a Multnomah County grand jury as result of the skirmish at the Portland bar. The grand jury voted not to indict him for felony assault after police said the other party had needled Trent and threw a drink in his face.

* * *

Through mid-March, the Blazers had accumulated 40 technical fouls in 64 games, the second-most in the NBA. Anderson led with 11.

"When I get a tech, I know I deserve a tech," the point guard said. "If I feel like I'm going to get one, I just let it out. It can hurt us, though. I don't think we're liked by too many officials. I don't think we care, though."

Wallace had only seven technicals after drawing 21 during his rookie season, but it helped that he had missed 19 games due to injury. Carlesimo had only one.

"Given the nature of the team, I don't think I should be out there screaming," he said. "It's important to balance the way we are. We get on them, but I try not to go over the line. The last thing we need is me yelling on top of all our players yelling. I preach to them about staying in control. But they're going to lose it sometimes, and I understand that."

On March 15, the Blazers routed Cleveland, 96–73, for their eighth straight win. They did it without Rider, who was sent home before the game with flu-like symptoms.

On March 21, the Blazers (40–28) flew into Washington riding an 11-game win streak, which was equal to the second-longest run in franchise history. Carlesimo was featured on ESPN's *Sunday Conversation* with David Aldridge, and *Sports Illustrated* was at the team hotel to talk to the players.

"We're all excited," Rider said. "Everyone is feeling good about themselves right now."

On March 22, Portland's streak ended with a 108–104 loss to the Bullets at USAir Arena despite 28 points from Rider and 25 from Wallace. Robinson went scoreless, going 0-for-7 from the field in 41 minutes.

"Maybe it's good we lost one," Robinson said. "We were getting a little complacent."

Two days later, *Sports Illustrated* came out with a major piece on Rider, "Rider on a Storm," written by Phil Taylor.

> With the exception of the Chicago Bulls' Dennis Rodman, there is no player in the NBA with a reputation as bad as that of Rider, the Portland Trail Blazers' notorious shooting guard. No other player runs afoul of authority with such absurd regularity as those two. But Rodman is part clown; most of his transgressions are committed with a mischievous twinkle in his eyes. Rider's persona is far darker. His four-year NBA career has been marked not only by an assortment of fines and suspensions but also by the occasional arrest.

Taylor wrote how Rider's mother, Donna, raised J. R., his sister, and two brothers after a 1987 divorce from Isaiah Rider Sr., and how J. R. found refuge in sports. He was a catcher on the team that won the Babe Ruth League World Series when he was 14 and a star on the Encinal High football and basketball teams until his senior year when he was ineligible to play because of grades.

There was a good side to Rider, Taylor wrote, saying he was known in his hometown of Alameda for his generosity. He took children from economically disadvantaged families for back-to-school shopping sprees. He treated at-risk youths to sneakers and other gear with the proviso that any slippage in grades of school attendance would result in them being deprived of such privileges.

"He doesn't send out a press release every time he performs an act of generosity," Whitsitt was quoted as saying in the article. "He's not doing it with his image in mind, which makes it even more admirable."

But Rider had burned his bridges in Minnesota, especially with all the tardies and missed practice sessions.

"The kid has a great personality, but even in Minnesota, your pipes can only freeze and burst so many times," said Bill Blair, his coach with the Timberwolves. "He had about nine broken pipes and about 42 flat tires."

Shortly after the trade to Portland, Blair ran into Carlesimo at a golf course and warned, "You better have a nice vacation spot picked out. Because by December, that man is going to get you."

Rider was surrounding himself with the wrong people, Kevin McHale told Taylor.

"I like J. R., I really do," the Timberwolves VP/basketball operations said. "But it got to the point where every couple of weeks there was another incident, and we just couldn't depend on him. It's like having a friend who is always late to pick you up. You still want him as a friend, but after awhile, you stop asking him for a ride.

"You get the feeling he thinks he'd be selling out if he distanced himself from some of the people he came up with. I used to tell him he didn't have to turn his back on where he came from, but he had to be strong enough to say, 'Look fellas, I can't go to this place with you, or I can't do this with you. Because if something happens, if the cops come, it's going to be me getting in the paper.' He'd always nod his head and tell me I was right, but did I get through? I'd have to say no."

Rider defended himself in the article.

"People don't know who I really am," he said. "Sit down and listen to what I have to say and see if you still think I'm irresponsible. See if you still think I'm some kind of evil guy. I'm very intellectual, you know. Very smart. People think I'm this gangbanger, this monster, and I'm not. It's just that they don't know me. They don't understand where I'm coming from."

Rider vowed to improve his decorum.

"This summer is going to have to be different," he told Taylor in the *SI* interview. "I might not be able to hang out as much with some of the people I used to hang out with. I realize there is no more room for slip-ups. Period. No ifs, ands, or buts. No bad luck. No, 'I was there, but I didn't physically have anything to do with it.'"

Taylor asked for more time with Rider, and they made an appointment for the following day. When he was approached the next afternoon at the agreed-upon time, he said, "I want to do it. I just can't do it now. I have to take a nap."

In the days after the article appeared, with the Blazers headed toward the playoffs (currently the No. 5 seed), Rider told the Portland media he was doing all things he was supposed to do.

"To play hard, play well, and prove some of these people wrong," he said. "I don't want anybody to just totally ignore my mistakes but, at the same time, I believe I stand for the right things. I still have to work on the things that affect me, that affect the way people write about me, or the way people may applaud me at games. Whatever. I can honestly live with myself. I believe in myself. I believe in God. I believe in family. But I know there is still work to do."

That week, *The Oregonian* conducted a poll of eight NBA general managers, asking if they would have interest in acquiring Rider. Under condition of anonymity, seven said under no circumstances. The eighth: "I would find out how bad he has been off the court because he has been pretty good on the court. But if he [off the court] is the same way he was in Minnesota, you can't have a team."

One GM called Rider a "walking time bomb." Another: "I'd rather lose than have Rider or Rodman on our team." A third: "He's a headache. It's not worth it. We go after character as well as talent. The police blotter plays a large factor in our player pursuits."

* * *

With the season winding down, the Blazers were promoting Wallace for the NBA's Most Improved Player Award. The second-year forward was averaging 15.3 points and 6.8 rebounds while shooting .558, fourth in the NBA.

"The improvement he has made from one year to the other?" Carlesimo asked rhetorically. "It's clear-cut. He's deserving."

"That kind of thing doesn't matter to me," Wallace said. "I'm more into team goals than individual things. I'm just out there playing. I can't really sit back and say how many strides I've made since last year. My game is not where I want it to be, so I can't critique it."

On April 1, the Warriors ended a seven-game losing streak by winning 91–82 at Portland, snapping the Blazers' nine-game home win streak. Rider showed up late for the game and was fined.

Three days later, on a night in which the Blazers celebrated the 20th anniversary of the 1977 NBA title, the Blazers beat Milwaukee 108–93 for their 15th victory in the last 18 games. Bill Walton spoke to the Rose Garden crowd before the game, former coach Jack Ramsay tossed up the first ball, and Maurice Lucas—the beloved power forward of the '77 champions—made a half-court shot between the first and second quarters that earned a local charity $10,000.

"It was certainly a night we wanted to play well," Carlesimo said. "You feel especially good about being a Trail Blazer tonight. I felt it was important to play well in front of that team. It's the best team we've ever had here."

"After seeing them in the stands and hearing Walton talk, it gives you some excitement," Rider said. "It's like playing in high school when it's a big game, and you see a bunch of big-name college players or some pros come into the gym. You get pumped up. There's a little more adrenaline, and you want to play harder."

But it wasn't all good on that night. Wallace played only 17 minutes before sustaining his first ejection of the season. The Blazer forward received his first technical from referee Joey Crawford in the first half. Wallace thought he was fouled on a baseline jumper and yelled, "Make the call!" Crawford signaled the T and barked back, "Make the shot!" In the third quarter, after saying something to official Gary Benson, Benson ejected him.

"All I said was, 'Call it down there if you're going to call it here,'" Wallace said afterward. "It was a touch play. But I'm not sweating those cats [refs]. I'll be back playing the next game."

On April 5, Phoenix beat Portland 99–90 at the Rose Garden as Anderson was ejected in the fourth quarter after swearing at officials. Trent also drew a technical for taunting.

The Blazers closed out the regular season with four straight wins to finish 49–33, going 20–5 over the final seven weeks. But even the final week wasn't without drama.

On April 16, Portland blasted Denver 107–83 without the services of Rider, who had refused to go into the game in the second quarter. Rider had been nursing a bruised leg but did not start the game because he had been late for two practice sessions prior to the game. Mitchell Butler started in his place.

"I just wanted some of the other guys to get minutes," Rider explained the next day. "I didn't think it was significant that I play. I wasn't being defiant or anything. We were almost 20 points ahead going into the second quarter. I just didn't think it was that important that I go in."

Blazer management considered a suspension but decided only to fine Rider, given there was one more regular-season game on the schedule. Rider was not happy with the fine, which turned out to be $44,000, 1/82 of his $3.6 million annual salary.

"Ridiculous, considering my thinking on the situation," he said.

The Blazers assured themselves of their best record in four years by routing Vancouver 105–73 at GM Place in the penultimate game of the regular season. Rider didn't start and, in 24 minutes off the bench, scored six points on 3-for-5 shooting. There was no outward display of tension between player and coach.

"I think we're going to be fine," Carlesimo said after the Grizzlies game. "We've had incidents that have occurred all during the course of this year. I'm not happy when they occur, but it's wrong to say it's more critical now because of the time of year. I'm not going to minimize it, but I'm not going to go the other way, either."

* * *

With a 49–33 record, Portland entered the playoffs as the No. 5 seed in the West and would face the Los Angeles Lakers, the No. 4 seed.

The Blazers had knocked the Lakers down from the No. 2 spot with a come-from-behind 100–96 win in the regular-season finale on April 20. As the game ended, Rider and Robinson were two-stepping in front of a roaring Rose Garden crowd, Rider wearing Cliff's headband.

Portland had rallied from a six-point deficit with five minutes left to take a 97–94 lead, but Shaquille O'Neal's put-back with 7.7 seconds left cut the Blazers' lead to one, and the Lakers fouled Robinson intentionally. He split a pair at the line, and the Lakers got the ball back with six seconds left. Shaq was fouled going to the basket with 1.2 seconds left but missed both free throws. Robinson made two foul shots at the other end, and it was over.

Had Shaq hit the free throws, "it would have been a miracle," Anderson chortled. "It would have been raining elephants outside in Portland."

The Blazers had won the season series against the Lakers 3–1.

"Those guys wanted us [in the playoffs]," O'Neal said afterward. "Now they got us."

Carlesimo didn't quarrel with that train of thought. "We've won three of four [against Lakers]," the Portland coach said. "We know we can beat these guys. And we know we can beat them at the Forum because we've done it. I like where we are. I like the way we're playing right now. I like the fact that, deep down inside, we know we've played this team four times and three times we've come out ahead. But unfortunately, there are no guarantees. You start all over."

The Oregonian's Dwight Jaynes summed up the Blazers' regular season in a column the next day.

> There were stretches of ineffectiveness, outstanding play, and everything in between. There were countless episodes of players being fined, suspended, and otherwise punished for insubordination, missing practice, and other misdeeds. There were allegations of assaults and, in the case of Isaiah Rider, marijuana use. For a lot of the season, this was Team Turmoil, with Carlesimo taking the rap for everything but the noise-violation tickets on Gary Trent's car. Without some reversal of form against the Lakers, it will be a team remembered much more for its misbehavior than the brief moments of promise.

Before the playoff opener, Nick Van Exel said the Blazers had provided plenty of motivation for the Lakers.

"They talked trash while they were beating us [in the regular season]," the Laker guard said. "Rider, Trent, and Wallace the most. Are they annoying? If they're whipping your butt and talking trash, yeah, they're annoying. They have that right, sure. A lot of people feel they owned us during the regular season. But it's 0–0 now. We feel we haven't played our best ball against them, and they've played their best."

The Lakers opened the best-of-five first-round series with a resounding 95–77 victory at home. With the Blazers choosing to avoid double-teaming O'Neal, the Lakers 7-foot-1 behemoth scored 46 points, even making

12-of-18 attempts from the foul line. Rider, double-teamed often, had six turnovers. Robinson was 3-for-12 from the field, and the team was only 14-of-26 from the line.

Even after losing the opener, the Blazers were loose. As they were preparing for practice at Loyola Marymount before Game 2, Carlesimo got a call from Rider.

"Coach, I'm in Mexico, and I can't get out," Rider said. "They're holding me down here, and I'm not going to be able to get to practice."

Later, Rider chuckled, "I got him good. I could hear him over the phone, getting all serious. 'Really?' I got him. Don't let him tell you he didn't."

Carlesimo laughed, too, as he looked at Rider.

"You didn't get me," he said. "I hung up the phone and told the other coaches, 'Hey, that was a good one.' It was enjoyable. But you didn't get me. When you are really in trouble, you don't call. So I know when you call me, it's a joke. There was no chance it was real."

The Lakers won easily again in Game 2, 107–93, with O'Neal going for 30 points despite a sore left knee. Sabonis, abused in Game 1, wasn't any better, getting four points and two rebounds in 19 minutes.

Wallace scored 20 points, and Rider, double-teamed often, chipped in 18.

"We're not going to win with me shooting over three or four people," Rider said afterward. "The guys who aren't getting doubled have to step it up."

Asked if the Lakers' Eddie Jones was doing a good job on him, Rider said, "It's easy to do a good job when you know Shaq or Elden [Campbell] are coming to help. If you're watching the game, you know Eddie Jones isn't stopping me defensively."

But, Rider added, "We're flatline right now."

After the game, Van Exel suggested the Blazers might want to bring their brooms to Game 3 at the Rose Garden.

"I'm not thinking about that," Anderson said. "I don't think they can sweep up, but anything can happen in this series. Heck, we could win three straight. They've won two games. They're a pretty immature team. You expect things to come out of their mouths like that."

Portland extended the series by beating the Lakers 98–90 in Game 3 at the Rose Garden before the Blazers' 74th-straight playoff sellout crowd. Anderson came through with a playoff career-high 30 points, 17 in the first quarter.

"Now it's a war," Anderson said.

Sabonis played only 17 minutes, going scoreless on 0-for-7 shooting. The Lithuanian lug was so frustrated, he angrily threw his mouthpiece at Carlesimo's feet near the Blazer bench in the first half. Later, he bounced his mouthpiece off the floor and into the stands.

But Chris Dudley came off the bench for some important minutes, going toe-to-toe with O'Neal, who finished with 29 points and 12 rebounds. Wallace played him well for a spell, too, drawing a flagrant for sending him into the first row with a vigorous push to the back in the second quarter.

Despite going 1-for-15 from the field and getting outscored 32–14 in the final period (after being up by 31 with four minutes remaining in the third), the Blazers eked out the win.

Dudley remembers a moment at halftime, as the players filed to their respective locker rooms and Portland leading.

"J. R. sees Shaq and yells down the hallway, 'You ain't nothin'!'" Dudley says today. "I'm like, 'What are you doing? Don't wake him up—especially when you're not the one guarding him.'

"Rider was a character. I liked J.R. I liked playing with him. But he would get himself in trouble. He needed to be more of a leader at times. He didn't have the maturity then that he needed to have."

The Lakers were upset with Dudley's flagrant foul on O'Neal and said they would use that for motivation in Game 4. Coach Del Harris said Dudley's excuse—he didn't want Shaq to have a gimme inside—was like saying, "I killed somebody because otherwise he was going to get the promotion I wanted."

"That's a little dramatic," Dudley said. "Comparing it to murdering your boss? C'mon. With all the hype it's getting, you'd think I'd hit him with a baseball bat."

But the Lakers closed out the series with a 95–91 win in Game 4 at the Rose Garden, using a 9–0 run in the final 2:04. Wallace fouled out after scoring a career playoff-high 21 points.

"They were doing that flopping junk all game, but the ref [Steve Javie] said I bumped [Jones] too hard," Wallace said. "Sometimes a little ticky-tack foul like that is a back-breaker."

O'Neal and Elden Campbell each scored 27 points as the Lakers dominated the Blazers inside. Sabonis had a good game, scoring 23 points, but the Blazers suffered from 21 turnovers.

"I'm at a loss for words," said Anderson, who had a terrible game with six points on 1-for-8 shooting. "We were so close to getting the win, and we didn't get it. I wanted a Game 5. We all did. Everybody wanted to keep playing. This is the worst thing about the playoffs, knowing you're out. I screwed up. I'll live with this for a while. If I was going to go down, I should have gone down shooting. I just wasn't as aggressive as I had been."

Carlesimo was emotional in the postgame scene.

"I told our guys after the game that we worked hard all year, that I was proud of them," he said. "The Lakers are a great team, but we are a great team, too. If the critics were honest about what they said about the team at the beginning of the year, they would have admitted we exceeded in every way their expectations. We didn't exceed our own expectations, but I think we'll get there. We're very close. Bob has done a great job putting this team together. We're very young and don't have a lot of experience, but I like what we have."

* * *

It was wishful thinking on Carlesimo's part. Eight days after the final game, he was fired. Whitsitt called it a matter of coaching style. Observing from afar, Del Harris scoffed at that, defending his coaching counterpart.

"If you want somebody to coach trapping and pressing, that's pretty easy," Harris said. "You could fire any coach in this league and say you want a faster style of play. But the team that scored the most points in the league this year averaged 103 points, and the Blazers were two baskets away from that at 99."

In Philadelphia, where he had recently been fired as head coach of the 76ers, former Carlesimo assistant Johnny Davis defended his old colleague. "P. J. did a good job there," Davis said. "He had some volatile players. He handled it as well as it could have been handled. To win 49 games with that group demonstrates he is capable of getting the most out of his personnel."

Former player Buck Williams, now with New York, had an opinion, too.

"I think Whitsitt wants to have his own people in place, leave his own imprint on the team," Williams said. "P. J. was hired before Whitsitt was, and he was never Whitsitt's guy."

One of Carlesimo's friends, pro golfer Peter Jacobsen, said he was a victim of the "Beavis and Butthead show." He was talking about Whitsitt and owner Paul Allen.

At least one of Carlesimo's current players stood up for his coach.

"I'm disappointed," Dudley said at the time. "I thought he did a real good job. This year, especially, I thought he did a tremendous job. It wasn't an easy team to coach. You have to be pretty happy with the results. Most people thought going in—you know, with the 'Jail Blazers' and all that—it would have been mass chaos. It wasn't."

Today, Carlesimo looks back on his three seasons in Portland with fond memories but disappointment, too.

"We had three distinctly different teams," he says. "By year three, we had flipped almost the entire roster. I'm not saying [as a coaching staff] we did a great job, but we did a good job. What hurt the most, after the third year, we thought we had positioned ourselves well, and we won 49 games. But in all three years, we got beat in the first round of the playoffs.

"By year three, we thought we were as good as anybody. We had established a nucleus and it was going to be successful—and Mike [Dunleavy] did that after I left. They were in the West finals two years later. That was the disappointing thing. We had handled three different type of teams and had turned the corner and were headed in a right situation in the future. Bob felt they need to make a change, and that was disappointing."

In the last playoff series, Carlesimo said, "The Lakers were a little better than us. Our teams both got better as the season went on. They improved, and we were playing well going into the playoffs. The year before, Utah was a little better than us.

"We were not the favorite in any of those three series," he continued. "Part of the reason I got the job after the great success Rick [Adelman] had, they got beat in the first round a couple of times. Portland had been spoiled with the success they had. They were looking for playoff success.

"But we changed the team dramatically and were in a good position when we left. We left the franchise in a lot better shape than when we came in. I would have loved the opportunity to coach another year or two."

Does Carlesimo harbor regrets about his time in Portland? "Any time you could do something a second time, you'd treat somebody differently," he said. "In terms of how hard we worked and the staff we had, and whether we had our guys prepared for games, I'm arrogant enough to be comfortable with that. We worked our asses off. When we went into games, our guys were prepared."

Carlesimo's teams won 44, 44, and 49 games (a 246–137 overall record for a .557 winning percentage). His demise was tied to going 0-for-3 in three first-round playoff series.

"My memories of the three years in Portland are really good," he said. "I'm proud of what we did. The best thing about it was the relationships. Every time I go to Portland, I feel good going into [Moda Center]. So many of the people are still around. That fan base and their relationship with the team is among the two or three best in the whole league. I'm proud to say I was the coach of the Trail Blazers."

Anderson wishes the Blazers had faced any team but the Lakers in the first round. "Shaq was dominant," he says today. "That year, we had played everybody in the West tough, but the Lakers were our Achilles heel. We were the fourth-best team in the West. We were 3–1 against them in the regular season, but we didn't get it done in the playoffs. It just didn't work out for us."

Chapter 3

NO SO EASY RIDER

(1997–1998)

"We can go 40 miles down the road and they're probably still hanging
people from trees."

—J. R. Rider

On May 14, 1997, the Blazers hired Mike Dunleavy as the team's new head
coach, replacing the recently fired P. J. Carlesimo. Dunleavy, 43, had served
as general manager and coach through four losing seasons with Milwaukee.
Prior to that, though, he had two successful seasons as coach in Los Angeles,
taking the Lakers to the NBA Finals in 1991. Dunleavy was coach of the
Laker team that survived the seven-game series with the Blazers in the
Western Conference Finals that year, including the unforgettable Game 7
in which his team rallied from a 15-point deficit to win and move on to the
Finals.

"The reason I'm here is that I want to win a championship," Dunleavy
said.

Dunleavy hired a strong coaching staff, with Elston Turner staying on
from Carlesimo's staff, joined by veterans Bill Musselman and Jim Eyen, and
the young Tony Brown.

Assistant general manager Jim Paxson, who sat in with GM Bob
Whitsitt on the Dunleavy interview sessions, says today that Whitsitt had
Dunleavy in mind all along.

"P. J. had enough talent to get us to the first round every year," Paxson says now. "Part of the reason Bob made the change was we couldn't get beyond that. Mike had done that [with the Lakers]. We didn't interview a lot of people. Mike was going to be his guy."

Dunleavy would be taking over a Portland team with the youngest roster in the NBA.

Unlike Carlesimo, Dunleavy had NBA playing experience. He spent 15 seasons in the league as a player, including time as a reserve guard on the 1976–77 Philadelphia 76ers who lost to Portland in the NBA Finals. Dunleavy had even played seven games in two seasons while coaching the Bucks in 1988–89 and 1989–90. That experience, Whitsitt figured, would give him cache in working with his players in Portland.

"Mike was a really good X's and O's coach," says Jay Jensen, who served as trainer during Dunleavy's years in Portland. "That was his forte. He was a basketball coach, a gym rat. His favorite thing was, 'Let's go in and smell the gym.' Maybe you were coming off back-to-back games on a trip and some of the guys wanted to take a day off. He'd say, 'We won't do much; we'll just go in and smell the gym.' During a practice session, he was regimented. He was very organized.

"Mike cared about you. He was a good guy. I have nothing negative to say about him, other than he tended to think things were OK all the time, which is not a bad thing. But when there were things that needed to be dealt with, he concentrated on just the basketball things."

And, as Dunleavy went through his time as Portland's head coach, there were plenty of other things to deal with.

* * *

J. R. Rider made the news in late May when he was convicted of possessing less than an ounce of marijuana in Clackamas County District court and fined $500. That stemmed from charges in October 1996, when he was caught with three other men sitting in a car on a shoulder of Highway 43 north of Lake Oswego.

"I'm very surprised and disappointed," Rider said about the conviction and fine.

Soon thereafter, Utah president Frank Layden made a surprisingly frank observation to a reporter about an opposing team in the Western Conference.

"The Blazers are going through some troubled times, some angry times, some bad things, and they haven't learned anything from it," Layden said. "They're not handling it very well. I don't know Rider, but I feel sorry for him because it is a talent wasted. He was allowed to get away with things in college, so many he's not to blame as much as the people around him.

"He should have been slapped down sooner. I used to hate that type of guy. I used to hate Dennis Rodman and what he stood for, but now I realize the guy is an attraction. He's Godzilla. People love him, and we don't have many characters in the game. The guy puts on a funny costume and goes out and entertains, and he does it pretty well. He is probably laughing all the way to the bank. But I worry about these guys. They end up a bad statistic."

Forward Cliff Robinson was on the free-agent trail, seeking a long-term contract averaging between $7 and $12 million per season. In July, agent Brad Marshall lowered the aim but said his client would not accept a contract averaging only $5 million.

"I think we can get in the $6 million range, maybe a little more," said Marshall, claiming that Whitsitt was blocking a sign-and-trade option.

On August 26, prosecutors dropped charges of marijuana possession against Robinson after his brother, Torrey, pled guilty to the violation. On July 30, police had pulled Cliff over in his blue Humvee in downtown Portland after receiving reports of guns pointed out the windows of the car. They turned out to be paintball guns that Robinson, his brother, and two friends had in the vehicle. Torrey wound up pleading guilty to possession of less than an ounce of marijuana, which was also found in the car.

The next day, Robinson wound up signing a one-year, $1-million contract with Phoenix, which was all the Suns could offer under the salary cap. His departure meant the end of an era, as he was the last remaining piece of the Portland teams that reached the NBA Finals in 1990 and '92. He would go on to play four seasons for the Suns.

Robinson had come to Portland as a multi-dimensional 6-foot-10 player from Connecticut who had been disappointed to be taken with the 36th pick of the 1990 draft. Robinson had fully expected to be taken in the first round, and it was never explained exactly why he fell to the Blazers in the second round, though some deportment issues at UConn were clearly part of it. There were even some concerns in NBA circles, it was said, about his "scowl."

Robinson made an impact with the Blazers as a rookie, quickly earning Coach Rick Adelman's confidence with strong play at both ends and his versatility. He was long and could play all three front-line positions. He could score inside, had 3-point range, and wound up being the sixth man on the Portland team that lost to Detroit in the NBA Finals.

Two years later, in 1992, was when Robinson's enduring nickname, "Uncle Cliffy," was born. Friends noticed a dance he was doing at a nightclub.

"Somebody said, 'You should call that the Uncle Cliffy,'" Robinson says today. "It was funny, but it wasn't a big deal. Then, after we won the Western Conference finals against Utah that year, I did the dance in the locker room. Somebody asked me what it was called. I said, 'The Uncle Cliffy,' and it stuck."

The nickname took on a life of its own. Robinson feels there was a negative connotation to it for a while, that the young players such as him weren't taking things seriously enough. As the years passed, though, it became a term of endearment with the fans. Robinson was one of their own.

"Many people call me 'Uncle Cliffy' these days, and I have no problem with that," Robinson says. "It comes with the territory."

There were off-court behavior issues with Robinson during his early years with the Blazers, notably an incident in which he decked a female police officer during a brawl outside a nightclub. He pleaded guilty to misdemeanor assault and was sentenced to a year's probation, with a $250 fine and 50 hours of community service. There was also the matter of a speeding ticket he and teammate Alaa Abdelnaby both picked up—Robinson in his 1992 Mercedes—for racing home at 110 mph from the Hillsboro Airport following the Western Conference Finals–clinching win over the Jazz.

Robinson played hard off the court, but he always played hard on the court, too, and worked his tail off to get better. By 1992–93, he had become the NBA's Sixth Man of the Year, ranking second on the Blazers in scoring behind Clyde Drexler at 18.1 points per game that season. The next season, Robinson would surpass Drexler and become the team's leading scorer with a 20.1-point average, joining Clyde at the NBA All-Star Game.

When Anderson, Rider, and Wallace were brought on before the 1996–97 season, Robinson knew he would no longer be a 20-point scorer. He wouldn't need to be.

"We had a lot of good, talented players," he says now. "I knew with those guys coming in, my role was going to change. I was willing to make the adjustments to my game so everybody else could fit in and fill the voids. I knew I wasn't going to be taking all the shots anymore."

Robinson now looks back and reflects on being a member of a group of players who were being hailed as "the Jail Blazers."

"I was a little disappointed in that," Robinson says today. "I knew what type of guys were on that team. Some situations happened where people were making judgments about folks, like my paintball incident.

"I've never owned a gun in my life other than a paint gun. To get pulled over SWAT style in the middle of Front Avenue, blocking traffic. . . . It was blown way out of proportion. The only thing found in the car was a half a joint on the passenger side. And the word around is that Cliff was riding around shooting at people. You can see how the story gets blown up."

Robinson says incidents were scrutinized more heavily because Portland was a smaller-market city, with no other Big Four pro sports franchise.

"Things were magnified because we were here in Portland, where the Blazers are the biggest thing in town," he says now. "My early years with the Blazers, we had older guys, and we didn't have that kind of problem. When one or two things would happen with the new group, it was going to get blown up. Everybody had good character. They just got into some bad situations."

"Cliff had so much talent, at times he may have taken it for granted," says Johnny Davis, an assistant coach with the Blazers for two seasons during Robinson's time. "And he was not a bad guy. Youthful exuberance played a part with him in whatever problems he created. Beyond that, I didn't see him being detrimental in any way."

Robinson got along well with the major personalities on the team, including Rider and Wallace.

"J. R. was extremely talented," Robinson says, "but I didn't know how he was going to be acting from one day to the next, if he was going to go out of his head over something or not. It took a little while to learn how to handle J. R. But I'm the last one to be talking about somebody showing up late. I had my string of tardiness in the early part of my career. If someone is holding the plane up, yeah, it's a distraction. That's going to be uncomfortable.

"I really enjoyed playing with Rasheed. I knew he was going to be an extremely good player. We competed hard against each other at practice, and hopefully, he picked up some of my tricks as he went throughout his career. When he lost it over an official's call, I would find myself thinking, 'Come on, Sheed, let it go.' But at the same time, I knew what kind of person he was. If he believes in something, he's going to push the envelope and try to get his opinion across."

Spending his first eight seasons in Portland, Robinson was surprised Whitsitt and owner Paul Allen didn't want to keep him when he became a free agent.

"I was disappointed," Robinson says, looking back. "The Blazers never even offered me a contract. Bob talked Chris Dudley into opting out of his contract, and Chris thought he was going to get a new deal. Bob ended up letting both of us go. That's when he signed Brian Grant. I was looking forward to continuing to play with Rasheed and Sabonis and Kenny and those guys.

"I never got an explanation from Bob, but I never looked for one. I was more disappointed that Paul let it happen. Bob was trying to make his mark on the team and take it in the direction he thought was best. But I played well with those guys. It wasn't like I didn't have a good year [in 1996–97]."

When looking back to his first few years with the team and the years before he left, Robinson can see a stark contrast in feel between the two.

"Bob put together a nice group of talent around the pieces that were there," he says. "He also alienated himself with the players and didn't make it feel like it was that family atmosphere like it had been before he got there. When Geoff Petrie [Whitsitt's predecessor] was there, you always had straight-up dealings with him. He didn't say one thing and do another. Bob and I never had that kind of rapport, to be able to talk to one another or have those kinds of conversations.

"It was a colder atmosphere than it was prior to him getting there. His attitude toward the players was the biggest problem with him."

* * *

In August, the Blazers replaced Robinson by signing Brian Grant to a six-year, $56-million free agent contract.

The 6-foot-9, 250-pound Grant, 25, opted out of his contract after three years in Sacramento to sign with the Blazers. A bruising, blue-collar power forward, Grant had played only 24 games with the Kings the previous season due to a knee injury. However, Whitsitt and Dunleavy saw him as a good fit alongside Sabonis and the more finesse, perimeter-oriented Wallace on the front line.

Work ethic was ingrained in Grant, who was raised in rural Georgetown, Ohio, where from the age of 11, he spent summers toiling in the tobacco fields of his relatives.

"When I first started, I was too small to cut tobacco, so I laid the sticks down the rows," he said after coming to Portland. "When I was 14 or 15, I started cutting tobacco. You could work eight or nine hours a day for about $3 or $4 an hour. You were out in the hot sun. It was real humid, and there are always a lot of insects all over you. You were covered with dirt and tobacco gum, which is real sticky and takes about a year to get off your hands.

"The taller I got, the more it became back-breaking work to bend over and cut. But we enjoyed it. It was a time for us to bond. You would spur each other on by saying, 'You ain't working hard.' It was a way to show everybody that I could work."

During the second of his three seasons in Sacramento, the Kings made the playoffs but lost to Seattle in the first round. The next season, 1996–97, the Kings were also-rans at 34–48.

"We fell apart and had a horrible year," Grant says, looking back. "I had to get out and test the water. When I heard Portland was interested, my first thought was, 'Can I play in that rain?' But when I looked at all the players, I felt like it was a team I could fit in with that's going to go somewhere. They said, 'We want you to defend and rebound. We want you as a role player.' I didn't have to be the man. I always liked playing hard while having good players around me."

Gary Trent served as Grant's backup and started 13 games until a mid-season trade to Toronto.

"Gary was one of those guys where, if he likes you, he'll go to bat for you all the way to the end," Grant says. "If you did him wrong, he was going to retaliate. I got to know him and his story and what went on with his family, and it was difficult. His father [who had been in prison] came out and stayed with him that season. I remember having a conversation with him. He had gone through it all and was able to tell Gary, 'You better keep your life on the straight and narrow.' Gary was lucky. Gary listened to his dad—and maybe nobody else."

Before training camp began, Trent avoided prosecution when he made an out-of-court financial settlement with Theron Hall. Prosecutors had accused Trent of a "vicious" July 24 attack on Hall, punching and choking him outside of Self Enhancement, Inc., where Hall worked as a counselor. After Hall had tripped Trent's home security system, it resulted in a $500 fine for a false alarm.

Trent had been charged with fourth-degree assault and had to spend a few hours in Clackamas County Jail in January for failure to pay or respond to repeated fire alarms at his house and was eventually fined $2,650.

Trent said Blazer management hadn't talked to him about the incident.

"That's something I already knew as a man, anyway," Trent said. "They don't have to babysit me."

On September 30, Wallace signed a six-year extension worth more than $80 million, beginning with the 1998–99 season when he would make $10.8 million.

"I'm glad I'm going to be locked down here in Portland for the next few years," Wallace said. "I love the guys we have here—J. R., Gary [Trent]. I wasn't even thinking about going to another ballclub."

* * *

Rider, 26, entered his fifth NBA campaign hoping to be a team leader.

"I've always been a leader, in some way, on every team," Rider said. "This year, I have to be extremely vocal and take my leadership role to another level."

Dunleavy applauded the concept. "J. R. has a strong personality," he said. "It would be positive if he took more of a leadership role on the team. He has the respect of others because of his talent."

At the league meetings in New York, team officials were shown slides of six recent newspaper sports sections that were embarrassing, to illustrate how players' poor behavior was hurting the league's image. Four of the six headlines involved the Blazers.

To help the transition to the NBA of second-year forward Jermaine O'Neal, soon to turn 19, the Blazers hired George Glymph as director of player development. He had been a legendary coach in Columbia, South Carolina, and was O'Neal's high school coach and father figure.

O'Neal said he expected to be "10 times better than last season."

"I'm not afraid to make a mistake this year, and I know Coach Dunleavy isn't going to yell at me," O'Neal said.

O'Neal said he had felt slighted by Carlesimo during his rookie campaign, who brought him off the bench almost as a last resort. He had played a total of four minutes in the four playoff games. But O'Neal would still be in a logjam at power forward, vying for time with Wallace, Trent, and the newly signed Grant.

Sabonis would be the center, and Rider and Anderson the starting backcourt, with Augmon and rookie Alvin Williams the backups.

As training camp ensued, Rider endorsed his new coach.

"I love playing for Mike," he said. "He wants perfection, but he also just wants you to be yourself and do whatever is asked. P. J. did a pretty good job, but if you get along with your players, they'll respond better for you.

"Mike is a lot different. People respond a lot more to him. He knows how to cater to personalities but still be professional and stern. After a game, he smiles and cracks jokes. We talk about how cool it is playing for him. He's my type of coach."

After his three arrests over the summer, Rider made an assurance. "I won't let [the Blazers] down. I can definitely guarantee nothing like that will ever happen again."

On October 14, police ticketed Rider for speeding and driving without a license on Interstate-5 near Portland's Terwilliger Boulevard. Rider was charged with going 73 mph in a 55-mph zone.

Ten days later, Port of Portland police were called to meet an Alaska Airlines flight when it arrived from the Bay Area. A flight attendant complained that Rider was verbally abusive when the flight was delayed by fog in Portland, though no charges were filed. Said Darrel Buttice, the port's director of public affairs: "He got excited because of the delay."

The reason for the "excitement" was that Rider had been trying to get back in time to fly with the Blazers for an exhibition game in Spokane. He wound up missing the midday shootaround at Spokane Arena. Dunleavy took him out of the starting lineup and fined him an undisclosed amount.

With the preseason coming to a close, things got wild in the warm-up finale. Rider and Dunleavy were both ejected in the Blazers' 98–77 loss to Utah. Rider objected to a three-second call, was given two quick technicals, and was promptly ejected. Dunleavy went onto the court to argue the call and was tossed, too. Rider seemed glad the coach went with him.

"It seemed like [referee Gary Zielinski] panicked," Rider said. "He said

Mike bumped him, which he didn't. It wasn't three seconds, and then he throws Mike and me out."

"I was trying to take the brunt of it for J. R. and defuse the situation," Dunleavy said. "I was on the court, but that's usually just one technical."

Wallace also got a T after yelling at referee Jack Nies from the bench during a fourth-quarter timeout.

* * *

Rider began the regular season serving a two-game suspension by the NBA for a marijuana conviction and a no-contest plea on illegal possession of cell phones over the summer of 1996. The suspension cost him more than $100,000 in salary.

"I'm very aggravated," he said. "I tried to stay out of hot water last summer. It's rather ridiculous. I thought I had dealt with it, and now I have to deal with it again."

Was the league picking on Rider? "It definitely looks a little shady," he said. "It doesn't seem like it was thought out sufficiently and judged fairly. I'm not a wicked person. I'm not a person who holds a grudge. If there is a problem with J. R. Rider, it's that he needs to be on time, not that he's a gangster or a thug."

During the preseason, Whitsitt talked about his dual role as president of the Blazers and the NFL's Seattle Seahawks for Paul Allen, who owned both franchises. Whitsitt was in his second year as president of Football Northwest, which operates the Seahawks. How does he divide the time?

"I don't break it down," Whitsitt said. "I spend most of my time on the Blazers because that is where I have firsthand knowledge to try to do some things. With the Seahawks, my job is more to help get things organized, to keep adding people (to the administrative staff) to provide a little big-picture direction, but not as much day-to-day stuff."

Whitsitt said he left player evaluation and selection largely to coach Dennis Erickson and Randy Mueller, the VP/football operations. Whitsitt, a football receiver during his college days at Wisconsin-Stevens Point, had a condo in the RiverPlace area on the Willamette River but lived with his family in Seattle.

"Whether I'm in Seattle or Portland, I have computers everywhere and phones everywhere, so that's pretty much the way it works," he said.

Does it ever get overwhelming?

"I haven't really had time to think about it, but there have been some times when the gas tank has been a little low," Whitsitt confided. "Paul and I agree that the Blazers have to stay the No. 1 priority. My responsibilities with the Seahawks have mostly been to get things organized. Hopefully, a year from now I'll be even more invisible around there."

* * *

On opening night at the Rose Garden, Seattle closed on a 9–0 run to beat Portland 91–83 to send the fans home disappointed. Rider missed the game, and Anderson played only 15 minutes with a sore left ankle. John Crotty, starting for Anderson, outscored Seattle's Gary Payton, 17–16. Brian Grant began his Blazer career on a positive note with 19 points and 11 rebounds.

The following night, the Blazers won on the road, 82–74, against the Clippers. Anderson, his ankle feeling better, led the way with 20 points.

The next day, Rider missed practice because he went to the wrong site. Dunleavy had canceled a Sunday practice at Nike headquarters and rescheduled it for Monday at Sports Nation in Tualatin. Rider said he had gone to Nike on Monday, but Dunleavy said the Blazers had left a phone message for Rider, confirming Monday's schedule.

"It's up to him to find out where and when the practice is," Dunleavy said. "That's not a good enough excuse."

Rider was asked about it by reporters. "Bottom line, I made a mistake. I have to pay for it. You guys go ahead and have a field day with it."

Dunleavy still started Rider in the next game against his old team, Minnesota. Carlesimo had implemented a steadfast rule—miss a practice or shootaround, you sit out the first quarter of the next game. No exceptions.

"Different coach, different style," Anderson said. "Mike is going about it differently."

"Why punish the team?" Dunleavy asked. "We don't suspend guys for missing practice. Multiple offenses? Maybe."

Rider played well, scoring 20 points to help the Blazers whip the Timberwolves at home, 122–105, to improve to 2–1 on the season.

It was a wild one at the Rose Garden on November 14, with Phoenix pulling out a 140–139 win in quadruple overtime to end Portland's five-game winning streak. Danny Manning scored 35 points for the Suns, as did Rider, though the latter was only 5-for-20 shooting in the four extra sessions. Grant, starting alongside Wallace and Sabonis on the front line, contributed 34 points and 17 boards while Sabonis had 31 points before fouling out early in the fourth overtime after playing a career-high 50 minutes.

On November 20, in a 93–87 win at Detroit, a spectator near the court talked trash to Rider during halftime, and Rider spit on the fan. The league suspended him for three games and fined him $10,000.

In a written statement, Whitsitt said the penalty was too harsh because Rider was provoked. Rider had scored 24 points in the first half of the game and finished with 28.

Rider's teammates stood up for him, too. "If someone threatened my life and said something about my mother, I would have broken his neck if I could have gotten to him," Augmon said afterward. "J. R. let him off easy, I think."

"From the beginning of the game, you could hear the fans yelling at J. R.," Trent said. "As soon as he scored his first basket, they were on him. Maybe that's why J. R. did what he did. Fans think just because they buy a ticket, they can say anything they want. They think they can come up and disrespect you."

But Rod Thorn, the NBA's executive VP/basketball operations, who would be called upon often to explain sanctions against the Blazers in those years, said league officials interviewed "all the pertinent" people who witnessed the incident.

"The only thing anyone overheard were words to the effect of, 'You had a good first half, but Grant Hill is going to take it to you in the second half,'" Thorn said. "Numerous people are right there, and it did not come out that the guy was drunk. Every night, there are fans who say things to players. If a fan is unruly or out of control, security will take care of that. If you can't play without fans saying things to you, you're in trouble. And once you engage with fans, no good can come from it."

One of the biggest problems what that Rider had not returned a phone call when Horace Balmer, the NBA's VP/security, had called him about the incident.

"Anyone knows that if Horace Balmer calls, you call him back," Thorn said. "Mr. Rider was unavailable. Several messages were left for him. Then, through the trainer, he was spoken to about talking to Mr. Balmer. He refused to do it. Then later, he changed his mind and talked to Mr. Balmer."

Maybe Rider's actions were rubbing off on his young teammates. With 8.5 seconds left in the first half at Detroit, O'Neal, who had yet to play, would not check into the game when Dunleavy asked him to sub for Cato. Dunleavy instead inserted Wingfield.

"I was looking down the bench for someone to put in, and I just didn't get a quick enough response from Jermaine," Dunleavy said. "It wasn't a major thing, but when I look down there, I want you jumping up and ready to go. And if I don't see that in you, I'll pass on you.

"If I was playing and was at the end of the bench, I'd make sure I was standing up almost before my name was called, and I'd be tearing off my sweats to get in there as quickly as possible."

On November 28, former Blazer Clyde Drexler scored 24 points to lead Houston to a 98–89 win over his old team at the Rose Garden. Before the game, Drexler addressed a comment made by Whitsitt, who in speaking about Rider, had noted that Drexler had experienced problems with Coach Jack Ramsay as a young player with the Blazers.

"I'd appreciate it if he'd keep my name out of his mouth," Drexler said. "I don't respond to dumb comments but, at the same time, you don't let people take pot shots at you and try to defame you. Don't be a player-hater. We had a good history in Portland. What he has to do is try to top that in the future."

Rider, returning from his three-game suspension for spitting on the fan at Detroit, led Portland with 20 points.

A few nights later, on December 5, Rider left the bench unexpected in the third quarter of a 94–77 win over Utah at the Rose Garden, telling the team doctor he felt nauseous. Rider, who finished with nine points on 4-for-16 shooting, would not return. That surprised Dunleavy. "When I was in the league, I played a game with a stress fracture in my foot," the coach said. The following day, Rider told Dunleavy he was too sick to practice.

Needing an extra boost, the Blazers got a lift from Kelvin Cato, who blocked eight shots—including three by Karl Malone—in 19 minutes off the bench.

"He blocked everything in the building," Utah coach Jerry Sloan said. "If he had played more minutes, he might have blocked 30."

On December 8, after scoring 26 points in chest-thumping fashion in a 105–99 home win over the Lakers, Rider spoke to reporters about his All-Star Game aspirations. "It's been the media who for 2½ years have been painting a terrible picture and downplaying my game," he said. "But the league—there's no way they can avoid recognizing I'm a great player. I think Rod Strickland should have gone to the All-Star Game several times, but he never made it. I guess it was because of his past."

Seconds later, in a moment of clarity, Rider—who had been a no-show to at least two practices in Portland's first 14 games—admitted that making the All-Star Game "is a dream, but at this point in time, it's far-fetched."

Two days later, Wallace scored 10 of his 14 points in the final 10 minutes as Portland rallied to beat Indiana 93–85 at home, improving to 13–6. Rider, who had a team-high 15 points and helped hold Reggie Miller to 16 points on 4-for-10 shooting, had missed practice the previous day and was fined.

"He gave me a personal reason for missing practice, and it was a pretty good one," Dunleavy said. "Had he called before practice and let me know, it would have been excused. . . . But if he misses another practice, there is the possibility of a suspension."

On December 16, the Blazers were whistled for three technical fouls in a 94–87 loss to Sacramento, two by Wallace, who was ejected.

"We have to be mentally tougher than we are," Dunleavy said afterward.

"Our guys don't realize that the toughest job in the world is refereeing at the NBA level. You also have to realize the referees are human beings, and if you stick it to them, sometimes they stick it back to you."

Six days later, Blue Edwards stole the ball and dunked with 17 seconds left as the Grizzlies turned the tables with an 88–86 win in Vancouver. Grant was hit with two technicals and was ejected with 6:11 left, but he didn't complain about referee Tommie Wood's decision.

"He had a good reason," Grant admitted.

* * *

On December 28, after a 102–91 win over Utah, rumors were flying that Anderson would be involved in a deal with Toronto that would include local product Damon Stoudamire before the February 19 deadline. That didn't sound good to Anderson. "I'm going to chain myself to my locker," he said. "I'm not going anywhere."

Owner Paul Allen, in a wide-ranging interview (mostly about his Seattle Seahawks), was asked about Stoudamire. "He is a very talented young point guard," Allen said. "We already have one in Kenny Anderson. We're always looking for ways to get better. I challenge Bob and all the guys to improve the team if it makes sense.

"We have played well in spots. I'd like to see us improve a couple more notches. We have a lot of young players, some of them playing more minutes than they've played before. We haven't seen this team perform at the consistent level it is capable of. In spots, we've shown we're capable of beating anybody in the league."

* * *

On January 15, Rider showed up late for practice. Dunleavy chose to not start him the following night in a 96–86 home win over Utah, and Rider didn't look enthusiastic when he entered the game with 3:12 left in the first quarter.

"As you can tell, I don't like coming off the bench," he said after the game, in which he went for 28 points on 10-for-15 shooting.

"A brilliant coaching move by me to bring J. R. off the bench," Dunleavy joked afterward.

Three nights later, on January 18, the Blazers improved to 21–16 with a 94–82 home win over the Nuggets. Gary Trent had a big game, scoring a career-high 27 points on 10-for-13 shooting, while Anderson scored 23 points on 9-for-16 shooting and Sabonis collared a career-high 20 boards. But it was not a smooth night for the victors.

In the first quarter, Dunleavy looked exasperated when Anderson failed to pass to Trent on a 2-on-1 break. Later on, the coach yelled at him for not getting back to disrupt a breakaway layup. Kenny, visibly annoyed, snapped back, "I'm tired of this," as he plopped down on the bench during a timeout.

Rider picked up a flagrant foul early in third quarter when he tried to slap Nuggets rookie Eric Washington on the head. He thought Washington had popped him in the mouth on the previous play, but it was actually Denver's Dean Garrett.

Rider finished 1-for-9 from the field, was outplayed and outhustled by Washington, and eventually muttered to Dunleavy, "Get me out!" Rider spent the rest of the game on the bench against the epically bad Nuggets, who lost their 20th straight game to fall to 2–35.

Late in the third quarter, Wallace went ballistic after he was called for a foul on what appeared to be a clean block. After Eddie F. Rush called a quick technical, Wallace rushed the referee and slightly bumped him in front of the scorer's table. That drew another T and an automatic ejection. Dunleavy and Trent tried to get Wallace away from Rush, but he tore away from their grasp and let loose a stream of profanities. Some in the Rose Garden crowd of 19,964 began booing—not because it was a poor call, but because of Rasheed's behavior.

"We had to get through a lot of emotion to get the victory," Dunleavy said afterward.

Why did the Blazers struggle with emotions against the NBA's worst team? "If I knew the answer to that, I wouldn't have just majored in psychology," the coach said. "I'd have a Ph.D. by now and have written five to ten books. Some of our guys, in a tight game, react too much."

On Wallace, Dunleavy noted, "It's OK to get one, but you have to hold yourself in check after that. We overcame [his ejection], but I wouldn't want to have to do that too many nights."

On February 10, Rider made an unceremonious exit from a 117–105 home win over the Lakers, leaving the bench in the fourth quarter. Rider scored a team-high 24 points but walked off the court and into the locker room with 7:17 left after a quick exchange with Dunleavy. The Lakers promptly cut a 25-point deficit to five with 2:28 to go, though the Blazers were able to hold on.

Rider didn't start because he showed up late for the Blazers' pregame meeting—the third time that season he hadn't started because of being late for a team practice or meeting. In the fourth quarter, he had missed a long jumper early in the shot clock, and Dunleavy was unhappy with the shot selection. After a subsequent timeout, Rider said to the coach, "Put somebody else in," and walked to the locker room. Rider motioned to a woman in the stands—presumably a girlfriend—and was quickly gone. He was nowhere to be found when the doors were opened for postgame interviews.

"Talk to Mike," Bob Whitsitt said when asked about Rider's departure. Dunleavy: "It's terrible."

The team suspended Rider. Wrote *The Oregonian*'s Dwight Jaynes: "They should have fired him. Terminated his contract."

The next day, Rider held court with a media horde next to his automobile outside the training facility, lecturing reporters and not responding to direct questions. It was a rambling interview session that touched a variety of subjects and ultimately proved metaphorical for Rider's combustible three seasons in Rip City.

Asked why he left during the fourth quarter against the Lakers, Rider complained about lack of support from the Blazers' fan base. "I have a killer instinct," he said. "[The Lakers] embarrassed us on TV the week before. I wanted to win by 30 or 40. But a combination of things has me fed up. The weight of the world has just got on me. I ran. That was how I reacted.

"I need more respect and more just due. The respect isn't there. I might be the best player on the team, but I get booed . . . I'm doing too well here for people to boo. I get booed when I get introduced. No one else on the team does. I think that says a lot."

Somehow the subject got on Dunleavy's predecessor, P. J. Carlesimo, and Rider's effect on his dismissal.

"P. J. and I didn't have a problem," he said. "P. J. is the way he is . . . I could have made that problem a lot worse."

With a crowd of media around him, absorbing every Rider assertion, he concluded, "I'm fed up right now. I want to go home, take a bath, and get my thoughts together. Can I take it like I've been doing for three or four years? Yeah, but it takes a toll."

Wrote Dwight Jaynes the following day: "He spun a mystical tale of being followed in strange automobiles, of high-speed car chases ('Is it a crazy fan? A media person? A racist sniper? It could have been a cop. Could have been an FBI man') and of the wife of a Blazer staffer giving him dirty looks before the game. He spoke about how unfairly he was being treated by fans: 'They don't boo Sabonis when he misses shots. They don't boo Kenny Anderson or Rasheed Wallace.'"

Though Anderson and Wallace, both black, were excluded from the fans' scorn, Rider opined that there "definitely" is racism in the Portland area, "just like Minnesota or certain areas of any city that are not integrated and is like this . . . Come on. We can go 40 miles down the road and they're probably still hanging people from trees."

Whitsitt gave Rider a one-game suspension after his remarks.

The shooting guard returned for the next home game, ironically against Houston. Former Blazer Clyde Drexler received a standing ovation while the Rose Garden denizens loudly booed Rider during pregame introductions.

The Blazers rolled to a 105–81 win as Rider led the way with 25 points. Early in the game, there were boos every time he touched the ball. Eventually, the boos dissipated, perhaps because the fans seemed to think they had made their point but, more likely, because Rider was playing well.

Meeting with the press afterward, he issued an apology, which indicated a bit of coaching from a higher authority had taken place. Whitsitt said he and Dunleavy had met with Rider for 90 minutes pregame.

"First and foremost, I realize I have a lot more fans than I thought," Rider said. "I always say I don't want to be judged and, for a few bad apples, I can't judge this whole place. That is totally unfair, and I regret what I said.

"I'm apologetic about the racism [reference]. There is no substance behind it. Nothing physically or verbally has happened to me, and I should not have let my personal problems get in the way. Bottom line, I think I was unfair to everyone across the state."

Rocket forward Charles Barkley had read Rider's comments. Afterward, in the visitors' locker room, he focused on Rider's contention that the wife of a Blazer employee was looking at him funny.

"Maybe she was just looking at him and thinking, 'What a dummy,'" Barkley observed. "I know when I look at him, I think, 'What a nitwit.'"

Dunleavy was hoping the moment might be a turning point for Rider and the Blazers, who had won three in a row and now stood at 29–20, the sixth-best record in the West.

"Maybe this can be a very positive catalyst for our team and for J. R.," the coach said.

* * *

On February 13, the Blazers pulled the trigger on the blockbuster trade that had been rumored for months. They sent Anderson, Trent, Alvin Williams, two first-round picks and a second-round pick, plus several million dollars, to Toronto for Damon Stoudamire, Walt Williams, and Carlos Rogers.

"We now have some more ways to go," Dunleavy said. "These guys will help us be an even better club."

For Trent, there were mixed emotions. He would miss Portland, but as a budding free agent, the Raptors would be in better position to give him a big contract, he said.

"On the inside, my heart is crying because I'm going to miss everybody," he said. "But Gary Trent has to do what's best for Gary Trent. There was pressure on [the Blazers'] organization. They didn't think they were going to be able to keep me here. Maybe they could have if they would have overpaid me in order to stay and play a backup role."

Twenty years later, Trent looks back on his 2½ seasons with the Blazers with fondness and gratitude.

"It was a beautiful experience," he says. "I really needed a Portland type of city, coming in that young and living alone. We were always playoff-bound. We just needed to come together. We had had solid rosters, good talent, but it was not like there were two or three All-Stars on the roster at one time. We could have used a superstar to take us over the top."

Trent says he had respect for Dunleavy as a coach. "He had played in the league, he had a great understanding of basketball, a great basketball mind. He had a demeanor almost like one of the guys because he had been one of those guys in an NBA locker room. He still kept his line of separation and professionalism, but you could relate to him as a former NBA player."

Was there a character issue with that group? "Maybe in other elements, but I don't think on the court. Every now and then, guys would get pissed off, but we had no internal hate for one another. There were some team fights, but guys still loved each other and would hang out the next day, almost as you do with brothers or kids in elementary school. You fight your friend and then you hang out the next day. I don't think there was any bad blood for one another."

Was Rider a distraction? "At times, there were a lot of things that were distractions [with Rider]. Some of them were public and easy to see. Most of them were behind the scenes that you don't see. Yes, it's a distraction when you're trying to get a scouting report together and prepare and guys are not there, or they don't know the game plan or how you're playing defense tonight."

Even so, Trent spoke highly of Rider, as well as Wallace. "He was very passionate about the game. He played the game with a lot of emotion. Sometimes he'd get carried away. J. R. was a great guy off the court. J. R. was young and spoiled and made some mistakes. I know he loved the game of basketball. It was his outlet. It was his life. He just made some bad personal decisions that affected him professionally."

Does Trent regret his own transgressions during his time with the Blazers? "You always regret anything you don't do right in your life. It could be on the court or off the court. You make those decisions when you're young and in the public eye, and that's what comes with it. You would like to retry that situation and make it right and go about it the right way. But you don't get that chance."

As the product of a very difficult upbringing, it was suggested, it could have been a lot worse. Right? "To say it could have gone a lot worse is an understatement," he says. "Oh yes."

Was the "Jail Blazers" tag unfair to that group? "I mean, when you are carrying on the way we were carrying on, everybody getting arrested and things of that nature? Nope," he says now. "That's what's going to happen. I wish we hadn't created that title from the way we were carrying on. People will never let it go. But everybody out of that Jail Blazer group is successful today. I have to laugh at that, but it's not like we're proud of it. No way are we proud of it."

Trent now lives in the Minneapolis area and works on player development and with some youth teams. One of his sons, Gary Trent Jr., was a freshman at Duke during the 2017–18 season, who was taken by Portland in the second round of the 2018 NBA Draft.

The senior Trent—who went on to play for Toronto, Dallas, and Minnesota, and later coached with the Timberwolves—calls his time in Portland "one of the greatest times of my life."

"When I come back to Portland, the fans to this day still embrace me," he says. "They'll always be a big part of me. I scored my first NBA basket in Portland. I bought my first house in Lake Oswego. That city will always be a special place to me."

* * *

On February 17, the newly added Stoudamire and Williams combined to help Portland beat Golden State 101–83 in their Blazer debut. Both players started—Williams for Rider, who showed up late to the Rose Garden and was benched. Stoudamire contributed 12 points, eight rebounds, and six assists in 36 minutes. Williams knocked down three 3-pointers and totaled 15 points, five rebounds, and five assists in 24 minutes.

Rider, who said he got stuck in a traffic jam, still led Portland with 24 points. And Jermaine O'Neal, making his second start in as many games, went for 18 points, 12 boards, and three blocked shots in notching his first career double-double.

The Blazers, 5–0 since the All-Star break and 31–20 overall, were flush with optimism—especially the newest member.

"We can definitely challenge in the West," Stoudamire said. "I think I can make it a lot easier for J. R. And Sabonis sets big picks. It's going to be nice to play with him and see what he does, to catch some of those behind-the-back passes and other passes he makes. In Toronto, I scored a tough 19 [points a game]. Here, it might be an easy 19."

Stoudamire was a hometown hero. He grew up in North Portland and, as a sophomore and senior, helped Wilson High claim a pair of state championships. After four years at the University of Arizona, where he was a first-team All-American as a senior, Stoudamire was the seventh overall pick in the 1995 NBA Draft. He was an immediate hit with the Raptors, claiming Rookie of the Year honors in 1995–96.

But he was about to become a free agent on July 1 and wasn't happy with all the losing that was taking place in Toronto, so it was unlikely the Raptors would be able to keep him. That helped facilitate the deal with the Blazers, who had all but promised to make him the highest-paid player in franchise history with a contract that could be worth $100 million over seven years.

"I don't think they have any intention of letting me go," Stoudamire said after his first game as a Blazer.

Scotty Brooks understands why. He was then with Cleveland in the 10th and final season of an unlikely lengthy NBA career, an undrafted 5-foot-11 point guard out of Cal-Irvine.

"Stoudamire was a problem to defend," says Brooks, now head coach of the Washington Wizards. "He was one of the toughest guards to play against. He was so aggressive and quick. He was offensive-minded, he could shoot, and he could get on a roll."

Brooks says the early Jail Blazers teams "provided so many tough individual matchups."

"That's as talented group of individual players as you can put together," Brooks says today. "Rider was as talented as any two guard in the league, take away Michael Jordan. When he was on, he could flat-out put the ball in the basket. I had to guard him a few times. He had the strength of a power forward. He had that low base that would back you down and put you in the bucket. You just didn't know what you were going to get from him night in and night out."

Brooks says an overflow of talent is OK, as long as the chemistry is, too. "I don't know if you can have too much talent, but if the guys don't want to play with one another, that's not good talent. That group [of Blazers] was probably all so strong-willed. From the outside looking in, with all the talent they had, they should have been much better. If the players are not willing to play for one another and commit to the coach's system, though, it's not going to work. But they came within minutes of getting to the NBA Finals [in 2000]. They were doing something right."

But Brooks noticed the problems those Blazer teams had. "It's hard to win when you have distractions off the court constantly. There are going to be times when things come up, but when it seems like it's happening monthly, or weekly, your team's focus is not in the right place. Only certain teams can handle that. The Bulls had Dennis Rodman, but they had the greatest player ever to keep him in check."

Brooks calls Rasheed Wallace "an interesting guy."

"I never played with him," Brooks says, "but everybody I know who did loved the guy. He's that wild card you can have on your team. If you only have one or two of them, you can be OK. He reminded me of Vernon Maxwell as a personality. Vernon had a reputation as a loose cannon, but he was loved by all his teammates. Vernon was one of my favorite teammates.

"Rasheed has those same type of qualities, but he also had the unselfish quality. He could have scored 20 to 25 points a game if he were focused on being a hungry scorer."

Brooks is now in his 14th season in NBA coaching, the last nine as a head coach. He believes he has learned a few things about chemistry and defined roles on a team. "Chemistry is extremely important. As a coach, you're always searching for it. When you have it, you do whatever it takes to maintain it. As a player, you must have respect and trust in your teammates and have each other's backs. It's critical to every team's success. Look at all the championship teams. They have a bond they'll have forever."

* * *

On February 22, Kenny Anderson was in Portland playing against his old team—but not for Toronto. The point guard had refused to report to the Raptors, prompting a trade to Boston. In his second game as a Celtic, Anderson scored 14 points on 5-for-9 shooting and had eight assists, but the Celtics were steamrolled by the Blazers, 121–96.

Stoudamire, in his fourth game with Portland, had 17 points and nine assists. Sabonis, Wallace, and Brian Grant combined for 51 points, 26 rebounds, and .647 shooting.

"Life goes on," Anderson told reporters after the game. "I'm a Celtic now, that's how I look at it. You just move on. I didn't leave here with any bad blood, and I'm not giving anybody bad blood. I'm fine."

Today, though, Anderson admits to feeling let down by the Blazers for sending him away after only a year and a half with the franchise. "I was hurt when I got traded from there. I did everything in my power to help that team, on and off the court. I did a great job. I just didn't understand. I really don't even today.

"Portland was great for me. I played extremely well, and I was comfortable. I was getting adjusted. I loved the fans. I had a great following. I had a seven-year contract. I thought I was going to be there for a while. After doing all the right things, I didn't understand the trade. I was like, 'Wow, what happened here?' I couldn't figure it out."

Was it just the opportunity to bring in a local product in Stoudamire? "I used to think that," Anderson says. "Bob Whitsitt had a good relationship with Damon. He was having a great year, too. That's the way I came to grips with it. We were both the same type of player. Maybe it was like, 'We can get rid of Kenny's contract and move on from there.' It was a push for them. I understand it more now. It's part of the business. But I was hurt then."

Anderson noted how the Blazers had closed with a rush, going 20–5 down the stretch of the 1996–97 regular season.

"J. R., Rasheed, and I were all new to the team," he says now. "For the first half of the season, we were trying to find ourselves. But I was excited. I was going to be the guy for the franchise, and I delivered. We got better as the season progressed. We got better with each other. We had Cliff and Sabonis to take care of the middle. We just started playing better. And I thought we would be even better the next year."

Anderson felt comfortable during his season with P. J. Carlesimo and assistants Dick Harter, Rick Carlisle, and Elston Turner. "I wish I was able to stay there under that staff. That was a great staff. That was one of the reasons I was comfortable. P. J. and I had ties together back home in New York. Rick was with me with the Nets. I thought the players were very good. We had great talent. We had young guys; we had some veterans."

The chemistry, Anderson says, "was good, though a lot of the guys had their growls about P. J. and how he coached. Well, different strokes for different folks. It was great for me. Some players didn't like it. They wanted to change the type of coaching we were getting. I thought that was the best thing for that group. When they got rid of P. J. and that staff and brought in Dunleavy, it was too loosey-goosey.

"I didn't understand it when they brought in Dunleavy. He had his own collection of players he wanted to bring in, to play his style. The players were running the show a little bit more than under P. J. That's what they wanted to do somewhat—loosen it up a little bit. P. J. was more of a disciplinarian than Dunleavy. That was what Bob Whitsitt wanted."

Rider's antics, Anderson says now, "were a little bit of a distraction, but he had so much talent. That trumped everything. He and P. J. collided every now and then, but that's the NBA. The great coaches can deal with things like that and not let it affect the team. I didn't think it affected us that much. But I'm older now. I can see that, with those type of guys, if you don't wrap them up, it can get worse. P. J. was able to control them somewhat, even though they were going at it with him at times."

Anderson remembers the good more than the bad during his brief time in Portland.

"We won a lot of games," he says. "I was happy with everything the first year. We could have done a better job in the playoffs, but our first year together was a success.

"It would have been different if we'd kept P. J. He was hired before Whitsitt was. Usually, a GM is going to bring in his guy. That's how it works in the business.

"But I have nothing but love for the organization, and definitely for the city. That was the first game jersey I had framed for my mother, Joan Anderson [who passed away in 2005]. I have the jersey in my house now. I see it every day. She used to come visit me in Portland. She thought it was a great place for me to be, get away from everybody."

* * *

On February 26, Rider nailed a pressure 3-pointer with 41 seconds left, the key to a huge 106–101 win over Chicago at the United Center, the Blazers' first win there in four years. Rider scored 22 points against the defending NBA champions, while Stoudamire contributed 24 points and 11 assists. Sabonis went for 21 points and 20 rebounds as the Blazers improved to 33–22.

"We feel like we're on top of the world," said Rider, as the Blazers started a three-game road trip with the biggest win of the year.

Michael Jordan had 15 of his 33 points in the fourth quarter. "He just went into a zone," Rider said, but it wasn't enough.

Dunleavy didn't take kindly to the suggestion by a Chicago writer that the Blazers had stolen one.

"I don't think we stole one," the coach said. "What we did was come in here and play our butts off. Chicago's a great team. They're my favorite to win it all, until somebody puts them out."

Before the game, Rider spoke to Chicago reporters about his reputation.

"It bothers me the way I'm perceived," he said. "For years, I've been getting drilled. Some of has had some substance and was well-deserved. If something happens, you have to report it. But most of it, I'd say 65 to 70 percent, is garbage."

After winning nine of their previous twelve games, the Blazers were unable to sustain their momentum. On March 1 came a crushing defeat, a 102–101 loss at Boston, in which the Celtics rallied from 25 points down with 10 minutes to go.

"It's like we were brain-dead or something," an irritated Dunleavy said afterward. "We did some things out there [in the fourth quarter] I haven't seen us do even in practice. I've never seen us play with so little poise."

During pregame introductions, Rider ducked out, ostensibly to go to the bathroom. He didn't get back to the court in time for the opening tip, and Dunleavy was forced to insert Stacey Augmon in his place. Later, Rider got called for a technical from the bench—big in a one-point loss. He seemed surly most of the night as his teammates spent time clustered around him, trying to calm him down.

Two days later, Stoudamire was on crutches after spraining his ankle in a 98–83 home victory over Phoenix.

On March 12, Sabonis went for 28 points and 20 rebounds, including the winning basket with 7.2 seconds left, in a 95–92 home win over Minnesota. Rider had promised he would celebrate his 27th birthday with "a very, very, very big game" against the team that traded him, and finished with 15 points on 5-for-18 shooting.

Three days later, the Blazers hit a low point for the season with a 92–82 loss at Denver to the 7–58 Nuggets. Johnny Newman, a 34-year-old journeyman, came off the bench for 33 points.

The Nuggets had extra motivation. They were still seething from the way the Blazers gloated in their last meeting, a 117–82 Portland romp in a dunk-fest at the Rose Garden on February 15.

"That left a bad taste in our mouths," Denver center Dean Garrett said. "It's easy to kick a dog when he's down, and that's what they did. We were down 30, and they were laughing and giggling and trying to get Jermaine O'Neal his career high. We've been down to a lot of other teams, and those teams handled it differently."

"There is a level of humility and class I feel should be accorded, no matter what the situation is," forward LaPhonso Ellis said. "Even when we were real good a few years ago, we never, ever tried to run up the score or showboat the way they did."

On March 18, Cleveland romped past the Blazers 96–82 at the Rose Garden behind 20 points from Shawn Kemp. With 8:43 left in the game, Rider launched a 3-point airball attempt that drew a few scattered boos. He waved his arms, asking for more boos, and mouthing, "Bring it on." Then he didn't take another shot for 6½ minutes.

Three days later, with Stoudamire still idled by the ankle injury, the Blazers were bounced 102–87 at Orlando to fall to 37–29. Grant collected 21 points and 16 boards, but Rider had words with Dunleavy during a first-quarter timeout and was all but a no-show throughout the rest of the game.

Afterward, Dunleavy held a long team meeting and issued an ultimatum to the players, saying that he wasn't going to put up with anything more resembling insubordination.

"I told our guys I wanted them to have a more professional attitude," Dunleavy told the media. "I said from this point on, I want us to tighten the ship and get ready for the playoffs, that things aren't going to be tolerated that could affect our chances."

Stoudamire returned on March 26, and the Blazers celebrated with a 90–73 win over Sacramento, pounding the Kings on the boards, 56–37. Rider scored 24 points, and Grant hurt his old team with 19 points and 14 rebounds.

On April 1, Karl Malone scored 24 points to lead Utah to a 98–89 win at the Delta Center.

Sabonis played only the first half before bowing out with a sore hip. Rider didn't play at all, as he was suspended after showing up late for practice.

"He was excessively late," Dunleavy said. "This is something we've addressed before." It was the seventh game in which Rider has been suspended that season.

Rider took responsibility for being late, telling the media, "Mike and I are fine, as far as I know. I was just late, and I had to pay for it."

After an easy victory over the Kings, the Blazers suffered another embarrassing loss to the Nuggets, falling 109–101. The Nuggets improved to 11–70, with two of their wins coming against Portland.

"That was a bad display," Stoudamire said. "I guess this is the reason why everybody loves to hate the Blazers. We can tease you. We can look so good one day, and the next day we're not even the same team."

* * *

The Blazers finished the regular season 46–36, the No. 6 seed in the West. That earned them a first-round best-of-five matchup with the Los Angeles Lakers, who had the No. 3 seed despite a 61–21 record. It was a rematch of the first-round series of the previous season, won by the Lakers. But the teams had split their four-game season series, and the Blazers felt good about their chances going in.

"You want to beat the Lakers," Rider said before Game 1 at the Fabulous Forum. "You want to shock the world. I want to be part of the team that breaks their hearts."

Shaquille O'Neal had outscored Sabonis 46–18, 30–4, and 29–0 in the first three games of the previous year's series. The Blazers were hoping for much more from their 7-foot-3 center this time.

"As you look down the rosters, you can't put it all on one key matchup," Dunleavy said. "Except I do know this: That matchup is one we have to contain. It's Shaq's mobility vs. Sabas's immobility. In most cases, Sabas has a size advantage. That's not true in this case, but still, with his versatility, Sabas should be a big part of any series. I don't think we're going to win the series if Sabas doesn't play well."

O'Neal had finished second behind Chicago's Michael Jordan with a 28.3 scoring average during the regular season. The Laker behemoth had the league's best field-goal percentage at .584. At 26, he was beginning the physical peak of his career. Sabas was a worn-down 33.

Stoudamire, in his first taste of the playoffs, was set to match up with veteran Nick Van Exel and young Derek Fisher, 23, of the Lakers. Meanwhile, Coach Del Harris was considering using 19-year-old Kobe Bryant some at point guard, too, though he hadn't played much, or consistently well, since the All-Star break.

Bill Walton, TV analyst for the series, said the Blazers must "come together as a team to beat the Lakers." The former Blazer center said Rider would be a key.

"He is a troubled and confused person," Walton said. "In last year's playoffs, he simply could not play at the mental level that the game was being waged on. He is going to have to change."

The Blazers lost a hard-fought opener, 104–102, after dominating much of first half. Rider scored 25 points in 43 minutes, and Sabonis got 15 points and nine rebounds despite playing only 24 minutes with foul trouble. Stoudamire contributed 12 points, 10 assists, and seven rebounds but on only 4-for-14 shooting. Wallace added 18 points but only three boards in 41 minutes.

O'Neal totaled 30 points on 13-for-20, shooting along with seven rebounds and three blocks in 41 minutes.

The Blazers were confident they could win Game 2 and go home for the next two games with the series tied, but the Lakers prevailed 108–99. Guard Eddie Jones had 21 points, but Rider, booed throughout the game by Forum partisans, scored 24.

"I feed off it," Rider said of the boos. "I shut the LA fans up. Shut everybody up. That's what the personal thing is all about. But I'm not going to go outside the team to outdo anybody. The bottom line is wins and losses."

Shaq got in early foul trouble and scored only 19 points with nine boards, but small forward Rick Fox came through with 24 points. The Lakers won the game at the foul line, sinking 34-of-52 attempts to only 17-of-21 for the Blazers.

Stoudamire finished with 17 points and 14 assists but also had six turnovers. Brian Grant collected 15 points and seven rebounds but Sabonis, hampered again by foul trouble, had only six points and seven boards in 14 minutes.

In the same position as they were a year ago, Portland now needed to sweep the final three games to win the series.

"They haven't done anything to make us believe we can't beat them," Stoudamire said. "They might think they have, but they still haven't beaten us in Portland."

Rider was asked about his team's chances.

"I'll be honest—we need a miracle," he said. "That's a tough team with a lot of talent. We're down 2–0. We need a miracle."

Stoudamire scored nine of his 18 points in the fourth quarter as Portland earned a come-from-behind 99–94 win in Game 3 at the Rose Garden. The Blazers trailed 72–69 heading into the fourth quarter but outscored the Lakers 30–22 over the final 12 minutes.

In the third quarter, Stoudamire told Dunleavy, "Run plays for me."

"I wanted to take it upon myself," the point guard said. "[The Lakers] are hedging out on me, giving me that lane. I was trying to go in the middle and make something happen. Luckily for me, it worked. I always dreamed about winning a playoff game somewhere, not necessarily at home. It feels good to get that first one."

Shaq had a huge game with 36 points on 16-for-23 shooting with 16 rebounds in 42 minutes. Sabonis battled him pretty well, collecting 13 points and eight boards before fouling out in the fourth quarter. Rider contributed 18 points and 10 rebounds but made only 6-of-19 shots. He sealed the win by going 4-for-4 at the line over the final eight seconds.

"The momentum has shifted a little," Stoudamire said. "Not a lot, but to where the Lakers feel they have to win the next game."

"Just a fraction of the pressure is off us," Wallace said. "We can't let them win any more games, or it's bye-bye Blazers."

The Blazers were 3–0 at home versus the Lakers for the season (including their Game 3 win). Rider, for one, thought that meant something going into Game 4.

"They're not the same team they were in LA," Rider said. "They weren't talking. They weren't hyped. They were a flat-line team emotionally, and they are a team that plays off emotion. They're a high-powered team, but they're human. They're beatable."

But history repeated itself with the Lakers rolling the Blazers, 110–99, wrapping up the series at the Rose Garden. LA led 56–30 at the half, and the game was pretty much over from that point.

Shaq was dominant again with 31 points on 13-for-17 shooting to go with 15 rebounds, five assists, and four blocks. The Lakers' bench outscored their Blazer counterparts, 48–15, led by Bryant with 22 and Van Exel with 14.

Stoudamire had a nice game with 22 points and eight assists, but the Blazers shot only .385 while the Lakers fired at a .581 clip.

"We didn't give them a run at all," Rider said.

The Blazers had become the first team in NBA history to lose in the first round six straight years.

"If there's anyone who doesn't take this loss hard, a season-ending loss, then they will realize it tomorrow when they wake up and realize it wasn't a dream," Stoudamire said.

"They were the better team tonight," Grant said.

Dunleavy agreed. "The Lakers are my pick to win it all. I mean, put the ring on their fingers."

That wasn't to be. The Lakers would get swept 4–0 by Utah in the Western Conference Finals (who would end up losing in six to the Bulls, winning their third championship in a row).

After his exit interview with the Blazer brass, Rider told the media about his goals for the following season and newfound relaxed mindset.

"I want to expand my ballhandling," he said. "That's my main focus. Each year has been a learning process, whether in basketball or just the game of life. I'm taking some knowledge into the summer. I learned to hang in there through adversity, to stand firm. I learned to be less hard on myself.

"I'm my hardest critic, and I don't need to put any added pressure on myself. I learned to be more easy-going, not take everything so seriously. And I learned to enjoy life, to kind of relax."

* * *

The end of the season marked the end of Bill Schonely's long run in the broadcasting booth. The beloved radio play-by-play voice—who had served the position since the club's inaugural 1970–71 season—had been removed at season's end and switched to a less prominent role.

In Schonely's autobiography, *Wherever You May Be—the Bill Schonely Story*, he painted the scene.

"My previous contract expired at the end of the 1996–97 season," Schonely wrote. "During the summer (before the 1997–98 season), I learned from Harry Hutt, our senior VP/marketing, that a change was going to be made at the end of next season. I would not be doing play-by-play anymore. I asked him whether I had done anything wrong. He said, 'Absolutely not. We still want you to be part of this organization for as long as you want to be.'"

The next season, the "Schonz" would host television specials, voice radio ads, do some pre- and postgame work, and serve as an ambassador while doing appearances on behalf of the club. Brian Wheeler was Schonely's successor, and over his successful 20-year run has developed an ardent following of his own.

When the bombastic Hutt delivered the news during the summer of '97, Schonely was "devastated," he says today. "I had no inkling it was going to happen. You could have knocked me over with a feather when Harry told me. I didn't want to retire. I thought everything was sailing along just fine. I wanted to go as long as I could. I was so damn mad, I walked out of the room."

What was the reason given?

"I never really was given one," says Schonely. He guesses age was at least part of it. He would celebrate his 70th birthday about a month after the 1997–98 campaign ended.

Maybe Whitsitt and Hutt were envious of the attention Schonely was getting. Perhaps owner Paul Allen was oblivious to it, since he lived in Bellevue, Washington, and flew to Portland primarily only for home games. Allen—who rarely listened to Schonely, since he was either watching a game in person or on TV—probably wanted to get some fresh blood.

When the Blazers released the news that the season would be Schonely's last, the reaction from fans was harsh—at least when they found out it wasn't

Schonely's idea. The Blazer front office was bombarded with calls and emails criticizing the decision. There were protests and signs at games through the season. Whitsitt and Hutt had underestimated Schonely's popularity. To some of the team's supporters, the affable broadcaster was the most important person ever in the organization, ahead of even Bill Walton and Clyde Drexler in the pecking order.

Schonely continued to work through the season. With a couple of months to go, Whitsitt and Hutt brought him in for a meeting to reiterate their plans—and also to chastise him.

"They said, 'We want you to stop organizing what's going on with the fans and the public,'" Schonely says now. "They thought I had instigated the whole thing."

Schonely tried to get them to change their mind.

"I pleaded with them," he says. "then I got so mad, I just shut up."

Schonely spent the next two summers calling play-by-play for the PCL baseball Portland Beavers.

"I was off the Blazer payroll for a little while," he says.

The court of public opinion demanded he come back, though, and by the time the 1999 season opened, Schonely was in his new role, albeit somewhat buried. It wasn't until Whitsitt was fired and Steve Patterson hired in 2003 that Schonely was placed in a more prominent role and his microphone "retired" to the rafters alongside the numbers of the franchise's greatest players.

In a newspaper interview after the season, Whitsitt addressed the Schonely situation.

He said the outpouring of fan support for Schonely made it harder for the veteran broadcaster to relinquish his job.

"When my fans are telling me I can shoot forever, I'm not going to tell them, 'No, I can't,'" Whitsitt said. "The whole situation is unfortunate for everybody. It's one of those classic lose-lose-lose-lose-lose-lose type of things. What he was supposed to try to enjoy this year was a last time behind the mike and then move on to other things and make sure he got to 2,500 games.

"A lot of the reasons [for replacing Schonely] are behind the scenes. Some of them are public. There are private issues that should not be shared publicly."

No, Schonely wasn't involved in a domestic case or sexual assault issue. He hadn't been arrested or done anything to embarrass the organization. To this day, Schonely has no idea to what "private issues" Whitsitt was referring.

"I can't really relate to broadcasting, but if I was talking about basketball, at what point do you retire?" Whitsitt asked the reporter. "Why do you retire? At what point do you become the sixth man? At what point do you take a different role? Who makes those decisions? How? Why? How many times have you written about the quarterback: 'I wish he would have retired three or four years ago, so I could remember him that way versus the other.'"

Whitsitt, basically, was saying Schonely was 42-year-old Willie Mays, stumbling around in the outfield in his final season with the New York Mets.

Schonely, who at 89 still works as a broadcaster/emeritus and ambassador for the club and is as popular as ever with the fan base, says he still hears from admirers and well-wishers who would love it if he were still calling play-by-play.

"I get it every day of my life," he says. "I still wonder why Bob and Harry did what they did. But guess what? I'm still working for the organization."

And they're not.

Chapter 4

THE LOCKOUT SEASON

(1999)

"Someday, I'm going to learn how to channel [players' emotions] to where it's positive and have us take it out on opponents and not the officials. That's my ultimate goal in coaching right now."

—Mike Dunleavy

The Trail Blazers couldn't wait to begin the 1998–99 season. Point guard Damon Stoudamire, acquired at the trade deadline from Toronto the previous season, would have his first training camp with J. R. Rider, Rasheed Wallace, Aryvdas Sabonis, and Brian Grant. With a season under his belt, Coach Mike Dunleavy felt he had the personnel to make a run at a berth in the NBA Finals.

But there had been labor discord for some time and, as the league's collective-bargaining agreement came due for renewal on July 1, 1998, the NBA and its Players Association were far apart on many issues. A six-year CBA had been in place since September 1995, but there was a three-year opt-out clause that the owners used to reopen the contract.

So a lockout ensued, and the issue wasn't resolved until early January. That left time for only a 50-game regular season.

There were some changes in Portland's front office and on the coaching front. Dunleavy added Tim Grgurich—whom he had tried to hire away from Seattle the previous year—as an assistant coach. Grgurich, who commanded one of the highest salaries for his position in the league, held an annual summer camp in Las Vegas that was popular on the NBA front, and he was reputed as a coach who built close relationships with players and helped develop their games.

After just one season as the Blazers' director of player development, George Glymph was relieved of his duties. Glymph had been brought on for one reason—he had been Jermaine O'Neal's high school coach, and the Blazers wanted him to help make the teenager comfortable in Portland and bring him along as a player.

Glymph later said he learned about his dismissal by reading it in *USA Today* and was "devastated." A couple of years later, after O'Neal was traded to Indiana, Glymph joined the Pacers' staff to work with Jermaine and a couple of other young post men, including Al Harrington and Jonathan Bender (both drafted out of high school).

Meanwhile, Jim Paxson left to become VP/basketball operations of the Cleveland Cavaliers. Paxson—a former All-Star shooting guard in the 1980s who is one of seven Blazers to score 10,000 points with the team—had begun as player development coach in 1993–94. When Whitsitt came aboard the next season, Paxson did some advance scouting for a season, then served as assistant GM for three years. Whitsitt found Paxson as a good sounding board and, at times, leaned on for advice.

"Our big trade was getting Rasheed Wallace [in 1996], a young player who was that talented," Paxson says now. "That trade set the course of moving forward. Also, bringing Arvydas Sabonis over [in 1995] was huge. Bob flew to Spain a couple of times to meet with Arvydas and convince him that was the time to do that. He was trying to lay the groundwork and accumulate as much talent as he could.

"I learned a lot during that time. P. J. Carlesimo was hired before Bob was, so he wasn't his coach, but Bob tried hard to make it work with P. J. There were challenges on both sides with that."

Paxson didn't know Whitsitt before he was hired by the Blazers.

"We didn't have a relationship early on," Paxson says. "He kept things pretty close to the vest at first, but he gradually got me involved. It was a great learning experience. If I wouldn't have those three years as assistant

GM in Portland, I probably wouldn't have gotten the opportunity to go to Cleveland."

Paxson worked with scouting director Mark Warkentien to search for talent. He and Warkentien attended practices for the McDonald's All-American Game when Jermaine O'Neal participated in 1996.

"Mark did a good job pinpointing talent—Jermaine, Gary Trent, and, the year I left, Bonzi Wells," Paxson says. "Bob trusted Mark's talent evaluation and draft guidance. Mark had a big imprint on all those players drafted through the years with Bob."

Paxson wasn't involved in the decision to take on J. R. Rider.

"That was a risk reward deal that Bob and Mark felt strongly about taking a big swing on," Paxson says. "He was a big talent who had plenty of issues, that's for sure. He was always very pleasant to me. He was just immature."

Paxson remembers getting a call from Whitsitt that Trent had been involved in an incident and to take care of it.

"We'd gotten a call from the Boys and Girls Club that, in front of 300 kids, Gary had punched out some guy. I had to address that with him. He told me it was a guy living with him, and he found out he was stealing from him. He said, 'What's a guy supposed to do?' I said, 'Well, that's not the way to handle it.'"

There were times Paxson was called upon to shield the Blazer players from the dastardly Fourth Estate.

"J. R. had an incident the night before a practice at Club Sport. All the media was waiting for him there. I told him, 'We'll go out the back door so you don't have to talk to anybody.'

"I was there to help the players work through things that were going on. Being an ex-player, I had a pretty good understanding of what was going on. You do everything you can to make it work. You also want to keep your players' value up until you trade them."

Another team official, who asks to be unidentified, says Rider was a paradox.

"I could never really figure him out," he says. "He was incredibly talented but was extremely moody. If you caught him at the wrong time, he could say and do some things that seemed a little illogical.

"Sometimes on the team plane, he would put a blanket completely over his head. They had booze on the team plane then. You'd see the blanket moving up and down as he's drinking out of a bottle. Sometimes he'd say something to the flight attendant that sounded like, 'Hey, bitch, make me a tuna fish sandwich.'

"He was passive-aggressive in the way he dealt with the fans. He went through a stretch when the fans had been hard on him, so he would react negatively when the crowd would cheer for him. He'd hit a shot and go down the floor with his hands flapping down, like, 'Don't cheer for me now.'"

Paxson was on the other side of a three-way deal in which he unloaded a bloated, drug-addled, overpaid Shawn Kemp to the Blazers before the 2000–01 season. Brian Grant went to Miami, and Cleveland received Chris Gatling, Clarence Weatherspoon, a first-round draft choice, and cash.

"I can understand why Bob did it," Paxson says now. "That group of players didn't get over the hump the previous season. Bob took one big swing to see if that would make the difference. He felt with [Shaquille O'Neal] with the Lakers, he needed more size and bulk to go against them.

"They probably should have held onto Brian. Shawn was never again the player he was when I had him in Cleveland."

Paxson offers mixed emotions on whether or not Whitsitt stockpiled too much talent.

"Bob's philosophy was to try and get as much talent as you can and let your coaches figure out how to best utilize it," Paxson says. "That can work, but sometimes it doesn't. The teams I was around in Portland didn't get beyond the first round of the playoffs. That's why Bob kept tweaking the roster and trying to give the coaches more talent. I know Mike was open to that.

"It's hard to keep everybody happy. I'm a big believer in chemistry. Chemistry and how you put teams together is very important, but Bob was a little bit ahead of his time in thinking you just go get the guys and try to make it work with as much talent as you can."

Seattle's backcourt that season was comprised of perennial All-Star Gary Payton out of Oregon State and veteran Hersey Hawkins, who would wind up as a long-time employee of the Blazers after his retirement as a player. Hawkins spent 13 years in the NBA, the first 12 as a starter, averaging 14.7 points in 983 games. Hawkins, who twice averaged more than 20 points a game at Philadelphia, was with the Sonics from 1995–1999.

"Talent-wise, the Blazers were one of the best teams around in those years," says Hawkins, now the player programs director with Portland. "Confidence-wise, they were as tough as they came. When you played against them, you knew it was going to be a dogfight. That's the way they played. Against those Portland teams, you knew it was going to be a tough night.

"It was one of the better rivalries in the league. I wouldn't say there was hatred, but it was close. There was mutual respect, but because you were so close, you wanted bragging rights in being the best team in the Northwest."

Hawkins was well aware of the Blazers' frequent off-the-court problems through those years.

"It got to a point where you weren't surprised when you read something that happened," Hawkins says today. "It was disappointing to see such talented guys and such a good team come apart because they weren't able to keep it together off the court. They had a lot of those players who wanted to have entourages. That's not good at any level."

When the Sonics and Blazers collided, Hawkins was often matched up against J. R. Rider.

"He was really talented," Hawkins says. "He was a little unorthodox. He could shoot the 3, he was strong, he posted up, he handled it well. He was a tough guard for me, because of all the things he could do. I never looked forward to playing against him, but I also knew defensively he wasn't going to put out the best effort. He may score 20 points, but I always felt like I could get 20 against him."

Hawkins respected Rasheed Wallace but saw a weakness there, too.

"Rasheed was an All-Star talent, a clutch player," Hawkins says. "He could do it all. But he was emotional. You knew if you could get under his skin or get him to react, maybe that would throw him off his game. He was a terrific player, but he lost his cool a little bit too much. I always looked at it as, 'There goes Rasheed again.'"

Hawkins thinks the Blazers of that era should have had even more success.

"Those were some of the best teams Portland has seen as far as collective ability," he says. "You don't get that kind of talent assembled very often. From 1 to 12, those teams were very talented. You thought they were good enough to win it all, but it never quite came together for them. You can have a few guys who test the boundaries, but you better have a group of veterans to bring them back."

* * *

An abbreviated 50-game regular season was to begin on February 7. About two weeks before the start of the season, eighteen Blazers gathered for a makeshift training camp. One of those on hand was rookie Bonzi Wells, a 6-foot-5, 215-pound guard out of Ball State who had been acquired in a trade with Detroit. The Pistons traded their first-round pick—11th overall— to Portland for the Blazers' first-round choice in 1999, which turned out to be No. 27 (Vladimir Stepania).

Wells had set the Mid-American Conference career record in scoring (2,485 points) and had also established a conference single-season record while averaging 3.6 steals as a senior.

"I like his size, I love his defense, I like his ability to take the ball off the dribble," Whitsitt said at the press conference announcing Wells's signing. "He's a typical Indiana kid—he loves basketball."

Typical Indiana kid. Sure—straight out of *Hoosiers*.

Gawen DeAngelo Wells grew up in Muncie, Indiana, a blue-collar city of about 70,000, and stayed to play in the state at Ball State. When it comes to his unique nickname, it's one he picked up as a toddler.

"When my mother was pregnant with me, she craved ice cream bon-bons," Wells explained. "She started calling me 'Bon Bon.' Somehow, 'Bonzi' came into effect soon after that."

Wells was a talented player at Muncie Central High and, as a senior, was runner-up for the state's "Mr. Basketball" award. But after the season, he was kicked off the Indiana All-Star team by a unanimous vote of his team-mates "because of his selfish attitude," wrote Doug Zaleski, who covered Muncie Central for the *Muncie Star-Press* during Wells's time there. Wells left the arena at halftime of his first high school All-Star game after an argument with the team's coach.

Shortly after being named Mid-American Conference Player of the Year as a sophomore at Ball State, Wells was arrested for domestic battery when a woman accused him of striking her because she refused to have sex with him. According to police reports, the woman suffered scratches on her arms, neck, and one leg, and some of her jewelry was broken. He was jailed briefly, then released, and the prosecutor's office, citing lack of conclusive evidence, chose not to file criminal charges.

As a junior at Ball State, he stomped off the court after a loss at Central Michigan, then delivered a slap to the head of the Chippewas' Jerry Glover, who had chased him down to shake hands. On the way to the locker room, according to Zaleski, Wells kicked teammate Randy Zachary down a flight of stairs as the two argued.

In an interview before his senior season, Wells, who had received eight technical fouls the previous two seasons, pledged better deportment.

"I watched a lot of film and saw I was acting like an ass out there," Wells told the *Star-Press* at the time. "I saw I was jaw-jacking at the referee or doing things that weren't right for us to do as a team. I can't lead the team in technicals, can't be yelling at teammates or not clapping when I'm on the bench. That's no leader right there. That's a crazy person—a Dennis Rodman."

But Wells also said this: "People who like me are the people who know about basketball or played the game or understand the game. Those who don't are probably just new fans who don't know much about basketball and don't understand how hard it is on the court."

Zaleski's read on Wells was not a complimentary one.

"He was the typical pampered high school and college athlete you hear about who thinks he can do no wrong," Zaleski said in 2002. "Everybody always bent over backward to make excuses for Bonzi and allow him to do things. He can be a snake charmer. Underneath the bull, there is a softer side, but he chooses not to use it. He can be engaging and funny. Kids from his neighborhood worship him. But for the most part, he is Eddie Haskell with money."

* * *

The Blazers went into the 1998–99 season stacked at shooting guard with Rider, newly acquired Jimmy Jackson, and the rookie Wells along with swing men Walt Williams and Stacey Augmon.

Jackson, 28, was signed to a bargain three-year, $6 million free-agent contract five days before the start of the regular season. Portland would be the fifth destination in just three years for the chiseled 6-foot-6, 220-pound Jackson, who had been with Dallas and New Jersey in 1996–97 and Philadelphia and Golden State in 1997–98.

Jackson had been a starter since his rookie season with the Mavericks, averaging 25.7 points his third season on a Dallas team co-featuring Jason Kidd and Jamal Mashburn. He came in knowing he would be expected to back up Rider, at least to start the season.

Four of the starters were set—Rider and Stoudamire in the backcourt, Sabonis and Grant on the front line. Dunleavy used Walt Williams at small forward on opening night but would employ Wallace, Jackson, and Augmon in that spot through the 50-game season.

With Greg Anthony backing up Stoudamire at the point and youngsters Kelvin Cato and Jermaine O'Neal there to provide support inside, it was a deep, veteran club.

Rider was ready to go for the regular-season opener coming off a strained hamstring that forced him to miss the final two exhibition games. He made it clear he preferred playing with Stoudamire as opposed to his predecessor at the point, Kenny Anderson.

"This is the first time in my career I'm playing with a point guard who is willing to pass," Rider told reporters. "I don't want to talk down on Kenny, but playing with him, he made a lot of people frustrated because he had to score and he had to make the play. Here, everyone is very unselfish."

Dunleavy was hoping Rider—who led Portland in scoring during the previous season with a 19.7-point average—would play well enough to merit All-Star Game recognition.

"The only thing that's lacking from his game is being a great ball-handler," Dunleavy judged. "If he handled the ball better, that would lock him into being an All-Star guard."

Going into the season, the Portland players were offended they weren't being mentioned as an NBA championship contender.

"I've looked at our schedule," Stoudamire said. "We should win at least 37, 39 games."

Most pundits were picking Portland to finish third or fourth in the

Pacific Division. One writer was a believer, however. Peter Vecsey of the *New York Post* picked the Blazers to win the title.

On February 7, Portland opened the regular season with a 91–88 loss at Seattle, a game in which the Blazers led by 14 points in the second quarter. Gary Payton went for 32 points for the Sonics, and his backup, Moochie Norris, hit four straight 3's in the fourth quarter. Rider had the chance to be a hero but, with the Blazers trailing by one, he missed an open 15-footer in the closing seconds.

"Before I shot, I said, 'Game over,'" Rider said afterward. "I make that shot 9 out of 10 times. It's a free throw. I got happy and overconfident."

Portland followed their opening night defeat with victories over Vancouver and Indiana, then a 105–100 overtime loss at Golden State to give former Blazer coach P. J. Carlesimo his first win of the season as the Warriors' coach after an 0–5 start.

Before the game, Rider was asked by the Bay Area press about Carlesimo.

"I laughed at P. J. when he got upset," he said. "With us, he was a yeller, and the organization took care of the problem [by firing him]."

* * *

Over the next seven weeks, the Blazers were the NBA's hottest club, winning 25 of their next 29 games to get to a league-best record of 27–6.

It started with a 99–84 home win over Dallas, a game in which Portland allowed a 23-point halftime lead to fritter to seven in the fourth quarter. Sabonis came the closest he would ever come in the NBA to a triple-double with 16 points, 10 rebounds, and a career-high 9 assists. The 7-foot-3 Lithuanian played 38 minutes after going 40 the night before against Golden State.

"He was so efficient, it was hard not to keep him," Dunleavy said. "But I don't want to have to continue to play him that much."

Dunleavy had pulled most of his starters in the second half, some of whom weren't happy about it.

"I told them I don't care," he said. "If that's their attitude, if they don't know they were part of the problem out there, that's their problem. It sounds like a personal problem to me. In the second half, we lost our poise. I wasn't played with our shot selection. We let them back into the game."

Dunleavy and Rider denied they were at odds after exchanging words in front of the Blazers' bench after the coach substituted for the volatile shooting guard.

"I wasn't arguing with him," Rider said afterward. "Not unless he says I was."

The Blazers went into a February 27 game at Washington without Rider, who was suspended for one game for leaving the bench during an altercation between Charlotte's Bobby Phills and Greg Anthony in the previous game. The suspension cost Rider more than $60,000.

Rod Thorn, the NBA senior VP/basketball operations, said Rider "went all the way to the free-throw line" as officials and coaches tried to keep Phills and Anthony separated after the former had knocked Anthony to the floor on a breakaway.

"Then I think it dawned on him that he shouldn't be out there, so he turned around and ran back," Thorn said. "But the penalty is automatic."

With Rider out of commission, Jackson started and hit the game-winning basket—a 20-footer with 39 seconds left—in an 82–81 triumph over the Wizards. It was the start of an eight-game win streak.

Rider was available for the next game and returned to his old roost as the Blazers beat Minnesota 100–93 to improve to 9–3. Rider had 12 points on 5-for-14 shooting and got into a postgame shouting match with Dunleavy in the visitors' locker room. The *Minneapolis Star Tribune* reported Dunleavy was heard to shout, "We're supposed to be a team!"

"We had some words over a substitution," Dunleavy told reporters. "But it all stemmed from something that happened in the heat of battle. It was really no big deal."

On March 2, the Blazers pulled out a nail-biter, beating Utah 102–100 in double overtime at the Rose Garden. Rider scored 18 points, including Portland's first five in the second OT.

"It was intense," said Grant, who battled Karl Malone tooth and nail all night. Malone finished with 20 points, seven rebounds, and nine assists. Grant had 13 points, 12 boards, and six assists.

"It was a playoff atmosphere," Grant said. "We wanted to win. They wanted to win."

"I'm impressed with what [the Blazers] did," Utah coach Jerry Sloan said. "They played very well. They're probably the most talented team in the league. They should play well."

Portland won another close one, this one on the road, the next night in pulling out a 97–93 overtime verdict at Sacramento.

"They are very deep, very physical, very good," Kings coach Rick Adelman said. "Right now, you're looking at Portland, Seattle, and the Lakers in [the Pacific] division. I don't see Portland going away, especially in a short season with a young team. They could get on a roll and stay on it."

Dunleavy was asked to compare the '99 Blazers with his 1990–91 Lakers who made it to NBA Finals. "My Laker team was more talented," Dunleavy said. "We don't have an All-Star. That team had at least one MVP [Magic Johnson]."

On March 9, the Blazers won their eighth consecutive game, beating Sacramento 103–98 behind 21 points by Rider. Nine days later they beat the Kings again, 88–78, and this time Rider provided some drama, as he was known to do. The erratic shooting guard was late for the morning shoota-round at Arco Arena and sat out the first quarter.

"I totally understand," Rider said afterward. "I could make excuses. There was a valid reason why I was late, but there are only one or two things that are excuses—like death. It has to be kind of serious. I'm mature. I'm not going to pout. I apologized to my teammates. This is the first time this year, and I want it to be the last."

Early in the second quarter, Rider gave Kings guard Jon Barry an open-handed shove as they argued moments after Barry had lost the ball on a drive. It wasn't the first time the pair had gotten into it. Nine days earlier in Portland, Rider had knocked Barry to the floor with a hard foul that was ruled flagrant. This time, the two had words as soon as Barry got up. Rider sent a right hand into Barry's face, drawing an immediate flagrant foul.

"I went to the floor, and he went by and kicked me," Barry said. "No one saw it, so that's why I got up and said, 'No need to kick me.' And he took offense and pushed me in the face."

Barry said the hard feelings go back to the previous season's play-offs, when "I was talking smack to him on the [Lakers] bench and he was offended."

"He walked into my face," Rider said. "He put his finger in my face, and I don't appreciate that. We just don't like each other."

Rider might have chosen to punch Barry, "but I don't want to get thrown out. I wasn't going to do anything to hurt myself or us in the next game."

Sacramento coach Rick Adelman felt Rider had already done so. "He should have been ejected," Adelman said. "I don't know why he wasn't. You can just slap somebody as hard as you want, and you're OK? One official told Jon to 'walk away; he's gone, anyway.' I assumed that meant [Rider] was ejected. Then the three referees got together, and he wasn't gone, and there is no excuse for that."

The rest of the night, the Arco crowd booed Rider's every move.

"I just laughed," Rider said. "It just wakes me up. If they boo, it makes you concentrate harder."

Sacramento's director of player personnel at the time, Jerry Reynolds, didn't laugh. He just shook his head. Reynolds served three years as head coach, three years as GM, 10 years as director of player personnel, and still works as TV analyst for the Kings.

"Rider should have been one of the three or four best two-guards in the league," Reynolds says today. "He was probably more talented than Mitch Richmond, but Mitch was way better for other reasons."

Reynolds also uses a Kings' frame of reference to evaluate Rasheed Wallace.

"A little bit like DeMarcus Cousins," Reynolds says. "What a talent, but he just couldn't control his emotions. He sincerely believed the refs were out to get him. It's a shame because he was a great player."

Reynolds got a close look at the Jail Blazers through the years.

"They were really talented, but they had too many problem childs," Reynolds says. "Every team has one or two, and you can work around that. But the Trail Blazers got in over their heads by having way too many. You like to have a bunch of good guys to lead the pack and the questionable guys will follow along. It goes the other way, too. If you have a lot of questionable guys, the other guys will become followers of that, too.

"Character has to figure in there. It's a talent league, but a lot of talent won't develop if they don't have good character."

Will there ever be another team like the Jail Blazers?

"I don't think so," Reynolds says. "That's it. That was a good lesson for a lot of people."

* * *

Rider was hit with a $7,500 fine and one-game suspension for the incident with Barry. NBA senior VP/basketball operations Rod Thorn declared that Rider "should have been ejected."

Little more than five hours later, Rider was in trouble again. After arriving in Portland on the flight from Sacramento, he received a citation for driving without a license and insurance and speed racing in Northeast Portland. It was his second multiple-violation traffic stop in five weeks.[1]

With Rider out of action again, Sabonis came up big with 28 points and 11 rebounds in 40 minutes against the Twin Towers of Tim Duncan and David Robinson in a 90–85 home win over San Antonio. Duncan also had an outstanding game, going for 29 points and 15 boards.

"Sabonis was the difference," Spurs coach Gregg Popovich said. "He got us tonight. We stopped everyone else, but we couldn't stop Sabonis."

Whether or not it had to do with the off-court issues, Rider was in a bit of a slump, averaging 8.8 points and shooting .266 over the previous six games.

"I think I've gotten a little complacent," he observed. "My team needs me, but if I don't score 20 or more points, it's not the end of the world

---

1   On February 13, he had been cited for speeding, careless driving, and driving without a license.

because we have four or five other guys who can make up the points. And defensively, I'm doing a good job."

On March 28, the Blazers survived the second of back-to-back games with the Suns, winning 88–86 at Phoenix.

Rider, who sat out the first quarter for missing practice the day before, had 18 points in 23 minutes off the bench. Sabonis contributed 18 points and 13 rebounds.

On May 30, Bimbo Coles scored 16 of his 24 in the fourth quarter to lead Golden State to a 93–90 win, ending Portland's six-game win streak.

But like clockwork, Rider was in trouble again; this time for going into the stands late in the game. Rider had sat out the fourth quarter and, with about two minutes to go, went about 10 rows into the stands. His brother and some of his friends were involved in an argument that had attracted the attention of security guards at Oakland Arena, which is near Rider's hometown of Alameda. NBA rules prohibit a player from entering spectator areas during a game.

Rider became the second player to violate the rule. The first came in 1995, when Houston's Vernon Maxwell went into the stands and punched a fan at Portland's Memorial Coliseum, drawing a 10-game suspension and $20,000 fine.

Rider didn't punch anybody, and Dunleavy didn't even know he had left the bench to go into the stands.

"When I heard about it, I thought at first it was after the game because he came into the locker room a few minutes later [than the other players] after the game," the coach said.

The NBA levied a one-game suspension, Rider's third of the season and his second in 12 days. It was to be the 12th game he had missed due to suspension in his 2½ years with the team.

Asked about it by the media, Whitsitt defended his shooting guard. "I think he's done a good job," the Portland GM said. "He has worked hard off the court. He has worked hard on the court. He has been suspended three times by the NBA, and they're all pretty self-explanatory."

Without Rider, the Blazers beat Sacramento again 100–86 at the

Rose Garden, their third win over the Kings in March. Wallace picked up a flagrant and a technical foul, and Augmon was ejected after his second technical during a dust-up with—ironically enough—Kings guard Vernon Maxwell in the second quarter.

"Our emotions can be very positive for us, but at times, they can also be very negative," Dunleavy said. "It's something we need to work on. I'm disappointed we're a team that has the best record in the league [at 24–6] and we're having to fight through things that we shouldn't have to fight through."

On April 6, Portland beat Vancouver 98–89 to improve to 27–6 overall and 17–1 at home. It was to be the high-water mark of the regular season for the team.

A week later, the Blazers rebounded from a loss to the Clippers to roll the Lakers 113–86 at the Rose Garden. Shaquille O'Neal had 24 points and 14 rebounds, while Sabonis helped little with four points and six rebounds in only 14 minutes. But Grant, Wallace, and Cato stepped up with important contributions.

"They played well," O'Neal said afterward. "I still think we can beat them."

Rider didn't start the game because he was late to the morning shoota-round. He still managed 16 points to share scoring honors with Stoudamire.

"He's like a little rocket," Kobe Bryant said of Stoudamire. "He gets out there and is able to create opportunities for his teammates and put a lot of pressure on the defense."

On April 24, Utah beat Portland 96–85 at the Delta Center to run its record to 33–10, a half-game ahead of the Blazers (31–11) in the battle for the NBA's best record. Karl Malone scored 25, including 13-for-13 at the line.

"We have more talent, man-to-man, than they do," Rider said afterward. "We have a lot more players. Their three players [Malone, John Stockton, and Jeff Hornacek] are smart, and their other players just fill in the blanks."

Two days later, the Blazers routed Denver, 92–77, to clinch the Pacific Division title.

"It's a good thing," Dunleavy said of the victory. "It gives you at least the second seed to start out. It's a good first step. But a Western Conference championship would be more meaningful to us."

In a win against the Spurs on May 1, Rider was introduced as a starter but made a race for the bathroom and didn't get back to the court until just before tipoff and not before the Blazers had Jackson ready to take his spot.

Was he sick?

"You'd have to ask him," Dunleavy said afterward. "I guess he was."

The next day, Dunleavy—clearly peeved at Rider—started Jackson instead in a 110–102 win at Denver. Jackson had 14 points and nine assists on 5-for-10 shooting. Rider came off the bench for 16 points on 6-for-14 shooting.

"I decided to go with J. R. off the bench for more scoring," Dunleavy explained.

The win improved the Blazers' record to 8–0 with Jackson starting at shooting guard.

Rider wasn't happy with the move.

"I came off the bench, we won, and we move on," he told the media. Asked if he could support Dunleavy's decision, he said, "I don't even think that's a relevant question." Asked how he felt about coming off the bench, Rider told a reporter to "shut up."

Three days later, the Blazers lost 87–81 at home to San Antonio, their third straight loss to the Spurs in 2½ weeks. Rider was late for team's pregame shootaround and didn't start.

"We started at 4," Rider said afterward. "I got here at 4:05. I guess that was enough to keep me on the bench tonight. I didn't miss anything [at the shootaround]. But I guess people are making points."

Rider wound up playing 16 minutes, scoring two points on 1-for-4 shooting.

"I can't say he was disinterested," Dunleavy said, "but I don't think he played very well."

With the win, the Spurs went to 36–13 on the season, clinching the Western Conference's No. 1 seed. With one game left for each team, the

Blazers were 35–14, but the Spurs held the tie-breaker by virtue of a 3–1 record in the season series.

The Lakers blew out Portland 119–91 in the regular-season finale at the Forum as Glen Rice bombed in 40 points. It had no bearing on playoff positioning, but it meant the Blazers closed with four losses in their last five games.

"I'm not happy at all," Dunleavy said. "That wasn't the attitude I was looking for. We needed a game to get ready for the playoffs, and we did not get it tonight. We didn't have it, mentally or physically."

"We quit, period," Anthony said. "Everybody quit."

Rider started for the first time in three games and had five points in 26 minutes. In his final 10 games, the unstable guard shot .351 from the field and averaged 11.5 points.

"We'll be fine," he said after the Lakers game.

The Blazers were 3–8 in their last 11 games on the road. After starting the season 27–6 overall, they went 8–9 to finish 35–15 to take the No. 3 seed in the West behind the Lakers and Jazz.

* * *

Portland's matchup in a best-of-five first-round series was with the Phoenix Suns, with whom they had gone 2–2 in the regular season. The Suns, 27–23, were just no match for the Blazers.

Wallace had started only 18 times in the regular season, but Dunleavy inserted him as a starter against Phoenix, and he stayed there through the playoffs.

On the eve of the series, Rider was asked if he felt his off-court behavior was a distraction.

"It's not distracting to us [players], it's distracting to you [media]," he said. "I don't read the paper or watch channel whatever, but I can feel the vibes when a lot of heat is coming on me. I'm a sensitive person, and it can affect me, so I just blank it out . . . I'm not a distraction to my teammates. We win this series, and everything goes away."

Portland opened the first round with a 95–85 win behind 25 points from Rider, who hit 10-of-17 shots from the field. He thoroughly outplayed Phoenix shooting guard Rex Chapman, who made only 3-of-12 shots and scored nine points.

"It's playoff time, gut check, time to get it going," Rider said afterward. "I love playoff games. All eyes are on you—will you be scared, or will you be the player the organization wants you to be, a step-up player?"

Rider's offensive repertoire had been too much for the Suns.

"When Rider is taking those fadeaways that start at eight feet and end up at 20, there isn't anything you can do about that," Phoenix coach Danny Ainge said. "But we can do a better job trying to defend him, for sure."

Rider thought he knew a way. "I don't know why they didn't double-team more," he said.

While Rider carried the team in Game 1, Stoudamire came up big in Game 2 by going for 22 points with 13 assists in a 110–99 win. Grant scored a career playoff-high 22 points to go with eight rebounds.

Two nights later, Portland completed the sweep by defeating Phoenix 103–93. The Blazers lost all of an 18-point first-quarter lead, then outscored the Suns 34–21 in the fourth to take command for good. They overcame emotions, two technicals, and a bunch of silly turnovers to complete the sweep.

Rider dominated Chapman, averaging 20 points while propelling the Blazers to the second round of the playoffs for the first time since 1992.

"J. R. was the whole series," Wallace said. "We owe this one to J. R."

And, to not much surprise, the Blazers almost didn't have him for Game 3—at least to start the game.

As the players were loaded on the bus, waiting to drive from the hotel to the arena, they realized that Rider wasn't on board. Nor was he answering the phone in his hotel room. Dunleavy sent a team official to go to check on him. The official pounded on the door. Rider was inside, and it sounded as if he was having sex with a woman.

"J. R., we're on the bus, waiting for you," the official said.

"OK, I'll be right down," Rider said.

Rider made it down in a few minutes, but it's fair to wonder about priorities.

That night, the Suns were physical with Rider, who scored 18 points. He was fouled hard on breakaways by Cliff Robinson and Danny Manning, and Tom Gugliotta received a flagrant as he dove into Rider going for a rebound in the third quarter, injuring Rider's knee.

Rider sat out for seven minutes but came back in the fourth quarter.

"I was motivational when I came back," he would say. "I was definitely Willis Reed."

Rider absolved Robinson and Manning. "I know those guys," Rider said. "They came right to me and said they didn't mean it."

Gugliotta? "I mean, we're not playing football," Rider said. "It's one thing to make hustle plays. It's another to dive into someone's knee. I was scared. My knee feels funny, kind of loose. The doctors want to do an X-ray tomorrow. . . . I played with Tom [in Minnesota]. I thought we were a little better than that. I asked him about it, and I didn't like his response."

Wallace laughed off the suggestion that the Blazers had gotten too emotional.

"Emotion can be a good thing," said the forward, who had two technicals in the three-game series. "It just depends on how you direct that energy—positive or negative."

Even with a solid win and the sweep, there was still controversy as the NBA investigated an incident behind the Blazer bench late in Game 3 involving rookie guard Bonzi Wells, who did not play.

"He was standing up a lot and got into it with a fan," said the director of America West Arena security, George Bevans. "My security person got between them, and [Wells] pushed him. We asked [Wells] to sit down, and he wouldn't. He didn't sit down the rest of the game."

"The fans hated me for loving my team," explained Wells. "I got to cheering, and people told me to sit down. I accidentally bumped [the security guard] and apologized to him."

* * *

The Western Conference Semifinals matchup was with Utah, which had gone 37–13 in the regular season and had survived a five-game first-round series with Sacramento.

The Blazers went into the series aware that the veteran Jazz knew how to draw fouls.

"These guys, when they finish their careers in the NBA, they can go right to Hollywood," Dunleavy said before the series. "I've tried to bring to [Blazer players'] attention not to get caught up in a situation of taking any dumb fouls, not letting Utah irritate them into taking any fouls.

"When [John] Stockton starts flopping and they start playing their tricks, when [Karl] Malone starts locking you up, try and raise your hands in the air. That's the best way to bring it to the officials' attention—'Hey, it's not me bringing this on here.'"

Malone collected 25 points and 12 rebounds as Utah prevailed in a wild, rugged opener 93–83 at the Delta Center. The Blazers blew a 15-point third-quarter lead and made no field goals with just five points in the fourth quarter, the lowest-scoring quarter in playoff history.

"They missed a lot of shots," Utah coach Jerry Sloan said. "I don't think it was our defense. I saw some wide-open shots missed."

With the game turning early in the fourth quarter, Wallace lost his cool after being whistled for a flagrant foul on Bryon Russell. He drew a technical foul, and a four-point possession tied the score at 78–78. Portland never led again.

"That right there opened the door for us," Utah's Shandon Anderson said.

"It gave us the momentum," Jazz swing man Bryon Russell said. "It changed the whole game. From then on, it was smooth sailing."

"I didn't lose my composure, not at all," Wallace said afterward. "I was trying to plead my case that it wasn't a flagrant foul."

Down the stretch, Greg Anthony stuck a foot out and tripped Hornacek in the middle of the floor, which earned him a flagrant as well.

Sloan thought it was a dirty play, shouting expletives toward the Blazer bench after running onto the court to check Hornacek's status.

"Our motto is, in the playoffs you keep your mouths shut," Russell said. "You stay off the referees and concentrate on your game and keep your composure. Our experience and leadership really helped us. I don't think [the Blazers] have a leader."

Dunleavy had little to say on the subject of his players' on-court deportment.

"We've addressed that issue all the way through the season," he said.

Grant picked up a personal foul when he got tangled up with Malone in the third quarter. Upon review, the league assessed Malone a $10,000 fine for elbowing Grant in the mouth on the play.

"I just know it wasn't a foul," Grant would say later. "You can't foul somebody with your chin."

It was a struggle at the offensive end for the Blazers, who made only 2-of-11 shots from beyond the arc. Rider, playing through a sore knee, made 6-of-14 shots and scored 12 points.

"We beat ourselves," said Grant, who led the team with 19 points. "It wasn't like they just came out and beat us. We let one get away, but something crossed my mind. 'Man, we can beat this team—all day, all night.'"

In Game 2, Rider scored eight straight points down the stretch, finishing with 21 of his 27 points in the second half of an 84–81 victory at the Delta Center, tying the series.

"I won't lie," said Rider, who had been listed as "day-to-day" with his knee injury. "It felt good. You relish and cherish these opportunities. I was dead tired, but I wanted the ball. I felt if I had the ball, I dictated what would happen to us. I wanted to be aggressive. I refused to lose tonight."

But Rider had his irascible moments, too. Late in game, Dunleavy called a play for Anthony rather than Rider, who became irate and barked "What is he doing?" to no one in particular.

After the game—a day after Dunleavy had been named as the NBA's Coach of the Year—*The Oregonian*'s Dwight Jaynes called out Rider for it.

"Getting this far with Isaiah 'I won the game' Rider is a single achievement that, by itself, should get Dunleavy all kinds of coaching awards," Jaynes wrote. "Many fans, of course, suddenly love Rider—because he has helped the Blazers win games. That, in their eyes, justifies his tardiness, his suspensions, and his ugly behavior, on and off the court. Being a sports fan today often requires a certain suspension of reality."

Portland returned home to claim a 97–87 victory in Game 3 for a 2–1 series lead. Malone had another big game with 25 points and 14 rebounds, but no other Jazz player scored more than 12 points. Grant took Malone on, blow for blow, collecting 16 points and 15 boards.

"Brian Grant has done a great job in the series so far," the Mailman said afterward. "He works very hard."

"It's an honor to take him on," Grant said. "He's one of the best players in NBA history. I look forward to the challenge. He's going to get his points. You just try to contain him the best you can."

The Jazz shot only .389 from the field after shooting .387 in Game 2.

"I don't know if I've ever played against a better defensive effort," Sloan said. But the veteran Utah coach claimed Wallace threw a "roundhouse" at forward Thurl Bailey and filed a complaint with the league office.

"We just got locked up, and I was trying to free my arm," Wallace said. "I'm not sweating it. That's their master plan, to send Thurl in there. I'm the emotional one. Send him in there to get me heated. I might get a foul, but I'm not going to get ejected from the game. I'm not going to bite on it like that."

"My problem with Wallace is there have been four situations in which he has been involved," Sloan countered. "What does that tell you? It tells me he has gotten the game out of perspective. I'd just as soon lose if we have to play that way. I've told Karl Malone that."

Dunleavy supported his player.

"That's not a punch," he said. "That was the weakest swing. That was a roundhouse swing? There's nothing to it. That would be like me coming out and saying, 'Malone and Stockton are real cheap-shot artists with the elbows and the things they do.' They take it to the limits, and they're smart about how they do it."

In Game 4, the Blazers shot .344 from the field, made only 22 baskets, and committed 18 turnovers, yet still turned back the Jazz to win 81–75 and seize a 3–1 series lead. Rider hit five of six free throws in the final 14.7

seconds and scored seven points in the final 29.9 seconds to clinch the victory.

"That was probably our best win of the season," Dunleavy said. "We won more with our hearts and our brains than physical. If you'd told me we would shoot 34 percent and make 18 turnovers, I would have said we don't have a chance to win."

Needing to stay alive, the Jazz returned home and came out winners with an 88–71 victory in Game 5. Portland shot only .343 from the field, including 2-for-14 from beyond the arc. Malone had 23 points and eight rebounds while Russell chipped in 22 points and nine boards for the Jazz.

Dunleavy was ejected with 8:45 remaining after rushing the court to argue a technical foul call against Grant.

After the game, Rider said Malone should keep his eyes open in Game 6. Grant needed six stitches to mend a cut that came from a Malone elbow early in Game 5.

"We have to have certain ways to get him back," Rider vowed. "We have to send somebody off the bench who doesn't get a lot of playing time. Somehow, someone has to be a designated guy to get in Karl's head.

"Brian is mad. Brian wants to get back at him, but we can't let him. He wishes there was a way to get him back legally. There is nothing he can do but get a bunch of points and rebounds, and we'll get a win."

In Game 6, Rider scored 24 points, and Jackson came off the bench for 17 as the Blazers beat Utah 92–80 at the Rose Garden to give them their first West finals berth since 1992.

It was a banner day for the Blazers, who were 22-for-22 at the foul line. Portland shot only .406 but outrebounded Utah 51–40. It was the end of the line for the Jazz, who were the West champions the previous two years.

Grant helped hold Malone to eight points on 3-for-16 shooting and seven rebounds.

Rider was 10-for-10 at the line in the fourth quarter and 14-for-14 for the game.

"Tonight was my biggest night in basketball," Rider said. "We silenced the world. Utah is America's team, and everyone was rooting for them."

Rider said Dunleavy had been calling more plays for him in the playoffs, a "night and day" difference from the regular season.

"My teammates are going to give me the ball," he said. "That's why, instead of getting 13 points a game, I'm getting 20. The ball is coming to me, and I'm taking advantage of it. It will be the same in the next series, hopefully."

Dunleavy said he had been merely exploiting matchups with Rex Chapman and Jeff Hornacek.

* * *

The Western Conference Finals would be a duel between the Blazers and the San Antonio Spurs, who had beaten Minnesota in the first round, then swept the Lakers in four games in the semis. The Spurs had watched on TV as the Blazers celebrated their Game 6 win over Utah, complete with the shirtless dancing of Rider, the hopping of Williams, and the general hoopla from the rest of the team.

"I understand they beat Utah, but you have to go more than two rounds to celebrate like that," said Spurs guard/forward Mario Elie, who had played with the Blazers during the 1992–93 season. "I know they are a young team. I know they are fired up. But did you see us against the Lakers? There was no celebrating. We know we still have eight wins to go."

During the regular season, the Spurs lost the first meeting, then swept the next three against Portland. They had held Rider to 7.7 points in his three games against them.

In the series opener, the Spurs won 80–76, with the Twin Towers doing most of the damage. Tim Duncan had 21 points, 13 rebounds, and five blocks while David Robinson chipped in 21 points and 10 boards. They outscored the Blazers' Grant and Sabonis 42–13, and it was still barely enough.

With the Spurs leading 78–76, Wallace missed an open 20-footer with 5.4 seconds left. The Spurs rebounded, Elie sank two free throws, and the win was secure in front of a crowd of 35,165 at the Alamodome.

"I don't know if my wife's heart can take this," Robinson said.

"Neither team did anything very well," San Antonio coach Gregg Popovich said.

The Blazers were shocked when Wallace's game-tying attempt went off.

"When the shot left my hand, I thought it was good," Wallace said.

"I would put my money on that shot any time," Dunleavy said. "It was a high-percentage shot. It just didn't go in."

Wallace had a huge game to that point and finished with a career playoff-high 28 points along with eight rebounds in 42 minutes. He had thrived in the playoffs as a starter on a huge front line featuring Grant and Sabonis.

It didn't take Wallace long to get his first technical of the series—four minutes into the opener while jawing at a referee after Rider was called for a foul.

"It might have given our team a little spark," Wallace said. "After I got it, that's when we got a little kick-start."

"Someday, I'm going to learn how to channel [players' emotions] to where it's positive, and have us take it out on opponents and not the officials," Dunleavy observed afterward. "That's my ultimate goal in coaching right now."

Rider, who scored 13 points on 6-for-14 shooting, was optimistic in defeat.

"As bad as we played, we still had a chance to win," he said. "If we play even 'C' basketball, we walk away with a win in this one. That's the good thing, the funny thing about it."

In Game 2 on May 31, San Antonio won, 86–85, in a game dubbed by *San Antonio Express-News* columnist Buck Harvey as the "Memorial Day Miracle."

Sean Elliott's off-balance 3-pointer from the right baseline over a hard-charging Stacey Augmon with 9.9 seconds gave the Spurs their first and only lead of the game. At the other end, Robinson blocked Jackson's eight-footer from the baseline, Williams missed a 10-foot rebound shot, and the Blazers walked off the floor crushed and trailing 2–0 in the series.

The Blazers had led 52–34 in the third quarter.

How did Dunleavy feel? "You could go with gut-wrenching," he said.

On Elliott's game-winner: "An incredible shot. I've got $100 right now to see if he can make that shot again."

Elliott scored 22 points on 8-for-18 shooting, including 6-of-7 from 3-point range. Two decades later, now a TV broadcaster for the Spurs, Elliott reflects on what was probably the individual highlight of a long, successful career.

"They outplayed us in both of the first two games, they really did," Elliott says today. "Somehow we were able to win Game 1. In Game 2, they were taking it to us. We were down the entire game. We were down 18 in the third quarter, and we had the history of always flubbing it in the playoffs. The sentiment around the arena was, 'Here we go again.' So that was a game of frustration and satisfaction."

Elliott had a feeling a big day was coming.

"In my career, I'd had games like that where I felt like I was hot before the game," he says. "Before the game that day, I took my 25 3-point shots, five from each spot, and missed only two of them.

"In that game, I made my first two 3's. I felt like I couldn't miss that day. I was frustrated because I wanted more shots. I got some looks down the stretch in the fourth. I got a couple of 3's off from right in front of the Portland bench. I figured I had to be more aggressive with my shot selection; I wasn't going to get wide-open looks. Even if a guy got in my face, I had to let it go."

The Spurs trailed 85–83 when Elliott launched the game-winner.

"I caught the ball along the sidelines," he says. "When I got the ball, I thought I was going to fall out of bounds. The crazy thing is I never saw [Augmon]. All I saw was the rim. Maybe subconsciously I let the ball go higher because he was coming to try to block it. I was supposed to catch it and throw it in to David on the low block to tie the game. But I gathered, and I saw the rim was open, and I just let the ball go.

"I told the guys in the huddle [in a timeout before the final possession], I had one more in me. After I made it, I pointed at Mario Elie and said, 'I told you.' I wasn't surprised I made it. If I got a shot, I was going to make it.

"That win catapulted us. They had the talent to beat us, but it doesn't always come down to talent. We gained confidence and cohesiveness, and it took a little bit of air out of the Blazers."

On that day, the Spurs knew they were fortunate.

"Portland deserved to win," Elie said. "But we didn't quit. That's the sign of a champion."

"Sean has never been a shooter," Rider said. "A shooter is someone who is a designated 3-point shooter, and he's never had that role. We just hope it's a one-game thing."

The Blazers, indeed, were crestfallen.

"This was by far the toughest loss of the season," Stoudamire said in a sullen Blazer locker room.

Nearly 20 years later, Blazer forward Walt Williams hates the memory of Elliott's game-winner.

"That shot Sean hit was demoralizing," Williams says today. "We had that game. We were riding high. We went into the series very confident. We came off a fantastic regular season. Even in the first game, we had opportunities to win. We were thinking, 'If we win the second game, we're 1–1 going back to Portland.' For him to hit that shot, it was like, 'God is on their side.' I think it affected us for the rest of the series. But in that series, they were the more disciplined team."

Rider, whose sore right knee had locked up during the game, finished with three points on 1-for-4 shooting in 22 minutes.

The Spurs had now beaten Portland five straight, by a total of 20 points.

"We know we can still win this series, and that's half the battle," said Rider before Game 3. "We feel like we've got their number."

After averaging 20 points against the Suns and 19.3 against the Jazz, Rider had scored a total of 16 points in the first two games vs. the Spurs.

"The first two series, the offense went through me," Rider said. "This series, the offense is going through Rasheed. I accept that role. You can't ask for everything. I want the ball. I know I can turn it on at any point. But if the offense isn't geared for me, I don't want to go out there and take all kind of crazy shots just because I did well in the first two series. I still want to play within the confines of the team."

The Blazers returned home expecting to win the next two games and make it a series. Instead, they fell with a thud, losing Game 3 by an embarrassing score of 85–63.

"They dissected us," Stoudamire said.

The Blazers were outscored 24–8 in the third quarter. They shot .247 from the field, setting a franchise playoff record low for fewest made field goals and field-goal percentage. The 63 points tied for the second-lowest output in NBA playoff history. As things went from bad to worse, they heard an avalanche of boos from the home crowd.

"We never thought we'd have a game like this," Rider said.

As the game went on, the Blazers barked directions at one another. Wallace yelled at Dunleavy when the coach tried to prevent a tantrum. Soon after, Wallace got a technical. It was his seventh tech in 12 playoff games. After he fouled out, he bypassed the bench and stormed directly to the locker room, not watching the final two minutes.

"We were in such disarray, it was like a time bomb waiting to explode," Anthony said. "We never gave ourselves the opportunity to be in the game. Poise and patience go a long way, and we displayed none of that tonight."

There was plenty of finger-pointing and accusations in the Portland locker room after the game. NBC reported that Jackson—who scored five points on 1-for-6 shooting in 21 minutes—challenged Dunleavy about playing time.

"Nothing internal is bothering us," Rider said. "If it is, it will get addressed in the summertime. But right now, we're not breaking down internally."

How big a mountain did the Blazers have to climb?

"Mt. St. Helens, Mt. Rainier, any of them," Jackson allowed.

There would be no mountain climb for the Blazers, who went down 94–80 in Game 4 as the Spurs swept the series to write themselves a ticket to the NBA Finals. Robinson had 20 points and 10 rebounds while Duncan collected 18 points and eight boards for the Spurs, who led by three after three quarters but opened the fourth on a 16–4 run.

Stoudamire finished the series with a nice offensive game, scoring 21 points on 9-for-13 shooting to go with six assists. He got far too little help, however, for the Blazers to climb any mountain.

Wallace averaged 20 points, for the series but everyone else was subpar offensively, as the team shot only .392 for the series. Rider wound up averaging 9.5 points on .357 shooting.

Later, Jackson—who was traded to the Hawks in the offseason—fessed up to his locker room confrontation with Dunleavy after Game 3.

"I was frustrated," he says now. "We should have beaten them. I felt the game plan was flawed. It was like throwing in the towel. I exploded in the locker room. As a competitor, I felt our window of opportunity to win a championship was right then. As I look back on it, it was my fault. I accept the blame, and I paid for it by getting traded. That's part of growing as a person and a professional."

Elliott offers perspective today in going head-to-head with the Blazers from 1989–2001.

"They always had a collection of talent," Elliott says. "They were one of the teams I always thought had a chance to make a deep run in the playoffs. They were a dangerous club but, for some reason or another, someone was always able to knock them off.

"Whenever you have issues like they did, it holds you back. Whenever you have guys who are struggling away from the court, it carries over to how you play on the court. It's always in the back of your mind. It's hard to separate stuff off the court from what happens on the court. That's why guys with personal problems generally don't play as well as those who don't have them."

After Elliott's rookie season, Spurs assistant coach Gregg Popovich invited him to attend the draft with the team's coaches and management team.

"I was in the war room and saw all the names are on the board, the top 30 guys at every position," Elliott says. "In the corner of the room was a small chalkboard. At the top, it said, 'Not a Spur.' Underneath it were about 15 names. It didn't matter if those guys were super talented; they were not a Spur, and we were not going to draft them. We were going to draft guys with character."

Elliott had respect for J. R. Rider as a player.

"He was immensely talented," Elliott says. "He was extremely difficult to guard. He could do pretty much everything. There are so many guys who come into the league who are talented, but their troubles get them out of the league prematurely. You know somewhere along the line, throughout the course of 82 games, there are going to be breakdowns. And you know you're going to eventually get to some guys mentally.

"You want to get good people in your organization because you're goin to be around them seven to eight months a year. If you get guys with personality issues, it's almost impossible to be around them for an entire season. That starts to leave its impact on the court. Our mentality with the Spurs was, if you don't have high character and guys have matured on the other team, they're eventually going to crack."

Elliott chuckles at the thought of Rasheed Wallace.

"Away from the court, he was a great dude. I really like Rasheed. But when the lights came on and they got between the lines, he became Mr. Hyde. That's the case with a lot of guys. They can't turn it off no matter what. I had a little bit of that, so I can understand how guys have more of it than others.

"Rasheed was still a very effective player, but it probably detracted from his game in the sense that officials are human beings. They get tired of guys constantly going at them. He probably didn't get as many calls, or the benefit of the doubt, as if he wouldn't have been so aggressive with officials."

* * *

There were plenty of unhappy campers on the Portland side, including Jermaine O'Neal, who had only played a total of 23 minutes in the San Antonio series. O'Neal, who averaged 8.9 minutes a game through the regular season, was heading into free agency. He said he would return only for more money and playing time.

"O'Neal won't be back; Anthony won't be back," Rider predicted in the days following the series. "We can't afford Greg. He's going to get a bigger contract somewhere else.

"I may exercise my option, but hopefully, Portland will take care of me, and I'll be fine. If not, we'll see what happens. My contract is up. I've been waiting six years, so it's time."

Nostradamus Rider wasn't.

During the summer, the Blazers re-signed O'Neal for four years and $24 million. They brought back Anthony, too, on a multi-year contract.

Guess which Blazer wouldn't be back for the 1999–2000 season?

Chapter 5

THEY STARTED LIKE A
HOUSE ON FIRE

(1999–2000)

"I'm Public Enemy No. 1 . . . [the refs] have my face on a wanted
poster. . . . If I see something out there that I don't think is right, I let
[the officials] know. My reaction is letting them know it is full of BS
out there. I come at them with logic, and I guess that burns them up."

—Rasheed Wallace

Through the early summer of 1999, rumors swirled that the Trail Blazers
were seeking to trade J. R. Rider, who had one year left on the seven-year,
$26.5-million rookie contract he signed with Minnesota in 1993.

Normally, a player with his offensive statistics would be in high demand.
Rider averaged 20.4 points in his second season with the Timberwolves
(1994–95) and 19.7 points in his second season with the Blazers (1997–98).
But he had worn out his welcome as a serial transgressor, offering a poor
reflection on both the franchise and the city of Portland, and general manager Bob Whitsitt was on the lookout for a deal.

During summer league play at Salt Lake City, guard Bonzi Wells told a
reporter that he would be "very hurt" if Rider were to be traded.

"He has been the perfect mentor for me," Wells said. "He took me
under his wing. He never treated me like a rookie or a threat. He taught me
everything it takes to make it in this league. He is one of my best friends on
the team.

"If me and J. R. were on this team together next season, we would kill all the other teams' guards. If they want to keep us, I would have his back, and he would have my back. Me and J. R. are kind of the same person."

In a July interview with *The Oregonian*, Rider—who would never as much as make an All-Star team—spoke about how he ranked among the best shooting guards in the NBA. "With Michael Jordan gone [to baseball], it's wide open," Rider said. "You've got Penny [Hardaway] and Ray Allen, plus myself, Kobe [Bryant], and a bunch of other guys. It's a matter of whether your organization wants you to be the best. I can be the best two-guard in the league, but you have to milk the people you want in that position."

Had the Blazers only used Rider properly, he'd have been halfway to the Hall of Fame, he figured.

A week later, on August 2, 1999, Portland traded Rider and guard Jimmy Jackson to Atlanta for guards Steve Smith and Ed Gray. Gray, a 6-foot-3 guard who had played 30 games with the Hawks in each of the previous two seasons, was traded by the Blazers two months later and never played in another NBA game.

Rider was Portland's leading scorer in two of his three seasons but was also suspended for a total of 12 games and accumulated more than $600,000 in fines and lost salary. But yes, teammates seemed to like him.

"You can say all you want about J. R.—people think he doesn't care about anything—but he helped me through all my situations," Jermaine O'Neal said. "I'm really going to miss him."

Many in the organization, though, didn't share the same feeling.

"I wouldn't have missed this," one member said before the press conference announcing the trade. "It's the greatest day in the history of the franchise."

The front-office type wouldn't miss seeing Rider with a towel over his head at the end of the bench when he was having a poor game, or proudly tugging at his jersey to reveal a tattoo of a heart when things were going well.

"He would say all kinds of things to get out of practice," said one Blazer official, who asked to remain anonymous. "He felt like he could do any-thing, because there were no or few boundaries."

Bob Medina, the team's strength and conditioning coach, had been with Rider during his college days at UNLV. Medina got along fine with Rider but understood the issues that blocked his path to success.

"He came to Portland at a bad time, right behind the Clyde Drexler/Terry Porter era, where fans expected players to behave in a certain way," Medina says. "J. R. was the polar opposite of those guys. He was not a good teammate. He was always late for practice. You could get 30 points out of him one night and three the next. He was a selfish player.

"He was one of the guys where you could see his skill level diminishing, as he didn't take care of his body. I'd put him in the same category as Rasheed [Wallace] in that respect. You could just see it start to deteriorate. Teams will put up with your crap while you're producing. Once you're not producing anymore, they're not going to, and they'll move on."

With his contract down to its final season, Rider became easier to trade.

"There was a great deal of discussion about leaving him off the team's playoff roster [in the 1999 playoffs]," *The Oregonian*'s Dwight Jaynes wrote. "He had gone through all kinds of late-season ups and downs that included quitting on the team two or three times during games. He was constantly in the doghouse. There was sentiment within the organization to make a state-ment and go without him in the postseason. It didn't happen.

"Rider was being showcased much of last season for exactly the purpose he served on Monday—to bring the team a better player. And in the end, after all the suspensions and unpredictability, that was the best thing he ever did for the Blazers."

At the press conference, Whitsitt put his spin on the deal.

"We gave up absolutely nothing to get J. R., and we got three produc-tive years from him," the Portland GM said. "He grew, and we helped him grow, on and off the court. He had a bumpy, rough road, but he improved while he was with us. He got better each year."

That wasn't true, of course. During his final season with the Blazers, Rider had a much lower scoring average (13.9) and shooting percentage

(.412) than he had in the previous two, and he had become a major burden for coach Mike Dunleavy for both his on- and off-court antics.

That was unlikely to be the case with Smith, 30, a 6-foot-7 shooting guard who had averaged 18.7 points for Atlanta during the 1999 season after better than 20 with the Hawks the previous two, making the All-Star Game in 1998. Portland's Brian Grant was honored as the NBA's J. Walter Kennedy Award winner for citizenship and community service in 1999. The previous winner was Atlanta's Smith, considered by all a solid citizen. That, if nothing else, would go over well for the Blazer faithful who had grown weary of the not-so-easy Rider.

* * *

Steven Delano Smith grew up in a tough neighborhood on Detroit's east side. His dad, Don Smith, wanted to keep him away from gang activities.

"I took a liking to basketball," Smith said. "My dad figured if he could keep me in the backyard, that would keep me out of trouble."

Smith's mother, Clara Bell Smith, died of cancer during his rookie season with the Miami Heat in 1992. In 1997, Steve had honored her at his alma mater, Michigan State, placing her name on the academic study facility for athletes on campus. He donated $2.5 million to help pay for the academic center while also funding a scholarship for a student from his other alma mater, Pershing High, for a full ride to Michigan State.

Smith had played five seasons for Atlanta after three years in Miami before coming to Portland. There was speculation the Hawks let him go because of the condition of his knees, as he had undergone surgery on his right knee to repair torn cartilage in 1992. In the lockout-shortened 1999 season, he played in 36 of 50 games.

"I got bumped on my left knee last year," a clearly annoyed Smith said during his initial press conference in Portland. "That's not a knee problem. There was nothing I could do about getting kneed in the knee, then have it swell up. It was the other knee than the one I had surgery on. But according to everybody, I still have knee problems."

Smith wound up missing one game in two years in Portland, though he would come off the bench for much of his second season.

Whitsitt, careful not to gloat about dumping Rider on Atlanta, said the trade was partly a numbers game.

"We have a very deep and talented roster, and one of the things we wanted to try to accomplish was to thin it a little bit," Portland's GM said. "We also wanted to try to increase our leadership ability."

Atlanta GM Pete Babcock, who immediately took some heat for taking on Rider, hinted that he couldn't pass up a talent like the former UNLV standout and that fans would like the results.

"People care about wins and losses," Babcock said. "Unfortunately, that's the way our society is."

Rider would average 19.3 points in his one season with Atlanta, in which the Hawks went 28–54, the third-worst record in the NBA. It would be his last season as a starter. He came off the bench for the Lakers in 2000–01, then played 10 games with Denver in 2001–02 before leaving the league for good at age 30.

Meanwhile, Smith was chomping at the bit to get started in the City of Roses.

"We have a great chance to win a championship in Portland," he said. "It's a great situation for me to go to a team loaded with talent. Maybe I'll be the one to get them over the edge and win it all."

* * *

The Blazers had plenty of talent, and they added more the first week of training camp when Whitsitt pulled off a six-for-one trade with Houston, acquiring Scottie Pippen for Kelvin Cato, Walt Williams, Stacey Augmon, Carlos Rogers, Brian Shaw, and Ed Gray. Only Cato, Williams, and Rogers would play for the Rockets that season. They waived Augmon, and the Blazers—who knew the move was coming—re-signed him.

Part of it was a money issue. The Rockets were all too happy to get rid of Pippen's contract, which called for him to make $53 million over the next four years.

Pippen, 34, and the Rockets had become unhappy with each other after one turbulent 1999 season. Pippen sought a trade during the offseason and, after it happened, teammate Charles Barkley—who had taken a pay cut to make room under the salary cap for Pippen's five-year, $67.5-million contract the previous season—referred to Pippen as a "turncoat." Barkley, Pippen retorted, was "fat" and "selfish."

Pippen played well during his only season with the Rockets, averaging 14.5 points, 6.5 rebounds, and 5.9 assists while making the All-Defensive team for the eighth straight year.

Chosen as one of the top 50 players in the NBA's first 50 years in 1997, Pippen had been Michael Jordan's sidekick as they won six league titles in Chicago in the '90s. Pippen was hoping to add a seventh one in Portland in 2000.

"When I was a free agent [in the summer of '98], I had my opportunity to look at the Blazers, but I didn't want them to have to dismantle their team to bring me in," Pippen said. "I was looking for a situation to come in and be a complementary player to a club, knowing I could do whatever it takes for us to win."

During his introductory press conference, Pippen declared, "This is far more talented than any team that has been assembled in the league . . . as far back as I can remember. We're far more talented than the Lakers and far ahead of where the Lakers are trying to get to. I would probably have chosen this team [over the Lakers] because I feel it is more on the verge of winning a championship. There had been a great chance to win even without Scottie Pippen."

He added: "It would be great to win for this group of coaches and players and staff, and for the fans. I think this city deserves it. I'm looking forward to the challenge."

Scottie Maurice Pippen grew up in Hamburg, Arkansas, population 2,700, the youngest of 12 children born to Preston and Ethel Pippen. Preston was a mill worker; Ethel had her hands full with a houseful of kids.

Scottie learned basketball in the neighborhood with his older brothers, but he was never a star, in no small part to his stature. He was always slim and only 6-foot-1 as a high school senior. He didn't make the starting five on the varsity until that year and—amazingly—didn't even play as a junior because he was student-manager on the football team.

"They wanted me to work through the winter with offseason training," Pippen recalled. "It was something to do back then. Small town. No entertainment."

Pippen received no scholarship offers, but Central Arkansas—150 miles from Hamburg—offered to pay for school through a work-study program if he would serve as student manager for the basketball team. In short time, it evolved into an opportunity to walk on as a player.

By the time his freshman year was over, Pippen was 6-foot-3 and good enough to play. By the start of his sophomore season, he was 6-foot-7, "and it was over," he said.

As a senior, Pippen was a 6-foot-8 swing man who earned consensus NAIA All-America honors in 1986–87. Ironically, Whitsitt—then the GM in Seattle—took him with the fifth pick in the 1987 draft, then traded him to Chicago for the eighth pick, center Olden Polynice, and two second-round choices.

"I guess I owe Bob twice," Pippen quipped.

Pippen became a starter during his second season with the Bulls and was a versatile offensive player and lock-down defender for six NBA championship clubs under the direction of coach Phil Jackson.

With Jackson and Jordan gone after the 1997–98 season, Chicago was in rebuild mode and didn't want to pay Pippen. In a salary dump, the Bulls sent him to Houston for Roy Rogers—the 6-foot-10 forward, not the TV cowboy—and a second-round draft pick. Rogers wound up playing in Italy.

Portland also signed 14-year veteran forward Detlef Schrempf, 36, to a two-year free agent contract for $4.2 million. Schrempf had averaged 15.0 points, 7.4 rebounds, and 3.7 assists for Seattle the previous season.

"Scottie, Steve, Detlef—what can you say?" Brian Grant asked of the new additions. "If you had told me last year we'd be acquiring these guys, I'd have definitely said it would not happen. If we can't get it done now, I don't know when we ever will."

* * *

Owner Paul Allen was paying to put the pieces in place, though. The Blazers would go into the 1999–2000 season with the NBA's highest payroll at $73.9 million, with the Knicks second at $71.3 million and Indiana far back in third at $54.2 million. Portland's payroll was more than double the league salary cap of $34 million. The starters combined to command $52.7 million, more than all but the top three teams.

Portland was also the second-oldest team in the league, with Schrempf, Pippen, Sabonis (34), Gary Grant (34), and veteran center Joe Kleine (37) the senior members. Greg Anthony was turning 32, Augmon was 31, Smith was 30, and forward Antonio Harvey 29. There was a young element, too, with Brian Grant (27), Damon Stoudamire (26), Rasheed Wallace (25), Bonzi Wells (23), and Jermaine O'Neal (21).

"We had the young guns—Damon, Rasheed, Bonzi, Jermaine," Harvey says now. "That group was really tight. Then the middle-aged guys—me, Smitty, and Augmon. Greg and Brian kind of bounced between the two groups. Then the old heads—Scottie, Sabonis, and the next year, Dale Davis.

"But there was a tight-knit nature to that whole team. We went out together, we went to dinners together, we hung out together. It was not uncommon to see Scottie in the same place as Damon and Bonzi and the rest of the group. That helped forge a bond to get us as far as we did. That was an accomplishment in itself. It speaks to how tight a group we were and how much we enjoyed being around each other."

Kleine was the ultimate journeyman. The 6-foot-11, 260-pound center was playing for his eighth team in the final year of a 14-year NBA career. Kleine, who was to play in only seven games that season, was on the roster mostly as insurance.

"I loved it there," Kleine says today. "Wish I could have gotten there when I was younger and could play a little bit. I always knew Portland was a good town and the Trail Blazers were a great organization, but it blew me away how much I liked living and playing there. I didn't play much. I was at the end. I knew it. I was an old man by then. But all the sellouts and fantastic fans and how everything was. . . . Coming in and out as a visiting player, you didn't quite get it. When you were living there, it was pretty cool."

Kleine had played for 50-win teams led by Larry Bird in Boston and 50-win teams led by Charles Barkley in Phoenix.

"That year in Portland, the talent was as good as there has ever been from a depth standpoint," says Kleine. "We were 10, 11 deep, with very strong players. You're coming off the bench with guys like Schrempf, Wells, Grant, and O'Neal. That's four All-Star-caliber players. That made it competitive in practice. Practices were really good.

"The problem was, the young guys like Bonzi, Jermaine, and Damon were really eager to show what they could do, as all young players are. They wanted to play 40 minutes a night and make the All-Star team, and Mike [Dunleavy] didn't need them to do that. There was a little conflict there.

"I didn't totally understand it. When I was sitting in the locker room with all of them, I'd be thinking, 'You're all getting paid. They're rewarding you. You're making All-Star money. That's the main thing.' But at 24, 25, if I'd have been as good as those guys, I'd have probably felt the same way."

* * *

The initial plan was for the starting five to be comprised of Stoudamire and Smith in the backcourt, with Grant, Sabonis, and Pippen on the front line. That would leave a deep bench with Wallace, Wells, Schrempf, Anthony, O'Neal, and Augmon.

Wallace, who was second on the team in scoring coming off the bench the previous season, didn't seem to mind the idea of being a reserve again.

"You have to keep a positive attitude," he said before the season. "I'm more of a team player, not a personal or selfish player. If I get a couple of minutes or whatever, as long as we're winning, that's my bottom line—to get the W."

But Grant, coming off knee surgery, was unable to start the season, which meant Wallace slid into the starting lineup and wound up being the Blazers' leading scorer for the season at 16.4 points per game.

Wells seemed on the verge of making an impact off the bench after playing sparingly—and being left off the playoff roster—as a rookie.

"This is what I've been waiting for my whole life," Wells said. "If [opponents] don't know me, that's OK. I'll be a silent assassin. I'll quietly do my part and kill the other team. I'm going to show [the Blazers] what they slept on last season."

Wells would earn his playing time, but so, too, would a lot of his teammates. Eleven players would average in double-figure minutes. This time, Portland wouldn't be catching the experts unaware.

"The versatility the Blazers have is going to be unmatched. They can go big, small, young, or old," Turner studio analyst Kenny Smith said before the season. "No other team in the NBA can do what they can do. To me, they're the favorite to win the whole thing."

"They're one of the top three or four teams in the league," ESPN's Jack Ramsay said. "The only area of concern to me is how Sabonis defends the big, quick centers like [Shaquille] O'Neal and [David] Robinson. For the Blazers to get to the Finals, he is going to have to get past at least one of them. But it's a very good, deep team, and if they can get past that hurdle, they have a great shot at winning the title."

Dunleavy said he wasn't going to pay attention to the pundits.

"Pressure gets you when you're not prepared for something," Dunleavy said. "The only pressure I feel is, I want to win a championship. You can predict us to go 82–0 or fourth or fifth in our division; I'm oblivious. My job is to get this team in the right frame of mind to compete when it counts. I welcome all of this. I envision it being a team that can play the way I want to play, and not having to sometimes skirt around the issues. We can go full-out on both ends of the court.

"We haven't won anything yet. But we are in pretty good condition to contend, and we have a tremendous opportunity, a big window, over the next two to three years."

* * *

The Blazers bolted out the gates quickly, winning 10 of their first 11 games, and never let up. They would be at or near the top of the Western Conference race the entire way, finishing the regular season 59–23.

On November 13, J. R. Rider returned to Portland for the first time since being traded to Atlanta. Rider, who received a mixture of boos and cheers during pregame introductions, scored 14 points on 5-for-15 shooting and was no factor in Portland's 131–95 blowout win.

Jimmy Jackson, the other piece in the Rider-to-Atlanta deal, took a shot at Whitsitt before the game.

"I'm bitter," said Jackson, who scored five points on 2-for-11 shooting off the bench. "I made a commitment and a sacrifice. What sacrifice did they make for me? None."

Jackson said he was surprised to be included in the trade. He had been traded three times in a 12-month span and said Whitsitt persuaded him to sign for less money and a reduced role by promising stability. "He told me I was going to be [in Portland] and I was an important part of the team, and I believed that," Jackson said.

Jackson again apologized for the blowup with Dunleavy during the Western Conference Finals but said it occurred "in the heat of the battle. Check my track record for the whole year. If you [make a trade based on] the one time I had an argument with the coach, then it was a bad decision on their part."

A six-game winning streak would end on November 23, when the Blazers lost to the Cavaliers 103–100 at Gund Arena. Portland (10–2) had chances to send it into overtime, but Wallace and Schrempf missed hurried 3-point attempts in the closing seconds.

On November 30, Indiana came into the Rose Garden and stole away with a 93–91 win, handing the Blazers (13–3) their first home loss of the season. Jalen Rose scored 22 points, Dale Davis came up with seven offensive boards, and Reggie Miller stole an inbounds pass with 2.8 seconds left to seal the victory.

"We had no scrap," Brian Grant said. "We're a great team, but everybody has to get tougher. We should have won tonight. We should have won all of our games, really. Sometimes we think we're just going to get by because we have big-time people. But [opponents] don't care about that."

On December 3, the Blazers laid their first real egg of the season, falling 93–80 to the Lakers at Staples Center. Kobe Bryant scored 23 points, and Shaquille O'Neal collected 21 points, 16 rebounds, and six assists for the Lakers (13–4), who held Portland to .342 shooting.

"I don't think you can fault our defense," Schrempf said, "but our offense was atrocious."

Lakers coach Phil Jackson got a dig in on the Blazers (14–4) afterward, calling them "the best team that money can buy." He added: "Are they going to improve? They're going to have to improve to beat us in the course of the year, or else we're going to overtake them."

On December 29, Wallace scored 24 points, and Pippen totaled 19 points, seven rebounds, and six assists while doing a nice defensive job on Gary Payton in a 94–89 win over Seattle at the Rose Garden. Wells, donning a red headband for the first time, scored 14 points in helping the Blazers erase an eight-point third-quarter deficit. One clever scribe, mindful of Sonics' history, referred to Wells as "Thick Watts."

"He looks like a Ninja Turtle, doesn't he?" Dunleavy said with a laugh.

"I'm a power guard," Wells said. "Coach told me to throw my weight around. As long as I keep my quickness and savvy, I should be fine."

The next night, Wells went for career highs in scoring (16), rebounds (seven), and steals (five) in 24 minutes, scoring 14 points in the fourth quarter of a 108–90 win over Philadelphia at home.

"Bonzi was the difference," said 76ers coach Larry Brown, who was ejected in the first half. Assistant John Calipari took over for Brown, who watched the second half on a monitor in the visitors' locker room.

Wallace scored 23 points and grabbed 11 rebounds, which caught the notice of fellow North Carolina alum Brown.

"Rasheed is the most underrated player in our league, among the real stars," Brown said. "People don't appreciate how good he is, understand what a great kid he is. He is incredible. As good a player as he is, he's a better kid. That's the thing that's so sad. His tantrums detract from his ability and also from his character. They give people the wrong impression."

On January 3, Portland dominated Chicago in an 88–63 beatdown at United Center, dropping the woeful Bulls to 2–26 for the season. Jermaine O'Neal, who came off the bench for eight points in 18 minutes, said he was happy he chose not to sign with the Bulls, who were offering more money and plenty of playing time.

"I thought about signing here, but the bottom line is, I want to win, and I don't want to learn bad habits," he said with unintended irony. "It would have been hard to go through a whole year here."

On January 14, the Blazers bounced Phoenix 105–83 at America West Arena on a night in which they were whistled for eight technicals. Portland (28–8) broke open a tight game by outscoring the Suns 33–13 in the fourth quarter. Sabonis, fighting through a chest cold, led the way with 23 points and 10 rebounds as the Blazers opened a five-game road trip.

Dunleavy received a technical 21 seconds into the game for arguing that a foul should have been called when the Suns stripped Sabonis of the ball. Wallace received two T's and an ejection early in the third quarter, then went after referee Ted Bernhardt and had to be restrained by Pippen. Shortly after Wallace was tossed, Dunleavy questioned whether a jump ball was tossed up straight and got a hook, too. The NBA fined Wallace—who now led the league with 16 technicals—$7,500.

"We fined him for not leaving the court in a timely fashion and for verbal abuse of the referees," explained league senior VP Rod Thorn. "He went across the line."

The next night, Wallace was ejected again in a 113–105 loss at Dallas. Wallace picked up two technicals just 1:02 apart in the third quarter, exiting with 11 points and two rebounds. Dallas (12–24) led 65–43 early in the third quarter before the Blazers began to make a charge, getting to within two with 54 seconds left. Portland dropped to 28–9, 3½ games behind the Lakers (32–6).

"We lost our best scorer and rebounder, and we're down 16 at the time,"

Pippen said. "Rasheed feels like he's not getting the calls, but he can't keep letting us down."

With 18 technicals in 37 games, Wallace had more than all his team-mates combined and was closing in on his career high of 21 set in 1995–96.

"It's a problem we have to solve," Dunleavy said. "Somehow, he has to get it under control. We can do all the talking we want to Rasheed, but he has to make a decision that he wants to channel his emotions in a positive way. He understands that it's hurting our team, and I don't think he wants to do that.

"It's to the point now where he has to be careful because [opponents] will try to bait him, if they know they can get to him like that. It could be like in the old days, where coaches would send in some stiff to try to rile a guy and get him ejected."

Pippen said he had spoken to Wallace about the problem with referees. Was Rasheed hearing what he was saying?

"Does it look like it?" Pippen asked.

Rasheed's family members had talked to him, too.

"My mom wants him to stop, but Rasheed is going to be Rasheed," said his brother, Malcolm. "He is not hurting nobody. He will grow out of it. He is a mature young man now, but as he matures more and gets a rapport with the refs, it will get better."

* * *

On January 27, Jermaine O'Neal came off the bench for 14 points and eight rebounds in 23 minutes while putting in some solid defensive work against Karl Malone as Portland beat Utah 85–75 for its eighth straight home win. O'Neal had played a total of 11 minutes in the previous five games.

"His best game as a pro," Dunleavy said of O'Neal, who helped hold Malone to 12 points.

"It was the best I've played all year," Jermaine agreed. "That was definitely a confidence-booster. I was waiting for a game like this to show people I can contribute in a big way."

Two nights later they stoned San Antonio, 81–67, as Duncan managed only 12 points and two rebounds in 28 minutes.

"They have done a great job of keeping me from getting into any kind of rhythm," Duncan said after the game.

On February 2, Wallace was added by coaches as a reserve to the West team for the All-Star Game, becoming the Blazers' first All-Star since Cliff Robinson and Clyde Drexler made it in 1994.

"It's cool, but nothing to jump for joy over," Wallace, who was averaging 15.9 points and 7 rebounds, told reporters. "It's not my ultimate goal. Winning a championship is my bottom line. That's bigger than any All-Star selection, MVP Award, whatever . . . that ring sums it up. That's what I'm after. Once I win a championship, then I'll feel like I've accomplished something."

The following evening, the Blazers opened a four-game road trip with a 98–88 loss to the Knicks at MSG. Wells came off the bench to keep the Blazers (34–11) alive by scoring all 18 of his points in the fourth quarter.

Wallace was ejected for the fourth time in 10 games, being thrown out for making a comment from the bench to referee Joey Crawford, picking up his 21st technical of the season. Wallace tossed his wristband toward Crawford on the way to the locker room.

"Instead of griping and moaning to the referees, we should have made the Knicks pay for it," Dunleavy said. "Until we are able to control ourselves, we're not going to get all the way to winning a championship. We could get frustrated along the way."

"I just hope we can build some toughness, to where we just play the game," Pippen added. "When things don't go our way, we start bickering at the officials and a chain reaction sets in. And before long, all the officials are pretty much turned against us."

The next night, the Blazers blew a 49–35 third-quarter lead but held on to win 97–90 at Atlanta, kicking off an 11-game win streak. Smith scored 21 points in his first return to Atlanta since being traded, and J. R. Rider got a double-double with 10 points and 10 rebounds, though he went 4-for-16 from the field and drew boos from the hometown crowd for his shot selection.

Grant, still working his way into form after offseason knee surgery, said he was content with his role off the bench since the Blazers were 38–11 going into the All-Star break. Grant's averages had dropped from 11.5 to 7.1 in points, 6.2 to 5.5 in rebounds, and 31.8 to 20.6 in minutes.

"If anybody has complaints, they don't need to be here," Grant said. "When you come off the bench, you have to work your way into the flow. I'm learning to watch the game more, find out what the flow is and what it is I need to do when I step on the court."

* * *

Wallace took part in a players' interview session with reporters prior to the All-Star Game in Oakland, as required by the league. By this time, he was giving few interviews and calling himself "Public Enemy No. 1" and declaring "[the refs] have my face on a wanted poster."

"Come playoff time, that's when it all counts," Wallace told the media. "The regular season, it's cool, it's all right. A lot of things go on in the regular season that don't go in the playoffs. Right now, I could have a million techs. I don't care. Come playoff time, that's when it all counts. I have never been thrown out of a playoff game, and I never will be."

Wallace said he didn't mind being the league leader in technical fouls. "It don't bother me. It's no big thing. It's part of the game. It's just fire, that's all. Just wanting to win. That's the bottom line. It's like, can you read or type without your glasses? I'm a fiery type of player. People say I have an attitude problem, but I don't. I hear my teammates, but that doesn't stop the will to win."

Wallace said he simply was alerting referees to their mistakes. "If I see something out there that I don't think is right, I just let [the officials] know. My reaction is letting them know it is full of BS out there. I just come at them with logic, and I guess that burns them up.

"Honestly, I don't care what no one else thinks of me, except for people in my inner circle—my teammates, my family, my wife, and my kids. Outside of that, it don't matter. The things I do, I do for me, not for no publicity stunt or cameras or whatever. Whenever we do something with my family,

I don't care if the media is there. I am still going to do it, and I am going to be me."

Wallace said he looked at his technicals as a "positive thing" for his team. "If we're down or we're out there lollygagging, I might get upset or get kicked out," he said. "From the games I've seen, the team plays harder. It bothers my wife more than it bothers me. It don't bother me at all. I'm not worried about that. That's more on [the refs]. I don't care what anybody says about me. I know what type of person I am. As long as I can look my family in the face every day, and they know what type of person I am, I'm cool."

Looking around at a room full of reporters, he added, "Because everybody that's here, when I'm finished with basketball, I won't see any more."

Wallace was co-hosting a party Sunday after the All-Star game, celebrating the launch of his record company, Urban Life Music.

"The most exciting part of my weekend is going to be Sunday night," he said.

Wallace came off the bench for nine points and four rebounds in 21 minutes in the West's 137–126 win over the East on Sunday afternoon. That night, he danced the night away.

* * *

Portland came out of the All-Star break with back-to-back wins over Golden State.

The victory at home (after winning 92–83 the night before) was their 12th straight home win despite a season-high 26 turnovers. Down 86–78, the Blazers ran off 14 straight points to take a 92–86 lead with 2:17 left, eventually winning 99–95.

"We can't take it for granted we can turn this thing on and off like a faucet," Dunleavy said. "Teams are not going to come in here and fall down. It's the opposite. You come in here and win, it's like two or three wins for you."

Sabonis celebrated Independence Day in Lithuania with 20 points and 11 boards; not bad for a 35-year-old in the second of back-to-back games.

"Sabonis was the fulcrum to the wheel," Warriors coach Garry St. Jean said afterward. "You have to respect his ability to catch the ball on the block. It sounds simple, but it's not. Larry Bird, Magic [Johnson], Kareem [Abdul-Jabbar]—when they get the ball down there, everything revolves around them. It's that way with Sabonis with this team.

"I always tell people I'd have loved to play with Sabonis at 25 years old," Stoudamire said. "But I will take the one at 35 any time."

On February 27, Portland beat Utah 101–92 at the Rose Garden in a rugged affair marked by five technicals and the ejection of Jazz center Greg Ostertag.

With 6:21 left in regulation, there was an incident involving Wells and Karl Malone. The Jazz had rebounded a Blazer miss and Malone started upcourt. Wells clung to his jersey and Malone threw him to the floor. Wells sprang up for a staredown with Malone, each drawing a technical. As fans booed and officials jumped between them, it ended there.

"He was on my arm," Malone said afterward. "You can't ride me with a saddle out there, can you? But it was no big deal. I've had my kids do more to me while I was asleep in bed."

A minute later, Smith and Ostertag got locked up under the Utah basket. Wallace joined in, and suddenly, a dance became a melee, with all 10 players, the two coaches, and three officials together in what amounted to a rugby scrum.

"Greg said [Wallace] swung over the top of his head; then he got a little excited," Utah coach Jerry Sloan said.

Two nights later, the Lakers won a slugfest, 90–87, to regain first place in the West at 46–11. It was the Lakers' 12th straight win and ended the Blazers' 11-game skein overall, their first home loss in 17 outings. Portland shot only .404 from the field, including 4-of-17 from 3-point range.

"This is the best defense we've played this year against a team of this caliber," Lakers coach Phil Jackson said. As if there were a lot of teams "of this caliber."

Shaquille O'Neal collected 23 points and 10 rebounds while Kobe Bryant contributed 22 points and seven boards for the Lakers. Pippen had

19 points, nine rebounds, four assists, and four steals, but he and Smith both missed 3-point attempts with a chance to tie in the closing seconds.

Before the game, Jackson said Pippen should have been an All-Star that season. Jackson, often playing mind games with his comments about the Blazers, might have merely been standing up for his former player in Chicago.

"The fact that he was snubbed by the rest of the coaches in this conference is a shame," Jackson said. "I voted for Scottie, and I think anybody who has a conscience says this is still one of the greatest players in the game."

Pippen demurred on the All-Star subject but addressed his role with the Blazers, referring to himself in the third person.

"If you want me to score 20 points a night, I can do that," he said. "I can get my shots. But it means more to me that we execute as a team and to not worry about individual stats. I am still one of the best players in the game, and I am a winner. That's what this game is all about.

"Tell me who is a better small forward in the West. I am one of the few players with six rings. You can say I got them with Michael Jordan or whatever, but what I do stands out, and if you are too blind to see it . . . Scottie Pippen has been on the stage for a long time, so it is time to wake up and recognize that what I do is not a fluke."

Pippen also addressed the subject of his Portland team, which stood at 45–12, a game back of the Lakers. "We have a nice team, but we haven't done anything yet. We have a long way to go before this team can be compared to any championship team. With my Chicago teams, I had an opportunity to grow and learn and take the time to develop. Those things mature over a period of years. I can't compare that to what I'm doing now.

"We haven't put that much time in on the court together yet. The challenge is there for us to win a championship, and we have as good a chance as anybody."

Perhaps the worst news of the night was that Grant sat out the game with a bout of plantar fasciitis. The injury would keep the power forward out of action for all but eight minutes over the next month.

After an overtime loss to the Pacers (127–119), in which Wells scored a career-high 29 points off the bench, the Blazers responded with road wins over Detroit and Washington. Reserves Wells (14 points on 6-for-8 shooting), Anthony (15 points on 5-for-6 from 3-point range), and O'Neal (six points and nine rebounds) played pivotal roles against the Wizards.

"That is a very good team," Washington coach Darrell Walker said. "I don't know if we should be more worried about their first or second unit."

"Bonzi and Jermaine are the future of the ballclub," Pippen said. "In a few years, the torch will be passed to them."

On March 16, Portland native Terrell Brandon scored 25 points, and Kevin Garnett came through with 17 points, 12 rebounds, and eight assists as Minnesota scored a rare victory in Portland, beating the Blazers 96–92.

Pippen scored 21 points and Smith 19, but Pippen missed three straight free throws in the final 3:04, while Wallace missed two. Rasheed, who had 17 of his 19 points in the first half, was ejected for the fifth time in the season, running his technical total to 28, the last one with 5.1 seconds left in regulation.

"We let the officials take us out of the game a little bit," Dunleavy said, his message a broken record. "When you get some calls down the stretch you don't like, you have to play through it."

Things took a downturn for a while. On March 28, Portland's home losing streak hit four games with an 89–85 defeat to San Antonio. After a 45–11 start, the Blazers had lost eight of their past 14 games.

"Nobody in here is trying to lose on purpose," Stoudamire said.

"We're not where we want to be, physically or mentally," Anthony said. "We've been tagged like a prizefighter who has taken some tough blows. We have to hold on until we can come back around."

The Blazers would close the regular season in strong fashion, however. On April 1, Stoudamire scored 18 of his season-high 31 points in the first quarter of a 113–79 rout of Milwaukee, matching the franchise record with seven 3-pointers.

The next night, the Blazers survived an early ejection by Wallace to complete a four-game sweep of Seattle with a 95–82 win.

Two technical fouls gave Wallace 34 for the season, a new NBA single-season record, breaking the mark of 32 co-held by Charles Barkley and Dennis Rodman. Wallace got one for throwing the Sonics' Vernon Maxwell off him with a forearm and the second for a remark to referee Joey Crawford and finished the night with a single point scored.

"We're counting on Rasheed to not get thrown out in the playoffs," Smith said.

"He consistently tells me it's not going to happen in the playoffs," Pippen said.

Co-captains Pippen and Smith were the primary conduits between Dunleavy and the players.

"I'm the guy who keeps a happy medium between the coaches and players," Pippen said. "If the players get yabby-yabby, I'm the one to say, 'Let him coach. Be quiet. Do this.' I have to make sure everything is well-oiled and greased. But it's a collective effort—myself, Steve, Detlef, and Joe [Kleine]."

Pippen told a reporter he felt the Blazers could win a title. "It's not just about getting to the finals and shaking the tree. You want to shake the branch and get all the apples off the tree."

On April 13, Portland beat San Antonio, 93–77, to set a franchise road record for wins in a season, climbing to 28–12 away with one game left in the season. Wallace led the way with 27 points for the Blazers (57–22), who clinched the second-best record in the West and home-court advantage against any team except the Lakers. The Spurs, going without the injured Tim Duncan, fell to 50–29.

"It was like playing the Lakers without Shaq," Pippen said. "But to win this way was good for our confidence."

Wallace was hit with his 37th technical of the season for comments to the officials while sitting on the bench late in the first half. He was repeatedly booed by the Alamodome crowd of 30,651 and brought on more of it by pointing frequently to the stands or the scoreboard.

On April 16, at shootaround before a 102–95 win over Sacramento, assistant coach Bill Musselman talked to the players, revealing that a week earlier, he learned he had multiple myeloma. He was scheduled to go to the Mayo Clinic in Rochester, Minnesota, the following week to fight the bone marrow cancer.

"If it weren't for Coach Musselman, I wouldn't be here today," Wells said. "Just having him come talk to us brought tears to my eyes. If he can be tough for us, we know we can put it on the line for 48 minutes."

That night, Wallace picked up his 38th technical of the season arguing a call in the second quarter. Early in the third, Dunleavy jumped up from the bench and drew a T, ostensibly to take the officials' focus off Wallace and help keep him in the game.

Wallace was making no death threats, but there certainly were some four-letter words being thrown out there. With two games left before the playoffs, day-to-day battles of the long NBA season were taking their toll on Dunleavy.

"I'm like one of those recovering addicts—I'm only good for today," Dunleavy said. "Tomorrow is the next day, and you just try not to fall down again. There is no time when you can feel real comfortable."

In the regular-season finale on April 19, Nick Van Exel's 21-footer with 1.7 seconds left gave Denver a 96–95 win at the Rose Garden to deny the Blazers a 60-win season.

The team wound up with the second-best record in the West at 59–23, eight games behind the Lakers (67–15). Phoenix and San Antonio (both 53–29) were six games back of Portland in third place.

Wallace won the technicals title with 38, more than doubling runners-up Gary Payton and Vlade Divac with 18. Sheed also had more T's than the New Jersey Nets (32), even though illegal defenses counted. Portland led the NBA with 93 technicals, seven more than Sacramento.

* * *

Portland's best-of-five first-round matchup was against Minnesota, which had finished 50–32 and featured Kevin Garnett and Terrell Brandon. Brandon and Stoudamire—three years Terrell's junior—had known each other forever, both growing up in Northeast Portland.

Damon had been the batboy for Terrell's team in the Peninsula Park Little League. They had played together growing up at Irving and Unthank parks. Brandon led Grant High to a state championship in 1988; Stoudamire had been a member of Wilson High teams that won state crowns in 1989 and 1991.

Now Brandon and Stoudamire would be matched up against each other in a seven-game series.

"We love each other, and it means a lot to us to represent Northeast Portland," Brandon said. "We talk about it all the time."

The teams had split their season series, 2–2, but the Blazers weren't just thinking about getting by the Timberwolves.

"We want to go all the way," Smith said. "You don't want to just get to the conference finals. This team did that last year."

NBC analyst Peter Vecsey predicted Dunleavy would be fired if the Blazers did not advance to the West finals.

Asked about it, Dunleavy, said, "If that's the case, that's a decision for Bob [Whitsitt] and Paul [Allen] to make. All I know is, I work as hard as I can work. If that's not good enough, then God bless them. Find the next guy who can do a better job."

NBC's Bill Walton predicted Portland would overpower the Timberwolves on the boards and advance.

"The Blazers' perimeter guys are pretty boys—Scottie Pippen, Steve Smith, Detlef Schrempf, Damon Stoudamire—and they're awesome," the one-time Portland pivot said. "But it comes down to who is going to win the battle underneath the basket. And that's what Sabonis, Grant, and Wallace do."

But Walton said the Blazers' playoff run would end when they met the Lakers in the conference finals. "They could play great and still lose. That's how good the Lakers are."

Walton shared an opinion on Wallace, too. "Rasheed is going to have to learn that the psychology of referee/player relationships is very important. If he doesn't, he's hurting himself, his team, the franchise, and the people who love the Blazers."

Portland drew first blood, winning a hard-fought opener 91–88 at the Rose Garden. Pippen scored 28 points and grabbed nine rebounds in 42 minutes.

"He's like the scrappy old Scottie," Garnett said. "He's getting steals, locking up his man, getting key rebounds, making crucial plays. It's amazing."

Stoudamire scored 18 points and Smith 17, while Brandon had 17 points and 12 assists for Minnesota. Even with Garnett guarding Wallace, the Wolves sent double-team help at times. Sheed finished with 15 points on 6-for-10 shooting.

"Rasheed is the most efficient offensive player in the league," Minnesota coach Flip Saunders said. "He probably scores more points per shot than anybody."

Even in the loss, Garnett had his first playoff triple-double with 12 points, 10 rebounds, and 11 assists, though he made only 6-of-20 shots from the field and did not get to the foul line in 41 minutes.

"Kevin just had an off day," Dunleavy said. "At 6-foot-11 with the skill level he has—the ability to go out on the floor and shoot and also post you up inside—nobody can stop him. We just tried to make him work really hard for what he got. Rasheed does a good job with his length to bother him some. We also double-teamed him, and it was effective."

Stoudamire, in his diary with me in *The Oregonian*, talked strategy.

> The thing that surprised me most was when Minnesota started the game doubling Rasheed every time he touched the ball. I guess they wanted to keep Garnett out of foul trouble. That allowed Steve, Scottie, and me to get some easy shots, and we knocked them down. Add that to what Rasheed is going to do, and we're a dangerous club. It was a good start for me and for the Trail Blazers. Only 14 wins to go.

Wallace, for his part, had nothing to say. He was pretty much not talking to the media, though he would make the occasional exception through the playoffs—primarily after series-clinching victories.

Pippen was big again in Game 2, scoring 12 of his 21 points in the second half to lift Portland to an 86–82 victory. The Blazers took the lead for good late in the third quarter and held off the Wolves to take a 2–0 series lead.

Garnett collected 23 points and 10 rebounds while Brandon scored 20 points with seven rebounds and six assists. Sabonis muscled Minnesota center Rasho Nesterovic for 19 points in a game the Blazers won at the 3-point line, making 6-of-12 attempts to the Wolves' 2-of-10. Wallace had nine points on 3-for-9 shooting and seven rebounds in 43 minutes.

In his diary, Stoudamire spoke in depth about his feelings about Wallace.

Rasheed has averaged 12 points and six rebounds in the first two games, but I can guarantee you we're not at all worried about it. Rasheed is matched up with one of the best players in the universe, Kevin Garnett. Just having Rasheed out there has caused the Timberwolves to double-team him almost every time he touches the ball. He is a big part of the reason the rest of us have been able to have so many open looks. Rasheed attracts so much attention. Rasheed might not be getting his 20, but give him credit for passing out of the double-team.

Rasheed has to take that as a respect factor. He still is our man, a big part of the team. Maybe some people say he is struggling; I say the Timberwolves have decided they are not going to let him beat them. He has been solid defensively. He has made Kevin work for everything he has gotten. Regardless of how many points he scores, Rasheed is always going to be playing hard, trying to help this team succeed.

Rasheed is one of my better friends on the team. His technicals have gotten a lot of attention, and he already has two in the first two playoff games. Sometimes I wish he could get a better grip on himself in terms of his temper, but that is Rasheed. As he gets older and matures more, I hope that will settle down. But emotion is what makes Rasheed go.

I am not going to lie and say that is a positive for us. It keeps you on an edge. We can't afford to be coming down the stretch of a playoff game and have him get a couple of T's and get ejected. We won't be able to win a championship if he's not there for us. He knows that.

He almost got himself kicked out [in Game 1] when he got so mad and tried to kick the ball and missed after he had already gotten one T. I was so glad the ball hit his shin instead of his foot. If he had gotten it, the ball would have gone 20 rows up in the stands, and Minnesota would still be shooting technicals. It's the kind of thing you can laugh about the next day, but at the time, we were all thinking, "Don't go crazy on us now."

But if we have an ultimate team guy, it's Rasheed. Some guys like the limelight, but that's not his personality. He just wants privacy. He doesn't care about numbers or accolades. He is always cheering for the rest of us when he's out of the game. In a lot of ways, you couldn't ask for a better teammate.

Garnett and Brandon had huge games in leading Minnesota to a 94–87 win in Game 3 at the Target Center. Garnett had his second triple-double of the series with 23 points, 13 rebounds, and 10 assists, while Brandon had career playoff highs in points (28) to go along with 12 assists. Garnett played 44 minutes; Brandon played the full 48 minutes.

The Timberwolves shot .535, including 6-for-10 from the 3-point line. The Blazers, meanwhile, shot .421 from the field, missing one dunk, eight layups, and 12 other close-range shots.

"We shot ourselves in the foot," said Pippen, who had 16 points, six assists, and five rebounds. "If we had made some of those layups, we'd have won by 10."

After suffering through his worst offensive game of the season—two points on 0-for-8 shooting with six assists in 28 minutes—Stoudamire offered a mea culpa in his diary.

> Give Minnesota credit. They played an excellent game from start to finish. They did what they're supposed to do, and we didn't. Terrell played an outstanding game. Everyone has been talking about the Rasheed-Garnett matchup, and it's a big one. But I think as Terrell goes, so go the Timberwolves. If Terrell plays well, it would be hard for us to beat them. He really stepped up his game Sunday. Everything he did worked well for him.
>
> I stunk up the gym. I don't think I've gone without a field goal once in my five years in the NBA. I don't know if it's ever happened going back to grade school. It's embarrassing, but the good thing is, we have another game Tuesday.

Between Games 3 and 4, Minnesota's VP/basketball operations Kevin McHale was asked by Portland writers about J. R. Rider, who had been cut by Atlanta late in the season. Rider, who had played his first three NBA seasons with the Timberwolves before being shipped off to the Blazers, had been cut by Atlanta late in the 1999–2000 season (due to his subpar play). McHale said he wouldn't be surprised to see Rider back in the league the following season.

"As many bridges as you burn in our league, you have to burn 29 to be out of it," McHale said. "He has burnt a few. Like I've always said, though, ax murderer by day, great player by night—you've got a job."

Portland outscored Minnesota 28–13 in the fourth quarter en route to a come-from-behind win (85–77) in Game 4 to clinch the series. All five Blazer starters were in double figures, led by Sabonis with 15 points and 11 rebounds and Wallace with 15 points and eight boards. Garnett had 17 points, 10 boards and nine assists, narrowly missing his third triple-double of the series.

"We had two chances to take control of the series, and we didn't take advantage either time," Saunders said. "Portland is the second-best team in the league."

The Blazers had dedicated the game to Musselman, who ironically was at the Mayo Clinic in Rochester, Minnesota, fighting bone cancer. The Blazers signed a game ball.

"It was basically us just digging down," said Wallace, who broke his silence with the media to talk about the highly regarded assistant coach. "We had to get this one for Coach Muss."

Musselman was to succumb to the disease three days later, on May 5, 2000, at age 59. Dunleavy learned of his aide's death on the eve of Game 1 of the Western Conference Semifinals series with Utah, after a practice session at the Rose Garden. He said a few words to the media about Musselman, then nearly broke down and had to walk away. The players elected to call off their scheduled 30-minute interview period.

Musselman had been recovering from an October 28 stroke when he was diagnosed with cancer. Son Eric Musselman, then an Orlando assistant, said his father had called each of the Blazer players as they were getting ready for Game 4 of the Minnesota series. Each player received a specific message, a mix of strategy and inspiration.

The senior Musselman felt well enough to watch the Blazers' series-clinching win on TV. The next morning, before he underwent surgery, Eric Musselman got word from Pippen that the players had dedicated the game to him. When son related the news to father, Bill responded with a thumb's up sign.

Musselman fully expected to recover from the surgery, begin chemotherapy, and return to Portland "to be with the team," his son said. But the next evening, his health took a turn from the worse. Hours later, he was gone.

* * *

The Blazers entered the West semifinal series with a payroll at nearly $74 million. Utah was at $49 million, ninth in the league.

"That's what money does—it can buy you a good team," Jazz forward Bryon Russell said, adding a reference to Portland owner Paul Allen: "We don't have somebody at Microsoft down here."

"They may have the deepest team in the league, and it shows you what money can buy," Utah center Olden Polynice said. "They have five guys who can start for any other team sitting on their bench. It's a nice problem to have."

Utah owner Larry Miller, who owned a string of auto dealerships throughout Utah along with several other business ventures, couldn't match Allen's pocketbook.

"I have great respect for Paul, but he has financial resources way beyond what I've got," Miller said. "Frankly, I don't think it's right that a team is allowed to spend more than twice what the [salary] cap is [$34 million]. It shouldn't be a case of the champion being the best team money can buy."

Portland had won the season series, 3–1, and the Blazers had a large advantage in depth. But Utah had Karl "The Mailman" Malone and John Stockton, perhaps the most dynamic duo in the NBA, even in their mid- to late-30s.

The Jazz were no match for the Blazers in the series opener, falling 94–75. With 6-foot-4 Jeff Hornacek trying to defend Pippen, the 6-foot-8 small forward scored 13 of his team-high 20 in the second half.

"This is a long series," Pippen said. "I don't know how long the matchup with me and Hornacek is going to last. We have to take advantage of that opportunity while it's there."

The Blazers won despite shooting .384 from the field. Utah was worse, shooting only .368 and making 3-of-13 from the 3-point line.

"Our guys didn't come to play," Utah coach Jerry Sloan said.

Portland rolled again in Game 2, 103–85, for its 13th straight playoff home win over Utah. The Blazers led by 21 at the half and by 33 in the fourth quarter while shooting .563 from the field. Smith scored 19 points to lead six Blazers in double figures. Malone, playing with a sore left knee, was the high-point man for Utah with 15.

"That's the best I've seen a team play against us since I've been in Utah," Sloan said afterward. "They were so good defensively, we couldn't get the ball near the basket. They just annihilated us defensively.

"Before tonight, I think there were a few guys in our locker room who thought we had a chance to win. I'm not sure there's anybody now. We looked like an expansion team trying to play against them. We're not good enough if we don't have a great effort for the full 48 minutes. They're just too talented."

Wallace had 14 points on 6-for-11 shooting and eight boards. He also picked up his fourth technical of the playoffs, protesting a non-call from the bench after the game had turned into a rout.

"I wish Rasheed could play with all that emotion and channel it all in a positive way," Dunleavy said. "I mean, just take it out on the opponent as opposed to the officials."

In the third quarter, Wallace collided with Utah's Armen Gilliam, who was knocked into Malone on the Utah bench. Malone suffered a minor knee injury.

"He hit [Gilliam] in the back and knocked him out of bounds," Sloan charged. "If I had to fight somebody, I wouldn't hit him in the back, I'd hit him right in the face. That's BS, but it seems as if that's acceptable today."

In Game 3, Portland blew a 21-point first-half lead, then took care of business down the stretch in a 103–84 victory at the Delta Center for a 3–0 series lead.

Portland led 53–32 late in the second, but Utah closed the quarter with a 17–2 run to draw within 55–49 at the half. The Jazz pulled even four times in the third quarter, but the Blazers used a 25–7 spurt to go ahead 88–72 in the fourth quarter, and by then it was over.

Sabonis had a big game, scoring 22 points on 10-for-13 shooting and grabbing eight rebounds for the Blazers, who shot .513 from the field.

Malone got untracked for 28 points and 11 rebounds, and Hornacek had 24 for the Jazz, who shot only .400. Portland reserves outscored their Jazz counterparts 35–2.

"We knew they were going to fight back," Pippen said. "Our bench gave us what we needed. Utah was able to come back with their starters, but they ran out of gas."

Asked to compare this Portland team with the Bulls championship teams of '97 and '98, Pippen gave the Blazers his strongest endorsement yet.

"This team is much more well-rounded," Pippen said. "From a talent standpoint, we're a much stronger team."

Utah prevailed in Game 4, 88–85, to avoid a series sweep and set up a Game 5 at the Rose Garden. The Blazers rallied from a seven-point deficit with less than two minutes to play and had a chance to send the game into overtime on their last possession, but Anthony missed from 3-point range.

It was a heated game, and there was a terrific battle in the trenches between Malone, who collected 27 points, eight rebounds, and seven assists, and Grant, who came off the bench for 20 points and 13 boards in 26 minutes.

The Blazers, who fired at only a .375 clip from the field, rushed shots, bickered with officials, threw the ball away, and got into foul trouble.

In the first quarter, Pippen and Polynice traded heated words as the two walked up court, and Pippen gave the Utah center a forearm to the chest. Both players were assessed technicals. Wallace drew his fifth tech of the play-offs for arguing an out-of-bounds call in the third quarter.

Wallace provided a moment of levity early, giving a long stare to a rotund heckler behind press row during a first-quarter timeout.

"You have BBs in your head. BBs!" the fan shouted.

Sheed shouted back: "BB? Stands for 'Big Belly.'"

The Blazers would have preferred the sweep but were now going to have to try to win the series on their home court.

"Maybe it's good for us to get this loss," Grant said. "Maybe it puts a little more fire under us. I know we are all angry at ourselves. If we win, maybe we're sitting on a high horse. Maybe this humbles us a bit and tells us, 'Look, you have to respect everybody.'"

"They won by three points," Wells said. "They played well, but they have to play well three more times. We have a lot of confidence. We know we can beat them. We weren't down 3–0; they were. We want to get out of Utah. Utah's not good for us. We have a bad vibe in Utah. We have to get back home and let our hair down."

The Blazers took care of business in Game 5, edging the Jazz 81–79 at home to claim the series, 4–1. Pippen's 3-pointer with 7.3 ticks left gave Portland an 80–79 lead, and Russell's two missed free throws with 3 seconds left were the difference.

Jazz coaches complained to officials after the first of Russell's misses.

"Someone was jumping up and down on the basket support," Russell said afterward. "I thought I'd get another shot."

After Russell's misses, Pippen was fouled and made the first of two free throws with 1.7 seconds left. Utah rebounded the second attempt and called timeout with 1.4 seconds left. Inbounding at midcourt, the Jazz got the ball to Russell. He launched a 3-point attempt as Wallace jumped into him, drawing some contact. But there was no foul call, the shot was off the mark, and the Blazers and their fans went into celebration mode.

Sloan said he thought the final play was a foul. Dunleavy disagreed. "At the end of the game," the Portland coach said, "you have to make the shot."

"I went up to try to block it," Wallace said in a jubilant Portland locker room. "Then I saw [Russell] bail out, so I put my hands straight up. I was just hoping they wouldn't call it."

Pippen scored 23 points to go with nine rebounds and eight assists. Sabonis had 16 points and nine boards. Malone had a monster game with 27 points, 11 rebounds, six assists, and three steals while Russell contributed 18 points and six boards . . . but the night was the Blazers'.

"This was the most exciting game I've played since I came to the NBA—even more so than the four-overtime game a few years against Phoenix,"

Sabonis said. "The last minute, I was thinking we might be going back to Salt Lake City."

* * *

Now it was on to the showdown with the high and mighty Lakers, led by unanimous league MVP Shaquille O'Neal and 21-year-old phenom Kobe Bryant and coached by the great Phil Jackson. The Lakers had won 65 games in the regular season, but they were pushed to the hilt in a five-game first-round series by Sacramento, then won their Western Conference Semifinal series in five games over Phoenix.

Participating in the Western Conference Finals for the second straight season, the Blazers salivated over a chance to play in the NBA Finals.

"We've been here before," Dunleavy said. "We want to take the next step."

"I came to Portland to win a championship, not just get to the Western Finals," Schrempf said.

"It will be everything everyone expects," Anthony said of the matchup. "And if we do the things we're capable of, we'll have every chance to win the series."

There was little to like from the Portland side as the Lakers dominated the opener, winning 109–94 at Staples Center. The Lakers, who were 7-for-10 from beyond the arc in the first half, outscored the Blazers 37–16 in the second quarter to roll into halftime with a 21-point lead. The Lakers boat-raced the visitors from there.

O'Neal played like an MVP, going for 41 points, 11 rebounds, seven assists, and five blocked shots while playing 47 minutes. Sabonis, meanwhile, went scoreless, going 0-for-4 from the field and collecting one rebound in 33 minutes.

O'Neal was 13-for-27 from the foul line, including 12-for-25 in the fourth quarter as the Blazers played Hack-a-Shaq. O'Neal made his first attempt, missed six in a row, then made seven straight to stake the Lakers to a 104–89 lead with 3:53 left.

"If we get down in a game, I don't think fouling him is a bad strategy,"

Dunleavy said. "Had we scored better, we would have given ourselves a chance to win."

Wallace had 11 points and three rebounds in 16 minutes before being ejected after sustaining his second technical of the game in the third quarter. It was a classic, too. Wallace got the second T after being told three times by referee Ron Garretson to stop staring at him.

"That's a first," Grant said in the Portland locker room afterward.

"Ludicrous," Anthony said. "But Sheed has to be more cognizant of the referees."

Wallace was laughing when approached by the media afterward.

"I ain't giving you all fuel for the fire," he said. "I ain't saying nothing."

After being whistled for an NBA-record 38 technicals in the regular season, along with six ejections, Wallace had promised he wouldn't get thrown out in the playoffs. After picking up five T's in the first two rounds without an ejection, "Mr. T" had now gotten the boot . . . and his coach wasn't happy about it.

"If Ron Garretson told him not to look at him and he looks at him, he's gone," Dunleavy said. "As much as that doesn't sound right and shouldn't be right, under those circumstances, we have to do whatever we have to do have him stay in the game. We can't have an All-Star sitting in the locker room with the game under 10 points in the last few minutes of a game. Even if he's right in any way as far as a bad call, that doesn't do us any good because he's in the locker room, and we're out on the floor playing.

"Bottom line: We're not going to win this series if he's not on the floor."

Two nights later, the Blazers didn't just win Game 2—they dismantled the Lakers on their home floor, winning 106–77 to square the series at one apiece.

Portland only led by three at the half (48–45) but outscored the Lakers 28–8 in third, including a 20–0 run. It was the fewest points ever scored in any quarter by a Blazer opponent in their playoff history.

"It started with the defense," said Dunleavy, pointing to the Lakers' .391 shooting. O'Neal had a serviceable game with 23 points—though he had only nine through three quarters—and 12 rebounds. Bryant managed only 12 points on 2-for-9 shooting with four assists and two rebounds in 42 minutes.

Sabonis struggled again, collecting five points on 2-for-8 shooting with five rebounds. But he blocked three shots and battled Shaq during his 17 foul-plagued minutes on the court.

Wallace, meanwhile, went for a career playoff-high 29 points and 12 boards in 46 minutes. Rasheed, who had been 8-for-50 from 3-point range during the regular season, went 3-for-3 from beyond the stripe in the third quarter.

"It was nice to have Rasheed in there for the full complement," Dunleavy said. "Having him around tonight for the full ride was nice."

Pippen had 21 points, 11 rebounds, three assists, and three steals for the Blazers, who had a huge advantage at the foul line, making 35-of-45 attempts to 17-of-32 for the Lakers.

Jackson was offended by the way the Blazers celebrated at game's end, making a big deal of it with the media afterward—for motivational purposes with his players.

"What we remember is the attitude Portland carried off the floor," the Lakers coach said. "They were jackals down there on the bench. We have to remember that when we go to Portland, that they might have been just a little bit too much so."

"Lose one game and it's like Armageddon around here," Bryant cracked after hearing Jackson's postgame "jackals" reference. "I expect Bruce Willis to walk in any time now."

Does Portland now have the advantage in the series, with Games 3 and 4 at the Rose Garden?

"Sure," Bryant said. "They have all the confidence in the world. They are going home now. The challenge is for us to match their intensity. This time of year, it is all about challenges."

There was a four-day break between Games 2 and 3. In Portland, prior to Game 3, Jackson spoke of his players' psyche after the pounding.

"I let them mope for a day or two—lick their wounds as a basketball club," Jackson said. "But they were able to sustain their feeling about their teammates. There is a tendency for players to blame their teammates, but they didn't. That gave me hope they would be able to come out and get inspired about playing again."

On the Blazers in Game 2, Jackson offered this: "That was quite a game by Portland. They didn't shoot that well, but they had a game plan that worked well against us. They pounded the ball in, drove it to the hoop, created foul situations, and put us on our heels. They played great defense, but our offensive execution was poor."

Returning to the Rose Garden wasn't what the Blazers had hoped for, as the Lakers prevailed 93–91 in Game 3, with O'Neal (26 points, 12 rebounds, three blocks) and Bryant (25 points, seven rebounds, seven assists) inflicting most of the damage. The Blazers led 61–49 early in the third quarter but then went stagnant offensively, scoring only 30 points over the final 21 minutes. Portland had a chance to force overtime, but Sabonis's driving shot in the lane was blocked by Bryant with 1.9 seconds left.

Wallace scored 19 points on 9-for-11 shooting, Stoudamire chipped in 19 points, and Pippen contributed 12 points, nine rebounds, and six assists.

Jackson dug the needle into the Blazers as he looked ahead to Game 4.

"If we can put another notch in our belt," the Lakers coach said with a wry grin, "they're really at death's door, and they know it."

The Blazers felt they had outplayed the Lakers in Game 3.

"We gave it away," Grant said. "We had every opportunity to win. We let them back into it. We got complacent as a team. We can't let it happen again."

In Game 4, the Blazers did it again, losing 103–91 as the Lakers took a commanding 3–1 series lead.

"That was a must-win for them," said Bryant, who had 18 points and seven assists, "and they didn't."

Wallace had a sensational game, scoring 18 of his career playoff-high 34 points in the fourth quarter to go with 13 rebounds. Smith scored 20 points, but the Blazers shot only .390 from the field, including 5-for-16 from 3-point range.

O'Neal had 25 points and 11 boards; the Blazers could live with that.

But Glen Rice knocked down 7-of-11 shots and scored 21 points with seven rebounds while Ron Harper chipped in 18 points with seven boards. The Lakers reserves also outscored the Blazers' bench, 19–8.

"We had some great stretches," Dunleavy said. "But we weren't good enough, not for the full 48 minutes."

"They thoroughly outworked us," Anthony said. "It was not a matter of us giving it away. They earned it. We have to stay together. We can't have any dissension internally because we have enough adversity externally."

The NBA fined Pippen for an incident with the Lakers' John Salley in the final minute of regulation. Pippen, angry when he and Salley collided, hit Salley in the back of the head.

"I fouled him, and it wasn't called," Salley would say later. "It wasn't like I did anything with malice. I guess it was just his frustration. He ran behind me and elbowed me in the back of the head."

At the next stoppage of play, Salley said he confronted Pippen.

Said Salley: "He said, 'Yeah, I hit you, and I am going to come down and hit you again. We don't need to play like that.'"

Said Pippen: "I retaliated. I'm not that kind of player, but I expect officials to protect me like they do other players. I wasn't protected on that play."

Pippen said the Blazers were down but not yet out, as they tried to become the seventh team in NBA playoff history to rally from a 3–1 deficit.

"Our backs are to the wall," he said. "We have to fight and sustain it for 48 minutes."

Pippen was all over the court in leading the Blazers to a 96–88 win in Game 5 in LA. The 34-year-old veteran had 22 points, six rebounds, six steals, four blocks, and three assists in a splendid 43-minute display. He scored 15 points in the first half and had 10 of Portland's first 17 points before dislocating the middle and ring fingers on his right hand in the first quarter—though that didn't slow him down.

"That is just Pip being a warrior," Wallace said.

Wallace collected 22 points and 10 rebounds, but he was just 7-for-21 from the field and was hit with his eighth technical foul of the playoffs—his 46th of the season—for arguing an offensive foul called in the first quarter.

It was a struggle offensively for the Lakers, who shot .380 from the field, including 6-for-27 from beyond the arc. Shaq had another stellar game, with 31 points and 21 rebounds in 46 minutes, but Bryant fouled out after scoring 17 points on 4-for-13 shooting to go along with six turnovers. Rice, who had 21 points in Game 4, scored only four while hitting 1-of-8 shots from field and 0-of-5 from 3-point range.

"It's disappointing, but not a surprise," coach Jackson said. "We're going to have to take a little more time to win this series, but that's good for us. This team has not grown up enough to understand some of the subtleties we're trying to do."

Jackson stopped Pippen—whom he had coached for 10 seasons in Chicago—in the final seconds of the game to tell him he shouldn't have been allowed to play.

"Cheap shot elbow to the back of the head [of Salley], and he just got fined $10,000," Jackson told reporters. "I told him it was a present, that he shouldn't have been here tonight.' He said, 'Thanks a lot.' I don't think he really meant it."

After the game, Pippen stomped off in a huff after reporters told him Jackson said he should have been suspended from Game 5.

"Phil is not my coach, so I'm not listening to him," Pippen said. "I am not listening to anything you tell me about Phil. Have a good day."

Bryant, who had averaged 22.5 points through the regular season, was averaging 17 points while shooting .406 in the first five games of the series. The fourth-year pro had a big game in Game 3, but in the other four was shooting .326 while averaging 15 points.

"Portland has done nothing but challenge us, force us to be better players," Bryant said. "Their defense forces us to pick up our level of play, mentally and physically. We have to be ready every night."

The Blazers returned to the Rose Garden for Game 6 with hope.

"We know in our minds and our hearts we can outplay that team,"

Pippen said. "We've outplayed them throughout the series. We feel like we're going to outplay them every time we go out on the court."

The Blazers got strong contributions from all five starters along with reserve Bonzi Wells in a 103–93 triumph in Game 6. There was electricity in the air in the Rose Garden from the opening tip. Clyde Drexler was on hand to watch the game, and when the JumboTron showed the former Blazer great in the stands during the first quarter, the crowd went wild.

Smith scored 26 points on 10-for-18 shooting and Wells came off the bench for 20 points in 19 minutes, hitting 8-of-13 shots from the field and scoring 14 in the final period.

"Steve is the heart and soul of our team from an offensive standpoint— him and Rasheed," Pippen said. "We run our offense through those guys. And when he comes out and plays like he did today, we're a dominant team."

The Blazers won the points-in-the-paint battle 48–28 and the boards 43–34 while holding O'Neal to a series-low 17 points on 7-for-17 shooting and 3-for-10 from the line. Sabonis had 10 points, 11 rebounds, and six assists in 45 minutes and was effective neutralizing his adversary for the first time in the series.

With tempers high, O'Neal was called for a flagrant foul on Pippen.

"Hopefully there won't be any cheap shots by the Lakers [in Game 7]," Grant said, "but we will be ready for them if they come."

Shaq was put off when Grant's comment was relayed to him afterward.

"I don't have to cheap-shot Scottie," O'Neal said. "He's not that important to me. If I wanted to cheap-shot him, I'd cheap-shot him in real life, not on the basketball court. If I want to cheap-shot somebody, I'll walk up to him man to man."

Now it was a one-game elimination for a spot in the NBA Finals.

"I'm not shocked this has come to a seven-game series," Jackson said. "The battle was lost tonight, but the war is not over."

And, ominously, Dunleavy was moved to offer this about Game 7: "The team that plays the full 48 minutes is going to win."

* * *

There are a handful of playoff games that stand out in the minds of long-time Trail Blazers fans. Game 6 of the 1977 NBA Finals comes to mind. Game 3 of a first-round series against Dallas in 2011, when Brandon Roy scored 18 of his 24 points in the fourth quarter of a comeback victory over Dallas. Damian Lillard's 3-point shot in Game 6 to clinch a first-round series against Houston in 2014.

But Game 7 of the 2000 Western Conference Finals ranks high on the list, and from the perspective of Blazer followers, it is the most infamous.

NBC analysts Bill Walton and Steve Jones—both with Portland ties—were set to work the game with the great Bob Costas. Walton was center on the Blazers' 1977 championship team. Jones, a Portland native and former University of Oregon standout, played the 1975–76 campaign with the Blazers.

They were at the mic for what some Blazer fans have chosen to call "The Collapse."

The Lakers, down but not out, rallied from a 16-point deficit over the final 12:04 to win 89–84 at Staples Center. They would head into an NBA Finals matchup with Indiana. The Blazers would return to Portland, then scatter to parts unknown.

The Lakers, who trailed 71–55 late in the third quarter, outscored the Blazers 31–13 in the fourth. Portland missed 13 straight shots as its lead dwindled, then evaporated.

"We realize we made cowards of ourselves in the fourth quarter," Pippen said in a deathly quiet Portland locker room afterward. "We played like we were fatigued, and they gained the momentum they needed."

In the 1992 Finals, the Blazers had blown a 79–64 lead heading into the fourth quarter of Game 6 at Chicago, and the Bulls won to close out the series in six.

"Very similar," said Jackson, the coach of that Chicago team. "However, I had much more confidence in that team. They had won a championship."

The Blazers, who led 42–39 at the half, used a 21–4 spurt in the third quarter to take a 71–55 lead. The Lakers' Brian Shaw—who, ironically, had agreed to be part of the trade that sent six players to Houston for Pippen the previous October—banked in a 3-point shot from the top with four seconds left, and Portland entered the fourth quarter leading 71–58.

In the final period, the Blazers missed 18-of-23 shots, including 13 in a row—six by Wallace, who was having a terrific game and finished with 30 points. Wallace also missed two free throws with 1:25 left and Portland trailing 81–79.

The Lakers scored 15 straight points in a 6:10 span to pull even at 75–75 with four minutes remaining. They held on despite hitting only 4-of-10 free throws over the final 32.9 seconds. Sabonis—who was effectively battling O'Neal—picked up his fifth foul with 8:35 remaining and departed with Portland leading 75–65. When he returned more than four minutes later, the Lakers had scored seven straight.

After feeding Wallace for a layup to give Portland a 77–75 lead, Sabonis fouled out with 2:44 left. Shaq made both free throws to tie it at 77–77. Bryant's two free throws with 1:28 left gave the Lakers a 79–77 lead and, moments later, when O'Neal slammed a lob pass thrown by Kobe for an 85–79 advantage, Staples Center was a sea of pandemonium.

Wallace knocked down a trey to cut it to 85–82 with 34.1 seconds to play, but the Lakers wrapped it up at the line.

"We just did not make shots in the fourth quarter," a stunned Dunleavy said afterward.

"The Blazers outworked us pretty good the last couple of games, and we didn't want to happen in a seventh game, particularly on our home floor," said Bryant, who was the best player on the floor with 25 points, 11 rebounds, seven assists, and four blocks.

The Blazer locker room was quiet as a morgue. A sober Pippen put the game in perspective.

"We wanted to be aggressive and continue taking the ball to the basket, but the momentum of the game shifted," he said. "When that happens, the officiating tends to shift, too. We didn't get the calls we were getting earlier. By that time, it was an uphill battle for us, even though we were in the lead."

When Sabonis came to the bench with his fifth foul, it opened up O'Neal's game, Pippen said. "Shaq was allowed to camp out in the lane much longer. The officials never focused on that. If you allow him to stay in the lane like that, when you have to sink back in and guys are shooting the ball as well as they did, they are going to be a tough team to beat."

Stoudamire's final entry in his diary had some soul-searching.

> We settled for too many jumpers. We quit going to the hole. It didn't help when Sabas picked up his fifth foul. That let Shaq roam around and he was able to do a little bit of everything. Once they got rolling, we could never sustain anything on our side. If just one or two of the shots would have fallen . . .
>
> Kudos to the Lakers. It was a hard-fought series. There are no quitters on their side. I know a lot of Blazer fans will say we were the better team. We can sit here and talk about being the better team, but it doesn't make any difference. We are going home, and we don't have practice today. The Lakers are playing for the championship, and not us.

* * *

To those inside the franchise, the loss reverberated.

"That was the biggest disappointment of my career," says Jay Jensen, who worked as an NBA trainer for 24 years, 19 in Portland. "I can't even watch [video of] that game. After the game, Scottie came into the training room and was crying like a baby. Scottie wanted a championship so badly. He won six titles in Chicago. He could have gotten out of Michael's shadow and won a title for himself. That game changed the course of two franchises. Had the Lakers lost, they have probably broken up their franchise. We lost, and we did."

"It was devastating," says Bob Medina, then the Blazers' strength and conditioning coach. "That cracked our franchise. We were never the same after that."

Toward the end of the third quarter of Game 7, reserve forward Antonio Harvey was certain the Blazers were going to win.

"Then Shaw banks in the 3 [at the end of the third quarter], and the Lakers started to feel like they had a chance," he says today. "We weren't built for it the way we thought we were. The only player on the roster ready for that moment was Scottie, but he wasn't Scottie of the Chicago Bulls, a guy equipped to carry that load when he was with Michael Jordan. Rasheed was the best player on the roster but, at that point in his life, I'm not sure he was ready to carry that load. Steve Smith was a great player but, physically, he wasn't what he once was. We were an ensemble cast of former great players, but nobody was in their moment at that time."

Reserve center Joe Kleine was sitting behind the Blazer bench that day.

"Through three quarters, they had no answer for Rasheed," Kleine says now. "We kept running a little cross pick and getting him the ball at his sweet spot. But he couldn't get it to go down in the fourth quarter. Rasheed just doesn't miss four or five turnarounds on the baseline, and Smith doesn't miss free throws—that just doesn't happen, but it did. Then it just snowballed.

"It was a real shitty feeling. To this day, when I watch [video of] the game, and Kobe throws that lob to Shaq, and I see him yelling, 'Our game,' I get pissed off. That was our series, but we couldn't close it out."

Assistant coach Jim Eyen will always believe the Blazers would have won had Sabonis not gotten into foul trouble and eventually fouled out.

"I was most disappointed for Arvydas because he was such a professional, and to have the game end the way it ended was terrible," Eyen says today. "He played only five minutes in the fourth quarter. He was whistled for three fouls in five minutes. The first three quarters, he did an unbelievable job out there defending Shaq and spacing the floor on the offensive end. Shaq had so much respect for him, he wouldn't leave him. Phil [Jackson] was yelling at him to drop down for help-side defense. Shaq would yell back, 'I'm not leaving him.'

"For three quarters, we had a lot of things going for us. You just wish we had not been impeded that fourth quarter by Arvydas's fouls, and that he had been able to play it out."

The game still leaves a bad taste in the mouth of Mike Rice, who worked as the Blazers' TV analyst for 26 years.

"I don't remember too many individual games, but I've never forgotten that one, especially with the arrogance of Kobe and Shaq," Rice says. "I don't think I'll ever forget that game. I tried to. It's difficult to get over. That had an effect on the franchise for a very long time."

"I remember Game 7 like it was yesterday," assistant coach Elston Turner says. "Double-digits lead deep into the fourth quarter, and we couldn't hold on. Mike did a hell of a job coaching the team that year. He had us right there. We have the lead, and then we have veteran guys who can't make plays—guys with a resume of making plays. But for that fourth quarter, nobody could make plays."

Looking back 18 years later, Bob Costas recalls how the Blazers came out from the opening tip of Game 7 looking like a team bound for the NBA Finals.

"They started that game like a house on fire," the Hall of Fame broadcaster says. "All the momentum was theirs, plus all the pressure was on the other side. The Lakers were the favorites, they were at home, and they were up 3–1 before losing Games 5 and 6. Everything was flowing Portland's way.

"Then Shaw hits that 3 at the end of the third quarter to get the Lakers to within 13. It's still a huge number to overcome, especially in a Game 7. But I felt at the time, not that I thought the Lakers would win, but it gave them a whisper of a chance. It seemed like it turned things a little and gave the Lakers a glimmer of hope."

Costas's feeling grew stronger as the score grew closer.

"The exclamation point was the lob to Shaq for the big slam," he says today. "That was the beginning of the baton almost seamlessly being passed from Jordan's Bulls to the Shaq/Kobe Lakers. What's interesting is, they had a really tough time with the Trail Blazers. Then they beat the Pacers in a six-game NBA Finals, but it could have gone seven.

"After that, the Lakers were a juggernaut. They beat the Sixers in five games [in the 2001 Finals] and the Nets in four games [in the 2002 finals], and if they'd played 40 times, they'd have won 40. Their biggest challenges in those years came in the West Finals from the Trail Blazers in 2000 and the Kings in 2002."

Costas searches his memory for comparisons in terms of a collapse with a big lead on such a big stage. He mentions the 2017 Super Bowl, when

Atlanta blew a 28–3 third-quarter lead to lose 34–28 in overtime to New England. And Game 6 of the 2002 World Series, in which San Francisco led the Angels 5–0 in the eighth inning and lost 6–5.

But a Game 7 of a Conference Final or NBA Final?

"I can't think of anything comparable to it," Costas says.

While Costas was aware of the Jail Blazers sobriquet, he's not sure it was applicable.

"The national image was more forgiving than that nickname, in part because guys like Scottie Pippen and Arvydas Sabonis and Brian Grant gave them a little bit of a good citizen's image," Costas says. "Pippen brought his cred from Chicago. Sabonis was an admirable talent who held his own against Shaq as well as anybody. Mike Dunleavy was a respected coach. To a national audience, they were among the faces of the franchise.

"Rasheed [Wallace] was a terrific player who was notorious. He had a chip on his shoulder that stretched from Portland to Los Angeles, from the Rose Garden to Staples Center. The whole league and the whole world were against him, and he set records in technical fouls, which obscured what a good player he was. Bonzi Wells and J. R. Rider and guys like that were alternately an asset and a detriment. But from a national perspective, I don't think they were as much the face of the team."

And, Costas insists, Portland's reputation as a good basketball city helped on a national level. "The passion of the fans in Portland was high. Games there just felt different. Arco Arena [in Sacramento] was like that during those years, too. The [noise] decibel levels were higher. It's not a coincidence that the Blazers and Kings are the only teams among our main sports leagues in those cities. All the focus goes there.

"The Jail Blazers nickname notwithstanding, they had a pretty good image. The idea of Portland being a good basketball town and a consistent contender during the decade, there was respect for that."

* * *

Across the country, people had paid attention to the Lakers-Blazers series. Among them was University of Michigan guard Jamal Crawford, a Seattle native who would be taken by Cleveland (and traded to Chicago) with the eighth pick in the 2000 Draft and go on to an NBA playing career that continues today.

"The Blazers were just as good as the Lakers that year," Crawford recalls. "And if they'd have gotten by the Lakers, they'd have had a great chance to win the title. Those guys had a chance to win it all. They went against one of the best duos ever in Shaq and Kobe, and it took everything the Lakers had to beat them. That Portland team was unbelievable. They were the deepest team I'd seen.

"I also remember how good Rasheed Wallace was. When I came into the league in 2000, at the power forward position, it was Kevin Garnett, Karl Malone, Chris Webber, maybe Antonio McDyess, and Rasheed. The other guys had more acclaim, but he was as good as anybody out there."

Long-time coach John Lucas thinks the fourth quarter of that Game 7 was one of the most important quarters in recent NBA history.

"One quarter defined the whole world for two franchises," Lucas says today. "It started Kobe and Shaq and the Lakers on their way to three straight championships, and it left an emptiness among everyone in Portland. It seems like the Blazers have never fully recovered from it. I don't know that Mike [Dunleavy] or any of them will ever admit that, but it left them unfulfilled and with a certain among of not life emptiness, but sports emptiness."

* * *

Three days after Game 7, as the Lakers prepared for their NBA Finals matchup with Indiana, Phil Jackson talked about how the Pacers would defend his team.

"They're going to crowd Shaq, but they don't have the athleticism of Pippen and Wallace," he said. "There is no better defender, and no better help defender, than Scottie Pippen."

Dunleavy watched video of Game 7 almost immediately.

"The only thing that saved me from a summer of misery was watching it," he would say months later. "You look for things to pick apart from that fourth quarter. What would you change? To be honest, not a thing, other than to have guys make shots. We made the right substitutions. All of our guys were rested. Our best guys were in good positions. Out of the 13 shots, there were maybe two I would like to have had better shots, but they weren't bad shots. We had one turnover and one misplay on defense. It was a mistake-free quarter, except we didn't make shots.

"Given those scenarios, you probably win 99 of 100 times. It's that high a percentage. Bottom line, we didn't have any fear going into Game 7. We were prepared. We felt good about ourselves. We believed we could win. We came back from a 3–1 deficit. That took a lot of character right there."

A few days after Game 7, Whitsitt met with the media.

"At the start of the season, I told everybody this team was on a two- to three-year window to make a championship run," he said. "This was Year One. We have a nice blend of talent, young and old. If you get lucky and have that mix of veterans on one end and a few guys who are developing, you can stay pretty competitive."

Wallace, Stoudamire, and Wells were still young. On the other hand, Smith was 31, Pippen was turning 35 in September, Sabonis would be 36 in December, and Schrempf was 37.

"Continuity is important," Whitsitt said. "Utah is an example of having players around a long time. One way to get better is if our players continue to work as hard as they're currently working. Young guys get better. There are still a lot of little things you have to learn when you are trying to be a championship team. We made great strides over the last year, but we are still learning."

Peter Vecsey's prediction didn't come true. Dunleavy wasn't fired after failing to get the Blazers to the NBA Finals . . . but he might have been.

Years later, Medina asked Whitsitt what his biggest regret was during his time with the Blazers.

"I should have let Mike Dunleavy go after that year," Whitsitt would say.

"There comes a point when the players on a team stop listening to a coach," Medina says. "You either have to get different players or move on from the coach. After that game, they stopped listening to Mike—100 percent."

There were several times the following season, Medina says, when Portland coaches would gather in a huddle during a timeout before approaching the players.

"Rasheed would tell the other guys, 'Don't listen to what this mother-fucker says. Let's just keep doing what we're doing," Medina says. "Coach Gurg [Tim Grgurich] would just tuck his head and shake his head."

After the season, Dunleavy was looking ahead to the 2000–01 campaign.

"I am very happy with the team," he said. "We have a shot at winning the title with the same group. Bob will explore the options, and we have some question marks with the status of some of our players. We aren't going to tie ourselves into not doing anything."

The players didn't want change.

"By keeping this team intact, we would have a good chance for a title again next year," said Smith, who would go on to help the US Olympic team to a gold medal that summer.

Change, though, was in the offing.

Chapter 6

MIKE DONE-LEAVY

(2000–2001)

"I wasn't a chemistry major in college; I was a sports major."

—Bob Whitsitt

In July 2000, Jermaine O'Neal said he wanted a trade—again.

The 6-foot-11 O'Neal, not yet 22 years old but entering his fifth NBA season, had proffered the "T" word in the past, citing lack of opportunity and playing time. This time, though, he seemed to be more serious about it.

"I don't want to go through what I went through last season, not knowing if I'm going to play," he told a newspaper reporter. "Bob [Whitsitt] is a brilliant president, and he's not going to let Arvydas [Sabonis] play out his last year without having another center to take his place. I'm not a center. I can play center, but I don't want to play center totally. I wanted to play the four, and Rasheed [Wallace] is doing such a great job there, it's tough for anybody else."

On the other hand, Whitsitt had O'Neal locked into a contract that still had three years left at a total of $18 million. Jermaine wasn't going anywhere, unless the club's president and GM wanted him to.

Meanwhile, Brian Grant's contract was up, and the Blazers put the word out that he had rejected a six-year, $70-million deal. Under NBA rules, Grant, 28, could get as much as seven years and $93 million from Portland via the Larry Bird Exception (which allows a team to sign its own free agent for an additional year and more money). Word was that a week earlier, Grant had turned down a max deal in a sign-and-trade with Cleveland for Shawn Kemp. Grant refused to play for the Cavaliers, who had gone 32–50 the previous season.

After an outstanding 1998–99 season, in which some saw him as the team MVP, Grant struggled through an injury-plagued 1999–2000 season. Knee surgery caused him to miss the first seven games, and he lost his starting spot to Wallace, finishing the season averaging 7.3 points and 5.5 boards in 21 minutes off the bench.

Grant was still a valued member of the team, though. Midway through the season, coach Mike Dunleavy had approached Wallace about going to the bench and moving Grant into the starting lineup, and Wallace was "way on board" with the switch, Dunleavy said. The trio had dinner together to discuss the move, but Grant demurred.

"The way Rasheed was playing, he deserved to start," Grant said that summer. "He beat me out of that spot. I didn't want anything given to me. Besides, if that was what a coach really wanted to do, he would have done it. A coach doesn't have to ask permission. He asked for my opinion, and I gave it. I told him, 'I don't think I should start, but I deserve to play some minutes.' After that, I didn't get to start, and I didn't get to play, either."

That wasn't fair. After returning to action from a plantar fasciitis problem on March 26, Grant played regular minutes until the Lakers series, when he averaged only 4. 4 points and 3.8 rebounds in 16.7 minutes.

"I was unhappy, like any player would be, but I stayed professional," Grant said. "I didn't bad-mouth Coach Dunleavy. He has a heck of a tough job. I have nothing but respect for him."

Grant's first inclination was to accept Portland's contract offer, but he didn't want to get dumped in Cleveland. Grant expected to be back with Portland until he learned Whitsitt was talking with Cleveland GM Jim Paxson about a trade to be made for Kemp in December, assuming Grant would re-sign with the Blazers. He would have to pass through a 90-day sign-and-trade period.

That set Grant's agent, Mark Bartelstein, into motion, looking for other potential landing spots. Grant was interested in the Knicks, but they had only a $2.25-million mid-level exception available, and the Blazers rejected all trade proposals. Miami had only the mid-level exception, too, but would have more room the following summer under the salary cap.

Grant initially thought he might go to Miami for the exception. Whitsitt, not wanting to lose his asset for nothing, swung into motion, helping facilitate a three-way deal with the Heat and Cavaliers after Grant agreed to a near-max seven-year, $86-million contract.

On August 30, Portland completed the trade, sending Grant to Miami and acquiring Kemp from Cleveland. The Blazers also sent guard Gary Grant to the Cavaliers, who promptly waived him. Miami traded Chris Gatling and Clarence Weatherspoon, along with a future first-round pick and cash, to the Cavs. Kemp was coming off a season in which he averaged 17.8 points and 8.8 boards despite being overweight and having to carry a downtrodden, shorthanded club.

But Kemp didn't come cheap; his contract called for him to make $71 million over the final four years of his contract.

Whitsitt and Dunleavy saw Kemp as a forward who could also play center and spell Sabonis.

Kemp, though, weighed more than 300 pounds at the end of the 1999–2000 season.

"I think he will be motivated to come to camp in better shape than he has the last couple of years, and I expect him to work hard," Dunleavy said. "We haven't weighed him, but I think we can get to where he needs to get to."

Actually, the Blazers had weighed Kemp—at 302. Whitsitt didn't want the figure to get out. Neither did Kemp, who would turn 31 in November.

Whitsitt seemed annoyed by reporters' questions about Kemp's skill set compared to that of Grant.

"We're not lining guys up," he said. "This isn't football. It's about matchups, switching, combinations. Shawn has played both [power forward and center] almost his whole career. When we had the great teams in Seattle [1992–1994], he played a lot of center. He played [Hakeem] Olajuwon all the time when Olajuwon was an MVP kind of guy."

Whitsitt felt he had gotten the best of the deal.

"I think we're a step ahead," he said.

A day later, the Blazers sent "The Kid" packing, too. Still only 21, O'Neal was traded—along with veteran center Joe Kleine—to Indiana for veteran forward-center Dale Davis.

"I finally get a chance to show what I can do," O'Neal said. "I don't think anybody really knows."

"We developed Jermaine, and we liked him, but he was frustrated and didn't want to be here," Whitsitt said. "I still think he'll be a really good player in this league. The book on Jermaine will be finished 10 to 15 years from now. We're trying to win a championship. We're close, and we're trying to do all we can while we're in that window."

The Blazers were getting something of value in return. The 6-foot-11, 255-pound Davis, 31, had been an All-Star in the Eastern Conference the previous season, averaging 10 points and 9.9 rebounds while shooting .502 from the field. Davis had led the Pacers in rebounding seven years running.

Meanwhile, forward Detlef Schrempf, 37, was leaning toward retirement. He was not on hand for training camp, but the Blazers kept a roster spot open in case he decided not to retire.

* * *

There was no doubt what the Blazers' goal was heading into the season. It was an NBA title or bust.

"Everything we do is pretty much based on that," Dunleavy said.

Garnett, who should have been hired as a publicist for the Blazers, was asked if they were the team to beat in the NBA for the upcoming season.

"Without a doubt. They almost made it to the Finals last year. Now they went out and added two beasts."

Davis had played his first nine NBA seasons with the Pacers, moving into the starting lineup late in his rookie season and never leaving that spot. He was an outstanding rebounder, solid defender, and high-percentage shooter, though it was all back-to-the-basket stuff. He was a quiet, proud man—liked by his teammates, the media, and the fans.

Davis never had a relationship with his father. He grew up in a single-parent family in Toccoa, Georgia, an hour outside of Atlanta. Dale's father left soon after he was born, and his mother, Carolyn Davis, raised sons Dale and Kevin by herself.

Carolyn worked for 21 years as a training instructor at Shaw Industries, until Dale made her retire after signing his first NBA contract in 1991.

"We didn't have a whole lot," Davis said after he arrived in Portland. "That's why I don't mind working for what I get. It wasn't always easy. Mom always tried to make sure we had food to eat, but there weren't a lot of extras, no name-brand shoes or clothes. I mostly wore hand-me-downs. It made me value things a lot more."

Dale was cut from his eighth-grade team but grew six inches the next summer, "and the next thing I knew, I had four basketball coaches in my living room," he said.

Kevin Davis grew to 6-foot-5 and played at Georgia State, and later in the CBA, the USBL, and in Europe. Dale played at Clemson, where he was an honor student and an All-American.

In Davis, Kemp, and Sabonis, Dunleavy said the Blazers "have three of the top 15 or 20 rebounders in the league."

But there would be a logjam for minutes up front.

"The problem with playing time only increases," Grant said before his departure to Miami. "I never looked at myself or Jermaine as superstars, but how will they find the minutes for everybody? I wish them all the luck."

Owner Paul Allen was paying his roster an NBA record in salary, a figure that would reach $86.5 million at season's end. Three of the players would be among the league's Top 10—Wallace at $14.4 million, Kemp at $12.7 million, and Damon Stoudamire at $12.4 million.

The only one being underpaid was Dunleavy, making a salary of $2 million in the fourth year of a five-year, $12-million deal. In Milwaukee, George Karl had just signed a two-year extension for $14 million, plus a one-percent piece of the Bucks.

There would be one change to Dunleavy's coaching staff. Assistant Elston Turner left to join Rick Adelman in Sacramento.

Dunleavy added Mike D'Antoni, who had been head coach of the Denver Nuggets in 1998–99. Dunleavy said D'Antoni, 49, would be "a jack-of-all-trades for us, on the bench some and scouting some."

Suddenly, with the departure of O'Neal and Grant and the addition of Kemp and Davis, the Blazers had the oldest team in the league. It was also perhaps the deepest roster, with seven players who would wind up starting at least 36 games in the regular season, with Stacey Augmon starting 23.

* * *

On opening night at home, the Lakers outscored the Blazers 29–19 in the fourth quarter to win 96–86. Shaquille O'Neal had 36 points, 11 rebounds, five assists, and four blocks for the Lakers, who shot .571 from the field. Coming off the bench to make a key contribution was former Blazer guard Isaiah Rider, who was 6-for-8 from the field and finished with 13 points, five rebounds, and three assists in 26 minutes.

Portland was without Arvydas Sabonis, who would miss the first eight games following offseason knee surgery. Wallace had 26 points on 11-for-17 shooting and seven rebounds in 47 minutes while Steve Smith scored 22 points, but the Blazers shot only .400 from the field, including 4-for-11 from 3-point range.

"We were lethargic," said Stoudamire, who had seven points on 3-for-13 shooting.

But that was an inspired effort when compared with two nights later when they were blown out by Phoenix 108–82 at the America West Arena; Dunleavy called it the sloppiest performance by his team since taking over in 1997. The Blazers had 26 turnovers in suffering their most one-sided defeat since a 119–91 pounding by the Lakers on the final day of the 1999 regular season.

"It looked like our guys are not even in shape," said Dunleavy, who wondered if his players "weren't getting enough oxygen in their brains."

Two nights later, on November 4, the Blazers broke into the win column, holding on to win at Seattle, 97–90, after blowing all but one point of a 21-point third-quarter lead at KeyArena. Wallace was ejected after picking up two technical fouls with 2:57 left and the Blazers ahead 85–78. Kemp stepped in to save the day by sinking back-to-back jumpers down the stretch against his former team, finishing with 18 points, 14 rebounds, and five steals in 29 minutes off the bench.

After a 79–75 loss at Sacramento, Portland returned home for a 97–88 victory over Atlanta in which the Blazers let an 18-point lead slip to seven with four minutes left.

"We have to play smarter basketball," Scottie Pippen said. "We lost concentration."

Wallace, who finished with 16 points, eight rebounds, six assists, and four blocks, injected some fireworks near the finish, drawing two technicals and an ejection with 35 seconds left.

"Got nothing nice to say," he told the media afterward.

The Blazers hit the road for a seven-game, 10-day trip with Sabonis, who had recovered from arthroscopic surgery on his left knee. They opened with a 94–82 win at New Jersey. Davis collected 12 points and 17 rebounds in a balanced attack that included solid scoring from Smith (17), Wallace (16), and Bonzi Wells and Kemp (15 apiece). Rasheed picked up his league-high sixth technical in eight games.

The next night, Jason Terry knocked down the game-winning short jump shot with 2.9 seconds left as Atlanta, which entered the game 0–7, came away with a 99–97 triumph at Philips Arena. Smith's 3-point attempt missed at the buzzer for the Blazers, who dropped to 5–4.

"Nobody thought [the Hawks] were going to go 0–82," Dunleavy observed drily.

"We just lost, man," said Wallace, who scored 25 points. "Nothing else to talk about."

On November 19, Wallace continued his hot hand with a 37-point outburst in a 110–102 overtime victory over Orlando at TD Waterhouse Center, the most by a Blazer since Rider had 38 against Toronto in February 1998.

"When he doesn't let officiating dictate his play, there's no one better," Pippen said.

"I always think he's going to make shots," Dunleavy said. "If I were his teammate, I'd put the ball in his hands every opportunity I could. I would look at him as an assist waiting to happen."

On November 28, the Blazers fell 105–93 at Seattle in Nate McMillan's debut as the Sonics' coach. The former assistant coach had taken over for Paul Westphal, who had been fired after a 6–9 start.

Sabonis missed the game with a sprained left knee, and Portland shot only .390 from the field on a night when histrionics were in full display, with referee Tim Donaghy in the middle of it all.

Dunleavy was ejected with two quick technicals after rushing Donaghy early in the fourth quarter, complaining that Wallace had been fouled on a missed shot. That started an 8–0 run that gave Seattle an 84–68 lead with 9:40 left.

With 4:38 remaining, Bonzi Wells got into it with Donaghy. He was given a technical and ejected when he tried to swipe the ball out of Donaghy's hands, then offered a few harsh words for the referee before assistants Jimmy Eyen and Tim Grgurich ran the length of the court to intercede. As Wells went by the bench on the way to the locker room, he rearranged some supplies, sending red Gatorade flying into the crowd. He was fined $10,000 and suspended one game without pay. It also cost him about $18,000 more in salary.

"I know I acted wrongly and I deserve some type of punishment—maybe," Wells said the next day. "But I can't help fighting for my team. I wanted to win so badly, and that's the way I want to play every night—hard, aggressive, and tough."

Two days later, Wallace scored 28 points after missing the morning shootaround in a 95–84 win over Dallas. The team called it an excused absence, but the 6-foot-11 forward did not start. He also picked up his league-leading eighth technical of the season.

Two nights later, on December 4, Phoenix scored 10 straight points in the final 1:30 of overtime to win 84–79 at the American West Arena.

Wallace, who finished with 16 points and 10 boards, picked up his 10th technical in 19 games for yelling at official Tony Brothers off the bench.

"Twenty-one games into the season, and it's already gut check time," Stoudamire said. "This isn't a sign of a team that's going to win even one round in the playoffs."

On December 13, Portland exacted revenge for opening night, handing the Lakers a 96–86 loss at the Rose Garden.

Stoudamire, scoreless at halftime, outscored Kobe Bryant 21–16 in the second half. Wallace had 18 of his 25 points in the first half, and Pippen contributed 18 points, 10 rebounds, and eight assists.

"This was a statement game for us," Pippen said. "We came out with energy and played hard. And we stayed off the officials."

Bryant finished with 35 points, and Shaquille O'Neal had 19 points and 13 boards for the Lakers (15–9), who fell behind the Blazers (16–8) in the Pacific Division standings.

"It's timely," Dunleavy said. "Certainly, it's a prestige win."

With Wallace averaging 20.8 points and 8.4 rebounds, he was looking at another All-Star appearance. Or maybe more.

"When you talk about Rasheed, you have to talk MVP," assistant coach Tony Brown said. "I don't know if there's anyone up there within in terms of inside and outside game. Kevin Garnett and Tim Duncan are good, but nobody scores consistently with the range that Rasheed has. And he has taken his defense up to another level this season."

On December 20, the Blazers' four-game win streak ended in a 106–101 loss at Dallas, where they received seven technicals.

Wallace earned his league-high 14th early in the game when he hung on the rim after dunking. Dale Davis picked up two T's, with Wells and Stacey Augmon drawing one apiece. Dallas also got four T's.

"This is an emotional game," Greg Anthony said. "This is what we do for a living, and we're out there trying to win. When things start going awry, it can have a negative impact. It did tonight in our case."

"A couple of the calls were tough ones, and we didn't stay disciplined enough," said Dunleavy, who was ejected after his second technical in the fourth quarter. "Both teams mixed it up and got into it. We took the brunt of it, and we let them take the game from us."

Wells thought the team's Jail Blazers image played a part.

"It's us against the world," he said. "A lot of guys probably give us that bad-boy image, and maybe a lot of people don't like us. When the momentum goes [the Mavericks'] way, everything goes their way—calls, calls, calls."

Kemp, who was fined for missing practice the previous day, did not play.

After a loss to the Nuggets two nights later (116–96), the Blazers fell to 17–10, and nobody was happy in the visitors' locker room.

"Disaster, disaster, disaster," Stoudamire said.

"We didn't play any defense," said Pippen, who scored a season-high 21 points. "We tried to outscore them, and they ran the ball down our throats all night."

The following night, before a home game against Washington, the Blazers held a team meeting during which Dunleavy and players vented at each other. After that, the coach seemed to back off and let the players call more plays on offense, and they seemed to give more effort. Portland went on a 10-game win streak.

Though the team would win on Christmas Day against the Lakers (109–104), the victory wasn't without controversy. Davis, unhappy after playing just five minutes, skipped the next practice, opting for a stopover in Las Vegas before the team's game at Utah.

"Mike and I talked about my status and contributions to the team," said Davis, who was fined for his transgressions. "I didn't communicate with him during the times when I was really frustrated. I know now what to expect."

After winning their first six games of the new year, Portland's 10-game winning streak came to an end against the Knicks on January 13. The Blazers finally had an off night, shooting only .397 as New York scored a 91–78 victory at Madison Square Garden.

* * *

On January 18, Detlef Schrempf, who had officially been on the injured list since the start of camp with a "sore neck," attended Portland's practice and seemed ready to go for the game that night against Miami. Schrempf had been home "recuperating" and collecting on the second year of the $2.2 million contract he signed before the previous season.

"Will I play this season? I don't know," Schrempf, who would turn 38 that week, told reporters. "Do they need me? Probably not. Not right now, anyway. I'm just staying in shape, and that's about it right now."

That night, Brian Grant made his first appearance in Portland since being traded to Miami in August, finishing with 11 points and four rebounds in 39 minutes in a game the Blazers won, 85–74. (The Blazers hiked their record to an NBA-best 30–11.) The "Rasta Monsta" was given 30-second standing ovation during pregame introductions.

Before the game, asked about Grant, Whitsitt had told reporters, "Brian was leaving us. We had no choice in the matter."

"I'll just say that is an untrue statement on his part and leave it at that," Grant said. "I perceive it as damage control, but I don't see any damage here. You guys have the best record in the NBA, and the team is rolling."

Two nights later, Wallace showed up Dunleavy after receiving a technical during a 111–101 home loss to Sacramento. Dunleavy, who had taken the bullet numerous times from referees to protect Wallace, tried to get him off the court to avoid an ejection. In a rage, Wallace brushed off his coach with expletives, then complained afterward that Dunleavy never backs him in disputes with officials.

Dunleavy had been asked prior to the game about the Blazers' depth, which inevitably led to some players feeling as they should be drawing more minutes.

"You are always much better off having talent," he said. "One of the toughest parts of this job is dealing with a player who doesn't understand why he is not playing. Sometimes there are valid issues. I know from having played. I have played through every situation these guys go through—everything from 12th man to a starting guard on a team that played in the Finals. You understand why they don't understand, but you do what you have to do.

"Bottom line with this group: We don't have any really bad guys.

Everybody wants to win. Ultimately, the guys are willing to sacrifice to do the things necessary to win."

Two nights later, the Blazers threw in an all-time lemon, falling 84–58 at Cleveland to a team they had beaten by 20 points the previous week. In the loss, Portland set team records for fewest points, field goals made (21), and field-goal percentage (.281). They also tied a franchise low with 24 first-half points.

"On a scale of 1 to 10, this was a bad 10," Dunleavy said. "We went off the scale as far as I'm concerned."

Wallace drew his league-leading 23rd technical in the third quarter. He finished with 12 points on 5-for-17 shooting. When approached by reporters afterward, he said, "Don't even waste your time."

In the third quarter, a shouting match between two fans and Grgurich turned into a scuffle, with Blazer reserves Gary Grant and Antonio Harvey providing physical support for their coach. Blazer officials said fans were throwing food at the players on the bench and that two fans were berating ex-Cavalier Kemp. Grgurich warned them what Kemp could do to them after the game. The debate escalated and soon the fans and Grgurich were grabbing each others' clothes. The fans were ejected.

Later in the week, Pippen had bone fragments removed from his right elbow. The diagnosis was he would be out for about six weeks.

"Scottie should be fine," Dunleavy said. "The injury comes when he was playing the best basketball I've ever seen him play, though. Taking that versatility out of our lineup hurts us on certain nights."

On February 1, the Blazers downed Phoenix 100–92 at home despite another ejection of Wallace, who was given the boot for throwing a towel that grazed referee Gary Benson. After drawing a technical, Wallace walked the length of the court near the scorer's table, spewing obscenities at the top of his lungs. He was ejected seconds later, then hurled a towel into the face of Benson before being restrained by teammates and coaches as he attempted to charge the official.

After the game, he was surrounded by staff members shielding him from questions by the media. Through 47 games, Wallace had sustained a league-leading 27 T's with three ejections.

"I was there. I saw it," an obviously disturbed Dunleavy said. "I don't need to see it anymore." The coach said his player's behavior would continue "until he decides to change."

Schrempf, who had finally been activated and played 14 scoreless minutes against the Suns, was asked about his teammate. "He has to learn how to control it because it's not just going to hurt us, it's going to hurt his career."

But Wells said it was no big deal. "It doesn't matter if he's suspended or not. Just look at our team. We have so many cats, it doesn't matter.

"What can you tell a grown man? Rasheed is his own person. If you really get to know Rasheed, he is a great guy. He would cut off his left arm for a friend. Sometimes on the court he gets so emotional, and he can't stop it. You like that fire, but sometimes, it becomes a forest fire. You just want a little campfire."

Should Wallace seek counseling or anger management courses?

"That's a question for Whitsitt," Dunleavy retorted, though the general manager declined comment.

PR director Sue Carpenter justified Wallace's actions this way: "This is not a case of Jason Kidd beating his wife. From 7 to 9 p.m. on game days, he wears his heart on his sleeve. Rasheed has two passions: basketball and family, and he will do anything to protect them and win."

One member of Portland's management team was willing to address the issue. "Am I concerned about the technicals?" assistant GM Mark Warkentien asked. "I'll take Rasheed on any day that ends in a 'Y.' I'm no more concerned about his technicals than I am for a technical for illegal defense."

In the other locker room, Phoenix coach Scott Skiles said he couldn't understand why Wallace wasn't ejected much earlier.

"He could have been tossed two minutes into the game," Skiles said. "He started going nuts. I felt like [the referees] showed no backbone and didn't throw him out until they absolutely had to. I didn't understand that at all. I got my share of technicals as a player, but that was one of the worst [scenes] I've ever seen. Every time something was called, he was just going nuts. It's unacceptable, in my opinion."

Wallace, surprisingly, had something to say when asked by the media.

"I'm not worried about it," he said. "I know who I am. The people in the league know who I am. If I don't get what I want here, I'll get it someplace else."

If Blazer brass wasn't interested, the NBA was. The league issued a two-game suspension and a $10,000 fine.

Portland (35–15) headed into the All-Star break leading the Pacific Division by two games over Sacramento.

* * *

The Blazers were one of the topics of discussion as players convened on Washington, DC, for the All-Star Game. Several All-Stars picked them as the team to beat in the West.

"Portland is the team everybody is looking at," Seattle guard Gary Payton said. "Look at their depth—Davis and Kemp, you almost forget those guys have been All-Stars."

"They have two starting fives in there," Dallas forward Dirk Nowitzki said. "Their second five could easily win some games in this league. They can throw a lot of bodies at you."

"Portland is incredibly talented," San Antonio's Tim Duncan said. "The Blazers have long, athletic guys all over the place."

Philadelphia 76ers coach Larry Brown (whose team was leading the East) said it should come to a battle between San Antonio and Portland in the West.

"It's been fun watching Portland retool and getting familiar with each other," Brown said. "They have so many weapons."

Wallace was Portland's lone representative at the All-Star Game, making the mid-season classic for the second straight season, and brought wife Fatima to the game.

"She is more excited than me," he said during a mandatory meeting with the media. "It's no big thing to me. Nothing I'm doing backflips over. Pip and Smitty were teasing me. Right now, they are in Hawaii. I would rather be there, honestly, for a chance to rest my body. If it was my choice, you better believe I wouldn't be here. I see it as a personal accolade. I want a team accolade. I don't care if it's 50 or 75 All-Star appearances, that can't beat a championship ring."

Did he feel guilty about the Blazers losing to the Clippers during his recent suspension?

"Nope," he said. "I played when we lost to Atlanta. It's not a big thing, just an 'L.' Take it on the chin. We play them again in a couple of weeks."

Wallace calls the fans "my best critics," saying he received positive feedback from "the people I grew up around, the everyday people in the community. All the corporate cats, I couldn't care less about. I know they're down [at the Rose Garden] just to watch the game and make the money."

Asked how much he'd like to play Sunday in the All-Star Game, Wallace said, "I'd rather it be just a cameo," he said. "I'm trying not to risk an injury. I would be satisfied with coming in, doing two or three minutes, and sitting down the rest of the way."

The West blew a 21-point lead and lost, 111–110. Playing for Sacramento coach Rick Adelman, Wallace played 21 listless minutes, more than any West reserve, and finished with two points and four rebounds, making 1-of-7 shots from the field.

"Don't make no difference to me as long as the fans enjoyed themselves," he said afterward. "I don't worry about it. It was all right, playing with a couple of guys I never played with."

* * *

The Blazers exited the All-Star break in good position, but Dunleavy's status seemed tenuous.

"There is a lot of pressure," Stoudamire said. "Sometimes you can see it in Mike's face. He would probably never say it, but at times, it must get uncomfortable for him."

"It affects him," assistant coach Tony Brown said. "He is not one to say it, but there are times when you can feel the stress. It's probably getting to him some. But he shakes it off; it doesn't linger."

Dunleavy wouldn't admit to it, publicly, at least. "I don't really feel any pressure. I'm in the financial position where [a firing] wouldn't be such a burden for me. I wouldn't have to worry about feeding my kids.

"The pressure I have is all from me. I want to win a championship. I want to be the best. I am always going to try to find ways to get better. I have never had a goal I haven't reached, and the main reason is, I haven't quit. I have had the door slammed on my face a number of times, but it hasn't stopped me from figuring out a way to get around to the back door, knock the front door down, whatever, just find a way to get it done.

"We have a logical percentage of a chance to win it all. We did last year, too. Sometimes you have to be a little lucky as well as good. As a coach, sometimes you tend to either overanalyze it or overestimate people's ability to see what you see, and it drives you crazy. Bottom line, that's where the pressure is."

Having 10 or 11 players who were good enough to play big minutes, and expected to do so, was both a blessing and a curse.

"He is always putting out fires everywhere," assistant coach Jim Eyen said. "He understands that is one of the jobs on the table for him here."

Pippen said he felt Dunleavy had handled things just fine. "He has done a tremendous job. He has had to deal with some unhappy faces after every game. It's hard to keep 12 players of this caliber happy. He has to do what he feels is right for this team."

* * *

On February 13, in the first game after the All-Star break, the Blazers won at home against Minnesota, 109–98, as Wallace—coming off the two-game suspension—contributed 18 points, eight rebounds, and six assists.

"You saw what he does for us," Wells said. "I mean, he's our team. He's our franchise player. We weathered the storm as best we could without him, but Rasheed is the biggest part of our offense, so it's great to have him back."

Two days later, the Blazers bombed Sacramento 105–81 at home, the Kings going without the injured Chris Webber. Stoudamire led six players in double figures with 20 points.

Wallace scored 10 points with eight rebounds and three blocks before being ejected early in third quarter. He was booted for arguing with referee Ron Garretson after he was called for an offensive foul for elbowing the Kings' Lawrence Funderburke to the court.

"It would have been nice if he was ejected with eight minutes to go in the first quarter instead of eight minutes left in the third," Sacramento coach Rick Adelman said. "He was complaining so much, it could have happened."

Three days after dropping a game to the Celtics, Wallace poured in a career-high 42 points in a 104–94 home win over Denver as the Blazers (38–16) remained 1.5 games ahead of Utah for the best record in the West. Wallace, who picked up his league-leading 30th technical of the season, was 17-for-27 from the field and scored the most points by a Blazer since Clyde Drexler had 48 in 1992.

Kemp did not play against the Nuggets. It was the veteran's first DNP/CD (did not play/coach's decision) since his rookie season with Seattle in 1989–90. Kemp had been having repeated problems arriving on time for meetings, practices, and team flights. He was fined and suspended for missing a practice in December.

Dunleavy gave it to Kemp straight: No more tardies for anything. Work hard in practice. Earn your minutes. If you do all that, we'll see about playing time.

For the short term, Kemp complied, even putting in extra work before and after practice.

"It's important to me, regardless of the time I get on the court, to prove to the coaching staff and the organization what type of person I am," Kemp said in an interview.

Kemp looked better physically, at least. He said he had lost 35 or 40 pounds since arriving in Portland in August and that he was down to 270.

"I am still a summer away from getting myself back into tip-top shape, but the work ethic is coming back—the hunger and the attitude," he said. "I am not afraid to admit I had let a little bit of that go. Maybe not playing so many minutes has given me a look at things from a different side and get that desperate need back. At this stage in my career, this is what I needed. I needed to challenge myself mentally to work harder than I had in the past, to change that attitude before I go in there and ask for more minutes."

* * *

After road wins over Houston and San Antonio, the Blazers (40–18) entered March on pace for a 56-win season, with Wallace performing at a Garnett/ Webber/Duncan level, Stoudamire playing his best ball in a Blazer uniform, and Wells emerging as an offensive force at shooting guard. They had the best depth in the league, with former All-Stars Schrempf, Kemp, Davis, and Smith coming off the bench along with veteran point guard Greg Anthony.

Portland would open the month with wins over the Clippers and Golden State to improve to 42–18 before the bottom would fall out. Things would happen on and off the court to affect the team's production, especially at the point guard position.

First, third-string point guard Gary Grant was arrested for DUI and speeding through downtown Portland. He would soon be cut and named as a "volunteer coach" for the rest of the season.

Anthony suffered a shoulder injury that would idle him for more than a month. Then on March 5, Rod Strickland—who had played for the Blazers from 1993–1996—was acquired after being released by Washington. Strickland, 34, would get the entire $2.25-million veteran's exception for 22 games.

Strickland had gone to the Wizards in 1996 in the trade that brought Wallace to Portland. His production had declined steadily, and his off-court transgressions had mounted.

On January 7, Strickland had been arrested for DUI in Washington— his third drunk-driving charge since 1998 (he was convicted of one charge, acquitted of the other). The previous November, he was accused of refusing to leave a nightclub after it had been shut down by fire marshals. That charge was dropped.

Through the season, the Wizards had fined Strickland nearly $20,000 for a variety of offenses, primarily for being late for workout sessions and team flights. He was suspended one game (losing more than $111,000 in salary) for missing a pair of practices, a doctor's appointment, and a team flight to a game in Miami.

Strickland had played in only four games—ostensibly due to hamstring injuries—since December 27 before the trade. His addition to Portland's roster crowded the point guard position, even with Anthony temporarily sidelined.

Whitsitt brought back the line he had uttered years before: "I wasn't a chemistry major in college; I was a sports major."

Stoudamire was left in a difficult position, and he wasn't happy about it. But he was saying the right things.

"I never will have a problem with Rod, so don't make it out like we have a problem," Stoudamire told reporters. "Everybody's question for me right now is, 'They are bringing Rod in, so what does that mean for me?' It don't mean nothing. It just means we have another body, somebody who can contribute. There's no rift between us . . . I don't want people to even get that in their heads."

When Smith was asked the question about Strickland's effect on the Blazers, he answered, "You never know. We do a lot of things around here that are different."

Around the league, people had opinions on Strickland's acquisition.

"Rod has playing skills, no doubt about that," ESPN's Jack Ramsay said. "But I don't know where they fit him into the rotation. What happens to Stoudamire? You can't play both of those guys. And what happens to Greg Anthony? I don't know. They already have too many guys who have to play."

"This is my big concern about adding Rod Strickland to the mess, err, mix," ESPN's Bill Walton said with, perhaps, a Freudian slip. "You can never have too much talent, but more important than talent is chemistry. The Blazers have such a dynamic group. They are the best team right now in the Pacific Division. And Rod has always been a chemistry-killer."

Portland Tribune columnist Dwight Jaynes laid the hammer on Whitsitt for the decision of adding another player requiring minutes to an already crowded cast.

Whitsitt has been hitting the rest of the NBA on the head with Allen's checkbook for nearly seven years now—the kind of power and financial backing other general managers can only dream about—and he's never even made it to the Finals. In fact, for some of that time, what he's stuffed into Blazer uniforms has embarrassed this city. Whitsitt never seems to let one group stay together long enough to stabilize and come together as a family, the way it's been for many great teams. Some of his players have performed with all the passion of hired mercenaries who have no sense of community, team spirit, or purpose and know they'll likely be somewhere else next season.

It seemed fitting that Strickland's first game in his second stint with the Blazers came on a night when the club was honoring his former teammate, the great Clyde Drexler, by retiring his number and naming a street near the Rose Garden after him.

Before the game, owner Paul Allen spoke to the media for what would be the only time all season—and reporters were instructed to confine their questions to about Drexler.

By that time, Allen had virtually blocked all media access. Weeks earlier, after a writer sought out Allen for reaction after a game in which Wallace was ejected, the Blazers installed a policy prohibiting the media from leaving the arena via the exit used by Allen.

Former teammates Buck Williams, Kevin Duckworth, Kiki VanDeWeghe, Kenny Carr, Darnell Valentine, and Mychal Thompson were on hand for Drexler's special evening. Speaking eloquently about his fondness for the community during a halftime ceremony, Drexler mentioned Whitsitt and owner Paul Allen only in passing. A standing ovation followed.

Less than two minutes into the third quarter of what would be a 105–97 loss to the lowly Vancouver Grizzlies, Wallace was ejected after drawing his second technical for arguing a call. He would finish with two points on 1-for-7 shooting. In the locker room afterward, though, Wallace acted as if he didn't have a care in the world.

Wrote Jaynes: "Every fan who buys a ticket to the game and sells out emotionally, pulling for victories, should get to see him joking around near his locker after one of these incidents."

Strickland played well in 16 minutes off the bench, hitting four of six shots while scoring eight points with five assists.

Asked if he would go to a reception honoring Drexler after the game, Stoudamire replied with a grimace, "I'm not sure I can look those guys in the eye after a game like that."

Dunleavy called his team's performance "disturbing."

"It's a major problem," Schrempf said. "It's a problem that should have been addressed a long time ago but it wasn't, and now it is definitely too late."

Stoudamire added a sentiment shared by many of his teammates: "We have to get it under control. If we don't win the championship, they're probably going to blow this team up in the offseason."

It started a stretch of five straight losses, beginning on March 8 when San Antonio defeated the Blazers, 93–79, after which Pippen would say, "We are breaking apart as a team, and we need to tighten up and pull it together. We need to play through this."

* * *

On March 8, San Antonio defaced the Blazers, 93–79, at the Rose Garden in a nationally televised game punctuated by emotional meltdowns by Wallace and Wells. Wallace didn't start, as he had missed the team's morning shootaround.

The Blazers, who trailed by 26 points in the third quarter, cut the deficit to 12 with 5:06 to play. Then Rasheed was ejected after drawing two technicals in a five-second span. It was the second straight game he had been given the heave-ho after a pair of T's.

A minute later, Wells was given a technical while arguing over a call, got into a scuffle with former Blazer Terry Porter, and both players were ejected.

It was the first ejection in the gentlemanly Porter's 15-year career. Wells and Porter had already received technicals, and Porter was in a discussion over the situation with officials.

"Wells came up and shoved me, and I shoved him back, and [Steve] Javie booted us both—I guess to get control of the game," Porter said. "No way did I deserve to be kicked out."

Porter was asked about the on-court behavior of his former team.

"I don't know if it's a way to fire each other up, but it doesn't seem to be working," he said. "On paper, they have great talent, but it's been a problem with them. Unless they get it under control, referees are always going to be watching them with a quick trigger. Championship teams have to have great composure and patience, and they haven't shown that."

Former Blazer guard Danny Ainge was working that night as an analyst for TNT.

"I just don't understand why [Wallace] feels the refs are picking on him," Ainge said. "Sometimes it's not even that bad of a call, and he explodes. It's one thing to get emotional. There are a lot of players who get emotional without getting technicals or getting kicked out of games. At some point, you have to change your approach to officials."

Ainge, who had coached Phoenix for 3½ seasons, said he didn't blame Dunleavy.

"Mike has a hard job, and I know there are politics involved," Ainge said. "The hardest thing for an NBA coach is covering all the bases—trying to keep players happy, taking care of your veterans, satisfying management, even showcasing players for future trades. Tonight, some of his substitutions were to keep people happy. But I don't blame Mike. When you have a payroll of $90 million and you're 15-deep, that's a really tough job."

TNT's Doug Collins weighed in, too.

"I have always said Bob Whitsitt is a rotisserie league general manager, and I don't mean that in a negative way," he said. "The philosophy is, 'I'll get the 12 best players I can get, and we'll see how it goes. If it doesn't, we can always change our team.' The big question is minutes and how guys fit in. Damon has played much better and has been much more comfortable this season. With Anthony being hurt, Damon knew those minutes would be there, and he settled in. If Rod cuts into the minutes Damon has worked so hard for . . . I don't know how that's going to play out.

"The other thing is, what kind of shape Rod can get in. Three years ago, he was one of the best point guards in the league, but I don't know where he is now. We know he can push the ball and is an underrated post-up player. If he gets into great shape, he can make the most of the situation."

On March 14, Portland fell to Phoenix at home, 84–79, for its fifth straight loss—its longest streak in three years.

"You're going to be disappointed any time you go through a stretch like this," Dunleavy said. "It's all about winning and great expectations. There are going to be some confidence issues—hesitation on shots or making plays. We have to play through that. We have to have more of a mindset of toughness."

With most championship teams of the era, the best player—Michael Jordan, David Robinson, Shaquille O'Neal—was an on-court leader. Portland's best player, Wallace, was either unwilling or unable to assume such a leadership role.

Portland's second-best talent was the young Wells, who earlier in the season had revealed his role models as a young player to be Wallace and J. R. Rider.

Some players resented Schrempf, who had taken playing time from Stacey Augmon since his return from inactive status the previous month. Whitsitt had given Schrempf permission to miss some weekend practices so he could spend time with his family members, who lived in Seattle. That hadn't endeared him with his teammates.

After breaking their losing streak in a win over the Jazz on March 16, the Blazers lost in San Antonio, 98–85, for their sixth setback in seven games, falling to 43–24 and third in the Pacific Division.

"We are not a contender," Pippen said. "How can we be a contender when we can't put a couple of wins together? There are a lot of teams playing well right now, and we're not one of them. I've been through it before. You can't just flip a switch in the playoffs."

The next night, Portland won at Dallas, 96–88, with Strickland playing his best game of the season for the Blazers, scoring eight of his 10 points in the fourth quarter and finishing with seven assists and no turnovers in 21 minutes. Kemp chipped in nine points and four boards off the bench, though he didn't play in the second half.

But Pippen was ejected after a second technical in the fourth quarter and fined $5,000 for failing to leave the court in a timely manner and verbally abusing a referee. Moments later, Wallace, who had 18 points and eight rebounds, tied his league record with his 38th technical while complaining about a foul call.

Even so, the Blazers won, and Dunleavy said, "This is the team we were used to seeing early in the year."

Speculation nationally was that Milwaukee's George Karl was set to take Dunleavy's job after the season. "This has always been a high-maintenance job," Dunleavy said. "There are a lot of high-maintenance personalities. But I don't pay attention to [rumors]. I know that I do a good job. I know how well I coach my team. That's all I need."

On April 1, Terrell Brandon had 30 points and 11 assists as Minnesota beat Portland 99–95. Wallace broke his own NBA record by picking up his 39th and 40th technicals of the season and was ejected in the third quarter with the Blazers trailing 69–66.

"Mr. T" had confronted referee Mike Callahan to argue a no-call and was given his first technical. As Wallace walked to midcourt, he continued to argue with another official, Bob Delaney, who heard a few magic words and issued the second T and ejection. One source said Wallace had threatened retaliation against the Wolves' LaPhonso Ellis.

It was the third straight game the Blazers had lost in which Wallace was ejected.

Afterward, Wallace sneered at advancing reporters, "Y'all might as well go back that way."

Minnesota coach Flip Saunders said Wallace's absence down the stretch helped his team win.

"It takes some pressure off you defensively," Saunders said. "One of the reasons we were able to hold them to 10 points in the fourth quarter was our defense wasn't so exposed."

Afterward, the Blazers fined Wallace and suspended him for one game for "inappropriate game conduct."

Two nights later, the Blazers lost 94–92 at Denver without Wallace or

Strickland. The league had suspended Strickland for one game as a result of a guilty plea in federal court in Alexandria, Virginia, for his January DUI charge.

"You're losing two guys in your top eight, and your go-to guy," Dunleavy said.

The Blazers were in a nightmarish four-day span, which would start with losing Wallace and Strickland to suspensions. That was followed by the news that Kemp was voluntarily leaving the team to go to Atlanta to enter a drug treatment plan. He would be lost for the season. A day later, Wells would be lost for the season due to a knee injury.

Kemp's substance abuse problems had finally come to a head.

"Players have covered for him," wrote Peter Vecsey of the *New York Post*. "Management, agents have looked the other way. Even now at the end, people around him did not want him to turn himself in because, of all things, he was going to lose his Reebok contract, the moral clause that's in his contract . . . and the only reason the players turned him in this time is that they were afraid he would actually die on the court."

Blazers' strength and conditioning coach Bob Medina worried about precisely the same thing.

After Kemp was acquired by Portland during the summer of 2000, he spent about a month with Grgurich and Medina in sweltering Las Vegas, attempting to lose weight.

"It never happened," Medina says today. "He just couldn't lose weight. He wasn't getting in better condition. We'd fly players in, and he'd work out with college guys, two-a-days. We'd be out running with him at 10 in the morning in 100-plus degree heat. As all the stuff surfaced about Shawn's drugs problems, it made me think, 'He could have had a heart attack. He could have died.' That scared me."

Medina didn't sense more drug use from the Jail Blazers than with other teams in the NBA at the time.

"I wasn't really privy to that, but I don't really think so," he says. "A lot of guys in the league at the time were smoking marijuana in those years. I don't think our guys were doing much more than that."

Soon, though, they would be getting caught smoking it more than any other team . . . while it came out that Kemp was also using cocaine.

"Yeah, and I hate to say it," Medina says. "I loved Shawn. I had him at the peak of his career [with Seattle]. When I found out about the cocaine, it broke my heart."

There were indications that Kemp was having serious drug issues. He would often ride in the back of Paul Allen's private jet, where there was a single captain's seat in a private room.

"You could hear snorting sounds back there at times," said one player, who asked to remain unidentified.

Another player, who also chose to be anonymous, said Kemp was going through pre-practice stretches and drills when he ran to the bathroom. When he returned, the teammate noticed a white mustache line under his nose.

While doing team laundry, an equipment manager found little packets of cocaine in Kemp's dirty socks.

Then, on a game day, Gary Grant came to team officials with a Crown Royal bag full of coke that he had found in a toilet paper dispenser in the players' locker room at the Rose Garden.

A players-only meeting was called the next day. When teammates confronted Kemp, he denied it at first, saying, "I might smoke a little weed, but I'm not doing any cocaine."

On road trips, one of Medina's duties was to walk the team bus after the players had been dropped off at an area.

"We were in Chicago," he says. "I saw a rolled-up bill in a seat with some white stuff on it. I took it to our security person and gave it to him. He asked, 'Where did you get this?'"

Medina heard no more about it. He doesn't know which player left it, if any.

"It could have been on the bus already, I don't know," he says.

After evidence was gathered on Kemp, NBA security met with him. Under the league's anti-drug program, he would not be fined or suspended if he went to a rehab program voluntarily. Kemp then turned himself in.

Everyone felt bad for Kemp, who was popular with players, coaches, and team personnel. But he was his own worst enemy.

"Shawn was the most amazing athlete I've ever been around," says one team official at the time, who asks to remain unidentified. "During his time with us, he was addicted to everything you could be addicted to. He'd be screwing all night, cleaning out the mini-bar, addicted to coke. And he'd still get you 12 and eight. I don't know how he did it."

Though Kemp's problems seemed to escalate during his time in Portland, his illicit behavior had been going on for years.

Asked one unidentified general manager at the time: "Didn't [the Blazers] even interview him before they made that deal? It's incredible they would take on that contract, knowing his weight problems and all the rumors about the off-the-court stuff. Didn't they see him play last year?"

The Blazers had turned into the NBA's living, breathing soap opera, coming to an arena near you.

"Those Jail Blazers teams kept me busy," says writer Vecsey, now retired and living in New York. "There were a lot of desperadoes on those teams. A lot of talent, too. Rasheed Wallace, my God—how could you like him? Rashweed, as I called him—such an asshole. It's amazing to me that these guys get on TV years later, and they don't remember how they acted."

Upon his return, Strickland still maintained a positive stance.

"You can say whatever you want to say about what is going on with this team," he said, "but the bottom line is, we are still capable of beating anybody."

But the ship was going down. On April 4, the Blazers lost 83–79 at Minnesota, their second loss to the Wolves in four days and their third straight defeat to fall to 47–28.

"This is just ridiculous what is going on," Stoudamire said. "At times, we look like we're not even going to the playoffs."

The Blazers flew to the Bay Area for a game against Golden State. Dunleavy canceled practice and called for a team meeting.

"I don't feel totally comfortable with the mood of the group," Dunleavy explained. "Everybody is very edgy, everybody is willing to look at negatives, and that's just not the way we need to be."

"There's a black cloud over us," Smith said. "There's so much negativity around the team right now. Everybody is on us, and we're a little bit down on ourselves."

The next night, the Blazers blew out Golden State at Oakland Arena, 122–91, shooting .597 from the field against the hapless Warriors (17–58). Sabonis went for a season-high 32 points, and Stoudamire collected his second career triple-double with 15 points, 10 rebounds, and 10 assists. But Wells injured his left knee and had to be helped off the court. Additionally, Wallace was inadvertently poked in the eye by Sabonis, giving him a shiner.

On April 8, with six games left in the season, the Blazers lost 98–89 at Sacramento to end their Pacific Division title hopes. The Kings (52–24) clinched the season series and took a 4.5-game lead over the Blazers (48–29). Wallace was suffering from blurred vision after being poked in the eye by Sabonis.

"I have felt great about my team all along," Pippen said. "I just wish we would look at the importance of the regular season and put forth the effort we need to win."

Was he confident the Blazers could get it done? "I wouldn't say that. We can't feel like we are just going to walk in there and flip the switch."

The next day, it was announced that Wells' injury was a torn ACL, and he would be lost for the season and playoffs. Wells had become a starter on December 29 and was averaging 12.7 points and 4.8 rebounds while shooting .533, second in the NBA.

With all the turmoil surrounding the team during the final week of the regular season, veterans Pippen and Schrempf came to blows during a practice.

"We're scrimmaging, everybody's going at each other, and you have a play where guys get into it a little bit," Dunleavy said. "It wasn't Lennox Lewis or anything like that. I took the biggest hit [trying to break it up]. Somebody struck me from behind. Nobody would own up to it."

On April 10, the Blazers beat lowly Golden State, 116–88, after hearing boos from the home fans in the first half. "That's what I like, for people to doubt us," Wallace said afterward. "Because then we get to prove them wrong."

Two days later, Houston tripped up Portland 109–103 at the Rose Garden to end the Blazers' hopes for home-court advantage in the first round despite Pippen going for season highs in points (28) and rebounds (13).

Prior to a Lakers-Blazers matchup in the penultimate regular-season game, Lakers coach Phil Jackson talked about the Blazers' collapse.

"I've been surprised," he said. "I measure my words carefully because they have lost some close games, they have had some guys injured, some guys out of service—there have been a lot of extenuating circumstances. Ultimately, they present a one-through-11 lineup that might be the best in the game. We know their talent and the quality of their coaching staff. This is a team that plays us well regardless of where we have been in the standings the last two years."

The next day, in an Easter Day battle at Staples Center, the Lakers scored the last six points to win 105–100 and hand the Blazers their seventh loss in 11 games. But the final score wasn't even close to the big news of the day.

During a third-quarter timeout, Wallace threw a towel in Sabonis's face. In Rasheed's mind, it was the culmination of frustrations over his teammate's reckless manner of flopping.

In the first half, Sabonis had taken a hit from Shaq, flopped, and accidentally smacked Wallace in the face with his hand, chipping a tooth. Later in the game, Rasheed showed displeasure with the Lithuanian lug, yelling at him after Horace Grant beat him for a rebound and an easy basket. As the players walked toward the visitors' bench during the ensuing timeout, Wallace lost it and threw a towel in Sabonis's face as they approached the bench.

Adding to Wallace's frustrations, Bob Medina says, is that the Blazers had played Sacramento the previous week.

"[Kings center] Vlade Divac would flop a lot, like a lot of Europeans," Medina says today. "He had flopped in the game and hit Rasheed when he flopped. So, in the Lakers game, as Arvydas flops, his fingers hit Rasheed in the eye.

"Later, we call a timeout. As the players come to the bench, the coaches are standing away from the huddle. Rasheed is rubbing his eye. Sabonis is sitting on the bench. Rasheed is getting his eye worked on. Rasheed throws the towel at Sabonis. Arvydas looks at him like, 'What's that all about?' Rasheed says, 'That's bullshit, flopping. You're getting somebody else hurt because you're flopping.'

"Rasheed wanted to win the game, but he was going about it the wrong way. The coaches said nothing to Rasheed, and they pulled Sabonis out."

Will Perdue was a backup center with the Blazers at the time.

"Sabonis had done one of his European flails and clocked Rasheed across the face," Perdue recalls. "Rasheed was pissed. Instead of letting it go, he gets in Sabonis's face and throws the towel. We're like, what? We spent the whole timeout defusing that thing, and we accomplished nothing. Something would set him off regardless of what it was. And once he got set off, there was no reeling him back in."

Medina says he will never forget what happened next.

"Detlef Schrempf is sitting on the bench, watching this happen with the rest of us," Medina says. "The timeout ends, and Detlef is standing with his hands folded in amazement. Detlef gets up, points at each of the four coaches, and tells them, 'You're a pussy; you're a pussy; you're a pussy, and you're a pussy.' Then he walks over and sits down at the end of the bench. Detlef was one of the most professional guys I was ever around, but he'd hit his breaking point."

To Sabonis's credit, he didn't react to the intentional slight.

Walton was working the game that day for ESPN. "It was one of the lowest moments of my life," the Hall of Famer would say later. "If I was any kind of man, I would have got up from that broadcast table and walked across the court and punched Rasheed Wallace in the nose. I let Sabonis, the game of basketball, and the human race down that day."

Back in the locker room after the loss, a loud and furious Wallace was yelling and saying he was going to "fuck up" Sabonis, teammate Antonio Harvey said. Sabonis looked calmly at Harvey and said, "I will kill him."

"Sabas gave me that Ivan Drago line," Harvey says today. "All I could think was, if he got his big hands around Sheed's neck, it would take an act of God to get him off."

After Dunleavy entered the room, he admonished Wallace, who charged the coach before being held back by three players. While Wallace was restrained, Dunleavy didn't back down, shouting to the players to let him go.

"He was emotional, and he ran at me, and some guys held him back," Dunleavy would say later. "I hollered at them to let him go. I don't think he was going to do anything. Two or three minutes after he did it, it was over. The next day, I told him, 'I know you are emotional, this is a part of you, but I can't let you get away with this.' There was no carryover to it."

Strickland was one of the players holding Wallace back.

"I remember pulling people apart in the locker room," he says today. "I was stunned by that."

Strickland enjoyed an excellent on-court relationship with Wallace. Rasheed called Rod "Strick Dime" (a play on the word "strychnine").

"He was so misread," Strickland says today. "If you get past all the on-the-court stuff, he was one of the most unselfish, kindest dudes I ever played with. I remember playing Dallas one time and he's on fire and Dunleavy is trying to feed Rasheed the ball. We get in the huddle, and he's saying, 'No, give it to Scottie.' He was a very unselfish player. He could have averaged 25, 30 points if he wanted to. He wanted to be a guy who just played basketball. But Rasheed is one of them dudes, when he doesn't trust you, it's over."

After the Lakers game, the Blazers boarded Paul Allen's "B-1" private jet for the flight home. The coaches were on board as the players filed by.

"Coach Dunleavy said, 'Hey Detlef, I need to see you in my office tomorrow before practice,'" Medina says. "Detlef turned and said, 'You can kiss my ass,' and continued walking to his seat. That was the beginning of the end for him. He had seen enough."

Schrempf's arrangement with Whitsitt allowed him to continue living in Seattle and return home to be with family on certain off days. It was, after all, the way Whitsitt handled it with his personal life.

"His teammates didn't see him as being all in," Medina says.

Sabonis and Schrempf were at a different point in their careers—and their lives—than their younger teammates.

"The young guys on our team—guys like Bonzi and Ruben Patterson—gravitated toward Rasheed when they should have gravitated more toward Pippen or Sabonis," Medina says. "I could tell Arvydas was near the end of it. He was a man, and some of the other players were boys. He couldn't relate to the things they were doing. They had their headphones on and were playing video games and going to strip clubs. He was way beyond those things."

Wallace was suspended for the final game of the regular season by the club for "conduct detrimental to the success of the team."

"It makes you sick to your stomach, what happened that day," long-time TV analyst Mike Rice says. "There's never a place for that. Among all the things that happened over the years, that probably hurt Sheed more than anything else. You just don't do that to a teammate. Everyone liked Sheed around the team, but he took it way too far that day."

It didn't help the team's chemistry or Dunleavy's standing as the Blazers' head coach.

"I probably should thank Rasheed," future Blazer Dan Panaggio observes today. "Without that incident with Sabonis, I may never have had a chance to coach in the NBA."

Panaggio would become a member of Maurice Cheeks's staff, which took over after Dunleavy was fired after the season.

The Blazers finished the regular season by losing 99–93 at home to a San Antonio team resting its regulars for the playoffs.

The end of the regular season coincided with a rap theme song released by the Blazers, which included a lyric by Wallace, who wrote, "So haters, just quit all the fightin' and fuss, 'cuz no one's ready to deal with us."

* * *

The Blazers entered the postseason knocked off their equilibrium. After mounting a 42–18 record after 60 games, they lost 14 of their final 22 games to fall to the No. 7 seed in the West.

"I can't remember ever seeing a team disintegrate so quickly," Dwight Jaynes wrote. "Not since Howard Hughes built the Spruce Goose has so much money been spent for so little return."

On the eve of the playoffs, Stoudamire took about as candid a look as possible at Whitsitt's construction of the roster.

"For most of the players, and coaching staff, too, this has to be one of the craziest seasons they have been through in their lives," Stoudamire said. "This is the craziest team probably that will ever be assembled in basketball in terms of just plucking people from here and there.

"When you look at the personalities and people on the team, it's kind of like picking apples from a tree. You have some who are ripe, then some who are not, still in the infant stage. It's a situation where you have brought in so many different personalities and egos, that regardless of what anybody says, it's going to be hard for anybody to swallow their ego."

The Blazers were matched up in the first round with the No. 2 seed Lakers, who had gone 56–26 in the regular season. The teams had split the season series 2–2.

The Lakers' Shaquille O'Neal was feeling plenty confident going into the series, having dominated Sabonis through the regular season. In the four games, Shaq had averaged 30 points and 14.2 rebounds to 8.3 points and 6.7 rebounds for Sabonis. Much like Muhammad Ali had been with Joe Frazier, Shaq waged verbal assault on his adversary.

"I own Sabonis," he told writers before the series. "It's kind of funny how a 7-foot-3 guy who weighs almost as much as me starts crying to the officials. 'Help, he's pushing,' he says in a little, whiny voice. I just have to back him down, then dog him out. That's the law of the playground."

Sabonis stayed mum on O'Neal but somewhat addressed the issue of the transgression of his teammate—Wallace—during the last regular-season meeting with the Lakers. Was he pissed?

"At the time I was, of course," Sabonis told a reporter. "But we have a job to do now. This is a hard time for everybody. Things are going bad."

Shaq said there was a wave of selfishness with the Blazers.

"Scottie Pippen wants the ball," the Laker behemoth said. "Stoudamire wants the ball. Wallace wants the ball. Smith . . . too many cats want the ball. Meanwhile, they don't have a go-to guy. That's what hurt them in Game 7 last year. Scottie didn't want to take over. Stoudamire was pissed because he didn't get the shots. Rasheed—too busy talking trash. Steve Smith—worried about getting fouled."

The Blazers had a couple of things going for them. Stoudamire had finished the regular season strong, scoring in double figures in each of his final nine regular-season games, including 28 points and one turnover in the finale against the Spurs. Over that span, Damon had averaged 16.3 points, 6.3 assists, 4.6 rebounds, and 1.3 turnovers while shooting .525 from the field and .400 from 3-point range.

And Wallace had played very well against the Lakers, averaging 28.8 points in the regular-season series. Dunleavy's plan was to get him 20 to 25 shots a game.

"It's a close matchup," Phil Jackson said on the eve of the opener. "We know it, and they know it."

But the Lakers came in having won eight in a row to end the season. They were hot, and the Blazers were not.

*　*　*

The Lakers won Game 1 at Staples Center 106–93 after trailing 72–70 late in the third quarter. At that point, the Lakers went on a 19–0 run. During that stretch, the Blazers went 0-for-7 from the field with three turnovers and a technical foul, failing to score on 11 straight possessions.

At halftime, O'Neal and Kobe Bryant were a combined 3-for-19 from the field, yet the Lakers still led 51–48.

Both of them came on in the second half, and Bryant scored 25 of his 28 points after intermission.

Portland, meanwhile, was a mess in the post. Sabonis finished 2-for-9 shooting. Davis fouled out in nine minutes trying to guard Shaq. The Blazers thought O'Neal was camped in the key.

"There or four times, I counted him in the key for five or six seconds," Dunleavy said. "He hardly every clears out of the lane when he goes through it. Then he leads with an elbow."

Appraised of the Portland coach's comments, Shaq responded, "Wish he'd stop crying all the time like a little girl."

Pippen thought it was more than bellyaching from a sore loser.

"If [the referees] allow Shaq to play like that, then no one's going to beat them," he said. "It was ridiculous the way they called the game. I don't know— maybe they wanted it to come out that way. If they are going to let him lead with his elbows and throw guys out of the way, we're going to have to change the way we play the game. No way officials should allow Shaq to play that way."

Wallace scored 24 points, but he had more technical fouls (1) than points (0) in the fourth quarter.

The Lakers had even less trouble in Game 2, winning 106–88 to take a 2–0 lead in the best-of-five series.

Things unraveled late for the Blazers, who had five technical fouls, a flagrant foul, and two ejections in the fourth quarter alone. To make matters worse, Wallace was wrongly accused by TNT reporter Craig Sager of scuffling with a cameraman after he was ejected with 4:42 left. After the game, Wallace, who watched the report from inside the locker room with Davis (who had been ejected earlier), told Sager, "Don't make that stuff up, man. It was cool for you to say the cats got ejected, whatever, blah, blah, blah. But don't add that other stuff. You're wrong, Craig."

Sager offered an apology, but Wallace said, "Don't apologize to me; apologize to the nation."

Sager said he would if Wallace would consent to an interview, but Wallace refused.

Wallace picked up two of the T's; Pippen, Stoudamire, and Smith were all tagged with one. Plus, Davis was ejected with 8:46 left after elbowing Robert Horry in the face while fighting for a rebound. Horry was called for a foul on the play but, after the whistle, the players became entangled and Davis whipped an elbow that knocked Horry to the court. Horry got up and went after Davis but was restrained by teammates.

By the time all the penalties were assessed and the players ejected, the Lakers were giggling on their bench.

"We're not really worried about what they are going through," said O'Neal, who finished with 32 points and 12 rebounds.

The Blazers headed home to Portland for what they hoped would be a pair of victories to even the series.

Portland would be shorthanded for Game 3. Davis and Stacey Augmon were both suspended; Davis was fined $15,000 and suspended for his elbow to Horry and Augmon was fined $5,000 and suspended for leaving the bench to come to Davis's defense.

Stoudamire was hoping for a resurgence from the aging Sabonis. "We're going to have to get Sabas some Ginseng, a massage, some acupuncture—a little bit of everything. We're going to ask a whole lot more than we have ever asked from him. Right now, he has to give that to us."

Extending the series beyond Game 3 was a pipedream. The Lakers won handily, 99–86, to complete the series sweep. The usual suspects came up big again—O'Neal had 25 points and 15 rebounds while Bryant added 22 points and nine assists.

After leading 26–23 at the end of the first, the Blazers trailed from the second quarter on. Stoudamire scored a career playoff-high 25 points, but Wallace had only nine on 4-for-19 shooting. Pippen hit just 3-of-13 shots and managed seven points.

The game was a public-relations disaster, too. A spectator, Katherine Topaz, was ejected from the arena for refusing to give up a sign that read, "Trade Whitsitt."

At halftime, a security guard—under orders from executive VP Harry Hutt—asked Topaz, sitting in the tenth row, to hand the sign over. When she refused, she and her eight-year-old stepson were escorted from the building.

Whitsitt brushed it off when asked about it by the media the next day, cracking, "I don't think you'd get anything if you traded me."

After the situation made national news, Whitsitt—who said he did not see the sign—apologized to Topaz and the team sent her a gift basket. The package arrived with $5.38 in postage due.

* * *

It was a disastrous end to what began as a promising season in Portland.

Pippen called the late-season collapse, "the worst thing I've had to deal with in my career."

After Game 3, Strickland was asked what changes should be made. "That's for management to decide."

What about getting rid of management? "That's for y'all to decide," he said with a grin.

"The first time Rod was with us (from 1992–1996), he was more of an instigator," says a team official, who asked for anonymity. "When he came back the second time, he was a totally different player and a different guy. It was at the end of his career. And he told me, 'These guys, they're off the chain.' All the stuff that was going on, he'd never seen anything like it. The stuff Rod had done was tame compared to the stuff he was seeing this time."

Schrempf seemed to put the onus for the failures on Whitsitt.

"I'm a strong believer in chemistry," the veteran forward said. "You can have a lot of talent, but you can't just throw it out there and win. It's embarrassing. The playoffs were an accumulation of the last six weeks of the season. We basically fell apart. We lost some tough games, but not in [the playoff] series. This was more embarrassing than tough. We gave it a shot, but we really didn't have a shot at it, the way we were going."

In the days after the series, there were plenty of opinions tossed about concerning the Blazers' plight. Many wondered about Kemp and why Whitsitt had taken a chance on him.

"Everyone in the league knew about Kemp's problem," said one NBA executive. "It was stunning he would take that one."

When he finally met with the media, Whitsitt said Kemp's drug use was a surprise.

"Even the Cleveland people made it crystal clear there were no issues about [drugs]," the Portland GM said. "If we could have it over again, of course you do a lot of things differently. We do a great job with research, but it doesn't give you the answer to every single question."

Looking back, Antonio Harvey believes the addition of Strickland and Schrempf was the team's undoing.

"There was such a tight-knit nature to that team," says Harvey, who would later spend many seasons as the Blazers' radio analyst. "It made me come to the realization of how fragile NBA egos can be. Whitsitt brought in too many guys. It sounds like a blame game, but it's not. When Schrempf and Strickland came in, it disrupted the chemistry. Rod was a great guy and player, and we enjoyed having him around. But it was just enough to throw our chemistry off-kilter, and we went into a tailspin."

* * *

That marked the end of Mike D'Antoni's lone season with the Blazers. Dunleavy's chief assistant would go on to stints as head coach with the Phoenix Suns, New York Knicks, and Los Angeles Lakers. He would strike gold in Houston, where he coached the Rockets to the best record in the NBA during the 2017–18 regular season.

"It was a chaotic year," D'Antoni says today of his season in Portland. "Mike helped me grow as a coach in a lot of areas, in terms of organization and things of that sort. That was really good for me personally.

"I learned a lot that year. It wasn't a great year, coming from the year they had the previous season. It looked like we had a chance to do a lot more than we did. The talent was off the charts. it was almost too much talent, trying to get it all to fit, having a lot of strong personalities. It was tough for everybody to get on the same page. It was a trying year for Mike, I know that."

Wallace set an NBA single-season record with 41 technicals, but D'Antoni didn't feel that was a major hindrance.

"It was a bit of a distraction," D'Antoni says. "But the biggest problem was the chemistry and where people were in their careers and how many guys needed to play. Sometimes you bring so much, the milk jug is almost full, and you wind up tipping it over."

The late-season incident between Wallace and Arvydas Sabonis "was nerve-racking," D'Antoni says. "It wasn't a good part of the season."

D'Antoni says he learned that season how important it was to have players with defined roles.

"Especially when you have a team with so many personalities like we did. Then chemistry is a very delicate thing. Nobody has an analytic answer to that, but that year for us, it didn't mix. We had a lot of veterans at the end of their careers, and sometimes they are tough to handle. It was hard to get a vision for every guy. When that's the case, it's really tough to be pulling in the same direction."

Were the 2000–01 Blazers capable of winning a championship?

"There was that chance. For whatever reason, we didn't. Maybe the year before, when they got so close, frustrations carried over. I felt we had the potential to do more than we did, but it just didn't happen."

* * *

Strickland would go on to play for five more teams in the next four seasons before calling it a quits in 2005 after 18 years in the NBA.

"I've always loved Portland," says Strickland, who now lives in Tampa. "It has always had a big place in my heart."

As he looks back, the second stint—21 games during the 2000–01 season—was a mistake.

"Oh my God, there was so much going on before I got there," he says today. "I came in there naive. Bringing me in compounded a bad situation. If I knew everything, I may not have walked into that. I was talking to the Lakers and Indiana. I almost went to Indiana."

Before he agreed on a return to the Blazers, he called Stoudamire.

"That's my guy. I had a lot of love and respect for Damon. From the outside looking in, it seemed crowded. Mike Dunleavy told me he needed somebody who could post pass. There was a need. But I knew they had Damon and Greg Anthony. I knew both of them very well. I knew Damon was the guy. If Damon didn't feel good about it, I wouldn't have come. Damon said he was good with it. Maybe out of respect for me, he had to say that. Maybe he wanted to say, 'Don't come here.' But he was like, 'If that's what you want to do, it's all good.'

"When I got there, things started to fall apart. The players were great with me, but I don't think they felt they needed anyone else. They felt they had enough. The environment was so polluted. They almost burned the place down, but it was only indirectly related to me. I was cool with everybody, but that broke some of those guys. It shifted the chemistry those guys were holding onto.

"That started some kind of dissension. Greg didn't play after that. I walked into something I wasn't expecting. It went downhill from there. I'll never forget feeling, 'I got enough on my back, and I walked into something that was too much.'"

Was there too much talent on that team?

"Yes, absolutely, 100 percent, and I added to that problem," Strickland says. "I'm not one of those arrogant dudes. I came in and respectfully played my position. But there were definitely too many people at too many positions."

Strickland sensed a problem almost immediately.

"I don't want to call it a dysfunctional group, but there was dysfunction. I don't know if the head coach and the players were in unison, if they felt good about each other. I know I was disappointed in Mike when I left. I felt like I was thrown under the bus. People were thinking, 'When I got there, things got worse,' and he let that stick. That was unfair to me. It was almost good for him to let me be the scapegoat."

* * *

On May 9, 2001, two years removed from winning the NBA Coach of the Year Award, Dunleavy was fired after four seasons at the helm of the Blazers, finishing with a 190–106 record and two Western Conference Finals appearances.

"Mike is a hard worker," Whitsitt said in announcing his dismissal. "He has worked hard every year he has been here. Coaching in the NBA is a very hard job. He is as frustrated as I am, or more so."

At the time, Stoudamire had plenty of thoughts about Dunleavy's firing.

"In the future, for him as a coach, he has to understand that relationships are important," Stoudamire said. "We are more than basketball players—we're human beings. He spent a lot of time preparing us for things on the basketball court, but the one thing the players wanted more of was communication between coach and player. You want to know where everything stands. That wasn't always there. For me, that was the most troubling thing."

Stoudamire said what so many people were thinking: "I don't think it was totally his fault, but [the firing] wasn't surprising. After a while, it wasn't *if* it was going to happen, it was *when*. That's the way it felt the whole second half of the season."

A few days later, in an interview with the *Portland Tribune*, Dunleavy was candid in his feelings about his situation.

"We had a bad season. I take part of the blame, the players get part of the blame, and management gets part of it—everybody. Everybody has to feel badly. OK, let's work through our mistakes and go forward."

Dunleavy never got that chance. He said he'd heard Whitsitt made up his mind in January to make a coaching change.

"I think I did as good a job as anybody, under the circumstances," Dunleavy said. "This year wasn't a fair measuring stick. A lot of things happened—Bonzi getting hurt, Shawn having his problems. I didn't ask for it, but we did talk about an extension. I guess I was hoping we could work out the situation. That's what happened in Utah [with Jerry Sloan].

"We had very good players, but a lot of them are somewhere on the back nine of their careers. We took a lot of veterans out of a 35-minutes-a-game range and asked them to drop back. Everybody says yes in the beginning because in their hearts they were willing to do it. But when it happens, in some ways, it's hard to take."

Dunleavy said he saw the demise of the team coming in early March after Schrempf and Strickland were added to the roster.

"The psychology of everything changed," Dunleavy said. "For whatever reason, that sent us into a downward spiral from a psychological standpoint. It was a free fall emotionally from there."

After Dunleavy's dismissal, Stoudamire outlined what he felt the next coach of the Blazers should have in his profile.

"We need an authoritative leader. We need a guy who is going to command respect from Day One and is going to get it, whether he comes at me, or Rasheed, or Scottie, or anybody. It ain't a matter of whether we like it. You have to do what is best to motivate people. The most important thing for this team is, we need a guy who isn't afraid to get into people's faces. I don't mean he has to fight anybody or call people out—but to get up into people's skin when necessary.

"We don't have a bad group of guys. We have a group of guys you have to stand up to. Rules are rules. Stick by your rules. Everybody is going to have to obey them. Don't change and don't waver. That's when you lose respect."

The man Whitsitt would hire would not fit those guidelines—not by a long shot.

Chapter 7

"WE'RE JINXED AGAINST THEM"

(2001–2002)

"We're not really going to worry about what the hell they think about us. They really don't matter to us. They can boo us every day, but they're still going to ask for our autographs when they see us on the street. That's why they're fans and we're NBA players."

—Bonzi Wells

The Mike Dunleavy Era was over in Portland, and as the Los Angeles Lakers and San Antonio Spurs were battling in the 2001 Western Conference Finals, all sorts of possibilities were bandied about as potential replacements.

Names such as Flip Saunders, Jeff Van Gundy, Rick Carlisle, Terry Stotts, Lionel Hollins, Dwane Casey, Del Harris, Mike Fratello, and . . . Mike Krzyzewski, who had been offered a five-year, $7.5-million contract before the Blazers settled for P. J. Carlesimo in 1994. Word was the club might be willing to proffer a figure some five-fold of that this time.

A couple of other potential candidates with some major name recognition also surfaced: Clyde "The Glide" Drexler and Earvin "Magic" Johnson.

Drexler, the greatest player in Trail Blazer history, had retired in 1998 after a Hall of Fame career that included two NBA Finals berths with Portland (1990 and '92) and an NBA title with the Houston Rockets in 1995. Drexler then stepped in as head coach of his alma mater, the University of Houston, from 1998–2000. After seasons of 10–17 and 9–22, Drexler had resigned.

But now he was interested in coaching his first NBA club, and after a

Isaiah "J. R." Rider defends Michael Jordan on a drive to the basket during the 1996–97 season. Rider always considered himself alongside Jordan as one of the better shooting guards in the NBA.

Rider wears a look of anguish as he talks with Bob Whitsitt, the architect of the Jail Blazers and the team's president and general manager from 1994–2003.

Photos courtesy of Tom Treick

Talented but trou-
bled point guard Rod
Strickland had a strained
relationship with P. J.
Carlesimo, his coach
with the Blazers from
1994–96. *(AP Images)*

Cliff Robinson was the final link
from the great Portland teams
of the early '90s, and remained
a mainstay on the early Jail
Blazers clubs until he left for
Phoenix as a free agent after the
1996–97 season. *(Tom Treick)*

(Above) Rasheed Wallace, sitting between teammates Rumeal Robinson (left) and Jermaine O'Neal, is dejected after fouling out in the waning moments of a first-round playoff loss to the Lakers in 1997. *(AP Images)*

(Right) J. R. Rider speaks with reporters as he leaves the Blazers' practice facility in February 1998, the day that he said, "We can go 40 miles down the road and they're probably still hanging people from trees." At right is a young Mike Barrett, then working for KXL radio and later to serve 14 years as the team's television play-by-play broadcaster. *(Mike Barrett)*

Rasheed Wallace wasn't backing down in this fracas with the Utah Jazz, which involved guard John Stockton, coach Jerry Sloan, and center Greg Ostertag in February 2000.

From left, Detlef Schrempf, Rasheed Wallace, and Brian Grant accept congratulations from Scottie Pippen after the Blazers' victory over the Utah Jazz at the Delta Center to take a 3–0 lead in the Western Conference Semifinals in May 2000.

Photos courtesy of AP Images

Jermaine O'Neal didn't play a lot during his four years as a Blazer, but he sets to flush one down on Jason Kidd of the Phoenix Suns during a game in 1998.

Blazers (from left) Bonzi Wells, Walt Williams, and J. R. Rider celebrate after a Game 6 victory over Utah in May 1999, clinching the second-round playoff series against the Jazz and propelling Portland into a Western Conference Finals match-up with the San Antonio Spurs.

Photos courtesy of AP Images

Scottie Pippen reacts in the closing minutes of the Blazers' Game 6 victory over the Lakers at the Rose Garden to square the Western Conference Finals at 3–3 in June 2000. That set up the infamous Game 7 at Staples Center, when Portland coughed up a 15-point fourth-quarter lead and suffered one of the most ignominious setbacks in franchise history.

Damon Stoudamire is perplexed as he receives instructions from Coach Mike Dunleavy during a 2000 game. Stoudamire had an up-and-down relationship in his 3 1/2 seasons with Dunleavy in Portland.

Photos courtesy of AP Images

For the 2000–01 season, GM Bob Whitsitt brought in veteran talent in Dale Davis (left) and Shawn Kemp, which created additional problems for Coach Mike Dunleavy in an overcrowded front court. Who plays? Who sits?

In November 2000, Scottie Pippen and teammates paint a house as part of the Blazers' "Home Team" program, designed to rehabilitate homes and revitalize neighborhoods in Portland.

Photos courtesy of AP Images

From left, Scottie Pippen, Rasheed Wallace, and Arvydas Sabonis were key cogs for the Blazers during the 2000–01 season. *(Steve DiPaola)*

Assistant coach Tim Grgrurich stands between Wallace and referee Steve Javie as Sheed gives the ref a piece of his mind during Game 2 of a second-round playoff match-up with the Lakers in 2001. Coach Mike Dunleavy stood up for Wallace, but to no avail as Javie handed Sheed two technicals and an ejection in the Blazers' 106–88 loss at Staples Center. *(AP Images)*

New coach Maurice Cheeks is surrounded by players in a publicity shot on media day at the Blazers' training facility in October 2001. Clockwise from left, Shawn Kemp, Priest Lauderdale, Rasheed Wallace, Rick Brunson, Derek Anderson, and Ruben Patterson. *(AP Images)*

It was Cheeks's first time as a head coach, and he was the first to admit he wasn't fully prepared for the rigors of the job—especially with the headaches provided by his cast of characters. *(Steve DiPaola)*

Blazers reserves Shawn Kemp (left) and Ruben Boumtje-Boumtje celebrate from the bench as the Blazers knock off the Lakers in double overtime in April 2002 at the Rose Garden.

Steve Kerr played only one season (2001–02) with the Blazers, but the future coach of the NBA champion Golden State Warriors made an impact nonetheless.

From left, Derek Anderson, Shawn Kemp, and Ruben Patterson watch from the bench in the closing seconds of the Lakers' Game 3 victory over the Blazers at the Rose Garden to sweep a best-of-five first-round playoff series.

Photos courtesy of AP Images

Damon Stoudamire prepares to read a statement at the Blazers' training facility as teammate Rasheed Wallace waits his turn. The players had been cited for misdemeanor marijuana possession on a drive to Portland from Seattle after a game against the SuperSonics during the 2002–03 season. Stoudamire wound up with three such arrests in an 18-month period.

Graphic artist Geoff Gilliam, a fan disgruntled by the behavior of the Jail Blazers teams, stands below his banner at his business in Portland. This was in the weeks following the Stoudamire/Wallace traffic stop and a domestic-abuse charge against Blazer forward Ruben Patterson.

Photos courtesy of AP Images

(Above) Rasheed Wallace is restrained by Coach Maurice Cheeks during a free-for-all at the end of a game at Golden State in December 2002. The incident developed into chaos afterward, with the Warriors' Chris Mills and associates trying to block the Blazers' bus from leaving the arena. *(AP Images)*

(Left) Not many happy faces in Blazer uniforms during a game against Peja Stojakovic and the Sacramento Kings in 2002. *(Steve DiPaola)*

Wallace gets a hug from Scottie Pippen after making the game-winning shot against the Warriors, seconds before Mills and the Blazers' Bonzi Wells get into it, touching off a wild melee. *(AP Images)*

Guard Jeff McInnis's nickname was "McNasty," which he wore on his arm band in this 2002–03 game at the Rose Garden. *(Steve DiPaola)*

Darius Miles holds his head in his hands in the final minute of a game against the New Orleans Hornets at the Rose Garden in 2004. The Blazers gambled in acquiring the enigmatic small forward, but it didn't pay off. *(AP Images)*

Ruben Patterson shows his hops, dunking over the Lakers' Shaquille O'Neal in a 2003 game at the Rose Garden. *(Steve DiPaola)*

Paul Allen watches from his front-row perch alongside team president Steve Patterson (left) during a game in 2004. Allen has poured billions of dollars into the Blazers since becoming owner in 1988, but has no NBA championships to show for it over three decades. *(Steve DiPaola)*

Ruben Patterson jumps atop the scorer's table to celebrate with fans after a Blazers' win at the Rose Garden. *(Steve DiPaola)*

There were days, too, when Patterson just felt like getting away from it all. *(AP Images)*

Zach Randolph posts up against Karl "The Mailman" Malone of the Los Angeles Lakers in a power-forward match-up in 2003. *(Steve DiPaola)*

Zach Randolph smiles and adjusts a hat proclaiming him as recipient of the NBA's Most Improved Player Award for the 2003–04 season. *(AP Images)*

From left, Zach Randolph, Nick Van Exel, and Ruben Patterson aren't digging a one-sided loss to the Phoenix Suns at the Rose Garden in December 2004.

Ruben Patterson hugs Damon Stoudamire after "Mighty Mouse" connects on his fifth straight 3-point shot in a game against Seattle in March 2005. In the background is Blazers center Joel Przybilla.

discussion with Portland general manager Bob Whitsitt, Drexler told the *Portland Tribune*, "If it were offered, it would be hard to say no."

But Drexler also had some misgivings.

"I had a nice conversation with Bob, but it's almost like, what's the deal?" Drexler said. "Are you using me to deflect the Dunleavy criticism, or is it serious?"

Drexler also confided, "To be quite honest, I'd like to have his job. I think I could do a better job."

That didn't play well with Whitsitt. Within the week, he issued a statement to the media that Drexler was not on his short list of coaching candidates and that there were no front-office jobs open.

In the statement, Whitsitt said he told Drexler he would get back with him when the list had narrowed. After that had happened, Whitsitt said he spoke with Drexler's agent, Steve Rosner, and informed him that Clyde was not on his short list. Whitsitt said he also left a phone message at Clyde's home.

"You know what that is? It's a bunch of rhetoric," Drexler said. "The guy never called me back. He is lying his butt off, and I'll tell him that. He's just mad because I blew the whistle on him. I mean, I smell something."

Drexler said after their phone conversation, Whitsitt had said, "I'm going to call you back in a couple of days with some hard, fast questions about the team." Three weeks later, Drexler said, "I hadn't heard from him."

"I don't want to deal with anybody like that," Drexler said. "I'm still going to talk to Paul [Allen] about being involved with the front office, but I refuse to talk to Whitsitt about anything. I mean, all I ask for is common courtesy. My whole intention was to be involved and bring some value to a franchise I love. If you're not sincere with your interest, I'm not going to be a pawn in that game."

Meanwhile, Johnson was interested, too. Magic's storied playing career with the Lakers had ended five years earlier, and he had one short stint as the team's coach in 1993–94 before resigning. Now he was vice president and co-owner of the Lakers. Coaching the Blazers would mean he would have to relocate with his wife Cookie and their two children, plus divest himself of interest from the club. But it wasn't out of the question.

"I haven't talked to Bob Whitsitt," Johnson told the *Portland Tribune*. "A lot of things would have to be worked out, but that is a job I'm interested in. My family is willing to adjust if the right opportunity comes along.

"There is a lot of talent on that team. That's been a great franchise over the years. The people have supported them. The fans are wonderful. It's always been a great place to play. It's on the West Coast, not far from LA. It would be a great place to coach."

Johnson's previous foray in coaching had been nothing short of a disaster. After the Lakers fired Randy Pfund in 1994, he took over for the final 16 games, going 5–11, with complete disgust for the lack of work ethic and competitiveness of his players.

"This would be a lot different," Johnson said. "In Portland, you have a team that wants to win. Our Laker team didn't want to do the things necessary to win. They had given up. They didn't care about winning. I know the guys up there do. They have the talent to win, and they want to win. They wouldn't have gotten to the Western Conference Finals [two years earlier] if they didn't."

If hired, Johnson said he wouldn't suggest player moves.

"They have a superstar in Rasheed Wallace. I would relate well to Scottie [Pippen]. They have a nice point guard in Damon [Stoudamire]. The biggest thing the players will have to do is sacrifice. I don't think they were on the same page this year. That is why San Antonio and the Lakers are still playing and Portland is not. You have to sacrifice those egos.

"Rasheed will only be a small problem. I've got a little magic up my sleeve."

Johnson said he expected a call from Whitsitt. "He has to bring in somebody who will command those guys' respect," Johnson said, reiterating what Stoudamire had said shortly after Dunleavy's dismissal. "It's something I know I can do. The same thing Larry did in Indiana. The same thing [football coach] Dennis Erickson did at Oregon State. They need to bring in a winner, even if it's not me."

* * *

Johnson would get no call from Whitsitt, who bragged to one media source, "Every guy I talk to will cut off his arm for the job."

Chuck Daly, who had retired after coaching the Orlando Magic in 1999 and won two championships with the "Bad Boy" Pistons (1988–89 and 1989–90), turned down an opportunity to speak with Allen and Whitsitt about the job.

From there, it seemed to come down to Flip Saunders or John Lucas. Saunders came to Portland with his wife and son for a look-see, but then re-signed with Minnesota for five years and $25 million. The Blazers were willing to offer five years and $30 million. By all appearances, Saunders had used the Blazers to get more money from the Timberwolves.

Whitsitt interviewed Lucas, who had been a head coach with San Antonio (1992–1994) and Philadelphia (1994–1996) and was currently working as an assistant coach with Denver. Lucas's playing career had been cut short by drug addiction and, after undergoing successful rehabilitation, had founded a program that helped many NBA players with their own alcohol and drug abuse problems.

"The job came down to me and Mo [Maurice Cheeks]," Lucas, an assistant coach with the Houston Rockets, says today. "Bob and I met for about 17 hours [over two days] in Seattle. Then we got on a private plane and flew to Beverly Hills to meet with Paul Allen. He was dating Monica Seles at the time, so we had a strong tennis connection."

Lucas was a championship-caliber athlete who had played World Team Tennis. He said he spent about four hours with Allen in Los Angeles.

"They were going to get back to me in 24 hours," said Lucas, who was also in the running for the Cleveland Cavaliers head job. "But I could never get an answer from Bob, and I was running out of time with the Cavaliers. I knew the situation there was about getting LeBron [James]. They were going to be doing all they could to get in position to get LeBron."

That meant downgrading talent and tanking enough to be in position for the No. 1 pick in the 2003 draft to net James, then set to begin his junior year in high school in Akron, Ohio.

Lucas withdrew from consideration for the Portland job and signed as head coach with the Cavaliers.

"I wasn't going to wait [on Whitsitt]," Lucas says now. "When it got to be crunch time for me, there were no choices, really. Would I have been their guy? I don't know.

"I thought I would have been right for that group. They needed somebody to help pull them together. I felt the type of players Portland had, I'd be [the right fit] based on my recovery."

Finally, in the days leading up to the NBA draft, Maurice Cheeks was interviewed for the job. On draft day, he signed a four-year, $6-million contract, second-lowest in the league behind the Clippers' Alvin Gentry (four years, $5 million).

Cheeks, 44, started his playing career as an underdog. He had one scholarship offer out of high school—West Texas State, where he enjoyed a fine but unspectacular career. He turned out to be one of the best draft picks Philadelphia ever made. Cheeks spent 11 of his 15 NBA seasons with the 76ers, earning four All-Star Game selections and five All-Defensive Teams. Cheeks was the point guard for their 1983 NBA title, setting the table for Julius Erving, Moses Malone, and Andrew Toney.

He retired in 1993 after a career that would lead him to a Hall of Fame selection in 2018. When Cheeks retired as a player, he was the NBA career leader in steals and fifth in assists. His .523 field-goal percentage was best-ever for a guard who played a substantial time in the league.

Cheeks had begun his coaching career in the CBA as an assistant to Dan Panaggio—whom he had never met—with the Quad City Thunder in 1993–94. The Thunder would win the CBA championship that season. "I just didn't feel I was ready to start right out in the NBA," he would say later.

A year later, Lucas would hire him as an assistant coach in Philadelphia. Cheeks would remain in that position for six years, the first three working with Lucas and ex-Blazer Johnny Davis, the last three under Larry Brown.

"I hate to lose him," Brown said when Cheeks was hired. "He is the most decent guy there is. I think he will do a heck of a job in Portland. Some ex-players don't want to work. Mo does. He went to the CBA and decided he wanted to coach. Every year he has been with me, I have seen tremendous growth. He is bright. He has studied to be a head coach."

Cheeks had never been a head coach at any level.

"The only way you get a chance," he said during his introductory press conference in Portland, "is if someone gives you a chance."

Experience helps, though, and Cheeks was woefully lacking.

Bob Medina was there for the Blazers' first game at the Las Vegas Summer League. Cheeks wasn't coaching the team but was there to watch his young players, rookies, and training camp hopefuls participate.

After the game, Cheeks pointed to some messages on a grease board: "Defend the ball. Block out. Play with toughness." Turns out they had been left by another team from the previous game.

"Who wrote this?" Cheeks asked.

"Ah coach, sorry, we hadn't had time to erase it," Medina recalls saying. "And Maurice said, 'Wait a minute. We need to do this stuff. Good points.' He was really learning on the fly."

Cheeks knew how he wanted to coach. "My style will be aggressive, especially at the defensive end. Defense is a major thing in the NBA. You win games by guarding people."

"Mo saw it from a former player's standpoint and from a defensive standpoint," says John Loyer, who joined Cheeks's coaching staff in 2002–03 and remained there through the coach's tenure. "He saw the game the way he played it."

Cheeks said he would not be a hands-on coach, especially with the experience in the Portland lineup.

"Veteran players know how to play," Cheeks said. "Especially in the transition game, you can let older guys do what they do best . . . not put a lot of structure on them.

"I'm not here to be in the spotlight. I have a job to do. I like my players to know where I'm coming from, but I've never been a major talker. That hasn't been something that's been easy for me to do. I'm not a guy to elicit conversation. I don't like a lot of meetings. I don't want the guys to get tired of hearing my voice. That's why I will let my assistants do a lot of work."

Cheeks said he wouldn't worry about keeping a professional distance from his players, the mode of operation used by most NBA head coaches.

"There is not a right way or a wrong way to do it. I am friends with my guys. I don't see why you can't be. You can scold them and love them at the same time. If you can be friends with them and win games, then that's the right way."

Stoudamire said he was juiced to have a former point guard running the show.

"We have something to prove," he said. "He has something to prove, too. This could be a perfect match. This should rejuvenate everybody."

Trainer Jay Jensen noted how popular Cheeks was during his time as the Blazers' head coach.

"Who doesn't get along with Maurice?" Jensen says today. "He was a players' coach. He was good with younger players. His strength was being a people person. He came from a players' perspective, and his players loved him for that. He genuinely cared about what's going on in their lives other than just basketball. I couldn't see anybody who had a disdain for him."

* * *

The Blazers also made a major administrative change prior to the 2001–02 season. Harry Hutt, who had turned off employees and burned plenty of bridges as the club's senior VP/marketing operations, shifted out of the Rose Quarter offices to focus on Paul Allen's Action Sports Cable Network. In his place was Erin Hubert, who should have carried the title, "executive VP/public relations and mending fences."

Hubert, 43, had served the Blazers for a decade in corporate sales, including the previous year as senior VP/sales and service. She would now be overseeing seven department heads, 300 full-time employees, and 1,500 part-time workers.

Estimates were that Portland would operate in the red between $30 and $40 million for the 2001–02 season.

"I want this company to make a profit for its owner," Hubert said.

The Jail Blazers had jeopardized that possibility, and GM Bob Whitsitt's disconnect from the fan base impacted it as well. Hubert, a respected and well-liked representative of the organization, wanted to do whatever she could to help.

"We definitely have image challenges," Hubert said. "Some things are within our control, some aren't. How the team plays isn't in our control. But what we do to put a great product out there, what we do to treat our fans or our employees like gold, is absolutely in our control."

* * *

Cheeks would inherit a roster with a wealth of experience, featuring returnees Wallace, Stoudamire, Bonzi Wells, Scottie Pippen, Dale Davis, and Shawn Kemp. Veteran center Arvydas Sabonis had decided to retire and returned to his home in Europe.

The key off-season addition was shooting guard Derek Anderson, a Portland target the previous season while he was with San Antonio. The Spurs wanted to keep Anderson and offered him a six-year, $42-million contract extension. But Anderson wasn't happy in San Antonio, and the Spurs wound up trading him and veteran guard Steve Kerr to Portland for Steve Smith. Via sign-and-trade, the Blazers gave Anderson six years and $48 million.

The Blazers also signed small forward Ruben Patterson to a six-year, $34 million deal. Portland extended an offer sheet to Patterson, a restricted free agent with Seattle, which the Sonics chose not to match.

Portland unloaded point guard Greg Anthony to Chicago for a second-round draft pick. They also added free agents Rick Brunson and Mitchell Butler while bringing back free-agent center Chris Dudley, who had played in Portland from 1993–1997, on a one-year contract.

In the 2001 NBA Draft, the Blazers selected Michigan State power forward Zach Randolph with the 19th overall pick.

Derek Anderson was the product of a difficult childhood, growing up primarily in the projects in west Louisville.

"I didn't know my father that well," Anderson said after he joined the Blazers. "My mother was on and off." They were never married. His father had 10 children, but Derek really knew only one, an older brother, and they weren't close. He said he was passed from home to home more times than he could remember, living for a spell in Flint, Michigan. He often lived with his great-grandmother, who was "the most stable person in my family. We were always on welfare. It was tough."

As a child in Louisville, Anderson said he had food on the table "only now and then." There were temptations of crime and drugs on every other street corner, friends and classmates who wound up in prison, or worse.

"A couple of guys are in prison now," he said. "Quite a few are dead. Most people didn't even make it alive out of where I came from. It was a very bad area. The guys in my group, we hung tougher and didn't get into no trouble. Regular fistfights in the neighborhood, yeah, but nothing against the law. No stealing, no robbing, no drugs, none of that. But it was bad. I was so hurt as a kid. I would hide all that frustration and disappointment. I don't ever want to see people as hurt as I was."

Basketball steered Anderson in the right direction. A prep All-American, he signed with Ohio State, but blew out a knee and, after two years, transferred to Kentucky to play for Rick Pitino. At Kentucky, he played with such talent as Antoine Walker, Ron Mercer, Tony Delk, Nazr Mohammed, Walter McCarty, and Jamaal Magloire. Anderson helped the Wildcats to an NCAA championship as a junior in 1995–96. Kentucky also reached the title game in 1996–97 but, midway through the season, Anderson tore an ACL in the other knee.

"It's amazing Derek is such an incredible young man, the type of background he had," Pitino would say.

"In 26 years of coaching, Derek has the most charisma of any kid I've been around. Just a tremendous person, on and off the court. Of all the players I've coached, he was the most fun."

Portland would enter the 2001–02 season as the NBA's oldest team (average age: 31.6) and would distribute the second-highest payroll to players. New York was at $85 million, with the Blazers close behind at $84 million—nearly double the salary cap of $42.5 million, and $31 million over the luxury tax threshold of $53 million. The third team, Philadelphia, was far back at $58 million. The two-time defending NBA champion LA Lakers were at $53 million.

The Blazers had four of the top 13 salaries in the league: Pippen ($18.1 million, fifth), Wallace ($14.4 million, fourth); Kemp ($12.8 million, 10th), and Stoudamire ($12.4 mil, 13th).

Portland owner Paul Allen would pay the $31 million luxury tax check, and there would be more to come. The Blazers' salary commitment for the 2002–03 season was already at $95.4 million, and $72 million was obligated for 2003–04. (The Blazers had paid part of Kenny Anderson's salary to get Stoudamire. They paid Detroit to draft Wells and swap draft picks. They were also paying off the final year of Dunleavy's pact.)

Allen could afford it, though. In 2001, the Microsoft co-founder's net worth was figured by *Forbes* at $28.2 billion, making him the third-richest person in America. Allen, 48, was behind only Bill Gates and Warren Buffett on the list.

Portland would be Anderson's fourth team in his first five years in the NBA, having also played with Cleveland and the LA Clippers.

Today, Anderson offers more insight on what would be a four-year run for him in Portland.

"We were unbelievably talented when I got there," he says. "We had every piece to win a championship.

"I never thought there was such a thing as having too much talent, though. It was about using it correctly. I had been the second-leading scorer in San Antonio the year before, and [the Blazers] wanted me to take a backseat. It was like, 'What did you get me for?'"

Assistant coach Herb Brown says today that Anderson should have been more open-minded about his role.

"Derek was a very good player, but he was set in his ways," Brown says. "He wasn't very flexible with how we wanted to use him, especially defensively. If you told him, 'This is the way we're going to play it,' he didn't always play it that way. And he was another guy who wanted to play all the time."

* * *

Kerr, who would turn 36 by the time the 2001–02 season began, was a throw-in on the deal with San Antonio that reaped Anderson. The 13-year NBA veteran had four championship rings—three with Chicago, one with the Spurs—and was the league's career 3-point percentage leader.

One of four children to Malcolm and Ann Kerr, Steve's father was a UCLA professor who took several sabbaticals to help education in the Middle East. Steve was born in Lebanon while also living in Egypt and France.

"The experience overseas shaped me," he said after joining the Blazers. "Living in different cultures gives you a healthier respect for other people and human life. You have a better feeling for people's struggles. Living in Cairo, seeing a million people living in poverty, has an effect on you. It makes you more thankful for what you have, more passionate about life. Maybe that had something to do with what I have become."

Lightly regarded as a high school player out of Pacific Palisades, Kerr had no major college offers after his senior season. But he impressed new Arizona coach Lute Olson enough with his summer-league play to earn a scholarship and became a star. As a senior in 1988, Kerr shot .573 from 3-point range, was a second-team All-American, and teamed with Sean Elliott to lead the Wildcats to the Final Four.

During Steve's freshman year at Arizona, while Malcolm Kerr was abroad serving as president of American University in Beirut, a terrorist group assassinated his father. It was a tragedy that would shape Steve's views of the world for the rest of his life.

Even then, at 6-foot-3 and 190, not equipped with speed or quickness, Kerr was a long shot to make it in the NBA. Phoenix made him a second-round draft pick.

"I never thought I would play in the NBA," Kerr would say after joining the Blazers. "Maybe my senior year at Arizona, I realized I had a shot. When I was drafted, I thought, 'Maybe I can hang on for a couple of years.'"

Kerr accomplished much more than that—of course, always as a capable reserve. After joining the Chicago Bulls in 1993, he was a key player off the bench for the teams led by Michael Jordan and Scottie

Pippen that would win three titles. He also became a fan favorite wherever he played.

Kerr was also a rarity for his humility. Many NBA players, coddled since their days in high school, would go on to adopt a condescending attitude toward the public.

"It bothers me because in a lot of cases, it is true," he said. "I have had some great teammates and known some great people, but I have seen a lot of guys in this league who are completely self-absorbed, completely without thought or care about social issues or being conscious of a fan. That is embarrassing. It's a problem.

"Parenting is a huge part of it. In general, the guys I have known in the NBA who are the most decent people are the ones who come from the most solid families—guys like Tim Duncan, Terry Porter, Larry Nance, Grant Hill, and Danny Ferry. You see the strength in their family. I feel incredibly lucky and reluctant to pass judgment on other people. I grew up in a really strong family. Who am I to ask, 'Why is this guy like this?' Maybe he wasn't so lucky."

Kerr's defining moment as an NBA player had come when he swished a 15-footer with five seconds left in Game 6 of the NBA Finals against Utah in 1997 to give the Bulls the championship.

Kerr would enter the 2001–02 season with a career 3-point percentage of .462, best at the time in NBA history. Today, he still holds the record at .454.

"I'm proud of it, but I am not the best shooter ever," he said then. "A lot of guys were better shooters, but the combination of being a really good shooter, having good shot selection, and being on good teams worked for me. Have had a lot of wide-open shots because I have played with great players."

Kerr said he benefitted from playing with Jordan, even though the two had a celebrated fight during the 1995–96 season.

"Michael was embarrassed by what had happened in the '95 playoffs, and he was fueling an unbelievably competitive situation that fall," Kerr said. "When we would scrimmage, you have never seen anybody practice so hard in your life. His team was beating up on our team one day, and he was talking all kinds of trash. I had had enough, and I started talking back—like a fool—and we just got into it. We elbowed each other, and he grabbed me, and our teammates got between us; he got a pop in and gave me a black eye. I am lucky our teammates pulled us apart. I would be dead right now. I would have no chance. But he definitely respected that I stood up to him. We got along great after that. He trusted me, I guess. I wasn't going to back down."

Kerr cherished playing with Jordan, but his favorite teammate in Chicago was Pippen.

"Scottie was everybody's favorite among his teammates there. It is almost like he was the mother of the team, and Michael was the demanding father. They were the unquestioned leaders, but their roles were so different. Michael was so tough on us, and here was Scottie, the other superstar, so easy to talk to, and unselfish and giving. They were the perfect complement to each other. After having to deal with Michael, you needed somebody who was going to be a little easier on you. Scottie was that guy. He looked after everybody."

Kerr would make $2.4 million during his one season with the Blazers.

"I don't even know how to describe it when I look at my career," he said after coming to Portland. "Couldn't have dreamt it. Four championships, some records from the 3-point line—36 years old and still playing? It's kind of a joke."

* * *

Whitsitt was taking a chance on Patterson, a 6-foot-5 rough-and-tumble small forward who had played the previous two seasons with Sonics. The previous May, Patterson had entered a modified guilty plea to third-degree attempted rape by forcing his nanny to perform oral sex on him. With the guilty plea, Patterson was ordered to register as a sex offender and the NBA had suspended him for the first five games of the 2001–02 season. It was a big part of the reason why Seattle chose not to match Portland's offer sheet.

It wasn't, however, Patterson's first transgression. He also had problems during his two years at the University of Cincinnati, including an aggravated burglary arrest and a pair of school and NCAA suspensions.

The NCAA suspended him for the first 14 games of his senior year, citing extra-benefit violations, including using a Bearcat booster's condo, having the booster co-sign for a car loan, using a vehicle belonging to a recruiter for a sports agent, using coach Bob Huggins's school card to place long-distance phone calls, and receiving free housing and meals during the summer before his junior season.

Patterson was the product of a broken childhood. Both parents and a sister fell victim to drugs, and his father spent time in prison. He was raised mostly by his mother, who died of a heart attack when he was at Cincinnati. At one time, his small Cleveland home housed 14 people.

NBA teams passed on Patterson until the Lakers chose him with the 31st overall pick in the second round of the 1998 draft. After his rookie season, the Lakers let him go.

Patterson then signed with Seattle, for whom he started and averaged 11.6 points and 5.4 rebounds in 1999–2000 and averaged 13 points and five boards mostly off the bench the following season. During his time with the Sonics, he broke a man's jaw during an altercation outside a Cleveland nightclub. The judge suspended his six-month jail term, placed him on probation, fined him $1,000, and ordered him to provide 80 hours of community service. The NBA suspended him for three games.

Ruben came to Portland with wife Shannon and their two children, aged seven and two. After the rape charge against the family's nanny, the judge had suspended all but 15 days of his one-year jail term. Patterson served it under house arrest in Cleveland.

Sonics president Wally Walker said the attempted rape conviction "made it prohibitive for us to bring him back here. It's an overall philosophy of how we want to run an organization."

There were others around the league who had no interest in signing Patterson.

"There was a red flag on him," said Danny Ainge, then the head coach of the Phoenix Suns, who added he was "disgusted" with Patterson's behavior.

"I don't know where you draw the line," Ainge said. "That is up to the owner of the team. Whatever image you want your team to display, if you want to win at all costs . . . those are the choices Paul Allen has to make. Ruben was on the list of many teams, but many chose not to pursue him."

The Blazers did, though not without a thorough background check, Whitsitt said.

"Clearly it was an issue," he said. "It is something I take very seriously. We are very concerned with some of the issues off the court. We spent a great deal of time talking to people who have coached Ruben who have known him for a long time, who have played with him."

Patterson had played 24 games with the Lakers as a rookie during the lockout-shortened 1999 season, often guarding Kobe Bryant in practice. Ruben took to calling himself a "Kobe-stopper."

"Everybody knows Kobe is a little cocky and arrogant, and I'm a hard guy, and he wouldn't accept that from me," Patterson said after joining the Blazers. "Every time he sees me, he's scared."

Bob Medina still chuckles when he thinks about Patterson.

"Ruben was great for me in the weight room," Medina says today. "He was a physical guy, but he was a one-trick pony on the basketball court. If he wasn't helping you in one sense, he couldn't help you in the others.

"He wasn't a great offensive guy. He was a 'Kobe-stopper' who I never really saw stop Kobe. I kept waiting for the Kobe-stopping to come. He fit the persona. He was a tough guy. But he wasn't talented enough to help us the way we needed to play."[1]

* * *

Zach Randolph came to Portland having just turned 20 after his freshman year at Michigan State. He was a 6-foot-9, 260-pound southpaw with an impressive on-court repertoire, a ready smile—and already a bit of a police record.

Randolph grew up in Marion, Indiana, a blue-collar factory city about 80 miles northeast of Indianapolis. He had no father figure. When he was in

---

1   In 23 games where Kobe Bryant and Ruben Patterson faced each other, Patterson's team had a 14–9 record. However, Kobe averaged 29.3 points per game, scoring over 40 points three times.

grade school, his biological father went to prison. His mother, Mae, raised four children, the family living on welfare through much of Zach's childhood. Her boyfriend, Pete Bledsoe, had been with her for 15 years and helped raise the four kids—Zach, Roger, Tomika, and Kelly.

"I call him my dad because my dad ain't never been around," Zach said upon joining the Blazers. "Pete took me under his guidance. Ma is kind of quiet. She always stuck behind me 100 percent. She would tell me when I'm right, tell me when I'm wrong. She demands respect. Any time I got in trouble at school, I would get a whupping. I grew up the hard way, but you learn how to handle adversity."

There were plenty of problems with the legal system. At 14, Zach spent 30 days in juvenile detention for shoplifting a pair of jeans from Walmart. At 15, he was sentenced to 30 days house arrest for battery.

Marion High was runner-up for the state championship his sophomore year. At 17, he was again placed in juvenile detention, this time for receiving stolen guns, which led to a suspension that caused him to miss most of his junior basketball season.

As a senior, Zach led his team to the state championship, was runner-up to Jared Jeffries as Indiana's "Mr. Basketball," and collected 23 points and 15 rebounds to earn MVP honors in the 2000 McDonald's All-American Game. He played in that game with Darius Miles—who would become a teammate with the Blazers—and they became friends.

After his lone season at Michigan State—he averaged 10.8 points and 6.7 rebounds off the bench for the Spartans' 2000–01 Final Four team—Zach was drafted by the Blazers with the 19th overall pick of the first round.

"He went to class, did all of his stuff," said his coach at Michigan State, Tom Izzo. "What I told [NBA] teams: 'You've just got to get him around good people.'"

Mark Warkentien, Portland's assistant GM and director of scouting, had bird-dogged Randolph since his high school years. Warkentien was born and raised in Huntington, Indiana, 18 miles from Marion. He took particular interest in Randolph and liked what he saw.

"Zach was the best rebounder I ever saw come out of the state of

Indiana," says Warkentien, now director of player personnel for the New York Knicks. "He stuck out like a sore thumb. I saw him in a national All-Star game in Indianapolis after his senior year, and none of the guys going against him could stop him."

Seattle had shown interest in Randolph as well and considered taking him with their 11th pick. They ended up backing off after he finished last among 20 or so prospects in psychological testing regarding personal habits, trustworthiness, honesty, and so on.

And there were those off-court issues to worry about as well. Warkentien knew someone in law enforcement in the Marion area, with whom he discussed Randolph at length. The Blazers hired private investigators, who came up with 85 pages of notes but nothing that incriminated Zach as unworthy of draft selection, Warkentien says.

"We were peeling the onion back several layers," Warkentien says today. "Members of my extended family were in law enforcement, and they knew law enforcement in the next town. We met with one of the police officers from Marion, and asked, 'What is Zach like?' He said, 'Zach's going to get in trouble. Nobody's going to die.' That's him in a nutshell. Zach had some knucklehead indiscretions on his record, but the locals vouched for him."

In June 2001, just before the Chicago pre-draft camp, Warkentien flew to Indiana to meet with Randolph— primarily to dissuade him from attending the camp and allowing other NBA clubs to fall in love with him.

"I had a three-hour lunch with Zach," Warkentien says. "I wanted to get his version of everything that had happened in his past. His account jibed with what the locals had told us and what the investigators had told us. In most cases, he told me how he screwed up, and I believed what he told me. There was no way you couldn't like the kid."

Randolph was very close to his siblings, and especially his mother. Bob Medina would spend a month during that summer in Indiana helping him prepare for his first training camp.

"It was the best thing for me, getting to know his family and his people and where he was coming from," Medina says today. "If I didn't know Zach, I'd have been scared for my life in Marion, Indiana. It was a rough town, a rough environment. It gave me a better perspective on the guy and what he went through to give himself a shot at the NBA.

"Zach made a lot of bad decisions, but he is a good human being. What a competitor. An old-school player. Couldn't jump over a napkin, but a very skilled player and a tough guy. I never had a problem with him in the weight room. Anything I ever asked him to do, he did."

Soon after he arrived in Portland, Randolph began relocating some of his friends from back home. They lived with him at his home out in the country in West Linn. Soon, he had a nickname (Z-Bo) and an entourage (the "HOOP" Family, an acronym for Helping Others Overcome Problems). Randolph wasn't a member of a gang, but he confided to friends that he liked the gangster mentality.

And through his time in Portland, some of his teammates weren't the best role models.

"The whole Blazers' culture at the time was . . . well, unique," says John Nash, who took over as Portland's GM in 2003 and stayed on through 2006. "It was atypical of the NBA. It may have given Zach a false reading as to what the league was all about."

But Randolph had an endearing personality, an almost puppy dog–like demeanor.

"Zach was so easy to get to know and like," long-time TV analyst Mike Rice says. "He'd smile and talk to you, a very pleasant guy. He didn't mind if you poked some fun at him—or maybe he didn't know. He had the bling around his neck and those diamond teeth. He'd look at me and say, 'What you laughing at?'"

* * *

Damon Stoudamire, set to begin his fourth full season with the Blazers, thought he had found a comfort zone. The Portland native was in the fourth year of a seven-year, $81-million contract he signed with the Blazers in 1998. Father Willie and uncle Charlie had both played football and basketball at Portland State. Through most of his formative years, Damon raised by his mother, Liz Washington. Willie, who left the family when Damon was in preschool and moved to Milwaukee, didn't come back into his son's life until he was at Wilson High. Damon had allowed his father back in his life, but a distance remained.

"By the time he came back, I had formed my ways," he said in an interview with the *Portland Tribune*. "When a kid is 14 or 15, there is nothing you can do to change that. He hadn't been around, and that probably isn't the way to come at a kid. What has happened in the past is past, and you can't get it back. As every young man grows up, he wants to know his father, regardless of the pain you might have."

He had enjoyed his best season with the Blazers in 2000–01, averaging 13 points and 5.7 assists while shooting .434 from the field, .374 from 3-point range, and .831 from the free-throw line. He hadn't missed a practice or a game all season.

"I am a responsible person," he said. "People can say things about me, but they can't say I am not professional. I always showed up for work. I never came late. I always did what I had to do. It is something I pride myself on."

Stoudamire was looking forward to working with Cheeks, but he was also appreciative of his time with Cheeks's predecessor.

"It might not have been easy for me the last three years, but I learned so much from Mike Dunleavy, it is unbelievable," Stoudamire said. "One thing I will always credit Mike on, he prepared us the right way. Mike prepared our team for every game. He taught me how to play a half-court game. Now that I am able to get back to the 94-foot game, the style I thrive in, I am still able to be effective in the other style, and my decision-making is much better."

Cheeks said he would be laying a lot of faith in Stoudamire.

"I am hoping Damon can run the team," he said before the season. "I believe he can. In order to have a successful team, we have to have a guard to tell the players what to do, where to go, and his teammates have to respect him. I'm putting that on Damon."

If as promised, it would be the most freedom Stoudamire had experienced since his time with Toronto.

"It's a great situation for me," he said. "I have a coach who understands my game and has my back. Doesn't matter what anybody else thinks as long as he believes in me."

* * *

As assistant coaches, Cheeks hired Dan Panaggio, changing places with the man he had assisted in the CBA; Herb Brown, older brother of Philadelphia 76ers coach Larry Brown; Jim Lynam, with a decade of experience as an NBA head coach with the Clippers, 76ers, and Washington Bullets, and ex-Blazer center Caldwell Jones.

"Maurice was such a loyal guy, it probably hurt him," says Medina. "Dan wasn't ready to be an NBA assistant. Larry Brown pushed Herb on Maurice. He hired Caldwell, who had no coaching experience. Later, he hired Bernie Smith, who was more of a buddy."

During camp, Cheeks announced team tri-captains—Stoudamire, Pippen, and Wallace. A few eyebrows were raised at the latter, given his on-court deportment issues.

"Rasheed is our best player," Cheeks said. "He has been an All-Star. He commands respect from that area already. I am hoping that will carry onto the court."

Stoudamire said Wallace had suffered from a lack of discipline under previous coaches P. J. Carlesimo and Dunleavy.

"Mo is demanding things nobody has demanded of [Wallace] in the past," Stoudamire said. Carlesimo and Dunleavy "just kind of allowed him to flow. Now, when Rasheed makes a mistake, he'll get called out for it. He respects that."

On media day, Rasheed told reporters: "I got something for all y'all. A lot of y'all here was talking about me, Shawn [Kemp], my technicals, and the team. I got something for y'all during the season."

What's that, he was asked.

"You'll see."

* * *

Kemp came to camp looking somewhat lighter and in a better frame of mind after his time spent in rehab.

"I apologize to the fans for leaving the team early last year," he said. "I feel I did the necessary things to make myself a better person. You are always going to go through obstacles. I have gone through several obstacles in life. That was one of the harder ones, but I did what I had to do."

Shawn had wed his girlfriend, Marvena, on July 4 in Houston, but passed on a honeymoon to focus on spending time at the John Lucas Treatment Center.

"You never get any satisfaction out of anything until you redeem yourself," said Kemp, who would turn 32 in November. "Until the games start, you go through everyday things, and you feel you have made some improvement, but you can't be sure."

The previous season had been embarrassing for the six-time All-Star who had been paid $11.7 million, more than all but eight players in the NBA. But he said he was glad he had addressed his drug problem.

"It wasn't easy what I did, but I did what I had to do because it was inside of me, and I wanted to. Sometimes you have to challenge yourself to do things that are very uncomfortable, but I did what I did because it was the best thing to do at the time. [Staying sober] is something I have taken very seriously. I will continue to find out more about myself and I hope I can mature as a better person."

* * *

Scottie Pippen was direct when asked how bad it had been with the Blazers toward the end of the previous season.

"It was almost suicidal to be a part of that team," said the veteran, about to begin his 15th NBA campaign. "It wasn't a professional team. There was so much slippage, so many fines for being late for practice, for team buses, games, and all kinds of mess. All that stuff took its toll on me as a player. There I was, being captain of a team with players who didn't want to show up for work or to follow basic rules of being on time and giving their all in practice and in games.

"We had players feuding with each other, feuding with the coach, and the coach and the players feuding with management. It was an unstable situation where you just didn't know what to expect every day when you went to work. If it wasn't one thing, it was another, and you'd go to work expecting the worst. It was my most difficult season, because I'd never been on a team with so many problems."

Pippen said Wallace had been a problem.

"We couldn't win without him in the game and he knew it," Pippen said. "We'd talk to him again and again, and he'd promise to apply more self-control. But our problems involved more than Rasheed."

For the upcoming season, Pippen was projected to start on the front line with Wallace and Dale Davis, with Stoudamire teaming with Derek Anderson in the backcourt. Wells, Patterson, and Kemp would get the bulk of the minutes off the bench, with Kerr, Dudley, and point guard Rick Brunson lined up for less regular opportunities.

On the eve of the regular-season opener, *The Oregonian* released results of a poll of 107 Trail Blazer fans asking how they felt about their team.

Fed up, no longer on board, good riddance: 57.

Big-time misgivings but still following the team somewhat: 27.

Go Blazers forever: 23.

* * *

With Patterson beginning his five-game league suspension, the Blazers lost their opener to the Lakers at Staples Center, 98–87. Portland fell behind 21–6 in the first seven minutes and never recovered.

"Our bad start put us in a hole," Cheeks said after his first game as an NBA head coach. "We climbed back, but it takes a lot out of you. Every time we got close, they would make a 3 or run off seven or eight points. But we played well, we played hard, and that's just a start. We'll get more passionate about playing."

Wallace finished with 22 points, 12 rebounds and three blocks. But "Mr. T" was also whistled for a technical in the first half, maintained a steady pattern of complaints with officials, especially Dee Kantner, and narrowly averted ejection.

"Hard-fought game," Wallace told reporters afterward, repeating it several times. "That's my statement."

Cheeks admitted to a pinch-me moment on the Blazer bench.

"I turned to Dan and said, 'Can you believe we are sitting here?'" he said. "I enjoyed it. It was fun."

Shaquille O'Neal was typically dominant with 29 points, 18 rebounds, and five blocks. He offered no opinion on the 2001–02 Blazers.

"As a homeowner, I never worry about anyone else's real estate," Shaq said. "I don't even look at other teams."

O'Neal paused, then quipped, "I had no idea I made Sabonis retire. I thought he was coming back, but he wasn't here."

Kerr played five seasons for Lakers coach Phil Jackson with Chicago, which came in handy when the Blazers' were facing Jackson's Lakers. In the second half of the opener, Jackson called a timeout.

"Coach Cheeks says, 'Steve, you know what they're going to run. Tell us,'" Medina says. "Steve grabs the grease board and draws a play. 'Shaq's going to be here; Kobe's going to come around a pick.' Coach listened to him and, sure enough, they ran what Steve said. He drew it up, just like it happened."

The next night, the Blazers beat Golden State 92–87 in their home opener. Lights were left on for pregame introductions for the first time in memory, for a ceremony to commemorate the 9/11 tragedies. A byproduct: An easier look at all the empty seats, despite the announced sellout.

X-rays had proved negative on Anderson's injured ankle, but he sat out the game, with Wells filling in—and what a job he did, scoring 27 of his career-high 33 points in the second half. Wally Pipp, where are you?

"Derek better get ready quick if Bonzi keeps having games like this," Cheeks said.

"He is determined to be a star in this league," said Pippen, who had a terrific game of his own, finishing with 26 points, nine rebounds, and five assists. Scottie was 10-for-14 from the field, including 5-for-5 from beyond the arc.

"I told Scottie if he'd played like this last night, we'd be 2–0," Cheeks joked.

Wallace missed his first nine shots from the field and finished 2-for-17, making him 12-for-38 in the first two games. No technicals, though.

Wells followed with a 30-point performance in a 106–90 home loss to San Antonio, but the big news was Steve Smith making a triumphant return as a member of the Spurs. Smith had one of the great shooting games of his career, bombing in 36 points while making 13-of-19 shots from the field—and 8-of-8 from 3-point range. Afterward, he trashed the Blazers in general, and Whitsitt in particular, making it sound as if he had asked for the trade to the Spurs.

"This is the first time in my career that I really wanted to get out of a place and let it be known," he said. "I didn't agree with a lot of what management was doing. I felt it was best for me to leave."

San Antonio coach Gregg Popovich surveyed the Blazers' roster and observed, "You can only play so many guys—six or seven, really—and five at a time. So, when everybody is healthy, they could run into the same problems they have had over the last couple of years. They have guys who want to play, who think they should play and won't, which could create discontent."

On November 4, Wells scored 26 points in a return date with Golden State at Oakland Coliseum Arena. But the Blazers, manhandled on the boards 65–37, lost 96–86 in a game in which the Warriors led by 20 points with six minutes left. Portland fell to 1–3 on the season, though you'd never have known it by the postgame scene in the visitors' locker room.

Wallace was in one corner smiling, dancing, and joking. Kemp, who had missed the team bus to the arena, joined Wallace in the laughter and playful teasing. Davis and Wells were mostly smiles. But Pippen was in another corner, seething.

"You'd think we won the game," he said. "It ticks me off. It says you accept losing. Winning should be when you earn the right to sit in the locker room and talk. You win, then that's fine. That's the way I've always been."

"I agree with Scottie to a certain extent," Stoudamire said, when asked for his take. "All that stuff bugs me. There are certain times you play, and there are certain times to be serious. This stuff is big. This stuff is serious. We have to take it that way."

Two nights later, Wallace scored 26 points and provided strong defense on Karl Malone in a 101–83 romp past Utah at the Rose Garden.

On November 13, Portland lost to the Knicks at Madison Square Garden, 89–82, to drop to 4–5, the team's worst nine-game start in 14 years. The Blazers led by three points with 4:30 minutes left but went 4-for-24 from the field in the fourth quarter and shot .356 for the game. Wells and Wallace combined for 20 points on 8-for-31 shooting.

Before the game, rookie Zach Randolph wound up in a conversation with New York sportswriter/broadcaster Peter Vecsey.

Says Vecsey: "Zach asked me, 'What does a guy have to do get any time in this league? I kick Shawn Kemp's ass in practice every day and I can't get into a game?'"

Three days later, Wallace scored 27 points and Davis contributed 13 points and 11 boards as the Blazers beat the winless Grizzlies (now in Memphis), 101–85 at The Pyramid. Stoudamire was hoping a rest would heal his injured right knee, and that time would heal his wounded psyche.

Damon had played poorly in the first four games, averaging 8.8 points while shooting .350 from the field. With the knee flaring up, he sat out two games. When he got back, Pippen had moved into his spot in the starting lineup. Stoudamire wondered if Cheeks was getting orders from Whitsitt to start Pippen.

"I don't think he had a choice, but I don't really know," Stoudamire said. "It is baffling to me. I don't understand what's going on. I don't know how it went one way to the next in four games."

In a *Portland Tribune* article, Cheeks talked about his first three weeks as an NBA coach.

"I have loved every minute of it," he said. "I have enjoyed the players, being involved in everything head coaching is about."

Cheeks had followed through on his plan to pal up with his players.

"He talks to us like a brother," rookie center Ruben Boumtje-Boumtje said.

"There's not a wrong or right way to do it," the rookie coach said. "I am friends with my guys. I don't see why you can't be. You can scold them and love them at the same time. If you can be friends with them and win games, then that's the right way."

On November 20, former Blazer Walt Williams bombed in 31 points—including six 3-pointers—to lead Houston past Portland 94–87 at the Rose Garden before a crowd of 18,210, the Blazers first non-sellout in 104 games.[2]

"Like everybody else has bad days at their jobs, we have bad days at ours," said Wells, who collected 28 points and nine rebounds. "This was a long night."

Three nights later, the Blazers got past Denver 97–90 to open a six-game homestand. Wallace led the way with 30 points and 10 rebounds, including 12 points in the fourth quarter.

"We need him to play that way in the fourth quarter," Kerr said. "He's our horse, our best player, so he needs to be the guy on the block who creates some shots for other people or can get to the line himself and really be dominant down there."

Brunson started at point guard, netting five points, six rebounds, and three assists in 20 minutes. Stoudamire came off the bench behind him for 10 points, nine assists, and seven rebounds in 28 minutes.

Brunson had logged 31 minutes in the previous game, a 95–83 loss to Sacramento. After the Denver game, Cheeks made a comment that would make him look foolish.

"Rick Brunson knows how to run a team," Cheeks told the media. "Damon Stoudamire is learning how to run a team."

Brunson was 29, in the midst of a journeyman career which would carve out parts of nine years—but only one full season—in the league. He'd done his first stint with the Blazers as a rookie, playing 38 games—and starting

---

2   Actually, there may have been other nights when the house wasn't full, but on those nights, the Blazers papered the house or simply announced a sellout. They believed the sellout streak was important to make tickets a more hot item. Truth be told, it was getting harder to sell tickets to a fan base that was growing more disgruntled with what it was seeing on the court, combined with the off-court shenanigans.

10—during the 1997–98 season. He would average 2.1 points and 1.9 assists in 8.8 minutes and 59 games with Portland during the 2001–02 campaign.

Today, Brunson says there is a "fine line" between accepting a role and being unhappy when a roster is filled with talent.

"And we had a lot of talent on both my Portland teams," Brunson says. "Guys are trying to make a living. It's hard to accept a role when you're better than some starters on other teams, and you're coming off the bench for your team.

"In Portland, there was just too much talent. We had guys on the bench who were better than some of the starters. But I understand where [Bob Whitsitt] was coming from—you always try to get the best talent. You have to put the onus on the players, too. In order to win, you have to give a little bit."

If Cheeks thought Brunson was more the prototypical set-up point guard than Stoudamire, at least the first-year coach admitted he was doing a lot of learning, too.

"Every day is a learning process," he said. "This is all new to me. Basketball is not new to me, but dealing with all the guys, all the games, that is new to me."

On November 27, the Blazers beat Indiana 96–90. Even with the win, it may have been the worst first half they'd played all season.

"I wouldn't argue with that," Cheeks said afterward. "That would be a good comment, because we played like . . . I'm not going to say it, but you know what."

The Blazers had trailed by 14 at halftime. Patterson scored 15 of his 22 points in the second half, 10 in the fourth, and Kerr had 13, including a key jumper with 44.1 seconds to go to give Portland a lead they wouldn't relinquish.

"This is our best win," Cheeks said. "It's a heck of a win, because we were down and it looked like we were dead. But we fought our way back."

Wallace, who finished with 26 points, four blocks, and four steals, was hit with a technical. But he played second fiddle on this night to Wells, who was ejected with 3:30 in the first half after getting two technicals from referee Bill Spooner. After Wells picked up his first T, season ticket-holder Harvey Platt sensed something bad was coming.

Platt, in the front row of section 101 behind the scorer's table, sat in front of Frank and Mary Gill.

"Bonzi is getting beat on defense in a terrible game and he gets a T," Platt says today. "I turn around to Mary and say, 'He's not going to last.'

"A couple minutes later, Wells gets charged with an offensive foul. He gets pissed and takes his gum and throws it into the stands. It hits my ear and lands on Mary's lap. It was like the Zapruder bullet."

About two minutes later, Wells earned his second T and got the boot. When Platt got home, he wrote Blazer VP Erin Hubert a long email stating that Wells had become disrespectful of the game, of the officials and of the fans, and that she should look into it. The next day, Hubert called Platt, who told her about Mary Gill.

"Erin asked for Mary's seat number," Platt recalls. "She apologized, which wasn't her job to do. Before the next game started, they escorted Bonzi—like the kid who was bad in fifth grade—over to Mary and handed her an autographed practice jersey and an apology letter."

Sometime later, Platt received a copy of the same letter.

It read: "Dear Harvey, I am sorry for the gum thrown in your direction at the game. Bonzi Wells."

Later, Platt was to find out that Hubert had actually typed up a letter of apology that read, "I'm sorry I threw the gum at you. It was my mistake."

"She took it to Whitsitt, who told her, 'We don't want to admit guilt,'" Platt said.

Wells would publicly address the situation with a ho-hum attitude.

"I apologized and gave him [actually her] one of my jerseys," he told the media. "I guess it's the price you pay for being in the front row. You get close to the action, hear the sound bites, and accidentally get hit with a piece of gum. But I apologized and let him know that we have love for him."

* * *

Through the early season, Kemp was mostly sitting but thankful to the Blazers for keeping him in an NBA uniform.

"I feel like I'm blessed to be here," he told the *Portland Tribune*. "I ask myself, if I were somewhere else, would I have gotten this type of support? I don't think so. That has made it a lot easier for me."

Kemp said he still felt guilty about leaving the Blazers the previous season to enter a rehab program after several years of dealing with drug and alcohol abuse.

"I felt like I let the team down from that standpoint," he said. "Maybe I could have helped the team in the playoffs. It was tough to leave the guys but, at the time, I was worried about myself."

After several months in rehab the previous summer, he felt he dealt with the problem.

"I would be a fool to say you are going to recover 100 percent and never have to worry about it," he said. "But I think I'll be fine. I'm drug-free. I don't drink. I have handled all my responsibilities. People have the right to feel however they feel about what I have done in the past, but I would ask that they judge me after seeing how I handle this year."

As the calendar turned to December, Stoudamire came to the realization that, since he arrived in Portland in February 1998 during Mike Dunleavy's first season as coach, only one teammate remained—Rasheed Wallace. The Blazers, hovering around .500, were looking like an also-ran.

"This is a crossroads for the whole organization," Stoudamire said. "Everything is going in a different direction, and not just from a basketball standpoint. Everybody within the organization is trying to find his role."

On December 1, Portland blew a 16-point lead and lost 97–83 to Phoenix at the Rose Garden. The Blazers managed only 30 points in the second half after scoring 31 in the first quarter.

Wells said the Blazers were hard to figure out. Why?

"Too many people," he said.

Is that a good or bad thing?

"Depends on what day it is," Wells said.

Ten days later, Steve Nash scored a career-high 39 points, making

12-of-16 shots from the field, as Portland lost 105–103 at Dallas to fall to 10–10.

"We should have won the game, but [the Mavericks] did and we didn't," Cheeks said. "That's a very disappointing loss. We did nothing down the stretch. We have to learn how to run plays down the stretch of a game, and we have not learned how to do that."

Wells finished with 21 points and a career-high 13 boards.

"Doesn't matter," he said. "It matters how you finish."

Soon enough, Bonzi would be in hot water again.

* * *

In the December 24 issue of *Sports Illustrated*, which was released earlier in the week, Jon Wertheim wrote about the Blazers in an article entitled, "Losing Their Grip." The subhead: "Their once-ardent fans turned off by the players' misdeeds and front-office ineptitude, the Trail Blazers are showing how quickly an NBA franchise can alienate its customers."

Wertheim had lived in Portland for several years and worked for the club's *Rip City* magazine. Wertheim caught Wallace acting like a dolt at a Christmas tree giveaway for needy families, which was held after a free pancake breakfast sponsored by the club. The writer detailed many of the players' individual transgressions in recent years, including one that hadn't made the local newspapers.

"In 1999," wrote Wertheim, "the team forced Greg Anthony to apologize to [*Oregonian*] beat writer Rachel Bachman for allegedly making inappropriate sexual comments. Anthony, who was traded last summer to Chicago for a second-round pick, says, 'The charges are absurd. I was told by team management that if I apologized the whole thing would go away.'"

Wertheim quoted Harry Glickman, the team's founder and president emeritus, as saying, "When players are getting paid as much as these guys, the fans have a right to expect them to behave themselves."

The writer interviewed Whitsitt, who had taken so many hits from fans he called himself "the Portland Piñata." Whitsitt defended his signing of

Patterson with, "When you get the facts, the situation is no different from other folks' whose stories haven't been publicized. He really is a good guy."

Whitsitt defended his right to live in Seattle while presiding over the Blazers, saying, "Red Auerbach ran the Celtics from Washington, DC." Wertheim noted that Whitsitt scheduled a family vacation during the regular season.

The most damning quote, though, came in regard to the fans' growing distaste for the players' on-court antics and off-court shenanigans.

"We're not really going to worry about what the hell they think about us," Bonzi Wells said. "They really don't matter to us. They can boo us every day, but they're still going to ask for our autographs when they see us on the street. That's why they're fans and we're NBA players."

Sports Illustrated received hundreds of emails and letters after the article appeared.

"The response was overwhelmingly anti-Blazer and supportive of the story," said Doug Goodman, *SI*'s news bureau manager.

In the *Portland Tribune*, Dwight Jaynes used the occasion to take a swipe at the man who ran the show for the Blazers.

Wrote Jaynes: "Wertheim's portrayal hints at the real Bob Whitsitt—a self-serving, arrogant whiner who rewrites history and believes he is being picked on unfairly by a bunch of small-town hicks who can't hope to understand how really smart he is."

The magazine came out on December 19 and, that night, the Blazers got raked 97–79 at San Antonio. They returned home for two days later for a game against Detroit under a barrage of criticism from fans and media over the *SI* article. Wells's comment about the fans proved a lightning rod for the anti-Blazer sentiment in the city. Dozens of letters were sent to *The Oregonian*, including one from Debbie Soderquist, which ended, "No, Trail Blazers, the fans didn't stop loving you; you stopped loving us. We're loyal, but we're not stupid. Is that what they call irreconcilable differences?"

The Blazers issued a statement to fans apologizing "on behalf of Bonzi Wells," steering the controversy in his direction.

"I want to sincerely apologize to the fans of the NBA and especially to the fans of the Trail Blazers for my insensitive remarks," Bonzi said in the prepared statement. "I should not have said them, and there's no excuse. The fans are the most important part of the game and, without them, I wouldn't be where I am today. The fans of the Trail Blazers continue to be the best fans in the NBA and the team has appreciated their support since 1970."

The day before the Detroit game, Wells was also forced to give one-on-one interviews to local media and was briefed on what to say by representatives of Blazer management.

Wells had made his comments to Wertheim after a 95–89 loss on December 6 to Charlotte at the Rose Garden. "After the game, we were all frustrated," Wells told the *Portland Tribune*. "All I said was, 'The booing hurt our feelings, but we can't worry about it. All we can do is play.' I told the guy that it was wrong that the fans were booing us. I mean, fans booing the home team? That's wrong.

"'That's what I was saying, but he used my comments out of context. Now people probably think I want to leave Portland. That's just wrong. I love Portland. I'll be in Portland my whole career if it's up to me. "I have nothing but love for the Portland fans, and they've shown me nothing but love. For this writer to come in one day and assess the whole problem like he's been here for four years like I have . . . I wish it would have never happened."

Whitsitt went for a little contrition, along with a back pat to himself for the Blazers nearly reaching the 2000 NBA Finals, as he answered questions from the media.

"In my mind, the article was ripping us apart on the past," he said. "But Bonzi's comment is what hit hard. The past is the past. All we can do is work harder to make things better. But to say something like that is inexcusable.

"Our bar is rated higher because of how great it has been for so many years in Portland. Are we as popular as we were two years ago? I would presume we are probably not, starting with the fact that we are not a jump shot away from the Finals. But I am hoping we can let people know how much we care about them."

Cheeks had no idea what to say when asked about the article.

"*Sports Illustrated* is what it is," he said. "There's nothing I can do about it. All we can do is win some games and try to keep our guys in the right frame of mind. Hopefully, the next time they write about us, it will be something good."

Kerr gave a thoughtful and even-handed response, comparing his previous team [the San Antonio Spurs] to his current one.

"I went from one extreme to another," Kerr said. "I went from the milk-and-cookies gang to the Trail Gangsters. It's just amazing going from one end of the spectrum to the other. But really, it was unfortunate, and it is exaggerated a little bit because of some things that have happened in the past. This is a pretty good group of guys, and we get along very well.

"If our team stinks, feel free to rip us, but don't rip us for having a Christmas party that gives 1,000 trees to underprivileged people, for hosting 500 kids for a pancake breakfast where we're singing Christmas carols. They took two pictures (of players looking disinterested) and put them in the magazine. All of those guys were a big part of the whole program, singing with kids, interacting.

"Don't use a Christmas party and some misleading pictures as a metaphor for our supposed lack of communication with the fans. The opposite was true. In my 14 years in the league, it was one of the nicest events I have been part of. It was really genuine."

* * *

The Blazers beat Detroit that night, 83–81. Whenever Wells was shown on the Jumbotron during the game, he was booed. Afterward, reporters asked Whitsitt why that would be.

"You'd have to tell me," he said. "I don't pay too much attention . . . I would think that's a normal reaction. It doesn't surprise me."

The next night, the Blazers lost at Phoenix, 102–89. The Suns' Shawn Marion dunked with half a second left, and the Blazers thought he was showing them up.

"If I were 6-foot-7, I'd have gone down and hit him in the mouth," Stoudamire said afterward. "I know the Suns organization knows better than that. This ain't the NCAA Tournament. I guess that's what people think about us, that they can get away with it."

"We'll all remember that," Patterson said. "Next time he tries to dunk on us, somebody will put him on his head."

Portland had led 84–80 before the Suns ended the game on a 22–5 run. Anderson said it was time for the Blazers to look inward.

"Nothing against the guys," Anderson said, "but you have to find somewhere down inside yourself to be mentally, emotionally sharp, even during the tough times. You just can't quit. Some of the guys quit tonight, and that's a shame."

It would be the start of a six-game losing streak. In the next game, the Blazers lost by 15 at Sacramento (89–74), scoring a season-low for points.

"The first half, we looked like we were just out there," said Cheeks in a rare criticism of his players. "The first play of the game, we didn't even run what we were supposed to. That was disturbing to me."

After the six-game losing streak, Portland would finish 4–9 in December, its worst record for a month since February 1996.

Injuries to Wells, Pippen, and Anderson hadn't helped. Wallace was again leading the NBA in technicals. As the new year turned, the Blazers occupied a spot just outside the cellar of the Pacific Division.

Stoudamire was growing increasingly frustrated. Cheeks had decided he wanted him to be a distributor—like Cheeks had been as a player—instead of a scorer. After a short time coming off the bench, Stoudamire was back as a starter, but with a wounded spirit. The 5-foot-9 guard was passing up shots, shooting .392 from the field, and averaging a career-low 9.9 points. But he was also averaging 8.7 assists, and his assist/turnover ratio through December was 5.46, second best in the league behind Minnesota's Terrell Brandon.

Stoudamire was hoping to convince Cheeks to play him alongside Pippen in the backcourt, with Scottie running the point.

"I have been begging Mo to give me some 'two' action," Stoudamire said. "I could play off the ball when we get stagnant. Sometimes at the point, I feel like the whole defense can see me. From the two-guard position, I could slash through the lane and do some of the things I can do. People saw that when Scottie and I played together [in the preseason]."

On New Year's Night, the young Clippers danced, dunked, and postured in a 112–97 humiliation of Portland at Arrowhead Pond despite the Blazers getting back two starters—Pippen and Davis—from injury. The Clippers, who led 64–50 at the half, shot .579 from the field for the game with future Blazers Jeff McInnis (23 points and nine assists) and Darius Miles (17 points) leading the way.

"It was a big party for them tonight," Wells said, "and a smack in the face to us."

"The most frustrating thing to me is, we are losing to a bunch of kids," said Stoudamire, who led Portland with 25 points and six assists. "They were acting like they'd won the national championship. We have to show some pride."

Added Stoudamire: "Right now, our spirits are broken."

The Blazers were four games under .500 for the first time in over a decade (the 1988–89 season).

"My job is to figure it out," Cheeks said, "and I haven't figured it out yet."

The next night, the Blazers lost at home to Toronto 95–84 to drop to 13–18. It was the first time they'd been below .500 that late in a season since the 1995–96 campaign.

"There's nothing like you kicking somebody's butt, and then they finally get you down and start kicking your butt," Patterson said. "That's what we're going to through right now. It's sad right now, man. We suck."

Meanwhile, Kerr asked for some perspective.

"We don't have the talent to win a championship," said Kerr. "The talent here is good enough to be a good team, but our talent is overrated, frankly. This isn't two years ago when we had Jermaine O'Neal and Brian Grant and Steve Smith and Arvydas Sabonis. We miss Sabonis desperately. We are talented, but not as talented as people are saying."

* * *

Portland was getting pounded around by Western Conference title contenders. The Blazers were a combined 0–7 against the Lakers, Spurs, Kings, Mavericks, and Timberwolves.

The Blazers were still adept, however, at drawing technical fouls. Wallace (10) and Wells (nine) were running 1-2 in the league. That despite officials being advised not to be unfair with Rasheed.

"We know we're under the microscope," said one referee. "You don't want to be too quick to hit him, because then it's your fault. He is a known entity. You make sure that you are fair with him, but you know what you are getting. Sooner or later, something is going to happen, and he doesn't listen. He just goes off. Don't try to talk to him. He doesn't accept that kind of conversation. It's a waste of time."

Amid his team's struggle, Whitsitt made a plea with the fans for patience.

"We wish our record were better right now, but it takes time," he said, ignoring the fact that his team had the second-highest payroll in the NBA. "You can just sort of feel it when it gets there. Maybe it takes you a year; maybe it takes you three years."

On January 5, the Blazers beat Philadelphia 96–88 at home to snap their six-game losing streak. Wallace scored 30 points—though he took 20 shots to do it—while Stoudamire contributed 19 points and 11 assists. Kemp came off the bench to score 10 points on 5-for-6 shooting to go with six boards in 13 minutes.

"Shawn gets the game ball," Cheeks said. "He stepped up tonight."

On January 8, the Blazers took a step back, falling 101–92 to a lousy (13–20) Atlanta team. Wells broke out of the funk he had been in since the *Sports Illustrated* article, going for 26 points and 14 rebounds. The Blazers hurt their cause with two technical fouls in the last eight minutes—Wallace drawing one and Cheeks the other. When a fan yelled at Cheeks to shut up, the first-year head coach turned around and barked, "You shut up."

Pippen, who had played only 19 minutes against Cleveland, played seven minutes in the second half against Atlanta, and none in fourth quarter.

"Scottie was tired, and I chose to go to somebody else," Cheeks said when asked about it after the game.

"Who was tired?" asked Pippen when told what his coach had said. "I wasn't tired. Who said I was tired?"

Portland got some revenge on Phoenix in a 108–99 win, then ripped the Clippers 113–93 at the Rose Garden, Stoudamire leading the way with 29 points. The Blazers shot .542 from the field and held the Clippers to only .370 shooting.

Anderson's shooting percentage had climbed to .438, but in a reserve role, he was averaging only 9.8 points, on pace for a career low. He began the season as a starter but had sprained his ankle when he stepped on Shaquille O'Neal's foot in the season opener, and it was still bothering him three months later.

"I think I'm still more valuable as a starter, but right now for us to win, we have to sacrifice," Anderson said. "That's what I'm doing."

Whitsitt's lieutenant, Mark Warkentien, disputed there was apathy for the Blazers in the community. But Pat Lafferty, who had worked as the team's TV play-by-play voice from 1986–1992, and director of marketing services from 1992–1994, begged to differ.

"He doesn't help his or the organization's credibility with his assertions," Lafferty said. "There are no better indicators than television ratings, which have been running with ratings around eight, with a low near six. In 1990–91, Blazers telecasts averaged a 30 rating. The next season it was 29. Losses of that magnitude are staggering by anyone's standards, especially when the games are available for free."

Even with the consumer having many more cable options a decade later, and the fact that all TV ratings were down, those were big drops.

On January 22, the Blazers hit the halfway point in the season with their eighth win in 10 games, a 116–110 victory over Sacramento to go over .500 for the first time in almost a month. Blazer fans seemed to have forgiven Wells, who bombed in 34 points as the crowd roared its approval. It was a veritable lovefest only a month after he had become a local villain due to *Sports Illustrated*'s scathing article.

"We are starting to feel pretty good about ourselves," Pippen said. "We are starting to play a little better, so our confidence level is up. Winning has a whole lot to do with it. We are not playing as well as we can, but we are probably playing as well as any team in the league right now."

Stoudamire was on a roll, having scored 19 points or more nine times in the previous 15 games. Things turned around when Cheeks began to use Pippen for major minutes at point guard, allowing Stoudamire to work off the ball, spotting up for jumpers or taking the ball to the basket. It was just what Damon had asked for.

With everyone healthy, the odd men out of rotation were Kemp and Kerr, who had played well the first two months.

"It's tough, but I've been doing this my whole career," Kerr said. "One week I play; the next week I don't play at all. One reason I've been able to stick around is because I can handle it. That doesn't mean it's easy. I don't think it's [Cheeks's] job to come to me every day and talk to me about playing. A lot of it is up to me. My job is to keep myself ready whenever he calls on me.

"Guys like Chris [Dudley], Mitchell [Butler], Rick [Brunson], and myself, we have added some sanity to a situation that seemed a little insane the last couple of years. You can't have All-Stars sitting on the bench. You must have solid veterans who come in and can play when necessary but will support the team when they are not playing. Derek [Anderson] and Ruben [Patterson] are the ones who had to accept their roles without wanting to. When those guys accepted their roles is when things started to change for the better of us."

Bob Medina says the 2001–02 Blazers had unusually good chemistry. He gives Dudley and Kerr some of the credit. The two veterans often sat next to the rookie Randolph on the team plane.

"They'd give Zach the business," Medina recalls. "Zach would have all his bling on, and Steve would say, 'Man, that's a great chain. Where did you get that? How much did you pay?' Zach would proudly go, 'Ah, like $10,000.' Steve would say, 'Man, I gotta get one.'"

"Chris was a stand-up guy. He was great with people. Very professional in everything he did. He mixed in fine with the younger guys, though he was his own man. He was a great influence, a father figure. He tried to help guys.

He never got caught up in the BS. He knew who he was. He was a voice of reason when we didn't have enough of that."

As a whole, Medina says, that was "a tight-knit group."

"The players did a lot of things together," he says. "Once on an off day in Houston, there was a park by the hotel, and most of the guys were out there playing touch football. They'd play paintball together.

"There was a black gentleman who worked security at the practice facility. He took part in a walk for the March of Dimes. He mentioned it to the players, and they were all in. He raised the most money in the state of Oregon—I think it was around $50,000. That was the type of guys they had."

Two nights later, on January 24, the Blazers obliterated Memphis 120–82 at home, shooting .558 from the field. In their next game, they overcame a 16-point deficit to beat Seattle 92–86 at KeyArena, their fourth straight win and 10th in the last 12 outings.

Davis had a sensational game with 20 points on 9-for-10 shooting to go with 14 rebounds, and Wells piled up 19 points, nine boards, and six assists. The Blazers bickered, baited the refs, and had four first-half technicals—which resulted in the ejection of Pippen—but they still pulled out the win.

Said Stoudamire: "When I came in at halftime, I told the guys, 'I don't know why you are all fighting with the refs. You know we aren't going to get anything. We are just putting ourselves in a hole.'"

Pippen was playing a lot of point guard, running the offense in long stretches. It was a good fit for Scottie at that point in his career, where he was capable of scoring only in bursts. Soreness in his back and a knee prevented him from spending much energy on creating for himself on offense. Plus, it opened up the opportunity for Stoudamire to get some minutes at shooting guard.

"I'm content with it," Pippen said. "We have guys on this team who can put the ball in the hole. Scoring is not my main concern. It's great for Damon. Putting him away from the ball allows him to get to certain areas on the court, where he can look for his offense."

In early February, All-Star Game rosters were announced, and Wallace was left off the list. It was fitting, because when he made it the previous season, "Mr. T" had told everyone that he'd rather have been vacationing in Hawaii.

And how did he feel about it now?

"I could care less," he said, meaning he couldn't care less. "I don't care about that All-Star shit."

Did he plan on being in Philadelphia, where the All-Star game was being held?

"Hell yeah, I'm going back," he said. "That's my home. I got big thangs. I'm going to enjoy myself—enjoy partying. Whoo!"

Did he feel the All-Star slight was a political thing, perhaps backlash from his negative reputation for on-court decorum?

"I could care less if it is," he said. "If George Bush himself is involved, I could care less."

In his seventh NBA season, Wallace had developed into one of the game's top talents. He was unselfish and a team player. But the forward refused to do the extra things the great ones did to make their teams better. Players such as Kevin Garnett, Jason Kidd, and Kobe Bryant provided intangibles and the leadership that offered teams their best chance to reach the top. Not Wallace.

"That's not who he is," ESPN's Jack Ramsay said. "Rasheed is a tremendously talented guy, but he doesn't want to be the guy to vocally lead the team. He is not a take-charge, give-me-the-ball guy. But if you give it to him, he does pretty good things with it. You just can't expect him to be something he's not."

On February 2, Portland's win streak ended at five games with a 97–96 loss at Utah.

The Blazers' went the final 18 minutes without Wallace, who was given two technicals and ejected by referee Hue Hollins—his league-leading 16th and 17th T's of the season, and his first ejection of the season.

"We responded like a family, like we're supposed to," said Wells, who scored 24 points. "We have to stick together through thick and thin. When our best player is out, everybody has to step up his game a little more."

As he left the court after his ejection, Portland's best player swung at a

TV monitor on press row, knocking the monitor off its perch and grazing the shoulder of longtime *Salt Lake City Tribune* writer Steve Luhm, knocking off his glasses.

"[Wallace] smacked the monitor pretty good, but I'm fine," Luhm said afterward. "He just lost his temper for a minute. I suspect the Blazers may get billed for that monitor, though."

Three days later, Portland lost to the lowly Denver Nuggets, 97–96, despite leading by 16 midway through the third quarter. Patterson had a monster game, scoring a season-high 31 points with six rebounds, six steals, and four assists. But the Blazers also picked up four technicals, and Wells was ejected.

* * *

At the All-Star Game in Philadelphia, some of the game's stars were asked for opinions on the Blazers, who were 25–23 at the break.

"I know those guys," said Indiana's Jermaine O'Neal. "I talk to Rasheed and those guys all the time, and they are not happy with a .500 record. They are going to put it together. They have a much better team than their records states."

"They are a scary team," said San Antonio's Steve Smith. "They can get on a roll and beat everyone in the league. You don't want to face the Blazers in the playoffs. They have something to prove. I hope they turn it around. Those are my guys—the players, not management."

Charles Barkley, now with TNT, was not quite as optimistic.

"It seems like they are going to be inconsistent all year," he said. "Every time I think they are over the hump, they go back to their old ways. Rasheed is frustrating because he should be one of the five best players in the world. He's not. It's a shame when a guy with that much talent doesn't reach his potential. You look at him from a skills standpoint, you can't name five better players in the world. A team with a guy that good should be above .500."

After the break, Portland came out of the game with a win over the Mavericks (114–03) followed by a loss to the Celtics (107–104). Then suddenly, Portland was unbeatable, going on a 12-game tear to improve to 38–24.

On February 17, the Blazers beat the Lakers 111–105 with Shaquille O'Neal on the injured list with an arthritic big right toe. Wells had 27 points and 10 rebounds while Wallace scored 25 points, but the biggest contributor was Patterson. The self-professed "Kobe-stopper" had 22 points and eight boards while also helping slow down, yes, Kobe Bryant. Bryant scored 28 points but made only 11-of-26 shots, including 1-of-7 with Ruben guarding him.

"Y'all seen the game," Patterson told reporters afterward. "Y'all didn't see Kobe score on me. When I was out of the game, he hit a couple of shots, but when I got on him, it was a different story. I took it personal. Kobe runs his mouth. You know he knows he's talking to the wrong one when it comes to playing basketball. I just tried to play physical with him and deny him [the ball]. He doesn't like that. He gets frustrated."

To Bryant, Patterson was like a persistent pimple he couldn't pop.

"If we bump into each other at a gym and we play one-on-one, I would demolish him," Kobe said. "But playing five-on-five, that's a different mindset."

Bryant conceded that Patterson's energy off the bench had been a factor in the outcome.

"That's what he does. He's a garbage player. He gets in there and rebounds, gets steals and easy run-outs, and he does that very well for them."

Patterson had played for the Lakers as a rookie in 1998–99 and felt they had unwisely let him go.

"Every time we play the Lakers," he said, "it's personal with me."

Phil Jackson was complimentary, though the Lakers coach was surely speaking at least partly tongue in cheek.

"Patterson was again the nemesis of the Lakers," Jackson said. "Whoever gets to the Finals should hire him immediately. He might be able to help anybody beat us."

Jackson threw out a lot of things in his assessment of the Blazers: "They have pretty good talent—athletic players, a lot of good shooting, and they can rebound. Scottie is in good health, which is a key for them. I anticipated better performances from them as far as the character of their team goes. I don't know how solid they are in the middle. It's one thing I wonder about—what their toughness would be like in a playoff series."

From there, the Blazers just kept rolling. On February 23, they beat Denver 101–90 for their fifth straight win. Pippen missed his second straight game with a viral infection, but Anderson stepped in with 17 points, eight rebounds, and four assists. Stoudamire had a huge game with 24 points, 11 assists, and six rebounds.

"I was disappointed he didn't have any blocked shots," Cheeks joked afterward. Wallace came up big, too, with 23 points, seven boards, and five assists.

The next day, Kemp left the team, suspended indefinitely for a violation of the league's anti-drug aftercare problem. Kemp, who had been playing his best basketball of the season in recent weeks, did not fail a drug test but had not fulfilled responsibilities regarding counseling and regular check-ins with medical directors in the aftercare program from his suspension and rehab the previous season. There was suspicion, insiders said, that he had been using again.

"He's a little sad, and a little disappointed in himself," Cheeks said of Kemp, who would return on March 4 and play out the season. "But he says he is going to do everything he needs to do to come back."

The relapse did not surprise assistant coach Dan Panaggio, who was assigned to Kemp detail while the team embarked on a four-game road trip.

"Shawn was heavy and way out there," Panaggio says today. "I volunteered to stay behind—we went 4–0 on the trip, wouldn't you know it—and chase him around Portland to get him in for two workouts a day. There was plenty of evidence something was wrong [besides excessive weight] . . . the odd behavior and all of that."

For two seasons with Seattle, Hersey Hawkins was a teammate of Kemp's.

"Shawn kept to himself a lot, but he was a really good guy," says Hawkins, now the Blazers' player programs director. "He was a great teammate, always supportive—never a negative type of person.

"But his substance abuse started the last year I was with him in Seattle. We saw signs of it. That year we had a meeting or two because we weren't playing as well as we were capable of playing. Everybody threw the iron out on what was going on personally. He would never admit anything was going on, but everybody knew. We were hoping he'd open up about it, but he never did."

On March 4, Portland won their 10th straight game with a victory over the Pacific-leading Sacramento Kings, 107–95. Wells led the way with 20 points, seven rebounds, four assists, and four steals.

"We've won 10 straight? I didn't know we've won 10 straight," said Cheeks, adding, "I want people to look ahead on the schedule and said, 'We have the Trail Blazers on this day.' It doesn't matter to me whether they fear us or not, but I want to them to be aware of us. And I think we have done that."

When the playoffs were mentioned to Wells, he said, "We try not to think about it. We just want to keep it rolling. We understand we can beat anybody. If you want to call us contenders, fine. If you don't, then we'll try to prove ya'll wrong."

Win No. 12 in the streak came at the expense of New Jersey, 82–73. It was the second-longest streak in franchise history behind a 16-game tear by the 1990–91 team.

"Who would have thunk it?" Cheeks said of the streak. "I certainly wouldn't have thunk it, [the players] wouldn't have thunk it, and I'm sure [media] wouldn't have thunk it."

The streak ended on March 9, in an overtime loss to Denver, 109–106.

On March 14, the Blazers had as impressive a win as they'd had all season, walloping Dallas 132–106. The Blazers scored 73 in the first half and finished with the most franchise points in a regulation game since 1994. The Midwest Division–leading Mavericks had come into Portland riding a five-game winning streak.

"Not a whole lot to say," Dallas coach Don Nelson said. "Just an old-fashioned butt-kickin'."

Wallace scored 28 of his 37 points in the first half, then received his

23rd technical of the season in the second half. Davis was ejected in the third quarter after taking a swing at Dallas center Shawn Bradley and wound up with a two-game suspension.

Pippen contributed 14 points and 12 assists in the rout. In a lot of ways, the veteran was the straw that stirred the drink for the Blazers. There were some who felt he was the one coaching the Blazers, not Cheeks. Even Cheeks acknowledged some validity to that notion.

"He has brought our team together with his knowledge and ability to run a team," Cheeks said. "Even at his age, he brings it. He controls our team. He commands so much respect on the court and in the locker room because of his credentials. I learn things from the guy. I listen to him, it helps me understand things that are going on the court, and I apply it to my coaching and the game."

Kerr, who had been a teammate of Pippen's for five years in Chicago, valued his presence as well.

"Without him, we wouldn't be any better than when we were 13–18 two months ago," Kerr said. "People ask me why we got better, and I say because we got healthy. When I say that, I am really talking about Scottie. We had Ruben and Bonzi and Damon out, but the constant that was missing was Scottie, and we could never develop that rhythm."

When a reporter told Pippen it appeared he had given up on the Blazers after their lousy start, he nodded.

"I'd probably agree with you on that," he said. "We were wearing attitudes on our shoulders and weren't playing together as a team. Until we changed our attitudes, things were not going to look up for this.

"Now we are a very scary team. If we are playing good basketball, I feel good about our chances against any team. But we have to play an almost perfect type of basketball, especially at the defensive end."

On March 16, the Blazers won their eighth home game in a row, 95–80, over Washington, with an unexpected player leading the way. Kemp, who had recently returned after a five-game suspension, started at center in place of the suspended Davis. In his first start in more than a year, Kemp had a season-high in minutes (43), points (21), and rebounds (14).

"I don't know if my game suffered [from the suspension], but it threw my timing off," Kemp said. "Dale has played so well, and Rasheed has had a great year, also. I accept my role without even thinking about it. When you have that opportunity to start, you try to make the most of it. You go out there and just try to have fun."

"What you saw there was a championship-level team put the screws down," Washington coach Doug Collins said. "Really good teams only have to play an inferior team hard for about 12 minutes, and that's what happened tonight. They sort of played along with us and then cranked it up and turned it around with a spurt in the third period. Championship teams can do that."

On March 23, the Blazers ended a four-game road trip (3–1) with an important 108–99 victory at Minnesota. Portland (43–26) came from 13 points down to win for the 18th time in 21 games since the All-Star break.

"I told the team if they don't believe in themselves after that win, then something is wrong, because that was a heck of a win," Cheeks said.

"We are warriors," said Stoudamire, who scored 21 points while hitting two crucial baskets in the fourth quarter. "We are soldiers. We have fought and dug ourselves out from a big hole when everybody had written us off. There's a lot of resiliency in this locker room, and we have been showing it."

The tables turned on March 25 when one of the league's patsies, Memphis, rallied from 25 down to overhaul the Blazers 103–100. Portland led 30–7 nine minutes into the game, 25 points in third quarter, and 19 heading into the fourth quarter. Grizzlies coach Sidney Lowe cleared his bench, and reserves such as Will Solomon and Rodney Buford led the comeback. Buford had 14 and Solomon 10 in the final period in the biggest comeback in Memphis franchise history.

There wasn't much the Blazers could say after their eight-game home win streak had ended.

"We gave that fucker away," Stoudamire said.

"We stopped playing with about 10 minutes left," Kerr said.

Cheeks was able to get that bad taste out of his mouth two nights later, when San Antonio came to Portland riding a 13-game win streak and took the loss, 98–93. The Blazers did it mostly without Wallace, who sat out the final three quarters due to a sore back. Tim Duncan scored 24 of his 34 points in the first half but was slowed by solid defense from Kemp and Patterson through the second half.

"I don't know if I can swear but that was a freaking great game," Cheeks said. "To beat a team like that, the way they've been playing—that's a heck of a win."

On March 29, the Lakers beat the Blazers 91–79 at Staples Center, with the usual suspects doing the damage. Shaquille O'Neal went for 34 points and 14 rebounds while Kobe Bryant had 34 points, seven rebounds, and six assists.

Without Wallace, Portland had no offense, shooting a season-low .326. The game was tied late in the third quarter, but the Blazers made only 4-of-20 shots in the fourth. Kemp, starting for Wallace, had 12 points and 16 rebounds, but the rest of the Blazers struggled. Pippen was 2-for-18 from the field.

"We should have won the game, even without Rasheed," said Patterson, who failed to slow Bryant down this time. "We can beat them. I'm not scared of them. They're not that good. We had the game in our hand. We let it go. If Scottie would have hit those shots, we would have been in the game."

* * *

April began with a 107–91 blowout loss against Golden State, one of the NBA's worst teams. Portland was outscored 30–13 and shot 3-for-16 in the fatal fourth quarter to suffer its third straight loss. For a team that had gone 15–1, they had dropped four of their last five.

For the first time all season, Cheeks unloaded on his players afterward.

"For the first time in three and a half, four months, we didn't compete," the first-year coach said. "We haven't done this in a long time."

"He was ticked, and he had a reason to be," Stoudamire said. "It wasn't pretty."

On April 4, the Blazers ended a three-game skid with an 88–80 home win over New York, in the process clinching their 20th straight playoff berth. It was the longest current streak in major league sports.[3] The last time the Blazers had missed the playoffs was 1982.

Wells was building a growing reputation with opponents for profane trash talking, clutching and grabbing, and the sort of bush-league tom-foolery that might be expected from an instigator in hockey. Wells and the Knicks' Latrell Sprewell got into several spats, and Sprewell wound up getting ejected.

"I'm not the type of guy who is going to take stuff off anybody," Sprewell said. "He was being a little too physical, and I responded."

On April 8, the Blazers lost 99–87 at San Antonio after falling behind by 29 points in the third quarter. Wallace had his worst offensive game of the season, finishing with five points on 1-for-13 shooting to go with eight rebounds in 34 minutes.

The Blazers were called for three technicals in the game, and Patterson was whistled for a flagrant foul.

"We talked about that after the game," Cheeks said. "Sometimes we let the officials get to us. We react to the officials; then we stand there and argue a call and give up a fast break."

The next night, Wallace upped his season technical total to 26 and was ejected in the third quarter of a 103–88 loss at Dallas, the team's seventh loss in 12 games. Pippen also got the boot after taking a swing at the Mavericks' guard Nick Van Exel in the fourth quarter.

"I turned around and Scottie was swinging, and the next thing I know, there's a melee out there," Cheeks said.

In a moment of clarity, Wells had some sage advice for his teammates, as well as himself.

---

3   The NBA record, 22 straight years, was set by the Syracuse Nationals/ Philadelphia 76ers from 1950–1971.

"It has nothing to do with the officiating; it's all about us," he said. "We have to quit chirping as much as we do and play the game the way it is supposed to be played. We have a lot of non-traditional players, but we still have to go out there and try to play and keep our mouths shut."

After dropping three straight, the last to Memphis on April 11, Wells scored 29 points and converted the game-winning layup with 19.2 seconds left in an 80–79 win at Houston.

"It's time for me and my teammates to get our shit together and start winning," Wells said. "It's playoff time. It's money time. That's what we call it. It's time for all of us to step up and prove ourselves."

Two nights later, the Blazers prevailed in double overtime, 128–120, against the two-time defending NBA champion Lakers, who were their probable first-round playoff opponent. More like a mini-series than a game, the second overtime finished more than three hours after the opening tip-off.

The Lakers led by 13 points in the fourth quarter, but Wells—who finished with 33 points and nine rebounds—knocked down four 3's in the quarter to force overtime. The Lakers scored the first eight points of the first overtime, but the Blazers came back, and Wallace sent the game into a second overtime when he hit a 3 with 2.5 seconds left.

O'Neal did his usual damage with 36 points and 11 rebounds, and Bryant finished with 23 points, nine assists, seven rebounds, and three steals in 51 minutes. But Bryant, harassed for much of the time by Patterson, made only 6-of-15 shots from the field and committed six turnovers. Patterson, meanwhile, contributed 17 points, 10 rebounds, four assists, and three steals in 44 minutes.

"You feel good about yourselves today," Cheeks said after the emotional win. "You feel like you have a chance [in the playoffs]. But you realize how much it took out of us to win this game, and we have to go to win three games against them to go further."

Pippen was ejected for the second time in less than a week. First, he threw a ball into the stands after a defensive three-second violation in the second quarter. After drawing a quick second technical, he tossed his sweatband at referee Bennett Salvatore as he left the court. Then Pippen grabbed a plastic tray used by waitresses at courtside and hurled it high into the air from behind the Blazer bench. It landed on the court in front of the NBC broadcast crew, including a startled analyst Bill Walton, on a day when the 1977 NBA champions were honored on the 25th anniversary of their title.

"[Salvatore] hit me with two technicals fast," Pippen said. "That's pretty much the way it is with this team—there are no fair shakes."

The Blazers received two other technicals in the game—Wallace for kicking a chair going into a timeout and Patterson for elbowing Robert Horry.

On that day, none of it mattered to the Blazers' coach.

"To me, technicals are just a part of our team," Cheeks said. "Our guys have a lot of passion, and I don't want to take away our emotions of playing basketball. I love the way we play. I love the way we compete. Some of that is we have a lot of fire in us, a lot of emotion.

"I talk to them about controlling things we can control. As time moves on, they will understand it. Sometimes in the heat of battle, it gets out of hand. We are not the only team that does that, but ours can be a little magnified because we are the Blazers."

The next day, the Clackamas County District Attorney's office confirmed that the Lake Oswego Police Department had submitted a criminal case for possible felony drug possession charges against Stoudamire, a case that was expected to go to a grand jury.

In February, Lake Oswego police had responded to a burglar alarm at Stoudamire's home and had found roughly a pound of marijuana. Stoudamire was in the process of a move from the Lake Oswego house to a home he had purchased in West Linn. He had not yet been arrested or charged with a crime. At the time, possession of more than an ounce was a Class B felony in Oregon. The maximum penalty if convicted was 10 years and a $200,000 fine.

"It's just one of those things," Stoudamire said, adding, "I'm hanging in there. I don't want anybody to feel sorry for me or anything. I've got more than my share of supporters out there. The timing is tough, but I don't think it's going to be a team distraction."

Portland entered the playoffs as the No. 6 seed with a 49–33 record, having gone 6–7 since its high-water mark of 43–26 on March 23. The opponent, as expected, was the No. 3 seeded Lakers (58–24). The teams had split the season series at two apiece.

Patterson gave himself the edge in the matchup of players at the wing positions—himself and Wells against the Lakers' Kobe Bryant and Rick Fox.

"Me and Bonzi have an advantage on their 2 and 3 guys," Patterson said, looking back at the Blazers' April 14 double-overtime triumph. "I wore [Bryant] down in the second half, just playing physical with him. It's a mental thing as much as anything. He knows I am going to have a plan against him, play hard and do what I do."

Cheeks had a little fun with it when asked about the matchup.

"I tell Ruben, after we beat the Lakers in a five-game series, then you are a Kobe-stopper," Cheeks said. "I don't know if Ruben is in [Bryant's] head, but I believe you let a guy guard a player he believes he can guard. Ruben really believes he can guard him. But Kobe is a great player. He will make adjustments to whoever guards him. He will take on the challenge. You don't become a great player by letting one guy stop you."

ESPN's Jack Ramsay predicted a competitive series.

"Phil Jackson fears the Blazers more than anybody else," Ramsay said. "They have a lot of weapons and flexibility and the capacity to challenge the Lakers in a number of ways. That high screen-and-roll with Stoudamire and Wallace is tough to defend, and Bonzi and Ruben play so hard to the hoop."

TNT's Doug Collins said the Blazers would miss Sabonis in trying to slow down O'Neal. Shaq had averaged 33 points and 14.3 rebounds in his three games against Blazers, missing one with his sore toe.

"They don't want to play the Lakers," Collins said. "They have no answer for Shaq at all. At least with Sabonis, they had a big body to keep him in front of you. They had their best chance to beat the Lakers when Sabonis was playing. My guess now is they will struggle."

O'Neal didn't seem worried about any challenge the Blazers might offer. Instead, he was already looking down the road.

"If I'm going to fight you in a boxing match, I'm not going to train," Shaq told the media. "I'm going to eat some doughnuts, and I'll beat your butt. But if I have to fight Mike Tyson, then I have to train. I know what my troops are capable of. Sometimes we are so good we get bored, but we know what we have to do in the playoffs. I want a challenge. I want to get a championship—blood, sweat, and tears style."

Jackson, who always liked to poke fun at his northern foes, couldn't resist a snide comment about the Jail Blazers.

"I'm always surprised that Portland people can actually root for their players, given the type of character they display on the floor, but they somehow manage," Jackson said. "Maybe it's the money that they're paying [that makes them] feel they owe allegiance to the team. And they carry the name of the town on their backs."

* * *

The Lakers opened the series with a 95–87 home victory. Though winning by eight, Portland led through much of the first half, and the score was tied early in the third quarter.

Portland kept the Lakers' lead to single digits most of the rest of the way, but the Blazers' half-court offense was anemic as they shot .366 from the field.

"The second half was indicative of the way [the Lakers] win championships," Cheeks said. "Their players step up. Every little thing about their game stepped up."

Anderson came off the bench—and out of nowhere, really—to sink 8-of-14 and score a career playoff-high 22 points. Wallace was only 8-for-20 but had 25 points and 14 boards; the rest of the Portland starters combined for 25 points on 10-for-34 shooting.

Stoudamire made his first shot, a 3-pointer, then missed seven straight to finish 1-for-8 from the field. He felt there was something wrong with the offensive system.

"Nobody is getting good looks," he said. "It didn't just start tonight; it started about a month ago. The offensive rhythm hasn't been there. I can't speak for anyone else, but if I take 13 or 14 shots in a game, I probably get six I want to take. The others are contested shots or shots with the [shot] clock running down."

Bryant had 34 points but made only 10-of-28 shots from the field. He had seven rebounds, three assists, three blocks, two steals, and only one turnover in 44 minutes.

Patterson, who had 13 points and three rebounds in 27 minutes off the bench, drew the loudest boos during the game from the Staples throng. Kobe-stoppers not welcome here.

Shaq contributed 25 points and nine boards and made 10-for-17 from the field, thoroughly outplaying Dale Davis. Davis fouled out in 24 minutes trying to defend Shaq, finishing with two points and five rebounds.

Patterson offered a suggestion for his coach.

"We should start going to Bonzi and me a lot in the post," he said. "The Lakers are going to have to double us. But when we swing the ball, guys have to hit shots."

The Lakers made it 16 straight wins overall, and 16 consecutive playoff games, at Staples with a 103–96 victory in Game 2. The Blazers, who trailed by 21 points with 5:39 left, again shot poorly at 40 percent from the field.

Bryant again struggled with his shot, scoring 19 points on 5-for-21 shooting, but Shaq hammered the Portland defense with 31 points and 14 boards.

The Blazers drew four technicals and a flagrant foul, causing TNT's Jeff Van Gundy to note that they had a "persecution complex." Davis drew a technical on a questionable foul call while guarding Shaq, then was ejected after booting the ball into the stands. Davis then ripped off his jersey and stormed off the court. Wallace had a technical and Patterson a flagrant and, before the game was over, Pippen and Wells were on the bench after fouling out.

"We lost our composure," Cheeks said.

All the Blazers had to do now to win the series was beat the Lakers three straight times, including Game 5 back at Staples.

"We're down 2–0," said Pippen after scoring 20 points with nine rebounds. "There's not much more needed to describe it. You lose the next one and you go home."

At shootaround before Game 3, rookie Zach Randolph provided a moment of levity, showing he didn't have a strong understanding of how the playoffs worked.

"Zach was talking with Steve Kerr, and asked, 'If we lose tonight, do we play out the rest of the series?'" strength and conditioning coach Bob Medina recalls. "Steve says, 'Yeah. In fact, if we lose tonight, Coach [Cheeks] was saying you're going to play in Games 4 and 5. You're going to start.' Zach's eyes got big, and he said, 'Don't mess with me, man. Are you serious?'"

Game 3 was at the Rose Garden, and it was a doozy. Portland led 91–86 with 33 seconds left, but the Lakers didn't give in. Robert Horry drilled a 3-point shot from in front of the Portland bench with 2.1 seconds left for a mind-numbing 92–91 win.

"This is probably a tougher loss than I've ever had," said Kerr, whose NBA career was at nearly 1,000 games at the time. "This probably tops them all."

Through 47-plus minutes, it appeared the Lakers let the Blazers creep back into the series. They'd let Stoudamire restore a little of his flagging confidence. They'd let Wells get his legs under him. They'd let Pippen have a big game against his old coach. They'd let Kerr become a factor off the bench. They'd let the Garden crowd get revved up. They'd let doubt filter into their own minds.

Then in a flash, it was gone. There were Wallace and Pippen each missing a crucial free throw in the final 17 seconds. There was Bryant bombing in a 26-foot 3-pointer with 12.7 seconds left. Then with 2.1 ticks left, there was Horry launching a high-arching 3 from the corner . . . splat. Game.

Pippen had drifted off Horry to help defend Bryant on a drive to the basket: "Kobe had gotten a step on Ruben," Pippen said. "I was going to cut him off at the basket. I didn't get out to [Horry], and it cost us the game, pretty much."

Bryant scored 25 points. O'Neal was held to 21 points, but the big man also had 11 rebounds and seven assists. The Blazers outrebounded the Lakers 53–37, grabbing 17 off the offensive glass, yet still lost.

After the opener, Cheeks had told the media, "If we don't make shots, we don't win."

The Blazers didn't make shots, firing at only a .383 clip for the series. Stoudamire averaged 5 points and 3.3 assists despite playing 33 minutes a game, making only 5-of-22 shots. Davis averaged 2.8 shots on 3-for-11 shooting. Wells (14-for-38) and Patterson (5-for-15) were off. Wallace averaged 25.3 points and 12.3 rebounds but shot only .406 from the field.

It was the third straight year the Lakers had eliminated Portland from the playoffs. The Lakers' 92–91 win was their seventh straight triumph over the Blazers in the postseason.

"We're jinxed against them," Wells said.

Cheeks said he learned a lot through his first season as a head coach, and he offered a mea culpa.

"We could have had five or six more wins had I been a more seasoned coach," he said. "That's just things you learn as time goes on. I hope next year I will be a lot better coach. Being in the league 15 years as a player and seven years as an assistant, you think you know a lot. Then when you sit in the [head coach's] chair, you don't know half of what you thought you knew."

Chapter 8

ARMAGEDDON, ALMOST EVERY WEEK

(2002–2003)

"No need to search the car. We already smoked all our weed."

—Rasheed Wallace, allegedly, during a traffic arrest

General manager Bob Whitsitt didn't make changes to the nucleus from the 2001–02 Portland team that featured Rasheed Wallace, Bonzi Wells, Scottie Pippen, Damon Stoudamire, Dale Davis, Ruben Patterson, and Derek Anderson. Whitsitt did add some pieces, however, that would further complicate things for coach Maurice Cheeks and give owner Paul Allen some additional luxury tax to chew on.

Whitsitt acquired a pair of veteran point guards—Antonio Daniels in a trade, and Jeff McIinnis as a free agent—and lured Arvydas Sabonis into a return after his one-year hiatus.

After six seasons with the Blazers, Sabonis had elected to take the 2001–02 season off, dividing time with family in Spain and Lithuania.

"My last season in Portland was a hard season—for the team, for me, for everybody," Sabonis would say after his return. "Maybe I needed to get away from everything. I did nothing for eight months. For five months, it was good. Interesting, something new."

Then he got bored. "All my life, I have been organized—wake up, work out, play basketball," he said.

Sabonis decided he was interested in a return to the NBA. The Lakers had tendered an offer to Sabonis's agent, Herb Rudoy, but could only provide the veteran's minimum—one year at $762,000. Through the Larry Bird Exception, the Blazers could offer a three-year contract starting at $7 million, with an option for both sides the last two years.

"When the Blazers were interested, that was it," said Sabonis—at least when the difference in money was that large. "I was here before. I knew everybody."

Sabonis, though, seemed creaky-legged and rusty from a year away. And he would no longer be a starter. He was expected to play 15–20 minutes a game behind starting center Dale Davis.

"I'm not in good enough shape," Sabonis said as the start of training camp harkened. "Mentally good, but physically, I need work."

The 6-foot-4 McInnis, who would turn 28 in October, had been the starting point guard for the LA Clippers the previous two seasons, averaging 14.6 points and 6.2 assists in 2001–02. Whitsitt, who signed McInnis to a three-year, $9.6-million contract, had promised an opportunity to earn a starting job.

Rasheed Wallace and McInnis had played two seasons together at North Carolina and were fast friends.

"Damon was our point guard," assistant coach Herb Brown says today. "When Whitsitt traded for Daniels, we thought it was as Damon's backup. The next day, he signed Jeff. The coaching staff didn't want to sign both, but he did. I think that's because Bob wanted us to sit Damon. I don't know if he interfered, but I wouldn't be surprised.

"Not that they weren't good players, but getting both Antonio and Jeff was a problem. Now we had two other guys, neither as good as Damon—and the other players knew it, which is a difficult thing. Scottie Pippen could also play the point, and he did. You can't have unhappy players coming to coaches all the time asking, 'Why am I not playing?' We had that."

The 6-foot-4 Daniels, 27, was in his sixth season in the NBA, mostly as a backup. Daniels, who played his college ball at Bowling Green, had played the previous two seasons in San Antonio. He started at the point for part of the 2000–01 season but drew plenty of playing time both years, averaging more than nine points and 26 minutes each season.

Daniels was acquired from the Spurs in exchange for guards Steve Kerr and Erick Barkley.

Whitsitt told a reporter that Kerr wanted to return to the Spurs.

"That bugs me because I did not ask for a trade," Kerr said after the deal was consummated.

During the previous season, Kerr's wife, Margot, and their three young kids had stayed behind at their home in San Diego. A week before the trade, Steve had called Whitsitt about his stability with the club; if he were coming back, the plan was to move the family to Portland.

"Bob told me nothing was going on," Kerr said. "He said he didn't expect anything to happen, to plan on moving up, but to call him again in a couple of weeks before we definitely made the move.

"I told him I really enjoyed the previous season and was looking forward to coming back, and my family was fired up about joining me. The trade caught me totally off guard. Crazy."

With the addition of Manu Ginobili, the San Antonio backcourt would be even more crowded, which wouldn't have set well with Daniels. Kerr, at the end of his 14-year playing career, would be more willing to settle for a lesser role.

"[Spurs coach Gregg Popovich] always has an eye on the chemistry issue and how everything fits together," Kerr said at the time. "Over the years, the Spurs have made some moves to unload guys when there is a logjam at a position. Pop probably made this move to make sure everybody was happy.

"Bob makes no bones about doing it his way—put the most talent you can out there, and then it's up to the coach to make it work. It has never been more true than now. Bob doesn't ever change his philosophy, does he?"

The Blazers would go to training camp with Stoudamire, Wells, Anderson, Daniels, McInnis, and Charles Smith in the backcourt, plus swing man Pippen.

"They have all those guards," Kerr said as he left the team. "I don't envy Maurice. Now he has a couple of more guys to keep happy. If they keep

Damon, neither he nor McInnis will be happy splitting time. And with his contract, it is going to be hard to trade Damon."

About that time, Stoudamire told the team's coaches that, if he wasn't the starter, the Blazers might as well trade him.

Before training camp started, McInnis sounded as if he felt the same way.

"To be honest, I can't see myself coming off the bench," he said. "If somebody can beat me out, they might as well get me out of here. It wouldn't be a good sight."

Kerr was gone, and so was Shawn Kemp, having agreed to forfeit about $16 million of the $46.5 million due to him in salary over the next two years in a buyout agreement. Kemp would finish out his career with a single season in Orlando.

Back for his second season was power forward Zach Randolph, who had another legal issue to clear up.

Over Memorial Day weekend in his hometown of Marion, Indiana, Randolph had been cited for underage drinking less than two weeks before his 21st birthday. Though he would plead guilty, he considered it a bum rap.

"I had one beer," Randolph said. "I wasn't driving. I was just out on the street. I wasn't causing no trouble. A cop came by. He knew who I was, and we had a conversation. I felt like I got singled out there. It was bullshit, really, a small-town thing."

Wells was a restricted free agent and wanted to stay put.

"My future is in Portland," he said during the summer. "Portland is the first team to give me a chance. I'm a loyal guy. The only way I won't be here is if they don't want me here. I want to be around here the rest of my life."

Just before training camp, the Blazers re-signed him to a four-year, $29-million deal.

Portland's payroll would wind up in the neighborhood of $106 million, an all-time NBA record. New York would be second at $94 million, with Dallas a distant third at $73 million. With the salary cap at $40.3 million and the luxury tax threshold expected to be about $53 million, Paul Allen's tax bill would be more than $50 million.

Cheeks also made a couple of moves on his coaching staff, letting Caldwell Jones and Neal Meyer go while adding John Loyer to veterans Herb Brown and Jimmy Lynam. The Blazers also kept veteran point guard Gary Grant in a workout coach role.

TNT's Charles Barkley was among those unimpressed with the work Whitsitt had done with the Blazers.

"They have to start over," Barkley said before the season began. "You can't be in the middle because you don't get good draft picks. You either have to play for the championship or be young and getting better. They are in a no-man's-land. I don't know Whitsitt well, but I know one thing: You can't be bringing in old guys who make a lot of money. It's a young man's game. Because of all those contracts, they can't make trades. They are in jail."

Wallace, who had led Portland in scoring (18.1) and was second in rebounds (8.4), had also piled up a remarkable total of 107 technical fouls in the three previous seasons. Cheeks was less concerned with that than getting Wallace to focus more on being a perimeter threat.

"I have no problem with Rasheed being on the perimeter," Cheeks said. "He has won games for us out there. A guy his size who can shoot like that, it's a plus. But he can get that outside jump shot any time he wants. It helps him, and it helps us, if he is down on the block a little more. If we can get him down there, and focus on getting him the ball, that is a double pleasure."

Pippen would be the starting small forward but, at 37, was no longer the physical specimen he once was. He'd had knee surgery during offseason, then had fluid drained after the knee swelled up about a month before camp started.

Eleven of the 18 players in camp had been NBA starters, and that didn't include Patterson.

"We have too many good players," said Patterson, echoing a familiar tone. "It was hard for me and [Derek Anderson] last year, to sacrifice our own minutes to help the team. Everybody says I should be starting, but that don't matter that much. I like coming off the bench, bringing excitement and energy if the first unit ain't doing it."

Not everybody was saying Patterson should start, of course. As it would turn out, Stoudamire would be the odd man out, and Anderson would reclaim his starting spot at shooting guard. He didn't know what to expect, though, as camp began.

"It feels like we have 1,001 players at my position," Anderson said. "I get that [Whitsitt] is trying to make us better, not tear us down. It still has to come to a point where you don't put coach Cheeks in a position where he can't find time for guys."

Beginning his 16th season, the Hall of Fame–bound Pippen, voted in 1997 as one of the NBA's top 50 players ever, was expecting to come off the bench for the first time since his rookie season with Chicago in 1987. His preference, to no one's surprise, would be to start and play 30-some minutes. But at that point in his career, injuries had become a fact of life. In 2000–01, his second season with Portland, he missed 18 games because of an elbow injury. Knee problems had sidelined him for 20 games in 2001–02, when he averaged only 10.6 points, a low since his rookie season.

Now in the final year of a five-year, $19.7-million deal, Pippen said he would accept any role.

"Doesn't matter one way or the other," he said. "We have guys who are capable and ready to step up. It's up to Maurice who he wants to put out there."

Pippen had become a mentor to Wells, who idolized him, and now to rookie small forward Qyntel Woods. The 6-foot-8 Woods, 21, had been taken with the 21st pick in the first round of the draft after playing two years of junior-college ball at Northeast Mississippi. The Blazers regarded him as a diamond in the rough.

"He is very talented," Pippen said. "It's going to be important to teach him as much as I can."

As the preseason wore down, Patterson sounded a more subservient tone.

"Guys were mad and disappointed about minutes last year, but everybody is accepting roles this year," he said. "We know who the key players are. We have Rasheed and Bonzi, then Damon, and then the rest of us."

"We all have to swallow our pride and be the best team we can be,"

McInnis said, now sounding like a real team player. "If Damon is out there, I can't pout. I may not be happy about not playing, but I still have to cheer for him. That has to be the attitude of everybody."

Cheeks would cringe whenever asked about distributing playing time. He said he planned to go on "feel" from game to game, depending on matchups and player performance.

The Lakers and Sacramento Kings would enter the season as the favorites in the Western Conference. Portland, San Antonio, Utah, and Dallas were expected to be the teams chasing them.

"We will find out the first few weeks what this team is all about," Stoudamire said. "In the NBA, successful teams almost always get off to a good start."

* * *

The Blazers, meanwhile, were having problems selling tickets. A run of 17 straight seasons of home sellouts at Memorial Coliseum (capacity 12,666) and the Rose Garden had ended (officially, at least) in 1995. Portland's run of 814 straight home sellouts remains an NBA record, with the second-best streak owned by the Boston Celtics (662 from 1980–1996).

When the Rose Garden opened in 1995, capacity was 21,538. The Blazers had fifteen sellouts that first season. During the second season, they announced average attendance at 20,800, third-best in the NBA behind Charlotte and Chicago. In 1999–2000, the arena was reconfigured to seat 19,980. In 2001–02, Portland's home attendance averaged an announced 19,044, with twelve sellouts in 41 games.

A *Forbes* magazine analysis said the club had experienced losses in each of their previous two seasons, showing a net loss of $19.3 million for the 2000–01 season—gross revenues of $101 million against expenditures at $120.3 million.

Through the '80s and '90s, the Blazers had been on a financial roll. Now the economy was more difficult, expenditures had increased dramatically, and advertising revenue had taken a dip. "Image issues are a factor," team vice president Erin Hubert admitted.

With their payroll at $106 million for the upcoming season, the sheet wasn't close to balanced. Hubert would not reveal details but admitted the club's net operating income fell off by 15 percent in 2001–02 after showing an annual double-digit increase for many years.

Trying to connect with fans for the first time, Whitsitt made himself available to answer questions at four open fan forums over the summer.

"For a while, we weren't addressing the issues with the team or acknowledging them," Hubert said. "Maybe it was denial. Those days are gone. We are doing things to be the best team and best corporation we can be. We want to show everybody we care about them and we care about the community."

Fortune estimated the value of the Portland franchise at $283 million, behind only the Lakers, Knicks, and Bulls.

There were those throughout the NBA who weren't unhappy to see the Blazers taking a financial bath as well as a first-round playoff ouster.

"Around the league, most teams are delighted to see the Blazers lose games and money," wrote the *Portland Tribune*'s Dwight Jaynes. "They're seen as the rich bullies who have tried to buy a championship. In the league office, there is a similar attitude—this is the franchise that doesn't play by the same rules as everyone else."

* * *

Unlike the previous two seasons, the 2002–03 season began on a high note with a 102–90 victory over the Lakers behind 28 points from Rasheed Wallace. Portland led 60–40 at the half and 84–61 after three quarters. The Lakers were shorthanded—Shaquille O'Neal missed the game with a toe injury, Rick Fox sat it out due to a suspension, and Kobe Bryant left late in the game with an ankle sprain.

"Everybody can say they didn't have Shaq and Kobe got injured, but the standings say they got a loss and we got a win," said Stoudamire, who contributed 16 points, six rebounds, and six assists. "Everybody has their problems."

"That was a great exhibition by us," Pippen said. "We have to build on that. Phil [Jackson] would like to put an asterisk by the W, but it doesn't matter to me. A win is a win."

Bryant scored 25 points and grabbed 10 rebounds in 37 minutes before his injury. A reporter touched a nerve afterward when he asked about Patterson's defense.

"He does a good job of staying in front of me at times, but nobody can guard me one-on-one," Bryant said. "That's not what I do. I don't play one-on-one basketball. If you want to play one-on-one, holler at me in the offseason. We will go down to Ruckers [Park in New York] and do that whole little thing. During 82 games of the regular season, don't even holler at me about that."

The Blazers were a much different team the following night, getting drilled 100–72 by Sacramento at Arco Arena. The Kings breezed even without injured starters Chris Webber, Mike Bibby, and Doug Christie, as Peja Stojaković led the way with 26 points.

Wallace, who picked up his first technical of the season, had 24 points and nine rebounds. Wells struggled offensively with 11 points on 5-for-15 shooting in 21 minutes, and the playing time topic was again rearing its ugly head.

"We have a lot of guys, and it's tough to find your niche," Bonzi said. "I know I'm not in a flow, and it's tough to find it when you're not playing."

Two days later, the Blazers lost 96–79 to Denver. Toward the end of the game, the players were greeted by a chorus of boos from the sellout hometown crowd.

"Disgraceful," Patterson said afterward.

Cheeks often shouted directives from the sideline only to complain that the orders weren't being followed.

"That was as poor a game as any since I've been here," said Cheeks, uncharacteristically critical of his players. "There was nothing there—nothing. There was a lot of standing around. A lot of holding the ball. A lot of one-on-one. We would post the ball and everybody would stand around."

After an overtime loss to the Lakers at Staples Center, the Blazers were 1–3.

"Terrible," Pippen said. "We should have started this season off 4–0. Now we're in our fifth game looking for our second win."

Phil Jackson offered a review of the Blazers and couldn't resist a dig as usual.

"If they can do what they do against us—trap the ball, force us to turn it over, and run out for layups—they are going to score some points," the Lakers coach said. "Otherwise, scoring will be difficult for them. A lot of it is lack of an outside game. It's not an easy game when you don't have shooters. You can throw it to the big fella and cut, and it will change things up.

"I was surprised they gave up on Steve Kerr. He was effective for them as a mid-range and 3-point shooter. They miss that. Everybody else is take it to the hoop, drive it in there, and go one-on-one. There is not enough room on the court or enough balls for all of them to do that."

Portland would beat Memphis 94–88 in its next outing, but Anderson would be lost for four games with a concussion, and Sabonis would be out for a couple of weeks with a strained hamstring. After the victory, Pippen spoke up about wanting to have a larger role.

"I would like to get back to being a starter," he admitted afterward. "It's better for the team. It's tough being a leader when you go out there and you're already down 10 points and you don't have at the momentum. It's tough to come off the bench and get yourself going. I don't like going out there trying to play catch-up."

On November 9, the Blazers were on top of it in a 95–76 thrashing of San Antonio at the SBC Center. Wells scored 19 points off the bench, including a dizzying third-quarter array in which he accounted for six straight Blazer baskets.

But what would a Jail Blazer victory be without a bit of controversy?

Jeff McInnis notched his first DNP/CD (did not play/coach's decision) and didn't hide his feelings when asked about it afterward.

"Yeah, I'm mad," he said. "I want to play."

There was also Wells spitting on the Spurs' Danny Ferry as they walked to their respective benches during a timeout midway through the fourth quarter. Ferry complained about it to official Nolan Fine through the timeout and later received a technical when he tried to continue a dialogue.

"I was walking off the court, and it caught me off-guard," Ferry would tell the *Portland Tribune* later that season. "The more I sat there, the angrier I got. It is ridiculous, but there is nothing I can about it now. The guy is nuts. You never know what he's thinking. Every time you play him, it's an adventure. This was just something else. It has no place in the game."

A Wells-Ferry altercation the previous season had resulted in a double technical. Ferry told teammates that Wells had taunted him in games dating to last season, using the words "fucking honky" multiple times.

When asked after the game about the incident, Wells's response was, "I'm cool." It's a phrase he often used when choosing not to speak to reporters. Later, he said, "I don't know what's up with Danny Ferry. He's just got a problem with me. I don't have a problem with Danny Ferry."

Wells initially denied spitting on Ferry.

"He told me he didn't do it," Cheeks said after the game. "All I can do is take his word."

But there were witnesses, including Steve Jones, the television analyst for the Blazers, who made mention of it during the broadcast.

"Unfortunately, I saw it," Jones said. "I don't know what caused it. Usually something happens to precipitate something like that, but I didn't see anything. All I know is, there's not a good history between the two guys."

Corroborating evidence was provided by Spurs center David Robinson, who said he heard the spitting action as he walked to the bench. Robinson said he then turned and saw the saliva hanging off Ferry's face.

"It's a shame when you have somebody who decides that the best way to compete is to spit on somebody else," Spurs coach Gregg Popovich said. "Bonzi showed a lack of class. I can't imagine why there is any room for that in the game."

There had been at least two other times when players accused Wells of using racial epithets toward white players. During an exhibition game in October, Golden State forward Troy Murphy said Wells repeatedly trash-talked him, using the word "cracker."

The previous April, after a Blazer game at Dallas, Mavericks guard Nick Van Exel said Wells had scoffed at the Mavericks as "a bunch of soft-assed white boys." The comment, made public by Van Exel, created a stir in Dallas.

"I'm not aware of it," Cheeks would say. "If I had heard him say something like that, I would have addressed it, absolutely. There is no sense in saying something like that. I don't know the purpose of it."

It was unusual to have racial epithets tossed about publicly in the league, at least in recent history.

"I can't say I recall such an incident in all my [20] years in the NBA," league vice president Russ Granik said.

The next day, Wells played dumb when asked about the incident with Ferry.

"Incident? What incident?" he deadpanned. "There was no incident."

The Blazers suspended Wells for the next game, an 82–73 loss at Dallas.

"It's unfortunate for us this situation with Bonzi came about," Cheeks said after the loss to the Mavericks. "We could have used him because he is one of our best offensive players."

Later, Cheeks added, "It's Bonzi's word against whomever. They suspended him for allegedly spitting on someone. I didn't see it. I don't condone someone spitting on someone else, and it's unfortunate. For whatever reason, things are going to happen. Not just with our team, but with teams, period."

The coach stood up for his player.

"I don't think a man's character should be decided by one incident," Cheeks said. "Bonzi has had some problems, has done some things he has regretted, but I believe his parents raised him the right way. I believe Bonzi has been a very good character guy."

McInnis, who had not played against the Spurs, scored six points in 20 minutes of action against the Mavericks.

"I'm not going to make it a bigger deal than it has to be," McInnis said about his playing time. "I asked [Cheeks] what's up, and he told me he was working on some things on the rotation, that he wanted to see something. I just told him I wanted my chance, too."

The logjam at point guard was to be a consistent problem through the season.

"Jeff and Antonio wanted to play," assistant coach Herb Brown says now. "Each would ask, 'Why am I not playing?' But I thought Damon should be playing. I loved Damon. Every one of those games he sat, he'd be at the Rose Garden at 3:30 before a game, playing two-on-two, working out."

Portland finished a four-game road trip with an 86–82 loss at Houston, going 1–3 on the trip and falling to 3–6 for the season.

Stoudamire was off to a poor start, averaging 7.8 points while shooting .346. He had sat out the final 18 minutes of the Houston loss after exchanging harsh words with Cheeks on the sidelines.

Was Damon's benching the result of their exchange?

"Absolutely," Cheeks said afterward. "But it was my choice. When things go wrong, I have to try to right the ship."

It was important to Cheeks to be liked by his players—and they did like him. They respected him for his long, successful playing career. He often took part in shooting games with them after practice. Cheeks was by nature reluctant to come down on players for their behavior.

"It's easy to snap at somebody, to say that's not the right way," he said. "You have to maintain some level-headedness at a time like this. When things are going well, you can step on a person, but really, that's not the way to be. My mom always said, 'Treat people the way you want to be treated.'

"I can't make guys be me. We are all individuals, but I mentioned to them that I'm pretty much a character guy. I like my character to stand up for what it is. Long after I am done coaching or being around this game, I want people to say good things about me."

Dwight Jaynes of the *Portland Tribune* didn't believe either Cheeks or Whitsitt were up to the task. He wrote that Whitsitt was "without question the most despised team official in the history of this franchise."

"That he is still here is an incredible story," Jaynes wrote of the Blazers' president and GM. "Almost daily, I'm asked how he is still able to fool owner Paul Allen, and I'm way past being able to answer that question. It's inexplicable. He's spent millions of Allen's dollars with nothing to show for it in this town but ill will and hurt feelings. He needs to go and needs to go in a hurry.

"So does his coach. I'm sick of hearing what kind of a player Maurice Cheeks was. I'm tired of hearing how much the players like him. I believe him to be one of the least qualified people ever to have been handed an NBA team. His team, by its actions, doesn't seem to respect him or itself. . . . Cheeks is in no way the caliber of coach it's going to take, long-term, to deal with all the problems inherent to what has become an embarrassment of an organization. It's time to clean house."

The Blazers came out of their doldrums with a 112–88 thrashing of the Clippers at the Rose Garden. Anderson led the way with 28 points and nine rebounds while Wells added 21 points. Stoudamire, meanwhile, sustained the first DNP/CD (did not play/coach's decision) of his eight-year career.

Cheeks, who had admitted benching Stoudamire after their on-court exchange of words in the Houston loss, wasn't honest this time. Damon had also left the morning shootaround for what the team deemed "personal reasons."

Pippen started at the point and had nine points, five rebounds, and three assists in 24 minutes. McInnis was only 1-for-7 from the field with four points and seven assists in 29 minutes off the bench, playing alongside Pippen, who moved over to small forward for a while. Daniels also played 12 minutes, mostly behind Anderson at shooting guard.

"It had nothing to do with Damon, period," Cheeks said. "It was more or less that Jeff had played with the Clippers [the previous two seasons]."

Cheeks said he could have used Stoudamire in garbage time but chose not to do that out of respect for his standing on the team.

"The object of the game is to win," Cheeks said. "I'm very sympathetic to Damon not playing, but my allegiance is to the team. I changed the lineup just to try to get us to have a chance [to win], that's all. And it worked."

Before Portland's 98–84 win over Orlando on November 20, former

Blazer Shawn Kemp spoke to the media. Kemp had sacrificed $16 million in guaranteed salary over next two years so he could sign a one-year, $1.03 million free-agent deal with Orlando. No player in NBA history had ever done such a thing.

"I talked it over with my family and decided it was just time," Kemp said before the game. "I had been [in Portland] for two years. When you have played as long as I have, you have a gut feeling about things. It was time for me to go."

Kemp, who had signed a seven-year, $107-million contract with Cleveland in 1997, was to make $21.5 million that season and another $25 million in 2003–04. Kemp agreed to a buyout that resulted in him forfeiting $16 million to gain his release.

"It wasn't about money," said Kemp, who would turn 33 the following week. "I have been blessed in that aspect of life. It was personal. I am not going to play basketball forever. They have some great players on [the Blazers], but if I sat on the bench for two more years, I would have been pretty much ready to retire. I didn't want to go out like that."

Kemp accepted a buyout of about $30.5 million—not the $20 million Whitsitt had released to one media outlet. That irked Kemp, who wondered about the GM's motives: "Bob is Bob," he said. "Bob is going to do what he has to do. His reputation speaks for itself."

Once one of the most imposing big men in the game, Kemp's reputation had been sullied in recent years by

1. A *Sports Illustrated* story detailing that he had seven kids with five women at the time.
2. The demons of substance abuse, which came to light in Portland and resulted in his suspension for violation of the league's anti-drug program.
3. A battle of the bulge, the excess weight robbing him of the legs that earned him the nickname "Reign Man."

"It wasn't the Blazers doing it to me," Kemp said. "It was me. I knew I had to do something about the situation."

Kemp said he no longer drank alcohol or used cocaine. He said he was putting in extra workouts and had a chef cooking him meals.

"I don't know if you can ever say you have something beat, but I am [clean]," he said. "And I plan on living a healthy lifestyle the rest of my life."

The man taking Kemp's place in the rotation with the Blazers, Zach Randolph, was now a solid contributor off the bench, at times the team's most reliable inside threat with his left-handed baby hook and soft touch from the baseline. The second-year pro, only 20, was shooting .507 from the field while averaging 6.4 points and 3.2 boards in 12.5 minutes.

On November 21, the Blazers pulled out an 89–85 win over Seattle at KeyArena to run their record to 6–6. It was a good win, the Blazers rallying from a 13-point third-quarter deficit. Wells contributed 16 points, nine rebounds, four assists, and three blocks. One night after playing four minutes against Orlando, McInnis provided eight points, five rebounds, and three assists in 27 minutes.

"Mentally, I think this turns the corner for us," McInnis said. "Now we know we can win. We stayed together tonight. Nobody was arguing with each other. We just played hard."

Due to fog, the Blazers had bussed rather than flown to Seattle after the Orlando game. After the win over the Sonics, Cheeks gave Wallace and Stoudamire permission to drive home rather than ride on the team bus.

A friend, Edward Smith, was driving Stoudamire's yellow Hummer H2 when they were pulled over by police in Lewis County in Washington on Interstate-5 heading for Portland. A radar gun had the car at 84 miles per hour in a 70-mph zone.

During the traffic stop, the officer smelled marijuana and discovered a gram in the glove box.

From Sergeant Rob Huss' report:

> I immediately observed a strong and obvious odor of marijuana coming from the passenger side of the vehicle. [At first,] all three occupants acted as if they didn't know what I was talking about, denying that they had or were in possession of marijuana. I directed Stoudamire to exit the vehicle and Smith and Wallace to remain in the vehicle. Smith sarcastically and in a disgusted tone responded, "Man, I can't believe you're going to play it this way."

Huss requested a second trooper to respond to the scene, then advised Stoudamire of his Miranda rights. "Stoudamire's eyes appeared bloodshot and glazed," the report continued. "He indicated he had been drinking a Smirnoff Ice in the vehicle . . . he hesitantly admitted marijuana had been smoked in the vehicle but said it had all but 'burned up and/or smoked.' He said if there were more marijuana in the car, it was put in without his knowledge, possibly by the driver. He was placed in his patrol vehicle." Minutes later, trooper Brian Dorsey arrived at the scene.

> Wallace and Smith were directed to exit the vehicle and given Miranda rights. Wallace admitted he smoked one "J," that the pot had all been smoked and was all gone.[1]

The three men were placed in Dorsey's vehicle. Later arrived a third officer, Central K-9 officer Tracy Murphy, and a dog who was trained in drug detection. A small leaf of marijuana was found on the right passenger floorboard, as well as a bag of marijuana in the glove box.

Huss went back to the patrol vehicle, handcuffed Stoudamire, and placed him under arrest for marijuana possession. Murphy and Dorsey removed Wallace and Smith from Dorsey's vehicle, handcuffed them, and placed them under arrest as well.

All three men were cited for misdemeanor drug possession. Officers allowed the trio to continue their drive to Portland after determining the driver was not under the influence. Smith passed a field-sobriety test but admitted he had been smoking pot, as did Wallace and Stoudamire.

---

1   Urban legend has it that Wallace remarked, "No need to search the car. We already smoked all our weed."

Evidently, the officers felt Smith was not high enough for it to affect his driving.

Wrote Huss: "Although they initially denied possessing, smoking, or having knowledge of marijuana in the vehicle, Stoudamire, Wallace, and Smith were polite and respectful during the entire contact."

It was the first of four marijuana-related arrests involving Blazer players over a 12-month span and Stoudamire's second bust in nine months.

"The frustrating part of that era was, it seemed whenever you'd get some good momentum building on and off the floor, it was only a matter of time before something happened to derail it, and you went into crisis control," says former sportscaster Mike Barrett, who began with the club in 1999 and served as the team's television play-by-play voice from 2003–2016. "The Wallace/Stoudamire incident sticks out in my mind. I remember getting a phone call after it happened. It was a punch to the stomach, a 'here-we-go-again' moment.

"But I always caution fans against being too critical about those teams. I don't recall the Jail Blazers tag being used as much until they started losing. Don't act too high and mighty because you were cheering really loudly for that same group."

Even so, Barrett says, "the off-court stuff was always embarrassing, to be in another city and have people poke fun at you because you were involved with the team. That's when the Jail Blazer stuff got old. Any misstep by any player and it would be like setting you back to square one. It was unfair in some ways but, in other ways, the nickname was well-earned."

In the days that followed after the arrest, in his only public comment on the matter, Wallace said, "All I've got to say is, on December 6, the truth will come to the light."

That was the players' court date. Eventually, Wallace and Stoudamire agreed to separate plea bargain deals, and the misdemeanor charges were dropped.

* * *

The Blazers lost their next game to Sacramento, 95–94. It was only the

Kings' fourth victory in their last 44 visits to Portland. "A great win for us," coach Rick Adelman said.

Wallace started the game and was greeted by a smattering of boos, along with signs ranging from "It's all good RashWeed" to "Sign My Weed, Rasheed." He still led all scorers with 30 points while adding nine rebounds.

Stoudamire didn't play for the third time in four games, yet he stayed involved and was part of the team's huddles.

"I have a feeling it is all going to change for me sooner or later," he told a reporter after the game.

Two days later, on November 25, Ruben Patterson was arrested on a felony domestic assault charge against his wife, Shannon, at their Tualatin home. She had called police to the couple's home, where they found her with a cut finger and marks in other places. The alleged assault happened in front of the couple's two children, aged 12 and 10, turning it into a Class C felony under Oregon's Abuse Prevention Act.

Patterson was booked in the Washington County Jail, where teammate Anderson posted his $1,000 bail.

Through agent Dan Fegan, Shannon released a statement the following day:

> I made a statement that was accurate but, in the heat of the moment, was incomplete. Ruben and I had a disagreement . . . I want the public to know that Ruben did not assault me. I love my husband, and this is a private family matter. I'm embarrassed that it became public. This is something we are working out privately.

Cheeks said he took the back-to-back incidents personally.

"I pride myself in being a character kind of person, and when you talk about the Trail Blazers, you talk about me as well," he told the media. "You talk about the Damon-Rasheed thing, you talk about the Ruben thing—now it's part of me because I am the head coach. I have to try and find a way to rehabilitate this whole situation. Can I? I don't know. But I am in it with them."

The day after Patterson's arrest, the Blazers beat Houston 77–71 before an announced Rose Garden crowd of 18,088. The large number of empty seats were noticeable.

Patterson sat out the game under a one-game team suspension. Wallace, paying tribute to his teammate by wearing a "Rube 21" sweatband around his left bicep, scored all of his 16 points in the second half. Wells, who had also gone scoreless in the first half, finished with four points on 2-for-10 shooting.

"It wasn't a pretty game," Cheeks said. "It was an ugly game, basically."

Sabonis was a bright spot off the bench, collecting six points, nine rebounds, six blocks, and three assists in 27 minutes.

"What? You act like I never blocked six shots before," he deadpanned to writers afterward.

Stoudamire, playing for the first time in three games, entered with 3:37 left in the first quarter to loud boos. He missed both of his shots and went scoreless in nine minutes.

Cheeks said he understood if fans decided they would no longer support the team.

"I wouldn't blame them," he said. "I would understand. That's their right."

Whitsitt sounded a tough tone as he met with media before the game.

"I don't want players in situations where we even have to talk about this stuff," he said. "If later on there is guilt, or things are done in a certain way, there will be penalties. There will be discipline. There will be appropriate action. It can go anywhere from big fines to terminating contracts without pay.

"We are not there yet. The system has to play out. But this is not what we are trying to promote. This is not what we are about."

The Blazers lost their next game to New Jersey, 93–86, falling to 7–8 on the season. During the game, a member of the arena security force confiscated a sign from a fan that referred to the drug arrest of Wallace and Stoudamire.

When Stoudamire entered the game, he was booed loudly every time he touched the ball. But the boos subsided when he wound up having a great finish, scoring 14 points in 16 minutes—with 13 points in the fourth quarter—to lead a rally that fell short.

"Too much, too late," Cheeks malapropped, adding that he was proud of his players for mounting "a moral comeback."

Cheeks said late in the game he pulled Damon aside and said, "I hope we win this game, but if we don't, I'm very proud of you."

Stoudamire was as politically correct as possible afterward in his first meeting with the media in some time, although he did take a poke at his detractors.

"It hasn't been as tough as people might think," he said. "In the last month, what really happened is I separated a lot of fake people from my real friends and family and everybody who loves me. All I want is to be around positive people right now. I don't need to be around negative people."

As for his playing situation: "When I get into a game, whether it's two minutes or 25 minutes, I just want to play as well as I can. I've been biding my time, sitting on the bench, cheering people on. I'm mad, but I'm not going to sit and pout and be angry and not be happy for my teammates when they're doing well. I'm trying to be a good teammate, trying to be supportive of them."

With his team down and out, trailing 67–49 in the third quarter, Cheeks left his seat on the bench and took a seat in the second row. Later, he talked about how hard he worked to keep his team from thinking he had given up.

"Even when we're 25 points behind, I always stand up on the sideline," he said. "I don't want them to look up and see me sitting down over there and think that I've given up on them."

Why did he sit behind the bench, then?

"Well, you can't stand up all the time," he said. "It was my good luck seat. Every time I sat there, we did well."

On December 4, Dallas whipped Portland 103–88 as Dirk Nowitzki went for 26 points and 15 rebounds while Steve Nash scored 18 of his 20 points in the second half.

Wells, who was 3-for-12 from the field, was asked if the team's 7–9 record concerned him.

"Should it?" he asked. "You can't win them all."

Two days later, domestic abuse charges against Patterson were dropped. Whitsitt still fined him $100,000 for his conduct.

"Hopefully," Whitsitt said, "it helps people understand the direction we want to go."

The Blazers responded with consecutive double-digit wins against the Heat, Raptors, and Wizards before dropping their second consecutive game to the Nets. Two nights later, after it seemed like the Blazers were steadying the ship, they were blown out 101–79 at Milwaukee to drop to 10–11. Randolph tied his career high with 17 points on 8-for-11 shooting, but Wallace (eight points, nine rebounds) and Wells (10 points, one board) had subpar performances.

"We're mediocre," Stoudamire observed afterward. "That's the way we are playing. We win two, lose two, win three, lose three, win one, lose two. That's mediocre, man. We can't fool ourselves into thinking we are better than we are."

* * *

Just when it seemed like the Blazers were doomed to fall apart so early in the season, they made a complete about-face to become one of the top five teams in the NBA. Starting with a win over the Timberwolves, they went on a 22–5 tear to improve to 32–16 at All-Star break.

Before the streak began, Pippen let Whitsitt have it for shaking up the Blazers' roster after the 2000 Western Conference Finals ouster by the Lakers.

"It is always changes in Portland," Pippen said. "We come as close as anyone to beating the Lakers, then they let Jermaine O'Neal go. They go get Shawn Kemp—that had to be the worst move in pro sports. They have done the wrong things for the community because they broke up a team the fans could get behind. As a fan, you want to see things gradually improve. That's the way it was in Chicago. But it's been going the other way since I've been in Portland. Maybe I'll be the next one off the ship.

"You have to build relationships. You have to build chemistry. You can't do that in one season. How do you think guys respond when you pay them that kind of money? They think they have to go out and earn that money. They think they have to score. That kills chemistry. We will win some games, but when the dust settles, we will be under the dust."

* * *

On December 20 came one of the wildest scenes in Trail Blazer history.

Portland beat Golden State 113–111 at Oakland Arena on Wallace's buzzer-beating 16-foot jump shot.

As Wallace launched his game-winning shot, Wells—who finished with 28 points, six rebounds, and five assists—and the Warriors' Chris Mills were jostling for position. They were still tied up after Wallace's shot went through.

As Wells and Mills exchanged words and began pushing each other, the Warriors' Troy Murphy entered the fray and began a heated verbal exchange with Wallace. Wallace briefly broke away from teammates restraining him and made a run at Murphy, yelling, "I'm going to fuck you up." Wallace was finally bear-hugged by Cheeks. As that was happening, Golden State's Jason Richardson threw a punch at Wells.

Referees and coaches broke up the scrum, but the situation was made worse by fans throwing wads of gum and plastic beer bottles as the Blazers headed toward the locker room. One man was handcuffed and subdued by four security officers. He threw gum at Wallace, sparking another confrontation with several Blazers. Wallace tried to retaliate by reaching over a plastic barrier, and Randolph and Daniels briefly went into the stands to try to get the fan who was being led away.

"It was an unbelievable scene," says Bob Medina. "It carried over into the tunnel. And then the fans . . . it could have been another 'Malice at the Palace.' The type of guys we had on the team, they weren't typical NBA players. Most NBA guys talk a big [game]. These guys were like, 'Let's fricking go.' They were ready to throw down."

Afterward, Mills tried to get into the Blazers' locker room but was restrained.

"There was an entrance from the back side of the visitors' locker room," Medina recalls. "As the game ended, they had the fight, and fans were throwing beer. Our video guy, Tim Grass, was in our locker room. You can lock the back door from the other side. Tim had locked the door. Mills was pounding on the door trying to get in."

"Mills wanted a piece of Bonzi," Portland center Dale Davis recalls. "Then things got inflated. But security did a good job of defusing everything."

Temporarily, anyway. It wasn't just Mills. He had help from two teammates.

"Mills, Erick Dampier, and Gilbert Arenas came around to try to get into our locker room to get to Bonzi," remembers Jay Jensen, the Blazers' trainer at the time. "The door was locked. They couldn't get in."

Mills wouldn't be deterred.

"I looked out of our locker room and saw Mills in the tunnel, wearing a long trench coat, with his foot up against the wall," Jensen recalls. "I said to our security guy, Steve Warner, 'We can't have him here with players walking out. He can't be that close to our bus.' Steve and one of the Warriors' security guys told Mills he had to go, which he did."

Or didn't.

"After a game, I always ride with the equipment truck," Medina says. "When I walked out there after the game, I noticed Mills out there. He was looking in our bus. He got into his Range Rover. He was parked there with the lights off. I called Jay and said, 'Just so you know, Mills is out here by the bus. You need to call security.' It was like a scene from the wild, wild west."

After the players were loaded onto the team bus, the driver pulled out, and Mills pulled out his car at the same time. Another car—presumably, friends of Mills—pulled out, too.

"We start out toward the freeway and the cars park in front of the bus, a few yards away from us," Jensen says. "We were blocked. We couldn't get onto the freeway. These guys get out of their cars and start walking to us. Zach [Randolph] and some of our guys are trying to get off the bus to go fight with these dudes."

Warner got off the bus, but Cheeks yelled at him to get back on, that "we can get by them," Jensen says. Warner instructed everyone in the traveling party to get on the left side of the bus, opposite of Mills and his comrades.

"Somebody yelled at Arvydas, 'Get your big head over to the left side of the bus,'" Jensen says.

The bus got by the two cars, "and we were bobbing and weaving, and those guys got back in their cars and started chasing us as we made our way to the airport."

Jensen called officials at the "FBO" the private terminal in which the Blazers were to fly to Portland.

"I told them, 'We're coming in hot to the airport. We have to make sure the gate is open,'" Jensen says. "We went cruising into the FBO to get into the airport, and the two cars were behind us, outside the gate as the gate closed, the guys shaking their fists at us."

More than 15 years later, Jensen still shakes his head at the memory.

"We almost got hijacked," he says. "It was a scary deal. Some of the players who knew Mills said he was packing [a gun]. It could have escalated.

"I got home and got to bed that night and it was frightful. It was chilling. Very easily there could have been something stupid that happened. For somebody to stop and try to hijack an NBA bus and stop it from getting on the freeway, that's just unconscionable. Some serious things could have happened. That guy should have been banned from the NBA for life."

Mills was given a three-game suspension and a $15,000 fine by the NBA. Wells drew a two-game suspension for the fight at the end of the game, and Wallace was fined $15,000 for attempting to go into the stands.

"I've never seen anything like that, that's for sure," Cheeks would say later. "I've never seen a guy do anything like that. That can be scary, because you don't know what's going through a guy's mind."

Did the incident further tarnish the Blazers' reputation?

"Is that possible?" Cheeks asked with a grin, adding, "All I know is, it would feel a whole lot worse if we lost the game."

Mills later told the Bay Area media, "Bonzi Wells is a straight punk, with a capital 'P.' He's tough on the court. And I'll give it to the Blazers, their unity was there. They had all 12 players on the floor. When they all stand up, he feels invincible. That's cool, but he tried to sucker-punch me. Then he moon-walked like Michael Jackson back toward the tunnel. That's a punk move, and he's a punk."

Back in Portland, Cheeks would comment, "It's unfortunate for two reasons. One, we've been playing pretty good basketball, and Bonzi has been a big part of that. And with him out for two games, it's a setback we have to overcome."

* * *

The next night in Portland, the Blazers won their second straight game on a final shot. Anderson knocked down a 3-pointer with 1.4 seconds left to cap a 27-point night in an 81–80 win over Seattle, the Blazers' fifth straight victory.

In the fourth quarter, the home crowd welcomed Stoudamire back as one of its own. When he entered the game with eight minutes left, it was his first action in a week. He'd had three straight DNP/CDs. In his first seven NBA seasons, Stoudamire had experienced zero of them. In fact, he had started all but a handful of games over that duration.

Since becoming a reserve over the previous month, Stoudamire had shot .313 from the field while averaging 5.2 points and 2.1 assists in 17.9 minutes. It wasn't that much worse than his nine games as a starter, when he shot .346, averaging 7.7 points and 4.3 assists in 29 minutes.

Stoudamire had not been a fan favorite since his arrival in Portland in 1998, and it wasn't clear why. Perhaps some fans thought he made too much money. Others thought he shot too much, and not well enough, for a point guard. Cheeks had his own questions on the latter subject, wanting to convert him from a scoring point to a distributor.

Damon hadn't done himself any good by pouting about his situation at times, and he had come off as whiny in the eyes of many fans. His two arrests for pot possession over nine months further sullied his reputation. Since his move to the bench, fans greeted his entry into games as a reserve with a cacophony of boos.

Until that night against Seattle.

The previous week, Stoudamire—a Wilson High graduate—had contributed $250,000 to the drive to save Portland Interscholastic League spring sports. That may have put fans in a forgiving mood, and his surprise entry in the fourth quarter was greeted by a big ovation.

"You chastise your kid when he messes up," Anderson said after the game. "Then they came back and cheered him like they are supposed to. That gave him some energy."

Stoudamire didn't do anything special, scoring two points with two assists in his eight minutes.

"We needed a little energy," Cheeks said. "I thought Damon was the one who could give that to us. I pulled a rabbit out of my hat."

There was still a bottleneck at point guard. Cheeks preferred Pippen's length at the point, with McInnis backing him up. Stoudamire and Daniels were the odd men out. Damon already had nine DNP/CDs in the season. In one stretch, he played only eight minutes in seven games.

"People want me to complain about it, but I'm going to stay professional," Stoudamire said after the game. "I don't understand how I can go from starting to not playing at all, but I'm not going to pout. I'm a firm believer that something good is going to come out of this. I might be on the floor for us or in another jersey—who knows? But I'm 29, with a lot of good years ahead of me."

On December 28, Wells came back from a two-game suspension and, shrugging off an ankle injury, scored 32 points to lead Portland to a 119–113 overtime win over Sacramento at Arco Arena, the Blazers' seventh straight victory.

"After sitting out two games, my ankle would have had to be broken for me to stay out," Wells said afterward.

Portland was now 17–11 and had moved within four games of the Pacific Division–leading Kings (23–9).

The Blazers started a four-game road trip on December 30 with an 85–74 triumph over Detroit at the Palace at Auburn Hills, using a 15–0 run to break the tie and notch their fifth straight road win and eighth overall.

"We are fighting the stigma that we are bad guys," Anderson said. "The world is against us. We have been left no choice but to think it is just us now."

On New Year's Eve, playing their fourth game in five days, the Blazers fell 102–87 to Chicago at United Center as 20-year-old center Tyson Chandler went for 27 points and 18 boards.

"It has been a great run," Pippen said. "We just ran out of gas."

Wallace had picked up his game and was asked about his chances to make the All-Star Game.

"If I make it, cool—it's good for my contract, or whatever," he said. "If I don't, it's three or four days I get to spend at home and relax."

* * *

Randolph had joined the rotation early in the season and made solid contributions, averaging 6.9 points and 3.5 boards in 13.4 minutes while shooting .475 in the first 32 games.

Randolph had improved his work ethic during his second NBA season.

"Last year, Zach didn't do it religiously at practice," assistant coach Herb Brown said. "He would do it sometimes. This year, he is doing it every day in practice. It's like a light bulb went off, that we don't have Shawn anymore and we need somebody to back up at the four. He dedicated himself over the summer to getting better, and he has carried it over to our practices."

While Pippen was one of the league's most overpaid players at $19.7 million—a makeup for being underpaid all those years in Chicago— he also might have been the Blazers' MVP in 2002–03. The 37-year-old veteran couldn't bring it every night anymore, but the small forward-turned-point guard knew how to play, commanded respect from his teammates, could still knock down the big shot, and was a savvy defender.

After recuperating from knee surgery, Pippen had joined the starting unit in the fifth game and averaged about 32 minutes.

After a double-digit win over the lowly Cavaliers, and in the midst of moving up the Western Conference standings, a storm was brewing; the cloudburst happened during and after Portland's 100–92 home win over Memphis.

Wallace had enjoyed a near-career game with 38 points on 16-for-20 shooting to go with 10 rebounds. In the third quarter, referee Scott Wall had called a foul on Wallace. Wallace tossed the ball toward Wall, who had his back turned. Referee Tim Donaghy saw it and thought he was throwing the ball at Wall, giving him a technical. Wallace was angry but stayed in the game.

"Donaghy should never have gotten involved," Portland assistant coach Dan Panaggio says. "Rasheed was talking to [referee] Steve Javie. They were having a reasonable conversation. If Rasheed was out of line, Javie never needed anybody to bail him out. Then in comes Donaghy from left field and T's him up."

As luck would have it, after the game, the three officials were leaving via the Rose Garden loading dock while Wallace was standing there chatting with Grizzlies guard Brevin Knight. According to witnesses, Wallace noticed Donaghy and shouted, "That was a bullshit call on the tech, and I'm gonna get my money back."

Donaghy shouted back, "Watch the tape." Wallace removed his coat, took some steps toward him, and said, 'No, you watch the tape,' and cursed at him, raising his arms as if to throw a punch. "I'm going to kick your ass, you motherfucker." When Donaghy flinched, witnesses said Wallace mocked him and made more threats before several people intervened, and the incident ended.

The NBA launched a two-day investigation following the altercation. Donaghy told league officials that when Wallace charged him, "my life flashed before my eyes." The league issued a seven-game suspension. Stu Jackson, the league's executive VP/basketball operations, said Wallace's "prior indiscretions" with referees were considered when deciding on his punishment.

"That Wallace could be so out of control in a situation like that speaks volumes about his poise, self-control, and intellect," *Portland Tribune's* Dwight Jaynes wrote. "Or lack of same."

Jaynes added: "Bob Whitsitt has built a franchise where boorish behavior has become commonplace. And it isn't just our city or the Blazer organization that is embarrassed by that. It is all of pro basketball."

There was some irony to Donaghy's involvement. In 2007, he would plead guilty to two federal charges that he had placed bets on NBA games in which he had officiated. He would serve 15 months in prison.

"Rasheed was a fortuneteller, wasn't he?" Panaggio says today. "He was trying to tell the world something."

Ironically, Wallace had gone from an NBA-record 41 technical fouls in 2000–01 to 27 in 2001–02 to only five in the first 30 games that season.

"I believe Rasheed has made some major changes," Cheeks said. "If he's going to change, the officials have to do some changing as well. I don't believe it's all on Rasheed. Two people had that exchange. It wasn't just Rasheed."

Referees did appear to be cutting him some slack. He continued to argue a great portion of his personal foul calls—and sometimes those of his teammates.

"Rasheed is better this season," said one referee, who asked for anonymity. "Instead of just yelling and screaming at every call, he has learned to pick his spots. But he is still a train wreck waiting to happen."

On January 18, as Wallace began serving his suspension, Kevin Garnett went for 31 points and 20 rebounds as Minnesota pulled out a 104–98 victory. But the Blazers rebounded with a five-game win streak, beginning with a 112–110 double-overtime victory at Atlanta.

They closed out their road trip 4–0 with an impressive 100–93 victory over Dallas. The Mavericks, who came in with the NBA's best record at 34-9, were outrebounded 50–34. Wells scored 18 points and tied his career high with 14 rebounds. Randolph scored all 16 of his points in the second half.

"Rasheed who?" quipped Davis, straight-faced before breaking into a laugh.

"We don't like it like this, playing without Rasheed," Wells said. "But it helps our character out a little bit."

It was the first four-game road sweep by a Portland team since 1991. In 24 years as a player and coach in the NBA, Cheeks said he had never experienced a 4–0 road trip.

With Wallace set for his return, the *Portland Tribune* polled six of the league's general managers with questions about Wallace. All of them requested anonymity.

"A hell of a talent who has helped his club win games," one GM said. "That said, he has serious lack-of-control issues. How do you control it? Wow, you're waving a magic wand there."

"The things I've heard about him are that he is a great guy off the court, a good family man," another GM said. "But he is an enigma in a lot of ways. It's not like he's some rotten guy you don't want. But he has been getting out of control for a long time."

Asked if they would want him on their team, five of the six said they wouldn't.

"The answer is a quick no," one said.

"We have a mature team with a solid sense of who we are and how we want to play and how we want to fit together," a second GM said. "I wouldn't take a chance on a guy who could disrupt that."

"Not in our situation, with our youth," a third GM said. "There is enough poison in the league."

But a fourth GM had a different view: "I'd be interested if I thought I could help him, because he is a great player."

* * *

With Wallace back in the fold and collecting 28 points and eight rebounds, Portland ended January with a 107–94 whopping of Chicago, its 19th win in 24 games. Sabonis was good off the bench, contributing 13 points on 6-for-11 shooting with five rebounds in 20 minutes.

Cheeks called the Lithuanian "our relief pitcher," but he was really more like a fireman, coming to the rescue when the Blazers smelled smoke. On the second of back-to-back games, he was often ineffective, but there were few players who could match him on his good nights.

"He does so many things for you," Cheeks said, "and some of them don't show up in the stat sheet. He can change a game. There aren't too many players you can say that about. Sabas is unique."

Cheeks played with another Hall of Fame center, Moses Malone, and so was familiar with dominant big men.

"Moses was brute force," Cheeks said. "Sabonis is big and strong, but he has some finesse. I didn't know until I got him that he had that kind of ability to pass. He has great hands and an understanding of the game."

* * *

With the February 20 trade deadline looming, Stoudamire had decided he wouldn't ask for a trade.

"I'm going to leave it alone," he said. "This summer, all parties will want to visit, but not right now."

There were still times, though, when he didn't know if he was going to play.

"This is the least fun time of my career," he said candidly. "Everybody knows I'm frustrated by the situation, but if I kill myself over it, it's just going to make me miserable. There's no need for me to go up to Seattle to holler at the dude [Whitsitt]."

Pippen was sensational in a 96–89 win at Orlando, collecting 25 points, 17 rebounds (one shy of his career high), and seven assists with no turnovers in 37 minutes. Wells and Patterson, meanwhile, used physical defensive play to hold Magic star Tracy McGrady to 10-for-26 shooting on the night.

"They are right there at the top [of the best teams in the league]," McGrady said afterward. "They have a lot of talent. When those guys put their minds to it, put that craziness behind them and go out and play, they are one of the best teams in the league."

Pippen followed the Magic game with another outstanding all-around performance, piling up 26 points on 9-for-14 shooting to go with six rebounds, four assists, and five steals in 34 minutes for a 101–87 win at Miami.

"Scottie absolutely dominated that game," Heat coach Pat Riley said. "He did everything he had to do to get his team over the top."

Wallace picked up a third-quarter technical after snapping at referee James Capers, then scored 10 points in the final six minutes of the period.

"Getting animated fueled Rasheed," Cheeks said. "I certainly don't want him to take it to another level and get thrown out of the game, but it picked up his game a little bit."

Portland won the game at the foul line, attempting 32 free throws to seven for Miami. Riley took offense at the kibitzing the officials did with the Blazer players.

"That was a travesty," Riley said. "I thought I was at the Comedy Store, watching some sort of comedy out there. It was so unprofessional from a standpoint of officiating a game and getting into dialogues and talking to players and smiling with them. It was absolutely a joke. I would like to have heard some of the stories that were being told. It was uncalled for."

Going into the All-Star break, the team that had started the season 10–11 went into the break with a 32–16 record, half a game back of the Pacific Division–leading Kings.

In one of Cheeks's typical malaprops, he remarked, "It's probably an unfortunate time for us to go on break, because we have been playing so well. But I guess we need a chance to rejuvenate ourselves."

Had there been any more spring in the Blazers' step, they would have been bouncing into orbit.

After making the All-Star Game in 2000 and 2001, Wallace was left off the West roster for the second straight year. His seven-game suspension hadn't changed his on-court deportment much, if at all. He may have toned down the language he had used during his record-setting technical spree in previous years, but he still found time to complain about virtually every foul called on him or his teammates or calls that weren't made against opponents.

After calling a foul against Wallace in one game, veteran official Ronnie Nunn mused to reporters sitting courtside: "And he agreed with it. That's amazing."

* * *

Portland came out of the All-Star break with a heart-breaking 116–111 overtime loss to San Antonio at the Rose Garden. Rookie guard Manu Ginobili hit a go-ahead 3-pointer—his only basket of the game—with 42 seconds left in the extra session. Tim Duncan was magnificent with 36 points, 15 rebounds, seven assists, and five blocked shots in 46 minutes.

All three of Sabonis's NBA coaches happened to be at the game against the Spurs. Besides Cheeks, P. J. Carlesimo was Gregg Popovich's chief assistant with San Antonio, and Mike Dunleavy was doing TV analyst work for the Spurs.

"The way he plays is like John Stockton—close to the floor," Carlesimo said of Sabonis. "The great players learn to do other things as they get older. I wouldn't be surprised if he's still playing when he's 48."

"Sabas has been that way for as long as I can remember," Dunleavy said. "His game has never been tied into speed and quickness. He has learned to play within his physical limitations."

Though Achilles tendon and knee surgeries had robbed Sabonis of the bounce in his legs years before, he was playing with more pep this season than he had during his final year playing for Dunleavy in 2000–01. He had missed only three of the Blazers' first 49 games, all because of a sore hamstring in early November. Cheeks was also limiting the giant's minutes; he had seen over 23 minutes in only four games all season.

"But sometimes he is so good," the coach said, "it's hard to take him out."

On February 21, the Blazers lost a rematch with the Lakers, 92–84, as Bryant exploded for 40 points. Bryant, on one of the great rolls of his career, hit the 40-point barrier for the eighth straight game, the first player to do so since Michael Jordan in 1986.

The next night, Milwaukee won 93–90 after the Blazers blew a 10-point lead with seven minutes to play. With 10 seconds left and the score 93–90, Cheeks brought on Stoudamire, who hadn't played all game. Damon had played only once in six games since the All-Star break and hadn't taken a 3-point attempt in almost three weeks. His game-tying attempt in the final seconds was short. "Damon is one of our best 3-point shooters," Cheeks said. "I know he hadn't been in the game, but I decided to put him in. I didn't know if he was going to get the shot, but I was comfortable with him shooting it."

The play was designed to get a shot for Wallace popping out high, or to Pippen along the baseline.

"We were looking at a prayer," Cheeks said.

Stoudamire took the inbounds pass, threw it to Wallace who, under heavy defensive pressure from Anthony Mason, threw it back to Damon.

"I was hoping I could decoy the whole play myself," said Stoudamire. Instead, he had to take the prayer, which went unanswered.

On March 2, Wells exploded for 37 points as the Blazers blasted Detroit, 103–86. Wells always used playing against the Pistons as motivation; they had drafted and then traded him to Portland for a future first-round pick.

"It was special going against the team that drafted me and let me go without giving me a chance to play for them," Wells said. "It was my way of saying 'thank you' for putting me in a better position. They traded me for nothing, and that leaves a bad taste in your mouth. Whenever I get a chance to show them what they gave up on, I try to do it."

Stoudamire moved ahead of McInnis for backup point guard duty, drawing a 21-minute stint off the bench. McInnis, who played four mop-up minutes, said the demotion caught him by surprise.

"I was a little surprised, too," Cheeks said in another one of his off-the-wall comments. "I just did it. I didn't go into the game thinking about it. I wanted some hard, on-the-ball pressure when they brought in Hubert Davis, and I automatically said Damon's name."

On March 5, the Blazers lost 98–92 to Phoenix at America West Arena, shooting only .383 from the field. In the second half, Wallace answered a Pippen comment with an obscenity as they walked to the Blazer huddle during a timeout. Pippen was burned about it but chose to keep mum afterward.

"I still have to live here," he told a reporter who inquired about the scene.

The next night, Portland bottomed out in an 88–60 beatdown by the 76ers, one of worst home defeats in franchise history. It was a one-man show by Allen Iverson, who torched the Blazers for 36 points. They were playing the second of back-to-back games, but that was no excuse for shooting .361

from the field, including 0-for-10 on 3-point attempts. It was the second-lowest scoring output by a Portland team, two short of the 58 scored against Cleveland in January 2001.

Pippen's knee was sore again. It seemed that when Scottie didn't play well, the team often struggled.

"If I can pick up my play," he said, "the team tends to play a lot better."

When things were going poorly for the Blazers—and that was certainly the case against the 76ers—Wallace and Wells weren't a pretty sight. They spent much of their time sniping at the referees. Cheeks was mostly an enabler, supporting his stars no matter what path they took. It was left to Pippen to try and keep his teammates in line. In many ways, he was "Coach Pippen."

"I just try to utilize my leadership," he would say after the game. "If that's considered coaching, I probably do a hell of a lot. I have to talk and communicate things, make sure we are all running at the same speed, executing the same things."

Portland improved to 41–22 with a 92–77 trouncing of Seattle at KeyArena on March 11. Wallace scored 23 points, Anderson had 18, and Randolph provided 17 off the bench.

Patterson started in place of Wells, who had been suspended for one game for insubordination following a practice run-in with Cheeks. "It's an isolated incident," Cheeks told the media. In fact, it was Bonzi's third suspension of the season.

Sources said Cheeks had pushed for a two-game suspension, but Whitsitt held it to one, hoping to make the transgression appear less serious to the public. Years earlier, Dunleavy had run into the same issue with Whitsitt when wanting to discipline Wallace.

"I don't expect any lingering effect," Whitsitt said. "I expect Bonzi to be ready to roll, full speed, tomorrow."

Wrote Dwight Jaynes: "The Whitsitt philosophy is quite clear. Minimize the public relations impact, not the actions. Cover up when you can. Spin the truth."

The following evening, with Pippen sidelined by a sore knee, Stoudamire gained his first start since November 3. "Mighty Mouse" came through with a 20-point, seven-rebound, seven-assist masterpiece in a 125–103 win over Toronto, hitting 8-of-10 shots from the field. Did it serve as a showcase game against a team that might want to regain his services?

"The thought definitely entered my mind," Stoudamire admitted afterward.

The Blazers shot a blistering .641 from the field, the sixth time in eight games they'd been better than 50 percent. Cheeks started Patterson ahead of Wells but said it had nothing to do with the practice spat between coach and player. After victories over Indiana and Seattle with Patterson as a starter, Cheeks said, he saw no reason to change. Ruben scored 14 points and helped hold Vince Carter to 21 points.

Would he continue to bring Bonzi off the bench?

"Could be," Cheeks said. "I'm not sure."

Two days later, the Blazers opened a three-game road trip with a 90–79 loss at Philadelphia, the second defeat by the 76ers in eight days.

Stoudamire, starting again in place of Pippen, scored 16 points. McInnis also sat out the game with an injury. Wells continued his bumpy transition from starter to reserve, going for season lows in minutes (nine) and points (two).

"My role is still the same," Wells said, which was not the case. "I just do my job when I get called, and that's all I can do. The coach is the main guy, and whatever the coach wants, I've got to roll with it. I'm a team player."

Then came some very bad news: Pippen needed surgery on his ailing left knee and would be sidelined for three weeks. The hope was that he would be able to come back for at least a couple of games before the playoffs opened.

* * *

It was a special occasion on March 25 at the Rose Garden. In his final Portland appearance as a player, the retiring Michael Jordan scored 25 points on 11-for-19 shooting, dishing out seven assists and grabbing five rebounds in Washington's 95–91 win before a standing-room-only crowd of 20,580.

A pregame video tribute included Phil Knight's playful admonition that if the NFL's Jerry Rice can go six more years, so should Michael. A long standing ovation during introductions inspired goosebumps, and a rousing ovation with Jordan at the foul line in the waning seconds was a final send-off.

"They appreciate the way I play the game here," Jordan told the media afterward. "It inspires me. It is a great way to leave the game. They don't have to give me any presents or single me out. Just the respect the fans pay me means a lot. I know I make a difference in someone's life."

Wizards point guard Tyronn Lue jitterbugged through the Portland defense for 21 points. Wells led the Blazers with 20 points and 10 boards off the bench. The loss dropped the Blazers (44–26) to 6–6 in March and allowed Minnesota to vault into a one-game lead for the No. 4 seed.

On March 28, the Blazers showed some life, clobbering the team with the West's best record, Dallas, 112–95.

Wallace led the way with 20 points, Stoudamire had 17 points and five assists, and Wells contributed 11 points, seven rebounds, and six assists.

"You're not going to win all the time in this league, but we are still in this," Wells said. "We are still one of the top four teams, and we still have time to prove our doubters wrong."

Davis scored all 16 of his points in the third quarter. "Probably the most I've scored in a quarter since high school," he said.

The reserve center had been playing poorly for a week, so he shaved his head before the game to change things up.

"Usually, when I'm in a funk, I go back to my old roots," Davis said. "I go penitentiary style."

Two days later, Qyntel Woods was arrested for driving more than 80 mph south of the Terwilliger curves on I-5 while smoking pot.

When police pulled over his 2003 Cadillac Escalade, they discovered warm ashes and smelled burnt marijuana. Woods didn't have a license or insurance and instead used two credit cards and his own basketball trading card for identification.

"Apparently, he left his Malibu Grand Prix license at home," wrote the *Portland Tribune*'s Dwight Jaynes.

In the police report, the officer said Woods told him that he had smoked pot for about three years and wanted to quit but was addicted. "He was very worried about how this would affect his NBA career," the report said.

Woods had driven in Oregon for six months without a license or insurance. His Tennessee license was under a one-year suspension after a DUI conviction in Mississippi. The suspension date had passed, but he hadn't reapplied for his license in Tennessee. The rookie forward was arrested for speeding, possession, and no insurance or registration.

Woods admitted in pre-draft interviews with NBA general managers that he had used marijuana, though he claimed that was "in the past." He slipped from a projected top-10 pick to No. 21, where the Blazers took him. At the time, Whitsitt had addressed the drug issue, saying, "It's always a concern. You spend a lot of time researching all the players. We were very tuned into it last year and the year before."

Woods was not suspended or placed in rehab. The Blazers used him for one minute the next night in a 100–86 home win over Golden State.

A couple of days later, Pippen—still rehabbing from knee surgery—unveiled some feelings during an in-depth interview with the *Portland Tribune*. The veteran was asked if he were embarrassed by the rash of incidents involving teammates.

"I hope it doesn't reflect on me, yet we are all members of this team," he said. "It looks bad when players are still getting caught up in the same old bullshit, instead of being at their houses where they are safe. What the fuck are they doing out there on the road? Why even go out to a party? Have your own party. If you have people you want to hang out with, you have a house—why do you put yourself in jeopardy? You are an icon in this community.

"People don't stand for that kind of behavior, and they shouldn't. You get into your fancy-ass car and start flying down the highway at those kind of speeds . . . I mean, yeah, it is embarrassing when shit like that happens.

People see us as a group and it's like, ah man, those knuckleheads, those Jail Blazers."

Pippen said it bothered him "a lot."

"I'm sure people look at it as if there is no leadership when the guys are off the court," he said. "As a player, you are your own man. You make your own decisions. You are responsible for your own actions."

Earlier in the season, Pippen had laid into Whitsitt. Did he have any regrets about his comments about the Blazer's GM?

"Hell, no."

Had things changed?

"Not that I've seen. He has no attentiveness to this team. He doesn't know what he brought in, how it is responding, what the practice habits are like, nothing."

Pippen had arrived in Portland in 1999 hoping to add at least one more championship to his resume. Did it disappoint him that he hadn't accomplished that?

"Not when they destroyed the team after my first year. That is the only thing that disappointed me. [Whitsitt] said he had all these warriors, and we were going to get all this stuff accomplished. I was thinking I was coming in to play with all these guys. He made the trade to bring me here, and he dismantled the team the year after. That is the one thing I regret about coming to Portland when he did that. We had nice players here. But I guess he has always done that. Bob is always going on trading sprees."

Pippen said he had tried to inspire his teammates to push themselves to the limit.

"But it's like beating a dead horse. All of a sudden, it will click. We will go on a spurt. Then it's like, 'OK, that's not us.' We can't get from A to Z."

Would Pippen like to see Wallace step up and share more of the leadership?

"Rasheed is who he is. You are not going to change him. He has played for a number of coaches here, and I don't see a lot of change."

Would Wells be capable of taking more leadership?

"Bonzi is a great talent, but he hasn't put himself at the level where he is consistent. If he were consistent, he could probably be an All-Star candidate. But you have to show that you have grown, that you have matured, that you can bring it for 82 games. Every single night. You are getting paid to perform. That is why our league suffers because they are paying all these cats all the money at a young age, but teams don't get the players' attention. They don't bring it every night. They don't have to now."

Pippen had done it at the highest level for a long time. He didn't suffer fools gladly, especially when they were teammates.

"Scottie was a professional," says Bob Medina. "The way he ate, the way he practiced, the way he carried himself, the way he helped other players.

"I remember his first game as a Blazer. We were ahead, but the opponent made a run. Rasheed and another player started to argue with two minutes left, Dunleavy called a timeout. Scottie said, 'Hey, calm down, we're going to win this game. We're going to get a stop here.' And we did. He was a calming presence."

* * *

As the Blazers swung into the final two weeks of the regular season, Cheeks said all the adversity would have a silver lining.

"Because of the things that have happened," he said, "we have become more of a family."

And then, there was a family feud.

On April 2, during a practice at the team's Tualatin training facility before a home game with Utah, Patterson and Randolph got into an altercation that would live in Blazer lore.

Patterson had a habit of giving the business to younger players, such as Randolph and Woods.

Randolph and Woods, says Medina, "were very close."

"They were always together," Medina says today. "They were like little puppies—pushing each other, horsing around. They were like brothers."

"Zach and Qyntel made a pact," says Herb Brown, then an assistant coach. "They told each other, 'If Ruben goes after one of us and tries to Bogart us, the other guy is going to stick up for him.'"

"It had been brewing between Ruben and Zach," says Jay Jensen, then the team's trainer.

It started during an incident the previous season.

"Sometimes horseplay would get out of hand," Jensen says today. "They were horsing around in the locker room before practice. You could hear them egging each other on. Rasheed was involved.

"Zach and Ruben started wrestling. Ruben was so dang strong. He picked Zach up and threw him to the ground, and it bruised Zach's butt. He could hardly walk for a while. He was limping. By the time practice began, Zach hadn't forgotten."

"He body-slammed me on my ass," Randolph would say.

The second incident happened as Cheeks was sending the players through a scrimmage session. Woods, who was on Randolph's team, was guarding Patterson.

"Qyntel was a pretty athletic guy," Medina says. "It was one of those days when he was getting the better of Ruben, and Ruben was getting frustrated. Guys on his team were giving him a hard time, like, 'Hey, stop the guy.'

"Ruben started playing more physical with Qyntel, fouling him, trying to post him up. Qyntel was a street guy. He was a fighter. He was a tough guy, too. It started to get physical. There were no referees. Ruben was backing Qyntel down and beasting him. It got into a push-and-shove thing."

Randolph threw an initial punch that landed. Players moved in to separate the two. Chris Dudley and Dale Davis grabbed Patterson. As Ruben was wrapped up, "Zach punched him in the eye," Medina says.

"Ruben went straight to the ground," Medina says. "For a few seconds, he was out cold. As he was coming to, Coach Cheeks moves in and says, 'Zach, you and Qyntel get out of here, now.'"

Randolph and Woods were hurried out the building by assistants Dan Panaggio and Jimmy Lynam, "before Ruben killed them," Panaggio says.

"Coach Lynam comes into the training room with blood all over his shirt, hustling Zach and Qyntel out the door," Jensen says.

A dazed Patterson, meanwhile, was sitting in a pool of blood from the sucker punch.

"As Ruben was coming to and seeing his own blood, he went into a fury," Medina says. "They couldn't hold him back. He took off running to the locker room. He was not going to let it end like that."

"Ruben escaped," Panaggio says. "He was like a raging bull. Jimmy and I looked at each other like, 'What do we do now?'"

"There were people trying to grab him and stop him," Jensen says. "Ruben was like a crazed animal. It was a horrific, surreal sight."

"It was bad," Dudley says today. "When you have big, strong men throwing real men punches, bad things happen. I'm sure if you talk to Zach now, he regrets it. I'm sure he would say, 'I was young and shouldn't have thrown the punch.'"

Randolph says as much . . . sort of.

"Just something that happened in the heat of things," he says today. "You regret lots of stuff, but things happen."

But Randolph knew he was out of line for being the third man in.

"It was a nothing thing between Ruben and Qyntel, just Ruben being Ruben," Panaggio says. "He was mischievous but had no bad bones in his body."

All of Randolph's teammates thought he was out of line.

"We have to accept Zach with open arms," Stoudamire, a team co-captain, said at the time. "What he did was wrong, but you still have to accept him because he's still part of the team."

The next day, Cheeks and Whitsitt addressed the situation to the media.

"I've been around a long time, and things happen in practice," Cheeks said. "But this one was more serious. I don't know if it will shake the team, but this is going to test my coaching skills, just in trying to keep us together. We've been on a pretty good roll, and it's unfortunate this has to happen. I have to make sure our family stays together."

In a prepared statement, this was Whitsitt's message: "While these types of disagreements happen at practice during the course of a season due to the physical and competitive nature of basketball, this instance crossed the line. This type of behavior will not be tolerated by our organization without the individuals being held accountable for their actions."

Randolph was suspended for two games and fined $100,000. Patterson, meanwhile, was on probation until May 14 from the case in which he entered a modified guilty plea on a sexual assault charge involving his nanny.

"Ruben couldn't afford to get in trouble about anything," Medina says. "The next day, we were playing Utah. He came to the Rose Garden before the game with his wife, Shannon. His eye was swollen. Jay Jensen was looking over Ruben, and Whitsitt came into the room. She saw him and said, 'Something needs to be done about what happened. Look at this man here. He's his kids' hero.' Ruben was sitting there like a little puppy, his head down."

Speaking to reporters, Patterson took the high road . . . sort of.

"I forgive him," he said of Randolph. "He's my teammate. He made a mistake, and I can't retaliate, try to fight him or beat him up, because I'm on probation and I would get in trouble. I was pissed about the situation, but we have to try to win, so I'm going to let it ride."

Patterson played 10 minutes with a swollen left eye in the 93–88 loss to the Jazz, going scoreless with no rebounds and two turnovers while complaining of obstructed vision. The next day, X-rays showed a fractured left eye socket.

"I'm an animal," he told the media, "so I'll be OK."

Two days later, after a 122–100 win at Golden State, owner Paul Allen released his own statement on the situation.

> As an owner, I take player behavior very seriously. We all expect a lot from our team, and the Blazers have to be accountable for doing what's right for the team, the fans, and the community—and players need to be held responsible. Let there be no mistake that unacceptable conduct will not be condoned. Everyone at the Blazers will tackle these issues head-on—and we are prepared to suspend players, levy heavy fines, and trade or release a player if that becomes necessary. The community deserves a team of which we can all be proud, and I am fully committed to improving the Blazers' conduct on and off the court.

The scene was ugly at the Rose Garden the following night as the Blazers fell 97–78 to Minnesota, dropping them to 47–29 and leaving them a half-game behind the Timberwolves in the battle for the No. 4 seed in the West.

Boos cascaded throughout the Garden among those still on hand for the final, sorry minutes.

There was a chill in the locker room afterward. A few of the players, including Patterson, left without speaking to the media. Wells shouted an obscenity to Randolph, who had three points and one rebound in 10 minutes, as he answered a few questions. Randolph and Patterson, dressing a few stalls apart, never spoke or made eye contact.

Patterson, who had two points on 1-for-8 shooting with three rebounds, later told writers he couldn't retaliate against Randolph "because I am on probation, so I would get in trouble."

The better thing, of course, would have been for Patterson to say he wouldn't retaliate against a teammate because it was the right thing to do.

"In a basketball sense, I am frustrated," said Derek Anderson, who rarely uttered a discouraging word. "The hard thing is, sometimes we understand the problem, but then it gets to the point where you have to fix it, and it doesn't get done."

A testy Cheeks walked out of media room in the middle of a question. Asked about Wallace's propensity to shoot from the perimeter rather than near the basket, Cheeks responded, "We always, for some reason, come in here and talk about Rasheed taking a jump shot. Yeah, Rasheed takes a lot of jump shots, and I would rather have him on the post more times than not. But let's make it clear—it wasn't why we lost the game."

After rehabbing following left knee surgery, Pippen had expected to make his comeback in a starting role against the Spurs on April 9. But he awoke on game day and noticed a buildup of fluid in his left calf, an apparent side effect from the March 18 surgery. He tried to run during the morning shootaround but couldn't go. "The calf is so tight, I can't even run," he said.

With four games left, the Blazers (48–30) now held a half-game lead over Minnesota (48–31) in the battle for fourth place and home-court advantage.

On April 11, Portland lost at Memphis, 96–93, squandering a 20-point lead in the process. Randolph, starting at center in place of an injured Davis, had a monster game with 31 points and 20 rebounds while Wells contributed

24 points and 10 boards, yet the Blazers dropped out of fourth place and into a tie with the Lakers for fifth in the West.

"It's the same thing, over and over and over again," Stoudamire said. "I don't have any answers. The worst thing is, we are going backward. We have to suck it up a little bit more."

The Lakers had won nine of 10, and the Blazers had lost seven of 11, but Portland came out victorious against its LA foe, 101–99, two nights later. Wallace gunned in a wide-open 3-pointer for the game-winning shot with 4.3 seconds left for the Blazers, who shot .519 from the field.

"I want home-court advantage," Wells said. "We were down a bit after losing to Memphis, but to come back against the world champions is big and says a lot about the character of this team."

Phil Jackson was always happy to rain on the Blazers' parade, and he did while speaking with reporters before the game.

"Bob [Whitsitt] delivers great talent to his coaches," the Lakers coach said. "He has been known for that for 15 years, in Seattle and now here, where he has gone out and said, 'Here's the best talent; you can sort it out and figure it out as a coaching staff.' On the one hand, that's a gift. On the other hand, it sometimes can be a burden, and perhaps it has become a burden here."

With the Lakers, Jackson added, "We always say you can have an outlaw or two on the team, but you have to have good characters, too. You can always have a couple of guys come in as long as they feel the presence of those players who are toeing the mark, and then they'll be persuaded to be in the right element."

On April 14, the Blazers entered the final two games of the regular season at 49–31 and in fifth place in the West, still in position to finish either fourth, fifth, or sixth. If they were to lose the final two games against the Suns and Clippers, they might avoid the Lakers and get Dallas, considered a more favorable first-round matchup.

"We're trying to win all our games," vowed Cheeks. "We're not trying to avoid anybody."

The following night, the Blazers roughed up Phoenix 120–102, shooting .571 while keeping alive hopes for home-court advantage.

Randolph, starting again in place of the injured Davis, scored 27 points while Wells went for 21 points, seven rebounds, and five assists. Pippen returned after missing 17 games, getting seven points, three rebounds, two assists, and two steals in 17 minutes off the bench.

"I have a great feel about us," Pippen told the media after the game.

Why? "Because I'm back," he said.

Portland went into the final game against the last-place Clippers knowing it would play one of three teams in the first round: the Timberwolves, Lakers, or Mavericks.

In the last way the Blazers wanted to finish the season, they were blown out by the Clippers 107–93 at Staples Center to finish 51–31 and fall to the West's No. 6 seed, setting up a first-round playoff date with No. 3 seed Mavericks. The Lakers beat Golden State, so if the Blazers had won, they'd have been matched up with Minnesota.

Cheeks delivers a long postgame speech to the players in the locker room afterward.

"It was a great speech," Anderson said. "It was the truth. And sometimes the truth might hurt. He said we have to do everything possible, that we have to give our all. We are not going to base our confidence on this game, or the two we had just won. This is a whole new season, and we know we can win."

Wallace's three-year run as the NBA's technicals king was over. After averaging nearly 36 T's the previous three seasons, he was rung up only 11 times in 2002–03. Wells led the Blazers with 13.

* * *

There wasn't much optimism throughout the country for Portland's chances of knocking off Dallas, which had won 60 games with an explosive offense led by Dirk Nowitzki and Steve Nash, as well as a deep bench.

ESPN's Jack Ramsay said he didn't like the makeup of the Blazers.

"I didn't like it from Day One," said the man who coached the Blazers to the 1977 NBA title. "I heard a lot of people say the Blazers had loaded up, but I didn't like the composition of the team. Too much duplication of positions. Forget about whether these are the right character guys. It makes it very difficult to coach a team where you have so many guys of relatively equal talent vying for minutes. You can only assume [Whitsitt] is doing this with the consent of the owner. Until the owner decides he doesn't like the way it's going, he'll keep doing it."

While Cheeks was in his second season as head coach, the Mavericks were being led by veteran Don Nelson.

"Cheeks has routinely been outcoached all season, and I would expect it to happen again," wrote Dwight Jaynes. "I can't imagine a Don Nelson–coached team losing to a Cheeks-coached team. It shouldn't be a Dallas sweep, though. It really ought to go seven games."

As players met with the media before the series began, somebody asked Wallace about rumors that he might be traded in the summer.

"I don't give a shit about no trade rumors," he said. "As long as somebody 'CTC,' I'm with them. For all you who don't know what 'CTC' means, that's 'Cut the Check.' I just go out there and play. Again, somebody just 'CTC.'"

It would be the last substantial quote the self-proclaimed mercenary would offer for some time.

* * *

After building a 10-point halftime lead, Portland lost to Dallas 96–86 in the opener at American Airlines Center.

"We had it, and then we gave it away," Wells said.

The Blazers shot 55 percent en route to a 52–42 halftime lead, then made only 13-of-42 shots and were outscored 54–34 in the second half.

"We got very stagnant," Pippen said. "We mostly just stood around."

Nowitzki was unstoppable, going for a franchise playoff-record 46 points—23 in each half—with 10 rebounds. He finished a point shy of the most ever scored against the Blazers in the postseason.[2]

---

2   The record was set by Charles Barkley in 1995, as a member of the Phoenix Suns.

"I got tired hearing his name [on the public-address system]," McInnis said.

Wallace scored 26 points, and Stoudamire chipped in 16 points in 25 turnover-free minutes off the bench. But Anderson went scoreless in 19 minutes, and Pippen, his knee aching, made 2-of-8 shots, scored five points, and had four turnovers in 32 minutes.

The leg was "like walking on eggshells," Pippen said. "It was probably going to break down sometime, but I had to try it."

Jaynes was critical of the man calling the shots for Portland.

"Once again, Maurice Cheeks's 'coaching' left plenty to be desired," Jaynes wrote. "It would be a problem for any coach to have too many players who need long minutes and to have too few role players. For Cheeks, it's a severe handicap. It's like a four-year-old with too many Christmas presents. He likes the ones he's looking at and sometimes forgets about the others."

Jaynes continued: "Why was Arvydas Sabonis getting all those [regular-season] minutes if he's just going to play nine minutes in a playoff game? I'd like to say that only Cheeks knows, but that's too easy. Cheeks doesn't know, either. He hasn't all season. He plays hunches more than he plays players. And, I presume, he plays whomever Bob Whitsitt wants him to play."

Commissioner David Stern attended Game 1 of the series and was asked by the media about the Blazers' deportment.

"I read Paul Allen's words about his concern, and I would say to you, take it to the bank that next season is going to be different, because Paul doesn't kid around," Stern said. "You are going to see an understanding by the players that people want to talk about basketball on the court, and not off the court. I don't want to be myopic about the subject, but I expect it to get better."

* * *

Another franchise playoff scoring record was achieved in Game 2, this time by Wells—though in a 103–99 victory by the Mavericks. Wells scored 45 points while making 16-of-24 attempts from the field, breaking Clyde Drexler's mark of 42 points set in 1992.

"I was feeling good," Wells said. "My shot was going down. If I stay aggressive like that, I hope to have more games like that."

No chance of that. But Wells was unconscious in Game 2, with Pippen watching from the Portland bench in street clothes. Anderson was injured and departed early in the game, leaving the Blazers' backcourt play to Wells, Stoudamire, and McInnis.

It was a knock-down, drag-out affair, with 17 lead changes and 10 ties. Nash (28 points, eight assists) and Nowitzki (25 points, nine boards) were the keys as usual—especially late, when the Mavs used the pick-and-roll almost exclusively in the final six minutes. The Blazers continued to switch and ended up with bad matchups.

Portland led 78–76 with 8:44 to play, but Dallas scored on 12 of its last 13 possessions.

"The Mavericks did what they are supposed to do—they defended their home court," Cheeks said. "We were looking to come here and possibly get one, but we didn't get it. Now we go home and defend our court."

* * *

They did anything *but* defend their home court, as Dallas came to the Rose Garden and put a 115–103 licking on the Blazers to go ahead 3–0 in the series.

Portland, going without injured starters Pippen and Anderson, led 85–84 after three quarters. The Mavericks outscored them 31–18 in the final period to win going away.

Nowitzki had another huge game with 42 points on 15-for-20 shooting with 10 rebounds while center Raef LaFrentz sank 7-of-11 shots—including 4-for-7 from 3-point range—and contributed 20 points. Dallas shot .506 from the field, including 13-for-29 (.448) from beyond the arc.

Patterson came off the Portland bench for 19 points and nine rebounds. Wells contributed 15 points, eight rebounds, and six assists but made only 3-of-16 shots from the field. Wallace also had an off night, scoring 11 points on 4-for-10 shooting.

"We wanted to come out with the same intensity we did the first two games, and that's what we did," Nowitzki said. "I'm glad we got the third win, but the series isn't over."

"We have to go out and play even though we are down 3–0," Stoudamire said. "We were in the game tonight, but we had breakdowns on defense that hurt us. The way Dallas is shooting in this series, it's anybody's guess if we can beat them."

Cheeks would become famous for what occurred prior to the game. The Blazers' coach came to the rescue of 13-year-old Natalie Gilbert, who forgot the words during her singing of the national anthem. Cheeks stepped in next to Gilbert and helped her finish the song, to the delight of the capacity home fans (who joined in to help as well).

"Maurice showed his character that night," center Chris Dudley says today. "He stepped up and rescued that girl."

Cheeks received national attention for his act of good will.

"The reaction from everybody took me by surprise," Cheeks says now. "Still today, people come up to me and mention that situation. I just didn't understand the impact it would have. I didn't know it was going to be that memorable. I just saw the girl was having trouble and thought I would try to help her out."

Heading into Game 4 at the Rose Garden, Mavericks beat writer Eddie Sefko of the *Dallas Morning News* was already chalking up a series victory.

"The Mavericks can start breaking down videotape of the Sacramento Kings," Sefko wrote. "Put the rainy Northwest in the rearview and get California in their sights. As for the minor detail known as Game 4 against the Trail Blazers, pay it no mind. When a playoff series becomes a walkover like this one, the victorious team can step back and take stock."

Cheeks, though, had other ideas.

"It's not over," he said, "until someone gets four."

That would take a while.

* * *

Attendance was at the Rose Garden capacity of 19,980, but there were plenty of empty seats for Game 4—more than ever for a playoff game in Portland. Those on hand saw the Blazers dominate in a 98–79 victory.

With three key players out due to injury—Pippen (knee), Anderson (knee), and Sabonis (back)—Cheeks shifted his lineup. In Game 3, he had started Antonio Daniels in the backcourt with Stoudamire. For Game 4, he moved Wells back to shooting guard, switched Wallace to small forward from power forward, and inserted Randolph at power forward.

Randolph overwhelmed LaFrentz, notching 25 points and 15 rebounds in 41 minutes (while LaFrentz had four points on 2-for-7 shooting).

"We needed an injection of something," Cheeks said. "I didn't know exactly what, but I knew Zach would play hard."

Stoudamire had his way with Nash in the point guard matchup, totaling 17 points and 11 assists while Nash went scoreless with three assists and four turnovers.

The Blazers broke it open after halftime, outscoring Dallas 33–10 in the third quarter to take an 82–62 lead after the Mavericks had led by three at the half. Portland won the game at the foul line, making 30-of-42 attempts to Dallas' 12-of-13.

"We just came in with some intensity," Cheeks said. "I think [the players] came in with a little more relaxed attitude."

All the starters except Davis played at least 40 minutes.

"That played a role in the way some of our guys played, including myself," Stoudamire contended. "We were able to get into a rhythm. It's great to go out there and know you're not coming out if you make a mistake. You're not looking over your shoulder."

The game ended a 10-game losing streak in the playoffs for the Blazers, who had been swept by the Lakers in the first round in both 2001 and '02.

The NBA required all players to conduct a postgame interview. Wallace, who had chosen not to cooperate before, came to the media room afterward. His response to every query was, "It was a good game. Both teams played hard" even when given the chance to say something nice about a teammate.

The NBA wound up fining him $50,000—$30,000 for the postgame scene and $20,000 for refusing to talk to reporters in practice before the game. The Blazers were also fined $50,000—$25,000 for each incident—for not ensuring their players comply with NBA media interview rules.[3]

No team had ever come back from an 0–3 hole to win a playoff series. The Blazers seemed to think they had a chance to make history.

"I think we messed with their heads a little bit," Randolph said.

"We are still in a hole, but they have something to think about now," Stoudamire said. "There's no quit in us, I'll tell you that."

* * *

Portland returned to American Airlines Center and stole Game 5, winning 103–99. The Blazers led for a total of 1:05 in the game, and they trailed by eight points with five minutes to go. Wallace drilled a go-ahead 3-pointer with 1:06 left, and Sabonis—who missed Game 4 with back spasms—scored in a tip-in off a Wells miss with 10.3 seconds remaining to seal the win.

Sabonis was asked if it was the biggest basket of his career.

"I think yes," he said. "It is not a last shot, but it is for victory."

Randolph, now firmly entrenched as a starter, led the way with 22 points and nine rebounds. Pippen, who hadn't played since the opener because of his bum knee, played 16 minutes off the bench, contributing nine points and five assists and some excellent defense down the stretch.

Nowitzki had another big game with 35 points and 11 rebounds while Nick Van Exel chipped in 25 points off the bench as Nelson used only seven players. But the Blazers bullied the Mavs—beating them on the boards 48–32 (20 off the offensive glass), taking the ball to the basket, and getting physical with them on defense.

Now the series was going back to Portland for Game 6.

"The Rose Garden is a tough place to play," Nowitzki said. "It gets pretty loud. Along with Sacramento, it is probably the loudest place on the

---

3 The league's media relations director, Brian McIntyre, would have T-shirts made up that read "Both Teams Played Hard." At the NBA Finals, he distributed the shirts to media members to commemorate the occasion.

road. But the crowd was fired up for Game 3, and we found a way to quiet them and win the game. That's what we have to do again."

The Blazers' confidence was growing, and doubt had crept into the heads of the Mavericks.

"They are a little bit nervous," Sabonis said. "If we were in their situation, we would definitely be nervous. It was 3–0, and now it's 3–2. And if they come to Portland and lose . . . we are still alive, and we have the momentum. This win will make us really believe we can win the series."

"I never doubted that we could come back, but we're not back yet," said Stoudamire, who scored 13 of his 19 points in the third quarter and again outplayed Nash. "We have to win one more game in Portland. That's the only game we need to concentrate on right now."

"I'm kind of pissed, actually, because it took us to get our backs against the wall for us to play," said Wallace, now talking to the media, if in limited doses. "It's always us against the world."

* * *

Back at the Rose Garden, Portland played its best game of the series, steamrolling Dallas 125–103 to force a deciding seventh game. Six Blazers scored in double figures, led by Randolph with 21 points. Patterson was terrific off the bench with 20 points on 8-for-10 shooting while Wells scored 18 points on 9-for-14 from the field.

Nash scored 21 points and dished out six assists in 24 minutes, but Nowitzki finally proved mortal, scoring only four points with no rebounds in 28 minutes, making 2-of-11 shots from the field.

The Blazers won the rebound battle 29–9 in the first half en route to a 64–38 halftime lead. Dallas conceded early, pulling its starters before the fourth quarter. In the closing minutes, Wallace led the sellout crowd of 20,602 in the wave with the fans chanting, "Go home, Dallas!"

"We believed from the beginning, and the fans here, they believed in us," said Wallace, suddenly talkative with a microphone in his face. "There were a couple of people who counted us out, but everyone was out here today, and they saw it. We were not ready for it to end."

"We could have rolled over in this series, but this team showed some pride," Pippen said. "We have some warriors here."

"We have no excuses," Nelson said. "We got a real butt-kicking tonight, but it happens in this league. It's a seven-game series, and Game 7 is on our home floor."

Randolph, at 21 the youngest player on either team, also had 10 rebounds. In the last three games, he had averaged 22.7 points and 11.3 rebounds while shooting .564.

"We knew all season that Zach just needed some minutes," Pippen said. "He has a great knack for the game. He always brings such a positive energy to the game with his hustle and enthusiasm. He's a live body."

The Blazers had given themselves a chance to become the first team in NBA history to rally from a 3–0 deficit and win a best-of-seven series. But no road team had won a Game 7 since 1982.[4]

The Blazers would have to go without Davis, who suffered a strained groin and abdominal muscle and played only nine minutes in Game 6. They would still go into the deciding game with confidence.

After Game 6, Patterson had told a reporter that the Mavericks "look a little scared. I see fear in their eyes." Nelson would use it to full advantage as bulletin-board material for the Mavericks.

* * *

For 44 minutes, Game 7 at American Airlines Center was a donnybrook. There were 13 lead changes and 21 ties. Then Dallas took over. Van Exel, who scored 26 points off the bench, hit a 3-pointer to break a tie and give the Mavericks the lead with 3:36 to play. They would score on 10 of their last 11 possessions en route to a 107–95 victory.

Nowitzki was a difference maker again, going for 31 points and 11 rebounds. Nash contributed 21 points and seven assists for the Mavericks, who were 13-for-17 from the field in the final quarter.

Stoudamire had a strong game for the Blazers with 17 points, nine assists,

---

4   The Philadelphia 76ers defeated the Boston Celtics in Game 7 of the Eastern Conference Finals in 1982.

and seven rebounds in 44 minutes, and Sabonis—subbing for Davis—collected 16 points, eight rebounds, and three blocked shots. Sabonis fouled out with 2:12 on an illegal screen call, with Portland trailing by two. He was distraught in the locker room afterward.

"Let the players decide the game," he said softly. "Maybe we still lose, but . . ."

"It came down to us trying to outdo them for the last 12 minutes of the game, and we weren't able to pull it off," said Pippen, who had five points, three rebounds, and two assists in what would be his final appearance in a Portland uniform. "We laid it on the line, but I would have to say the better team advanced."

Nelson chortled to the media about using Patterson's comments as pre-game motivation.

"Ruben Patterson is dumber than a box of rocks," the Dallas coach said. "We put what he said on the board, which helped us. Saying that he sees fear in our eyes—thank you, Ruben, for being dumber than a box of rocks and for getting us to where we need to be."

* * *

Even in defeat, the Blazers came out of the series feeling they had earned respect.

"We could have packed it in and been on vacation a week and a half ago, but we showed a lot of character and pride," Pippen said.

Wells had led Portland in the series in scoring with a 19-point average but shot only .395 from the field. He was terrific in Games 2 and 6, and he was 24-for-86 from the field (.278) in the other five games.

Stoudamire had an excellent series, shooting .484 from 3-point range (15-for-31) while averaging 15.3 points, 5.6 assists, and 5.3 rebounds. Regaining his starting spot with Pippen's injury, Stoudamire played good defense against Nash and averaged only 1.7 turnovers.

Assistant coach Herb Brown feels the Blazers erred by not playing Stoudamire earlier in the series.

"We wound up losing because Damon should have been starting the whole way," Brown says today.

"We would have been more successful in the regular season had we not benched Damon for those 23 games. That showed a crack in the dike. Everybody knew he was the best point guard. And he and Scottie could play together."

Sabonis was huge in the last two games in the absence of Davis, making 15-of-21 shots and collecting 16 points and eight boards in each game. The question was, would he return for the following season? He might not, in part because his family had stayed in Spain.

"It is difficult to move them over here again," Sabonis said after his exit interview with Portland coaches and management. "It is not just one kid. It's four. I'm going to have to think about it before I decide [whether to retire]."

* * *

For a decade, Whitsitt had made changes every season, using owner Paul Allen's considerable wealth to stockpile talent and chase the elusive NBA Finals berth he had never attained in 18 seasons as a general manager. Much of that talent had exuded questionable character, casting a shadow on the franchise in the eyes of the community.

Through the 2002–03 season, the longest stretch where a player wasn't arrested, suspended by the league or team, or the police weren't called to someone's home was 17 days.

It seemed to many that Whitsitt was never held accountable for it by Allen.

"Of course, Bob Whitsitt needs to go," Dwight Jaynes wrote after the season. "Of course, Rasheed Wallace needs to be traded. Of course, we could do without Bonzi Wells and Ruben Patterson. Do I think anything major is going to happen? Of course not. I don't think, in fact, that Whitsitt is in any trouble at all."

As it turned out, there would be change again this off-season—only Whitsitt wouldn't be orchestrating it this time.

One other thing would change. The Blazers, who had been a playoff fixture for 21 straight seasons, wouldn't make it the following year. They wouldn't, in fact, return to the postseason for six years.

Chapter 9

BUH BYE BOB

(2003–2004)

"They just want to draft niggers who are dumb and dumber . . .
straight out of high school. That's why they're drafting all these high
school cats—because they come into the league and they don't know
no better. They don't know the real business, and they don't see
behind the charade. They look at black athletes like we're dumb-ass
niggers. It's as if we're just going to shut up, sign for the money, and
do what they tell us."

—Rasheed Wallace

Three days after the end of the Trail Blazers' 2002–03 playoff series with the Mavericks, owner Paul Allen fired Bob Whitsitt, who had served nine years as the club's president and general manager.

"We are changing our approach," Allen said in announcing Whitsitt's dismissal. "It's not business as usual at the Trail Blazers. To some degree, we put talent and on-the-court ability first and hoped the players we brought in would improve the off-the-court stuff when they became Blazers. In the future, we will be much more focused on bringing people who are solid citizens. We have had a lot of success in the regular season, but the last year has been an unusual one, for the team and the fans. Everybody in management here, and Bob himself, felt that we needed to make a change."

Allen wasn't divorcing himself completely of Whitsitt. He would remain on the job as president of the Seattle Seahawks, where he would butt heads with coach Mike Holmgren, leading to Whitsitt's firing from that position after the 2004 season.

A release out of Allen's Bellevue, Washington, office twice mentioned that Whitsitt's successor as president and general manager would live in Portland. Whitsitt had chosen to remain with his family in Seattle during his time with the Blazers, renting an apartment in downtown Portland. "My office," he liked to say, "is my cell phone."

The Blazers got some mileage out of some of his deals, including trades for Damon Stoudamire and Scottie Pippen. The best deal Whitsitt ever made was erasing his own mistake—sending J. R. Rider, along with Jimmy Jackson, to Atlanta for Steve Smith. His biggest blunders were signing felon Ruben Patterson, trading away Jermaine O'Neal for Dale Davis, and a three-team deal that sent Brian Grant to Miami and brought in Shawn Kemp.

Among Whitsitt's PR gaffes was the removal of popular broadcaster Bill Schonely from his radio play-by-play job after 28 seasons, despite a mass protest from fans. Schonely left without any send-off by the club.

From his 2011 memoir *Idea Man*, Paul Allen went into more detail on his change in the Blazers' leadership. He wrote that Whitsitt had overhauled an aging roster, as he had once done in Seattle, by drafting young athletes with upside and acquiring veteran talent.

"A few of his moves were brilliant, like the deal that brought us Scottie Pippen," Allen wrote. "But there were too many times when Whitsitt operated like a rotisserie-league GM, piling up players with gaudy numbers. He openly professed that he only cared about talent, to the exclusion of character and other intangibles. 'I didn't take chemistry in college,' he told the media. With enough physical ability on the floor, team cohesion would take care of itself. It was a risky assumption for a sport in which five men share one ball.

"Whitsitt temporarily staved off decline by using my wallet to load up on pricey long-term contracts—players who were available because they were overpaid or had off-court issues, or both."

Allen noted players acquired by Whitsitt including Rasheed Wallace, Isaiah Rider, Damon Stoudamire, Bonzi Wells, Shawn Kemp, Ruben Patterson, Qyntel Woods, and Zach Randolph.

"Any one of them would have been a handful," Allen wrote. "Despite the presence of some notable good guys, like Arvydas Sabonis and Steve Smith, they became known as the Portland Jail Blazers. How could I tolerate this stew of instability? The short answer was that we kept winning."

During Whitsitt's tenure, the Blazers had never won an NBA championship or even made it to the Finals. They had made the playoffs each year, though, and twice reached the Western Conference Finals, "enough success to give me pause about shaking up the organization. I can be patient to a fault."

"He was also a great rationalizer. When I'd ask why a draft pick fizzled or a trade backfired, he'd respond, 'Just watch. Next year, he's going to be so much better.'"

The Blazers had twice reached the NBA Finals during the Clyde Drexler years in the early '90s. That had made Allen hungrier to win a championship. Allen wrote that during the Whitsitt era, the team was always one "big-salaried veteran away from contention, and our payroll ballooned. Deep down, I knew there was something wrong. In the playoffs, when the pressure peaks and higher-caliber opponents target your weaknesses, a player's makeup is revealed in performance."

Allen singled out the collapse in Game 7 of the 2000 Conference Finals against the Lakers, when the Blazers blew a 15-point lead in the fourth quarter.

"That seventh game exposed us as a team without leadership or discipline," Allen wrote. "I'll never forget that feeling I had when we boarded our plane—still festooned with 'Beat LA' stickers—and headed home, our season done. It was a crushing defeat, and it took me a long time to get over it."

By 2002, the Blazers led the league in payroll at $106 million, were $65 million over the salary cap and $50 million over the luxury-tax threshold.

"Our player salaries cost us an outrageous $156 million, all for a medium-to-good 50-win team that would lose yet again in the first round of the playoffs," the owner wrote. "Off the court, it was worse, as the Trail Blazers became exhibit A for all that was wrong in professional sports. I found myself reeling from one lowlight to the next."

Attendance, as well as the team's standing in the community, suffered, and TV ratings declined by 50 percent.

"Our wayward players showed little remorse ... You could see why parents weren't rushing out to buy Bonzi or Rasheed jerseys for their kids," Allen wrote. "One day I said to Whitsitt, 'What's it like in the locker room? How is the team reacting to the latest incident?' He said, 'Well, Paul, half our guys are normal and half are crazy. The good guys are all freaked out, but the crazy guys are crazy, so they're fine.'

"I'd heard enough. A team might be able to absorb one erratic personality, but who could win with a group that was half-crazy? Three days after our season ended, I fired Whitsitt and gave his successor, Steve Patterson, a mandate to clean house."

* * *

Scottie Pippen would not return to the Blazers, either. He would play one more season in Chicago before calling it quits after 17 NBA seasons.

Before he left Portland, Pippen had his say about the demise of Whitsitt.

"I would have to say it was a good move," he said. "The fans had been on him for a long time. The team wasn't getting any better, and it put a lot of pressure on him. When you are spending the type of money on salaries that he was, you would expect a team to be playing a lot deeper into the postseason than we have the last three years. I mean, you need to be sitting up there with the Yankees. You need to be bringing in some kind of championship."

Pippen said he would never forgive Whitsitt for breaking up the 1999–2000 team after his first season with the club. "I felt strongly about that team," he said. "I got one year, and 'Trader Bob' pulls the plug before I get a chance to sit on the pot. We were on a roll, and three years later we can't put a team out there capable of competing for a title. A lot of his changes set us back more than they helped us.

"I begged him not to trade Jermaine [O'Neal]. That was the crushing thing. He was more or less telling me about the trade after the fact instead of asking my opinion."

Pippen said Whitsitt wasn't around the players enough, in part because he wasn't living in Portland.

"He was totally out of touch," Pippen said. "The presence of a GM helps. It's like, as soon as the principal shows up, the students do everything in a straight line. Being absent as much as he was, it put a lot more pressure on the coach. With Bob, it got to the point where they guys didn't really respect him."

* * *

Whitsitt had one more taste of power for the Blazers. In late May, before Allen had hired his replacement, Philadelphia GM Billy King contacted Portland executive vice president Erin Hubert, asking permission to talk to Maurice Cheeks about the 76ers' vacant head coaching job. They were all but ready to hire him as Larry Brown's replacement.

With Allen in France attending Naomi Campbell's birthday bash and vice chairman Bert Kolde (somebody had to handle vice control with the franchise) evidently too busy trying to hire front-office types, Hubert forwarded the request to Whitsitt in Seattle. He told Cheeks—who had one year left at $1.3 million, with a team option for the 2004–05 campaign—he had to honor his contract with Portland.

"I was surprised," Cheeks would say later.

Had the subject of an extension come up when he talked with Whitsitt?

"I didn't get that far," Cheeks said.

On June 18, a week before the draft, Steve Patterson was named to assume the presidential part of Whitsitt's duties with the Blazers. Patterson, 45, had been Houston's general manager from 1989–1993 and had put together most of the pieces for the teams that won the NBA titles the following two years. In Portland, he was hired to run the financial side and would be tasked with trimming salary and expenses. He would leave the basketball side primarily to a general manager, whom he would help hire.

* * *

In July, Stoudamire spoke with the *Portland Tribune* about his situation with the Blazers, and his feelings about his hometown. The Wilson High grad had taken some early summer school classes in Tucson, Arizona, then headed for Houston until just before training camp in late September.

"I ain't coming back to Portland 'til it's time to play basketball," he said. "I ain't having no fun in Portland no more. I like Portland. I'm from Portland, but it's best if I get out of there. It's crazy, but I feel more embraced in other cities."

Stoudamire had suffered indignities that wounded his pride during the 2002–03 season. For the first time in his career, the point guard had played benchwarmer, with 22 DNP/CDs (did not play/coach's decision). He averaged career lows in points (6.9), assists (3.5), and minutes (22.3). He was offended that both of his coaches in Portland—Mike Dunleavy and Maurice Cheeks—had tried to turn him into a prototypical point man.

"My whole thing with Portland is, when you traded for me, you knew what kind of guard I was," Stoudamire said. "I played fast. I pushed the ball in transition. I shot transition 3's. Then you bring me in and change my game?

"You know my game. Embrace my strengths. Help my weaknesses, but don't try to change me. Don't nobody nit-pick their point guard like Portland does me. I have felt at times that nobody has my back. Just embrace what I do well, let me play the way I am capable of playing, and everything will be all right."

Stoudamire, who had two more years and nearly $25 million left on his contract, said he would ask for a sit-down with agent Aaron Goodwin, Cheeks, and the new general manager.

"I just want to know how Damon Stoudamire is going to be used if I am out there for Portland next season," he said. "If you ain't going to play me, I want to be out of here. If you are going to play me, let's talk about it."

* * *

The Blazers selected 18-year-old Travis Outlaw of Starkville, Mississippi, with the 23rd pick of the 2003 Draft. The 6-foot-9 forward came from good stock. His father, John, was assistant chief of the Starkville Police Department. But it seemed like an unwise pick.

"To bring an 18-year-old kid into that?" said a rival team's general manager. "Outlaw has good upside, and he could be a salt-of-the-earth kid, but I didn't understand that pick at all. As a talent, he's a lot like the player they got last year [Qyntel Woods]. It proves one thing: The old regime made that pick."

In early July, the Blazers and the affiliate Oregon Arena Corporation laid off about one-third of the club's employees. Between them, the two companies were expected to lose about $100 million in the financial year that ended on June 30, executive VP Erin Hubert said.

This was the beginning of an austerity program for Allen. The office staff would be cut from 293 to under 200, with an annual savings of $4 million, said Hubert.

Patterson and John Nash would trim the player payroll down to about $83 million for the upcoming season. With the luxury tax threshold at $55.4 million, Allen's tax would still be more than $27 million.

Allen's fortune had been nearly halved in just two years—from $40 billion in 2001 to $21 billion—by the decline of the stock market and failing or failed companies. He remained the third-wealthiest person in the US behind Bill Gates and Warren Buffett.

Patterson expressed confidence he could help turn things around.

"Every team I've worked for has won games, won championships, and made money," he said, sounding a bit like Whitsitt.

* * *

On July 3, wearing a white tank top and red sweatpants, Stoudamire was arrested and charged with misdemeanor possession of marijuana and drug paraphernalia at Tucson International Airport. Stoudamire was going through a security checkpoint with a traveling companion on a flight to New Orleans when he set off a metal detector. In his possession was a plastic bag filled with a half-ounce of marijuana wrapped in aluminum foil.

A beep sounded every time the security guard passed his hand-held metal-detecting wand past Stoudamire's pants. Damon denied several times he was hiding anything, but then he wiggled his leg, which dislodged something down the leg of his sweatpants. The bag dropped to the floor.

Stoudamire was arrested and charged with possession of marijuana—his third such arrest in 17 months.

Patterson subsequently suspended and fined him $250,000. The new Blazer president said he would work to help get Stoudamire into a drug rehab program.

"Actions like this are contrary to that effort and cannot be tolerated," Patterson said. "We are committed to changing this behavior and the image of this franchise."

Dan Wasserman, director of communications for the NBA Players Association, lodged a protest at the size of the fine, saying it "clearly exceeds by a wide margin the penalties and remedies that were bargained for in the instances of marijuana use."

Stoudamire's voluntarily entered John Lucas's "Next Step" program as part of the NBA drug rehabilitation system. The four-to-six-week program would take place at the same Houston clinic that Blazer forward Shawn Kemp had used two years earlier.

Lucas's own playing career had been impacted by drug abuse. He would go on not only to be an NBA head coach but also a mentor to hundreds of players fighting issues of their own.

"I was the original guy who brought attention to the drug issues back in '86, and the NBA began to put all the programs in place," Lucas says today. "I started working with player programs on March 14, 1986. Cocaine was my issue, and it was the big issue then. We didn't have a program to help the players. That's what [commissioner] David Stern had to clean up and get right.

"Our player programs have come so far because of those times. It brought the mental health issue—drugs, alcohol, and things like that—to the front. Everybody thought we were just young and dumb with a whole bunch of money. In some cases, there were life issues and family issues going on with us, too."

Patterson flew to Houston to meet with Lucas about Stoudamire, "and we got in a big old fight" about the $250,000 fine, Lucas says. The Blazers eventually removed the fine and allowed Stoudamire to donate $100,000 to the Albina Head Start early childhood program.

"Damon did a good job [in rehab] with me and became a great ambassador for the Blazers," says Lucas, now an assistant coach for the Houston Rockets.

But he was also among those involved with incidents that led to the Jail Blazers tag.

"During those years, things just seemed to happen," Lucas says. "Rasheed was having his thing with referees. There was a lot of drug stuff, the dogfighting stuff. It really harmed their reputation for a while.

"But it's funny. Perception isn't always reality. All the things you heard about those guys, they're not true. Every one of them would give you the shirt off their back. Zach Randolph is still playing. Now he's a role model and will get his number retired in Memphis. Bonzi Wells runs a program in Indiana for kids. Damon is coaching at Pacific. J. R. Rider is working with kids in Phoenix. They just had to grow up."

Lucas believes the Blazers got the "most exposure" because of Wallace's problems with the officials and the players' off-court issues.

"Maybe it was also because people were a little jealous of Bob Whitsitt accumulating that kind of talent," Lucas says. "Everybody was chasing the Lakers, and Portland got enough pieces to pass them. It looked like they were there. It reminds me of us now, trying to pass the Warriors."

* * *

After Ed Stefanski turned them down and John Hammond and Chris Wallace pulled out of the running, the Blazers hired John Nash as general manager on July 19, 2003. Nash, 56, had been serving as the Philadelphia 76ers' TV analyst for Comcast SportsNet. Nash had 11 years of experience as a general manager with Philadelphia, Washington, and New Jersey from 1986–2000.

"Paul Allen has made it clear: He wants a team that he and the city of Portland can be proud of," Nash said during his inaugural press conference. "We are not going to tolerate the behavior that has been here previously."

Ironically, Nash was GM when the Washington Bullets chose Wallace with the fourth pick in the 1995 Draft. The Bullets kept Wallace for only one season before trading him to Portland.

"I don't know he is the type of guy I would classify as a consummate leader," Nash said. "I'm not trying to criticize him because I haven't had the opportunity to talk to the other players and coaches. But this team hasn't had the greatest quantity of leadership."

Nash would last just three years on the job.

"Paul was a little different than the other owners I had worked for," he says now. "He was living in Seattle, so I couldn't meet with him face to face on a regular basis. He was involved in so many things, yet the Blazers were one of his priorities. No doubt he wanted to win, despite the fact that, when I was hired, he made it clear he wanted to clean up the situation. I don't think he was prepared to take a step backward."

On August 6, the Blazers announced reduced season ticket prices and a 25-point mission statement that would include a player code of conduct that would be part of any contract offered by the club.

"Which is nice," wrote the *San Francisco Chronicle*'s Scott Ostler, "but did you ever try to read one of those when you're stoned?"

The Blazers invited all of their 11,000 season ticket-holders to a meeting at the Rose Garden to announce the new steps. About 3,000 showed up, asking hundreds of questions of Patterson, Nash, Cheeks, and executive VP Erin Hubert.

The following week, the club announced the hiring of former Blazer Jerome Kersey as director of player programs. The job description was a 70/30 split between working with the coaching staff and players and with marketing and the public relations side. Kersey was expected to speak with the players about professionalism and deportment and would accompany the team on most road trips.

"I represent the establishment, but I'm here for the players every bit as much as management," Kersey said. "I'm not here to be a snitch, to follow a player around. I want to build a relationship with them. I'm trying to learn 12, 13 different personalities at the same time."

On August 11, Arvydas Sabonis elected to give up a $7 million contract for the 2003–04 season to stay in Lithuania.

"It's time for me to end my time with the franchise, my time in America," the future Hall of Famer said in a statement from Lithuania.

On September 5, Erin Hubert left the Blazers to accept a management position with Intercom Portland, which owned eight local radio stations.

* * *

On the eve of training camp, Bonzi Wells was turning 27. In an interview with the *Portland Tribune*, he said he figured it was about time to grow up.

Now in his sixth year with the club, Wells was third in seniority on the Blazers behind Wallace and Stoudamire. The 6-foot-5, 220-pound swing man said he was embarrassed about some of his actions, the kind that earned him three separate suspensions the previous season and had affected his reputation in the community.

"I want to get away from all that happened the first five years of Bonzi in Portland," Wells said. "All the stuff that has happened is just crazy."

For the first time, he came clean on the incident with San Antonio's Danny Ferry.

"I can't believe I spit on Danny Ferry," he said with what seemed to be sincere contrition. "I think about that sometimes. That was the most stupid thing I have ever done. They put him in the game to frustrate me, and I am going to say Danny Ferry did his job to the fullest. He should have gotten a pay raise. I fell to the pressure. This is my sixth year in the league. There is no time to fall to pressure anymore."

Wells had two young boys—Gawen III (5) and Christian (4)—who lived with their mother in Muncie, Indiana. Bonzi had spent time with them during the summer and said he came to an important realization. "My kids are watching me," he said. "I don't want them to go to school and have everyone talking about their dad in a negative way. They are at an age where they watch every move I make. I have to be a role model for them. I'm happy I am getting a chance to be a father. My father and mother divorced when I was young, but Dad [Gawen Wells Sr.] wasn't one of those guys who left his kids. We have always been close. I am going to be there for my kids, too."

Wells said he was trying to reconnect with his spiritual side as a member of Union Baptist Church in Muncie. "My grandfather and my uncles were reverends," he said. "My whole family grew up in the church. I have strayed away from it. I have acted wild at times, but that's out of character for me. I am a good person. I have a great heart. Being mad at people is for the birds.

"This year, I am going to stay focused. I want to stay off the referees. I want to be a happy man. I am going to pray that I can stay strong every day. Prayer will help me through it."

Wells had run a pair of youth summer basketball clinics in Indiana.

"I see how much kids look up to me, how positive my life could be if I just stay positive with what I do," he said earnestly. "A couple of kids asked me about all the incidents I was involved in. I didn't really have an answer for them. I didn't like that at all. I want them to have nothing but positives to say about me this year."

Wells said he wanted to be a career Blazer.

"I want to give the Portland organization a product they are going to want to keep," he said. "I want to play here my whole career. I want to be like Clyde Drexler, except I want to stay my last couple of years. I want to win a championship here. And I want to be a new Bonzi. From this year on, I am going to make strides. I'm not going to be perfect. Like I have been telling myself, I can't just talk about it. I have to be it."

* * *

Prior to the season, the *Portland Tribune* caught up former Blazer J. R. Rider, the forefather of the Jail Blazers movement during his time with the club from 1996–1999. Rider, still only 32, had played his last NBA game with Denver on November 19, 2001.

Now Rider, who had racked up hundreds of thousands of dollars in fines and suspensions during his NBA career, was hoping for another chance. He shifted between apologies and excuses.

"I feel bad about my reputation," Rider said. "I wish I could change some things. I hate being in this position. At the same time, there are guys since I have been out of the league who have done a lot worse. I hurt myself,

I can say that. But I am also maybe unfairly in this position with the things I have done.

"Everybody makes mistakes and screws around. My things have been mostly not being on time, or if I didn't play, I would get a little upset. I think it was a little unfair I was singled out, that I am now out of the league."

Rider, now the father of a one-year-old boy, called himself an "entrepreneur," with several projects in the works. He said he was working as an executive for Rider Records, and was beginning production on a new movie, to which he would serve as assistant director. And yes, he could still play ball, too.

"I'm in shape," he said. "If somebody brings me in, if somebody offers me the right kind of money, I'm ready to play ball. But I have other things in my life now. I have a child. I have a lot to look forward to. You know, it's 'Be Smart, Be Safe.'"

Five minutes later, Rider was back on the phone with the reporter.

"Please do not twist my words around," he said. "I'm out of the limelight now."

Another five minutes, another call: "This isn't 'Badgering Me' time, is it?"

Rider would not play another NBA game. Four years later, he would serve four months in Marin (California) County Jail for felony cocaine possession, battery, and evading police.

* * *

During training camp, Stoudamire showed a measure of contrition during a half-hour session with the media. He said he was there to "fess up" to poor decisions. He had spent nearly three months with John Lucas in his rehab center in Houston, working on both getting in shape and on his life in general.

"The common denominator has been [marijuana]," Stoudamire told reporters. "I went voluntarily into a program for 90 days. I wanted to see if there was a problem. For 90 days, I was clean. I couldn't do that if there were a problem [with marijuana use]. There has been a problem with the law and the decisions I have made."

After his third incident with marijuana, Stoudamire called Lucas.

"I have to find out if I have a problem," Stoudamire told Lucas. "Do I really need this stuff?"

"As my mind cleared, I was able to understand the whole thing better," Stoudamire said. "The reason I know I can eliminate marijuana from my life is, I'm dealing with the other issues now. Once you can alleviate the big problems, everything else falls into place. I don't need it in my life. People who do have irregular patterns or are unreliable. I have never shown those tendencies."

With Patterson and Nash aboard, "I feel like for the first time since I have been here, I have been embraced," Stoudamire said.

"Steve and John have had nothing but open arms for me, and I respect them for that," Stoudamire said. "I haven't felt that much love since I have been a Blazer. I've gotten a lot of support through all this, and it makes me feel good, because this is my hometown and I want to maintain a good reputation here. There are lots of things I would like to do for the community in the future."

* * *

Ruben Patterson would report to training camp, but he was not a happy camper. The small forward had asked Nash to trade him, but he had four years left on his six-year, $33-million deal.

Patterson was still seething from the previous April's practice altercation with Zach Randolph and said Whitsitt, Nash's predecessor, had promised him he'd be traded in the offseason.

"He knew my situation," Patterson said. "I told him I didn't want to be around Zach. This is a guy who blindsided me for no reason. Nobody would want to be around a teammate who sucker-punched you when you weren't looking."

Patterson had missed the next three games with a fractured eye socket, and Randolph was suspended for two games.

After the season, Patterson and his wife, Shannon, sold their Tualatin home and moved to Columbus, Ohio. He did not spend a day in Portland all summer, waiting to hear news of a trade. Nash said he had tried in vain to deal Patterson.

"He is perceived by some in the league to be a risk," Nash said, "and teams aren't anxious to bring on malcontents."

Patterson was entering camp in a poor frame of mind.

"I am very disappointed," he said. "I have not talked to the guys running the club now. I don't even know what Steve Patterson looks like. It upsets me. It's frustrating. They have known how I feel the whole summer [about Randolph]. Deep down in your heart, you want to kill the guy.

"I'm not going to go in there and beat him up or have somebody else beat him up. I am going to go in with a positive attitude. Yeah, it's messed up, but I have to do my job. I have to think about my family and my future and my contract. I have to go in and do my job and help my team."

After the incident, Randolph apologized to Ruben during a meeting attended by Whitsitt, Cheeks, and Dan Fegan (Patterson's agent). Randolph said as far as he was concerned, that closed the matter. Patterson disagreed.

"He didn't mean it," Ruben said. "It was a fake apology. I know he didn't mean it."

Nash said it might be necessary to have another sit-down with both sides, but Patterson said he was not interested.

"Nah. My main thing is, [Randolph] can talk to me on the basketball court. Off the court, I want no part of him. No friends, nothing. I hate to have that type of attitude, but we can't be buddies, we can't be anything but teammates. You can be cool with me on the court, but off the court, you can't be around me."

* * *

During media day before the start of training camp, Rasheed Wallace gave mostly stock answers to routine questions. When asked about his "CTC" comment during the playoffs the previous season—the inference being, all he cared about was getting paid—the response was interesting.

"If it was true that I just cared about the money, then my whole attitude would be different," Wallace said. "I want to win every game, and I want to go out a winner. If I retire from this league and I haven't won at least one championship, then I'll feel like all my years in the league would be a failure. It's a business and you can't put your personal feelings before that. That's what 'CTC' means. Whoever cuts that check, that's who I have to play for."

Asked if he'd like to stay in Portland, Wallace said, "I would like to be out here. My wife likes it out here, and she's established here. My kids have friends here and go to school here. I would say we're intertwined in the community. But if I have to go somewhere else and play, I'm not going to boohoo about it. I will still be able to do the things necessary to take care of my family."

Nash had made no trades over the summer. He was under orders to do what he could to lessen the payroll and didn't want to make a deal that would saddle the club with any long-term contracts. With Sabonis, Pippen, and Antonio Daniels gone, it would lop off about $30 million of salary.

Mark Warkentien, who had been Whitsitt's right-hand man through most of the previous nine seasons, was retained, though he would drop his assistant GM title and serve only as director of scouting. Warkentien, who wasn't on the same page with Nash from the beginning, would remain on the job for only one season.

Cheeks was in a lame-duck situation in the final year (at $1.3 million) of a three-year contract, with a team option for 2004–05. His assistants would be Dan Panaggio, Jimmy Lynam, John Loyer, and Bernie Smith, the latter who had been video coordinator the previous season. Herb Brown would leave to join his younger brother, Larry, with the Detroit Pistons.

"Mo and I had a falling out," Brown says today. "I said something at a meeting after the [2002–03] season at the Chicago pre-draft camp. Mo took it the wrong way and got pissed. He said, 'I don't want you at the draft.' I said fine. He was messing with me a little bit.

"The Blazers sent me a contract [for the 2003–04 season]. In the interim, I had talked with Larry. He said, 'Hey, come sit in on our meetings for the draft.' I did. After that, Larry said, 'You're coming here next year.' I said OK, but I didn't tell Mo for a while. I waited until I had the contract from Detroit. Then I left Mo a message on his answering machine. I said,

'Thanks for the opportunity. I appreciate the two years we had together. I've decided to take a new job.' He went ballistic."

The Blazers would enter the season versatile, athletic, and deep, though thin at the post. Only Dale Davis and third-year man Ruben Boumtje-Boumtje were left at center. The 7-footer from Cameroon wound up playing nine games that season and, at 25, never play another NBA game.

Randolph was entrenched as the starter at power forward with Wallace as the small forward. Patterson would come off the bench to back up Wallace, and the Blazers were hoping for a bigger contribution from second-year man Qyntel Woods, who led the Rocky Mountain Revue summer league with a 28 ppg average. Wells and Anderson were in competition at shooting guard and Stoudamire was back as the starting point guard, backed up by McInnis.

Nash was asked where he felt the on-court leadership would come from.

"That's a great question," the first-year GM said. "I don't know."

"You look at our roster now, nobody on this team has really been a leader," said Cheeks, asked the same question. "Until that leadership role is filled, the question will persist."

That role would be filled by Stoudamire, who would play all 82 games and more minutes than anyone on the team.

Woods offered no apology for his summer arrest in Portland, which included citations for driving with a suspended license and without proof of insurance. That after being arrested late the previous season for pot possession and driving without insurance.

"I'm not embarrassed," he said. "It is taken care of. I forgot to pay a speeding ticket [which led to the suspended license]. Now I have a personal assistant who will remind me and make sure that doesn't happen again."

Wallace skipped a preseason team function for sponsors held on Paul Allen's yacht, docked off the Willamette River near Portland's downtown. Players were required to attend, and Rasheed was fined $10,000. Team officials privately groused about the example he was setting for youngsters such as Randolph, Woods, and rookie Travis Outlaw.

For the first time in several years, the Blazers were not among the favorites in the West. No experts were predicting them to finish better than fifth in the conference.

"We'll probably sneak up on some people this year, which is fine," Stoudamire said.

* * *

Portland blew a 13-point third-quarter lead and fell 99–92 in the season opener at Utah to a Jazz team picked to finish dead last in the Western Conference per *Sports Illustrated*'s preseason issue. That despite dominating Utah 25–9 on the boards in the first half. The Jazz made their first 10 shots of the fourth quarter and finished 13-for-16 from the field in the period to claim victory.

"A terrible fourth quarter," Cheeks said. "At a certain point, our guys got comfortable out there. We let up. We did some things I just don't understand."

Derek Anderson missed the game with back spasms. Randolph scored 22 points with nine boards but was only 6-for-16 from the field.

Jerry Sloan had some interesting observations about the Blazers afterward.

"There have been some problems with their players," the Utah coach said. "Everybody knows that. But there's no question they have some great athletes. They just have to get a little bit of rhythm. Any team has to win a couple of games to keep their dobber up. Sometimes, you feel sorry for yourself and look like you lined up as a jackass at the Kentucky Derby. It looked like tonight they felt a little sorry for themselves at the end."

The Blazers roughed up Cleveland 104–85 two nights later in their home opener as Randolph led the way with 21 points and 13 rebounds. Jeff McInnis was good off the bench with 15 points on 6-for-8 shooting and Woods had a promising home season debut with 13 points in 16 minutes.

Wallace had only 11 points on 4-for-11 shooting with four rebounds in 29 minutes. Even after being fined $30,000 by the NBA for refusing interviews during the 2003 playoffs, he wasn't talking.

Asked politely by a longtime beat writer if he would answer a few questions, Wallace replied, "Good win, man, bottom line. I ain't got nothing much to say. It was a good win, and we needed it. That's all I'm saying."

Wallace was then asked for impressions of Cleveland's 18-year-old rookie, LeBron James, who had totaled eight points, six assists, and four rebounds in his third career game. "I just told you, it was a good win," he said. "That's what we needed, and that's what we got."

So he wasn't willing to answer a question about LeBron?

"That's what y'all want to talk about," Rasheed replied. "I don't get into that shit."

Late in that game, five weeks after promising to be a better Bonzi, Wells offered a single-fingered salute to two fans. The fans, seated behind the Blazer bench, had been launching catcalls at Wallace, prompting him and Randolph to fire shouts back at the fans. Wells went a step further, signaling to the spectators that he considered them No. 1. He would be fined $10,000 for the incident.

It had been a rough night for Bonzi, who had gone 4-for-14 from the field and had, in the first half, twice thrown objects onto the court—first a towel and then a water bottle.

The next day, in a group media interview, Wells denied making the obscene gesture, saying with a wink he didn't remember what happened because he sometimes "blacks out."

Later that day, after a meeting with Steve Patterson, Nash, and Cheeks, he admitted his part in the incident and accepted the fine. The next day, he told the *Portland Tribune* why he had not acknowledged guilt the day before. Reporters, he said, were "all around me, baiting me, trying to get me to talk about something they knew was on [videotape]. Everybody knew, and I wasn't going to play along with that, so I played with them a little bit."

A mistake? "Probably. I would handle it differently if I had it to do over again."

As for the incident, "I stepped over the line, and I was wrong for that," he said. "But [the fans] were over the line, too. They went overboard. Sheed and Damon were doing a good job of ignoring it, but I wanted to come to their defense. They are my teammates, the guys I go to war with."

Wells said he considered the incident "a little setback, but I hope not that much."

"I'm not going to be 100 percent perfect," he said. "There are things you go through as a player that are hard for people on the outside to understand. Still, I can't be doing those things. I slipped across the line, and I'm going to do my best to do right from now on."

Nash admitted the Blazers were shopping Wells.

"Bonzi has put another suitcase on the baggage cart," he said after the most recent incident. "His value was probably significantly higher at the start of training camp when he professed to have turned over a new leaf that obviously is no longer."

Wells had vowed that there would be only 10 percent left of the old Bonzi.

"I'm not sure his math was accurate," Nash quipped.

Even Stoudamire said he was disappointed in Wells.

"He is a player with a world of potential," Stoudamire said. "I get disappointed because he has more to lose than a guy like me. Bonzi is 27, with a lot of years left, and he has a big contract coming up. Beyond that, we need Bonzi. He's going to have to figure it out himself. Maybe rap with Maurice and go from there."

Cheeks told reporters he would finally have to put his foot down with his players.

"It is to the point where you have to say, 'No more,'" he said. "That's intolerable. This stuff shouldn't happen anymore." He said he would meet with his players to discuss the situation, but "I don't know when I will do it. I don't think it will be something I will plan. It will be impromptu, but it's going to come. I hope it happens before another incident."

Cheeks, who was genuinely sore at Wells, moved him to the bench. Beyond his behavior, Wells had started the season 0-for-8 from 3-point range (through the team's first 10 games)—at that point the only starting two-guard in the league without a made 3-pointer.

Portland Tribune columnist Dwight Jaynes wrote about the unusual, and increasingly frequent, in-game behavior of the Blazers' coach.

> Maurice Cheeks did his usual number on the sidelines—an act unique in pro sports. He's constantly bantering with fans, even turning his back on game action countless times to flash what he assumes is a cute grin when he delivers a punch line. When he yelled at Ruben Patterson to stay with his man, he turned to the fans and asked them to "watch him now. Watch what he does. You heard what I told him."
>
> Patterson—like the big family dog with no attention span who will follow anyone down the sidewalk—wandered away from the guy he was supposed to guard. "See," Cheeks said to the crowd. If I know a player wouldn't do what I wanted him to do, I'm not sure I'd play him. And I think I'd find enough happening on the floor to keep me so busy I wouldn't have time to chatter with the paying customers. But I'm old-fashioned that way.

A couple of days later, Cheeks was asked about his penchant for talking to fans during games.

"It's the damnedest thing," he said. "I don't know why I do that. I would never have thought I would do something like that. I have never seen a coach do it.

"I do it sometimes on the road, but I do it more at home. I don't know if it's a comfort zone or seeing some of the people who have been there every night or what. I will just be talking to them, and I get into it, and the fans get into it. I have fun with it a little bit. It takes me away from the game when we are getting beat or trying to get back into a game. I have a good time with it."

Does it ever distract him from doing his job?

"No, no, no," he said. "I only do it after something happens or when a player goes out, or maybe when he is coming into the game, or in a dead-ball situation, or when I am walking up the floor toward the action. I don't do it when it takes my vision away from the game."

"Mo wanted to be liked," assistant coach Herb Brown says today. "Talking to the fans was a defense mechanism. I don't think that would break his concentration. In a game, I don't think anything broke his concentration. It was just a release."

On November 8, the Blazers beat Atlanta 100–93 as Randolph scored 29 points and McInnis contributed 21 points and nine assists off the bench. Attendance was announced at 16,170, but the crowd looked much smaller. Wallace, Wells, and Stoudamire were greeted with some boos during pregame introductions.

Four days later, the Blazers picked up the option on Cheeks's contract, guaranteeing him $1.8 million for the 2004–05 season.

"It feels better to have security, no question," Cheeks would say. "But I figured, whether I had it or not, I'm going to go out and coach this team to the best of my ability. Maybe we don't end up being as good as I hope, and then they don't keep me, or they don't exercise my option, and then I go someplace else. At some point, I figured I would get another job. But it's always better to have security under your belt."

The next night, the Blazers pulled off their best win of their young season, rallying from a 24-point deficit to overhaul Sacramento 112–110 in overtime.

Randolph had the best game of his career with 28 points, 14 rebounds, five assists, and three blocked shots. His last block, on a jumper by Mike Bibby with 6.9 seconds left in overtime and Portland ahead 111–110, was the deciding play of the game. The Kings fouled Wallace, who made 1-of-2 at the line with 5.8 seconds left. Bibby missed a fadeaway jumper, and the Blazers had their third straight win to improve to 5–3.

"We have a lot of heart," Randolph said. "This is a team, baby."

Randolph had help as Wells was terrific, piling up 27 points, nine rebounds, four assists, and three steals. Wallace chipped in 26 points.

Two nights later, the opposite happened as Portland lost 101–79 to the Hornets when the home team closed the game on a 41–18 run.

"We were right there, playing nice. Then the next thing I know, it's 73–63," Wells said, adding with a smile, "It was like I blacked out again."

On November 20, Cheeks and Wells got into it during a practice session, with Wells winding up with a two-game suspension for the incident.

"I was the only [media] guy there when Cheeks threw Bonzi out of practice," says Mike Barrett, then in his first season as the Blazers' TV play-by-play man. "I went to practice a lot. You never wanted to be the only guy from the broadcast team watching practice, because if something went down—and it inevitably did—the story would get out, and the first guy [management] would look at was you. I never once told anybody about anything that happened during those practices. When something would start to happen, I would often just leave."

The following day, the Blazers beat Houston 85–78 despite shooting only .341 from the field.

The announced crowd at the Rose Garden was another all-time low— 14,634. The 2002–03 season-ticket base had fallen to less than 12,000, and Steve Patterson admitted they were down about 10 percent from that this season.

"Blazermania, as we know it, is officially dead," Dwight Jaynes wrote. "Buried. Portlanders are just about to the point where they not only don't like this team, but they hate it. It's criminal what Bob Whitsitt did to this team. The man should be extradited, brought back to Portland in a paddy wagon, and charged with grand theft—for stealing the hearts of basketball fans in Oregon. He is gone, sure. But the stench remains."

On November 25, the Blazers lost 81–80 to Washington, even without Wizards stars Gilbert Arenas and Jerry Stackhouse. Larry Hughes made a go-ahead basket on a driving layup with 10.4 seconds left. After a timeout, McInnis took a running jumper that missed with 5.9 seconds remaining. The Wizards' Brevin Knight rebounded with about four seconds left and dribbled out the clock.

"I guess the dejection of missing the shot kept us from fouling," Cheeks said.

Randolph continued his inspired play with 24 points and 15 rebounds, but Wallace finished with only three points on 1-for-6 shooting to go with one rebound in 40 minutes (though he did have seven assists). Wells, booed after returning from his two-game suspension, had five points on 2-for-11 shooting in 22 minutes.

* * *

It was a different era of Blazer basketball. During the Whitsitt years, the team always carried three healthy players on the injured list and the maximum 15 total, unless there were legitimate injuries. During the 2003–04 season, the Blazers were carrying only 12 players.

"It changes things in practice," Stoudamire said. "There are no subs standing on the sidelines anymore, which means a little bit of fatigue is involved."

On November 28, in a 97–93 win over New Jersey, Stoudamire scored 28 points on 12-for-17 shooting and dished out seven assists while Randolph had 26 points and nine rebounds.

The Blazers were shorthanded for the game. Anderson made an appearance in the locker room but said he was far from a return to action with a bulging disc in his lower back that had kept him out of action since the opener. He would not resume play until January.

In addition to Anderson's absence, Wallace was benched for most of the first quarter for missing the morning shootaround, and Patterson was under a one-game suspension for skipping a practice over Thanksgiving, having returned home to Ohio without permission.

Wells went scoreless, going 0-for-4 from the field in 17 minutes off the bench. He continued to be booed every time he touched the ball.

"It's been frustrating," Stoudamire said. "When Bonzi gets booed, I can feel that. Like I told Maurice, it's frustrating to me to see where the team was when I first got here to what it has become. I never thought I would be part of something like that, but I'm in it now, and we just have to fight through it."

On December 2, just when it seemed like he could do no wrong, Randolph was arrested for driving while under the influence of marijuana after being stopped by police for a traffic violation at 2:19 a.m. in Northeast Portland while driving his 2003 Cadillac Escalade. The officer smelled burning marijuana inside the vehicle. Randolph was also cited for not having a valid Oregon driver's license and insurance.

To that point in the season, Randolph ranked 10th in the NBA in scoring (21.6) and fifth in rebounds (11.1), fourth in offensive boards (4), and eighth in field goal percentage (.517). He ranked third in the league in offensive efficiency behind Minnesota's Kevin Garnett and San Antonio's Duncan. "I want to be an All-Star this year," Randolph had told reporters.

Management elected not to suspend Randolph after the arrest.

"In all fairness, there has been a cultural marijuana issue in the US for the last 40 years," said Steve Patterson, with a precursor of what was ahead in American culture. "We are also living in a state that has some of the most liberal laws in the land, so we have a considerable mixed message in this whole thing.

"Even so, our efforts have been toward enforcing a stricter policy on our players than the [collective bargaining agreement] would lead you to believe is permissible. But we can't just go out and suspend Zach at this time, with the lack of information that we have."

Randolph was making $1.2 million in a league in which the average salary approached $4 million.

"On a return-of-investment basis," Nash said, "Zach might be the best player in the league."

But now, another off-the-court screw-up.

"It's laughable, but it's not funny," Stoudamire would say. "It's a lot to deal with, and I'm speaking from firsthand experience."

"Another embarrassing moment," Cheeks told the media, coming on more strongly than usual. "It's always something. To wake up and be hit with something other than basketball, it's not healthy for me, it's not healthy for the organization. It's not easy to sit here and always talk to you guys about these situations. I do not enjoy being surrounded by this type of atmosphere.

"It's not a pretty image. I'm not especially proud of the names I hear of a team that I'm head coach of. All I can do is rehabilitate this team and try to make them people who people want to [watch play] and want to be around."

Jerome Kersey, the team's director of player programs, was asked of his take on the situation.

"There is definitely some kind of problem here, and probably has been since the J. R. Rider days," Kersey said. "When I was with the Blazers, we had guys to keep us in line like Jim Paxson, Kenny Carr, Mychal Thompson, and Caldwell Jones. Then when Clyde [Drexler], Terry [Porter], and Buck [Williams] and I were veterans, we policed the young guys. We have a shortage of veteran leadership on this [current] team."

One day after Randolph's arrest, Portland traded Wells to Memphis for small forward Wesley Person, a conditional first-round draft pick, and $1 million. Person was in the final year of a deal that paid him $7.7 million that season, so the Blazers would have the option to let him go into free agency after the season and pare their payroll.

Blazer management wanted Wells gone, at almost any cost. Team owner Paul Allen wasn't quite so sure.

"Paul didn't think we got equal value, and we didn't," Nash says today. "But Person was a decent player and a good person, and we got a first-round pick. Bottom line—Bonzi couldn't stay in Portland."

Had Wells been traded the previous summer, his value would have been much higher.

"Although Bonzi is a talented player, sometimes his talent was a little too much for us," Cheeks said in his curious fashion. The addition of Person was a "better fit for us."

Would Wallace be next on the trading block?

"That's a question we ask on an almost daily basis," Nash said. "It depends on the performance of the player and the team, as well as what the opportunities are. I have to consider trading everybody. Would we like to upgrade our roster? For sure. Are we going to be able to make a trade that conforms to the parameters we have established? I don't know."

There was one final indignity extended by Wells. According to *Oregonian* columnist John Canzano, Wallace had pulled Wells aside in their final shootaround together before the trade to Memphis.

"'Watch this,' Wallace told his teammate," Canzano wrote. "He then whipped the ball baseball style the length of the court into Ruben Boumtje-Boumtje, who was shooting jump shots with his back to them at the other end. As Ruben writhed on the ground, Bonzi and Sheed giggled like school-girls and ran away the moment their teammate hit the canvas."

That night, the Blazers came from five points down in the final minute of regulation to beat Indiana 97–95 in overtime. The fans were quick to forgive Randolph, who came through with a career-high 34 points and nine rebounds.

"I apologize to my teammates and the organization and the fans,"

Randolph would say when he met with the media. "I am embarrassed and disappointed for the team. It's something we don't need."

Two nights later, when Person checked into his first game as a Blazer against the Knicks at the Rose Garden, fans cheered for more than a minute. Person contributed eight points, three rebounds, and two assists in 15 minutes as Portland won 88–81.

On December 7, Portland opened a three-game road trip with a 93–79 loss at Memphis. Wells scored 10 of his 16 points in the fourth quarter as the Grizzlies, who tied a franchise record with 28 offensive rebounds, rallied from a 15-point second-quarter deficit to take the victory.

As the game ended, Wells walked to half-court and exchanged hugs with Wallace, Patterson, and McInnis, along with Portland assistants John Loyer, Jimmy Lynam, and Bernie Smith. Wells had already shaken hands with Cheeks after reporting to the scorer's table in the third quarter.

"It was fun," Wells told reporters afterward. "A lot better to win than to lose. Those guys are still my friends over there, but I wanted to beat them. Memphis rescued me. It's a breath of fresh air."

Memphis GM Jerry West was lavish in praise of Wells, lauding his skills as a player and downplaying his reputation as a troubled person. Was it a gamble to acquire him? "Absolutely not."

"Just to hear somebody talking upbeat about me was a blessing," Wells said. "It made me feel good in my heart, because everybody has been down on me lately. That recharged my battery. I just can't wait to get back to the love of the game."

Wells was now playing for Hubie Brown, the Grizzlies' 70-year-old head coach.

"This is the type of team I need to be on to show my true colors," Bonzi said. "The spacing is excellent, the coaching is excellent, there's a lot of unselfishness here. I don't have to worry about all the things I used to have to worry about."

Cheeks, asked before the game if he had mixed emotions about the trade, chuckled. "Mixed emotions? No."

It was a bad night for Cheeks, who was ejected for the first time in 25 years as a player, assistant coach, and coach, after drawing a pair of techni-cals. The third-year coach was incensed by what he considered a flippant attitude from referee Jason Phillips, who gave him his first T.

"I didn't even cuss at him until after I was ejected," said Cheeks, who was fined because he walked onto the court to confront Phillips, had to be restrained, and did not leave the court in a timely fashion.

"I guess I got my money's worth," Cheeks said. "I hope my mother wasn't watching."

Person scored two points in 13 minutes for the Blazers.

The Blazers would finish their trip on the wrong end of a 102–77 rout at San Antonio, the Spurs running a clinic on back-door plays for easy layups. Portland shot .333 from the game, and the debacle left Stoudamire in an ugly mood toward at least a few of his teammates.

"I'll go out there and ride me somebody tomorrow," he said. "If I have to get a technical foul at the beginning of the game to get cats going, I'm doing what I have to do. I'm tired of losing on the road."

After 20 games to start the season, Portland was 10–2 at home and 0–8 on the road, the worst road start for a Blazer team since 1980.

Wallace granted an interview to TNT's John Thompson, the former Georgetown coach, who asked him about his problems with referees. Wallace had not drawn as many technicals the previous season as he had in the past. He said there was a reason.

"I know with Mo Cheeks and his coaching staff, he's willing to fight with us as far as with the referees," Wallace told Thompson. "He'll get up off the bench and fight for us."

The same was true with Cheeks's predecessors, P. J. Carlesimo and Mike Dunleavy, of course.

Thompson asked if Wallace felt he deserved the amount of technicals he had been issued by referees.

"When I came into the league playing with the Bullets, they were giving me a lot of techs then," Wallace said. "I didn't understand it. I felt they were picking on me. I didn't come into the league with a reputation and, all of a sudden, all these techs coming out of nowhere.

"Some of them I deserved, yes. Some of them I didn't deserve. It's still like that to this day. I might cuss at a referee, you 'mf-er' or this and that, and I might get it back. No problem. But some refs if I cuss at them, they cuss at me. They want to bang me. C'mon, that's double standards. How you going to cuss at me AND give me a tech?"

> Thompson asked about Wallace's growing distaste for reporters.
>
> "I don't put the whole media in one perspective," he said. "There are good people in the media who will print what you say. They might say some bad things about you, but they'll even it out at some point in their story. The whole thing with the media, I don't read the papers out here. Everything I hear that they're killing us comes from my wife or my cousin or some friends. It's steady bashing, bashing, bashing. I just feel like I don't want to put fuel to the fire."

Public reaction was much greater on December 11, the day after the loss at San Antonio. *The Oregonian* printed a lengthy article featuring an exclusive interview with Wallace, conducted by Geoffrey Arnold. Wallace had been routinely refusing to speak with members of the media for most of the past two seasons.

The interview had taken place on November 26, the day after the Blazer suffered an 81–80 home loss to Washington, a game in which Wallace took six shots and finished with three points.

"I'm not worried about my shots," Wallace told Arnold. "I know if I wanted to, I could shoot the ball every time I wanted. I could shoot it 50 times if I wanted and not get cussed out. But what good is that? A, I don't hit more than half the shots, and B, we lose."

Wallace said criticism of his lack of leadership was unfounded.

"What they want as a leader is guys out on the court pointing fingers in people's faces," he said. "No, I do my talking out there on the floor, with ['help'] defense and trying to shut my man down and trying to help my teammates shut their man down. Whatever I have to do get the win. I'll say it when we're by ourselves. When it really matters in the locker room or at practice. That's when the leadership comes up."

Wallace, who had only four technicals through that point in the season, confirmed he hadn't changed his approach with referees.

"I still say the same things as before," he said. "I still do some of the same things I did before. I haven't changed, and I'm not going to change. Why should I?"

Arnold pursued the subject of technicals, and Wallace addressed it boldly.

"That's just the fire in me," he said. "I'm not scared of the NBA. I'm not scared of NBA officials. If I feel as though myself or my teammates have been dealt a wrong hand, I'm going to let it be known. I'm not going to sit up like most of these cats and bite my tongue. That's not me."

Wallace reiterated what he had told Thompson about his problems with officials beginning his rookie season.

"They came messing with me in the beginning, when I was with Washington," he said. "Why? I don't know. It's been an ongoing battle with them ever since. They can say what they want; it don't matter. It's not like it's going to make me go into my room and cry."

Asked about his image, Wallace responded, "I know I'm Public Enemy No. 1. Fifty percent [of the fans] hate me, and 50 percent love me, no matter what I do. I can't worry about that. If you're not part of my inner circle or family, it don't matter."

Wallace said he donated time and money to charitable events but didn't care to advertise it.

"I don't need a TV camera to let me know on the inside that I'm doing something good," he said.

After talking it over with his wife, Wallace said he regretted the marijuana arrest while driving home from Seattle with Stoudamire after a game the previous season.

"It was embarrassing from the standpoint of my family," Wallace said. "She was like, 'I know how you are. I know stuff like that doesn't really affect you too much. But it affected us.' She meant her and my kids.

"That made me sit back and think about it, and she was right. I have to think past myself. I got a family. Got a wife. She was telling me what was happening with my kids. After I talked to her about it, I regretted the whole situation. Until then, I didn't regret it. OK, we had gotten in a little trouble.

"Did that make me a bad person? Does that mean I'm a bad basketball player? Does that mean I don't want to win? No. That's what the media and others tried to make it seem like. The only opinions that matter to me in this world are my wife and my kids, my mom—my immediate circle."

Wallace said he didn't care that some fans said they would not renew their season tickets unless he is traded.

"I'm definitely happy with who I am, my personality, my lifestyle. I won't change it. Not one bit. Not for any amount of money. I'm going to be me, plain and simple."

Then came the part that triggered a firestorm. Wallace said he thought the white establishment of the NBA was exploiting young black athletes to enrich itself.

"I ain't no dumb-ass nigger out here," he began. "I'm not like a whole bunch of these young boys out here who get caught up and captivated into the league. No, I see behind the lines. I see behind the false screens. I know what this business is all about. I know the commissioner of this league makes more than three-quarters of the players in this league. . . . They just want to draft niggers who are dumb and dumber . . . straight out of high school. That's why they're drafting all these high school cats—because they come into the league and they don't know no better. They don't know the real business, and they don't see behind the charade. They look at black athletes like we're dumb-ass niggers. It's as if we're just going to shut up, sign for the money, and do what they tell us."

Reaction to the Wallace piece was swift and profound.

The following day, commissioner David Stern was on the phone for an hour with Steve Patterson, lobbying for the club to suspend or release the player. Patterson wasn't pleased with Wallace's comments but cited First Amendment civil liberties. Any disciplinary action would have been challenged by the players' union. And agent Bill Strickland was prepared to enlist support from the likes of Johnnie Cochran and Jesse Jackson should the Blazers attempt to come down on Wallace.

Football Hall-of-Famer and black activist Jim Brown, in an interview with AOL Sports, said "Rasheed should educate himself and learn something about blacks." Former Blazer Bill Walton, in an ESPN.com article, said that Wallace was an "embarrassment and a disgrace" to the city of Portland.

ESPN's Len Elmore said he was befuddled.

"Those are strange comments coming from a guy who gets paid

double-digit millions of dollars per year by one of those same owners," Elmore said. "But money can't buy dignity. That is why Wallace is way off base, especially since he failed to look in the mirror before indicting NBA management . . . in the last 15 years, the NBA has created more African-American millionaires than in any time during the civilization of man. If that's exploitation, then exploit me, please . . . so when Wallace says, none too cryptically, 'I know what this business is about,' I'm not sure he's as smart as he thinks. . . . Whatever we perceive as the legacy of Magic or MJ, every player today must closely examine their modus operandi: Win and infect the fans with the idea that you are enjoying yourself rather than the constant 'bah, humbug' attitude on the court that is synonymous with Rasheed Wallace."

On the local front, the *Portland Tribune*'s Dwight Jaynes let Wallace have it.

"He has been protected, pampered, babied, and catered to since people realized he not only was pretty good at putting a round ball into a round hole but also was going to be lucky enough to end up very tall," Jaynes wrote. "I am so tired of having to listen to this man. I am so tired of his ignorance, bad manners, and foul temper. I am so tired of his alibis, excuses, and his lack of effort to be a great player and a great person. And I imagine you are, too."

Two days later, before the Blazers' 112–108 home win over the Lakers, Wallace issued a statement.

> I made a few comments that some people found objectionable. Like everyone, I have a right to express my opinion, which I did. But I regret using street language to express my opinion because everyone has focused on those few comments when I said other things. It was not my intent to offend anyone. So if I offended any of my teammates, fellow NBA players, the Trail Blazer fans and organization, I apologize.

By December 16, Portland's field-goal defense had fallen to .470, by far the worst percentage in the league. It was a far cry from the four seasons under Mike Dunleavy, when the Blazers finished fourth, sixth, fifth, and 11th in succession. In the first two seasons of Cheeks, they were 23rd both years. Now they were even worse.

On December 22, after a 117–98 blowout loss at Sacramento, Cheeks called for a team meeting, saying he was tired of harping at the players about their responsibilities and that it was time for them to be accountable for their play on the court. After the coach's talk, each player took his turn offering observations and suggestions about the Blazers being under .500 (12–13) for the season.

"It was basically a reality check," Dale Davis said afterward. "It's not happy around here right now, and we don't like having these meetings, but sometimes they are necessary. Hopefully, we will respond to this one."

The Blazers were to win their next two games, but then dropped 10 of their next 12 contests. The bottom was quickly falling out.

On December 26, after Portland's 101–92 win over Minnesota at the Rose Garden, ex-Blazer Gary Trent entered the Blazers' locker room. Trent had come by to see Wallace, who had already dressed and left. But McInnis was still there, and Trent started a conversation.

Then he saw Vladimir Stepania, the Blazers' 7-foot reserve center, who had fouled Trent hard in the first half. Trent approached Stepania and warned him that he doesn't "put up with that shit." When Stepania stood up, Trent came twice more with obscenity-laced admonitions. The last time, Stepania told him to "get the hell out" of the locker room.

Trent eventually did, but not one Blazer player came to Stepania's defense. Stepania, who was contacted by NBA officials about the incident, would later say this: "It's not like it was a big fight or anything. A few words were said. I didn't appreciate it, but I don't think Trent is known as a great guy, so it's not that surprising. It didn't bother me that much."

On December 28, at the shootaround before Portland's 86–74 loss at Cleveland, Cheeks told a reporter he was pleased with the performance of the recently acquired Person. The veteran small forward was shooting .467 from the 3-point line while averaging 7.3 points in 20.9 minutes through 11 games.

"He's a breath of fresh air," Cheeks said. "His attention to detail, the fact that he listens, his professionalism—he is what this team needed."

Just as Cheeks began to elaborate, Wallace picked up a basketball and punted it the length of the court, four rows deep into the stands. Cheeks shook his head, exhaled, and continued with his thoughts on Person, "He understands about playing. And when you get to the fourth quarter, you need discipline, and he has that."

That night, rookie LeBron James, two days from his 19th birthday, scored 12 of Cleveland's final 14 points, finishing with 32 points, 10 rebounds, and nine assists as the Cavaliers made the Blazers 0–10 on the road for the season.

"I'm pretty pissed at them," Cheeks told the media afterward. "Poor effort. In the last four or five minutes, they outworked us, simple as that."

The following night at New Jersey, the Blazers ended their road futility with a 91–87 victory over the Nets.

"Ever since I've been here, that's the way it has been with this team," said Stoudamire, whose two free throws with 8.7 seconds left sealed the triumph. "We win when people think we won't, and we lose when we probably shouldn't."

* * *

Portland moved into the new year with a 106–96 home loss to Denver to fall to 15–16 on the season. For three quarters, Wallace was sensational, scoring 30 points on 12-for-16 shooting. In the fourth quarter, he missed all four of his shots and had his eighth scoreless final period of the season.

The next day, Stoudamire was talking to a reporter about the state of the team.

"I hate to say this, but maybe this is a bad mix of players," he said. "I remember one of the main things in me wanting to get out of Toronto was I wanted to go to a perennial contender, a team that consistently got things done in the playoffs.

"But right now, this is the most frustrated I've been in the NBA. We don't play for 48 minutes. We don't have full concentration for the duration. That tends to hurt us. We have breakdowns at key times—and in a five- or six-minute span, we lose a game, usually in the second half."

Ruben Patterson was asked if he thought it was time to make a roster move.

"Absolutely," said Ruben, who had maintained he didn't want to be involved in any deal.

The schedule wasn't getting easier. Beginning with a 119–108 overtime loss at Seattle, the Blazers would face a stretch where 13 of their next 17 games were on the road. Portland would lose 96–75 in a listless performance at Minnesota to fall to 1–13 on the road.

The Blazers played the Timberwolves without Davis, who failed to make the team flight from Portland after getting caught in a snowstorm that had enveloped Portland two days earlier.

Randolph was the one bit of good news for the Blazers. The third-year forward was among the NBA's top 20 in several categories, including offensive rebounds (3.8, third), rebounds (11.6, fourth), double-doubles (19, fourth), scoring (22.8, seventh), minutes (40, seventh), and field-goal percentage (.491, 16th).

There had been no blow-up between Randolph and Ruben Patterson after their ugly altercation the previous season. They coexisted under an uneasy truce.

"I try not to think about what happened last year," Patterson said. "I will never forget about it, but I am the older guy between the two of us. I am not going to sucker punch him or beat him up. I am going to try to play basketball and help us win."

On January 13, the Clippers beat Portland 103–96 in overtime at Staples Center. In the closing seconds of regulation and Portland holding a three-point lead, Cheeks had chosen not to foul. Eddie House then tied the game on a 3-pointer with 3.8 seconds left, and the Clippers went on to win in the extra session.

"I understand why Bob Whitsitt fired Mike Dunleavy and brought Cheeks in—it was an effort to appease Rasheed Wallace," Dwight Jaynes wrote afterward. "That was obvious from the outset. But it hasn't worked. Wallace has been just as lazy under Cheeks as he was under Dunleavy. And Wallace has taken advantage of Cheeks's buddy-buddy style by not getting to the low post as often as he did when Dunleavy was hounding him to do so. I don't understand why Cheeks was given an extension. It's obvious from watching this team that the coach is not motivating anyone. And he's not outcoaching anyone, either. Never has."

After the game, the subject of potential trades came up in the team locker room.

"A cloud is always over this team," Stoudamire said. "I don't really want to see Sheed go, but if you think that is what's best for the team, you should do something before the trade deadline. Don't let it play out."

That week, Wallace appeared on ABC's *Shootaround* show and was asked by host Mike Tirico about his comments in *The Oregonian* article. His response was about as close to contrition as Wallace would get.

"I was not attacking David Stern," he said. "It wasn't no personal feelings about him. When I did the interview, it just came out. If I would have known it was going to get this heavy and blow up out of proportion like the majority of people did, no, I wouldn't have said it."

* * *

On January 21, the Blazers made a trade—but not involving the player many had expected. Portland sent guard Jeff McInnis and reserve center Ruben Boumtje-Boumtje to Cleveland for 22-year-old small forward Darius Miles.

McInnis had seen ample playing time, starting 26 games while Anderson was ailing with back issues. But McInnis felt he should be the starter at point guard ahead of Stoudamire. Damon said there was no outward tension between the two, "but it was always kind of hovering over us. There is no denying he wanted to be a starter. In his mind, maybe he felt he should have been, or should have been playing a lot more."

The big news, though, was the acquisition of Miles, a slim 6-foot-9 wunderkind who came out of East St. Louis High as the No. 3 pick in the 2000 draft (chosen by the Clippers). Miles was raised by his mother, Ethel Miles, in a single-parent household in one of the roughest areas of the country, just across the Mississippi River from St. Louis.

As a youth, Miles had learned his game at "The Hole" playground, a three-minute bike ride from his home. He'd had a gun pulled on him there when he was 11.

"I felt my life could have been over," he said. "So many people were shot at places where I played basketball, it ain't even funny. I decided then I was going to make the best of it and try to lift my family."

By the time he reached the NBA, Miles was a high-flying dunking machine with limited shooting range and comprehension of the game. He became the first player taken straight out of high school to be named first-team All-Rookie, having averaged 9.4 points and 5.9 rebounds while shooting .505 with the Clippers in 2000–01. He was solid coming off the bench the next year, averaging 9.5 points and 5.5 rebounds while shooting .481.

The Clippers saw something they didn't like, though, and traded him to Cleveland in the deal that brought Andre Miller to the Clippers. Miles averaged 9.2 points and 5.4 rebounds for the Cavaliers but shot only .410 as a starter in 2002–03. Those close to the scene wondered if he spent too much time on the set shooting a movie (*Van Wilder*) the previous summer and not working on his game. He also hadn't properly rehabbed after offseason knee surgery.

During the 2003–04 campaign, Miles had averaged 8.9 points and 4.5 boards while shooting .432 as a part-time starter. But his star was falling. New coach Paul Silas had used him as many as 20 minutes in only three of nine games in January. After playing eight minutes against Utah, Miles missed the next practice, saying he had forgotten to set his alarm clock.

Now he would be joining his third NBA team in 3½ years, making $4.1 million in the final year of his rookie contract, destined to become a restricted free agent in June.

"Darius is a player with tremendous upside potential," Nash said. "It is a rare opportunity for us, with very little risk. We have 40-some games left. We get a short-term look at a player, but it's long enough to make an intelligent decision about his future with us."

* * *

On January 23, Davis lost his starting job and a bit of his good reputation, walking out of practice after learning the Blazers had docked him one game's pay—more than $100,000 from his season salary of $9.06 million—for missing the team flight on January 7 and the game at Minnesota the following night. Steve Patterson had not accepted Davis's excuse after he had gotten caught in a snowstorm.

"We offered to send someone to his home to get him out, which he turned down," Patterson said. "Do I think Dale put forth an effort to get out? Yeah, he did. But 30 other people in our traveling party made it. He didn't.

"We had warned all of our players two days earlier to be ready for what was coming. If you know you are going to have trouble getting out of your driveway, you take actions to avoid problems. Dale is a good guy. This is not a character issue. It was just a mistake. The guy missed the plane."

Today, Davis looks back at the situation with bemusement.

"Where I lived, on top of Forest Heights, it was bad," Davis said. "I had to go up and down and around the hill. I tried by myself first; couldn't get out. Then I had a friend come pick me up. It took us a couple of hours to drag those bags to get to where his truck was parked down the hill, then another hour or two to get to the airport. By that time, I was late [for the team flight].

"I finally got out the next day to Chicago through Seattle, but it was after the fact—not in time to make the game. And then the fine—that was painful. C'mon, man, I almost killed myself trying to get there."

Davis said he was informed of the fine via certified mail on January 22, which pissed him off and, after a short talk with Nash, caused him to walk out of the following day's practice, which resulted in an additional $5,000 fine.

The previous week, Cheeks had moved Wallace to the post and Davis to a bench role, starting Randolph at power forward and Patterson at small forward. With Miles on board, the rotation on the front line had become even more crowded.

Davis would eventually take the lost salary from the missed game to arbitration and win.

"Part of the reason was that Maurice testified on his behalf," Nash recalls. "He'd been fired by that time."

On January 24, the Blazers were clobbered 105–87 by Golden State, hitting the halfway point of the regular season with a 17–24 record. It was the club's worst start in 28 seasons. The Blazers would enter the second half of the season 6.5 games back of Memphis for the eighth spot in the Western Conference.

"We can't kid ourselves anymore," Randolph said. "We have become one of those bad teams."

"This is the breaking point," Stoudamire said. "We don't care about each other on the floor. We don't play basketball the right way. We don't help on defense. We don't make the extra pass. Paul Allen needs to take down those big ol' [reader boards] in the four corners. Take them down and don't put no statistics on the board. It's bad out there, man."

The Blazers would make a resurgence, winning seven of eight to get within one game of .500. When the Blazers beat Seattle 95–85 at home for their seventh win in eight games, Cheeks pronounced, "We're playing very good basketball right now."

Portland was relying on the inside presence of Randolph and Wallace.

"Rasheed's defense has been very good," Cheeks said. "He's a heady defender, and he gives us a shot-blocker in there."

"Rasheed has carried us," Davis said.

The next day, the Rasheed Wallace era ended in Portland.

* * *

On February 9, the Blazers traded Wallace and Person—who had come to Portland in the Wells deal—to Atlanta for center Theo Ratliff, forward Shareef Abdur-Rahim, and guard Dan Dickau.

Steve Patterson called it a "watershed day" for the franchise.

Wallace was informed of the trade as he was attending the WWE *Raw* pro wrestling event at the Rose Garden. Before he was summoned to Cheeks's office, Wallace was shown on the scoreboard and booed heavily.

"Rasheed wanted out from the day I arrived," Nash says now. "I was disappointed. I'd drafted him in Washington and recognized what a great talent he was. During his rookie year, I tried to explain how he was going to damage his career with all the technicals. Referees were going to gang up on him. He didn't care. He had a disdain for authority.

"His agent [Bill Strickland] told me almost immediately, 'Rasheed's not going to be happy in Portland.' He was very upset at the way he was characterized, but he created his own persona."

Wallace would play one game in a Hawks uniform, then be sent to Detroit, where he would help the Pistons win the NBA championship that spring and make two more All-Star Games. Even so, it was a good move for the Blazers; a bold move, one necessary for the franchise to move beyond the Jail Blazers era.

Rasheed had been one of the most talented, and polarizing, players in club history.

"There comes a time when an organization needs to make a change for the organization's sake," Cheeks said after the trade. "This was one of those times."

Wallace would never reach his Hall of Fame potential, in part because he didn't take care of his body as carefully as most of the greats. In his latter years with Portland, he had been fined $50,000 a month during the season because he refused to take part in mandatory weight-lifting sessions for all players. The fine for a missed session was $5,000. The players were required to lift ten times a month. Over the course of the season, that would add up to $300,000. Rasheed would bring in a blank check at the beginning of the season to cover it.

"I'm not going to lift during the year," he would say. "How much do I owe you?"

"I love Rasheed, but conditioning wasn't something he felt he needed," Bobby Medina, Portland's strength and conditioning coach at the time, says today. "At one point Rasheed was a better player than Tim Duncan. You could see Rasheed's skill level start to decrease as Duncan got better because Tim took better care of himself. Rasheed didn't take care of himself, and all those things started creeping up on him—back injuries and things like that.

"He was a guy who played himself into shape. If you ask him, I think he'd regret not taking better care of himself. It hurt him later in his career. It's almost criminal with the natural talent he possessed. I put it on myself, too. I wish I could have done a better job with him. I wish I could have made him more of a believer in it. That was a struggle."

Many of those who worked with Wallace loved him.

"I'd like to have his jersey on the wall at my house," says Jay Jensen, the team trainer during Wallace's years in Portland. "The dude was a competitor. He didn't care if he scored two or 50 points, he just wanted to win. He didn't care about getting any credit. He was great to people like me and Bobby. He didn't like people in authority. He had a little trouble with Dunleavy, but he loved Cheeks. You'd be hard-pressed to find any teammate who didn't love playing with Rasheed. He didn't care about stats; he just cared about winning."

Danny Ainge had been critical about Wallace as a player in Portland during his time as a TNT in the early 2000s. Years later, when Ainge was executive VP/basketball operations for Boston, he acquired Wallace. At age 35, Rasheed came off the bench for the 2009–10 Celtics, who lost in seven games to the Lakers in the NBA Finals.

"That year, in our series against Orlando and Cleveland, we were playing our best basketball we played during the entire Kevin Garnett/Paul Pierce era, and Rasheed was a part of that," Ainge says today. "He didn't have a very good regular season, but he had an amazing playoff run."

Wallace retired after that season, leaving some guaranteed money on the table.

"By that time, he had matured," Ainge says. "He was a different player than he was as a youngster in Portland."

But Wallace was still boisterous enough to lead the NBA with 17 technical fouls that season, even playing only 22.5 minutes a game as a reserve. He would sit out two seasons before, at age 38, coming back for 21 games with the Knicks in 2012–13 to pick up the final four technicals of his career. Wallace led the league seven times in his 15-plus seasons and accumulated 317 regular-season T's. He ranks behind only Karl Malone (332) and Charles Barkley (329) on the all-time list.

"It always amazed me when Rasheed started acting up on the floor, especially in a pressure-packed game at home," says Mike Barrett, the team's TV play-by-play voice during Wallace's final season. "His reaction would fuel the fans' reaction, and all of a sudden the entire arena was angry. One guy's behavior toward the officials tended to fuel the arena in a negative way. It's impossible to say that was not a distraction."

With the departure of Wallace, the Blazers had extricated themselves from part of the behavioral problem but not all.

Wrote ESPN's Chad Ford: "They've dumped Bonzi Wells, a repeat offender in Portland. Wallace is gone, too, which is great. But left behind are numbskulls such as Ruben Patterson, Damon Stoudamire, and, to a lesser extent, Zach Randolph and Qyntel Woods. While the face of the Blazers has undoubtedly changed, they still have more troublemakers on their roster than anyone else in the league. Let's not take down the Neighborhood Watch signs just yet."

Then there was the opinion of Ruben Patterson, who took news of the trade for Abdur-Rahim with his trademark class.

"If I lose minutes because of this," Patterson said, "I will definitely have something to say about it."

* * *

Nash got some outstanding talent out of the Wallace deal.

The 6-foot-10 Ratliff, 30, was a shot-blocking machine who had been an All-Star the previous season and would lead the league in blocks in 2003–04 with 3.2 per game. Abdur-Rahim, 27, was a 6-foot-9 two-time All-Star who had averaged 20.7 points and 8.3 rebounds while shooting .465 through his eight-year career. He was a member of the US Olympic team that won gold in 2000. Dickau, a local kid from Battle Ground, Washington, was a throw-in but a useful backup at the point.

"Theo had seven blocks in a win over Boston last week, and his blocks are momentum-changers," said Ratliff's coach in Atlanta, Terry Stotts, after the trade. "If there's a guy at the rim for a dunk, he'll block it. Shareef's talent speaks for itself. He's an outstanding mid-range shooter who can score in a variety of ways. He gives defensive effort. He pays attention to the game plan. The only knock on him would be that he hasn't been to the playoffs."

Just as important was the character of the three. There would be no middle-of-the-night calls about this trio.

"First-rate," Stotts said of the three. "Theo is good people all the way. Shareef is one of the best guys I've known in the game of basketball. It was really tough to part with him. It was a pleasure to coach him. Portland will be the best team he has been on. He has had to shoulder a lot of responsibility throughout his career and has done it gracefully and with a lot of class."

The trade, though, overloaded the Blazers up front, giving them Ratliff, Davis, Randolph, Abdur-Rahim, Patterson, and Miles on the front line. They were left with a dearth of shooting guards and perimeter shooters.

Even so, reaction to the trade throughout the league was positive.

"Considering the situation he walked into, John Nash has done a phenomenal job," Knicks general manager Isiah Thomas said. "He has a talented team and good character people, which is exactly what they were hoping for."

"They did pretty well," TNT's Magic Johnson said. "They got Theo to close down the middle. Shareef has always been 20/9 every night, every season, and he is going to draw some fouls. They got some guys who have the character they are looking for, but they got some talent, too."

TNT's Doug Collins was a former coach who was well-informed on the situation Nash had faced.

"Portland is a city that lives and breathes Trail Blazers, and there was tremendous criticism about them in the community," Collins said. "The organization has made a concerted effort to tell the fans, 'We are going to turn this around and change our team.' Now they will have to settle in and see how all the pieces fit. They weren't going to make any deal not in the best long-term interest of the team. You get rid of a player like Rasheed, you can't just get nothing in return."

Another TNT analyst, Steve Kerr, had been a road roommate of Rasheed's during his one season in Portland. "The trade had to be done for the team's image," Kerr said. "I am glad they made the move. It was a smart move, and I was surprised they could get so much in return for Rasheed at this point."

But Kerr also sounded a warning about both Randolph and Abdur-Rahim on the same team: "One of those guys, probably Rahim, has to guard 3's. Both Zach and Shareef like to be near the basket [on offense]. Miles has already been on two teams that were willing to give him away. He has a lot of ability, but nobody seems to know what position he is or what exactly he does. They are three pretty talented players, and one of them is going to have to come off the bench."

Indeed, the trade had to be done, but it wouldn't improve the Blazers in the short run. They wouldn't make the playoffs this season, nor would they get to the postseason again until 2009, after Brandon Roy and LaMarcus Aldridge had arrived and settled into their roles with the team.

Nash was in between a rock and a hard place. He was trying to upgrade the roster, but also keep the peace with his current players.

"The veterans on that roster were upset that they were being character-ized as they were in the media," Nash says today. "In some cases, they didn't feel it was justified. In many cases, they were difficult with the coach. We had to eventually move [Cheeks] out.

"The attitude in that locker room permeated even some of the good guys. There was a rebellion in the locker room against management and authority. It was a locker room with a lot of difficulties."

Stoudamire, though close friends with the recently traded Wallace, struck a positive note.

"I see potential," Damon said. "Once the new cats get a couple of prac-tices under their belt, they will be even better. There are going to be issues about minutes. I just hope it gets addressed in the right way. I hope the thing with Ruben doesn't become an issue, because we don't need that now."

Ruben Patterson was both disgruntled and confused.

"I was pulling my hair out with Ruben," Nash says. "He would get me confused with Steve Patterson. Before I had seen the Blazers play a single game, I got a call from Ruben. He asked for Steve Nash. He called me

Steve for a while. He made it clear he wanted out. It was hard to move him because of his prior legal situation.

"It was a difficult group of guys to work with, and it was difficult to try to get equal value. At one point, I thought we had a trade for Jason Kidd that didn't work out. Paul Pierce, the same thing. We were trying to acquire quality players, and we never got there."

* * *

On February 12, in their first game with the new alignment, the Blazers lost 107–98 to Denver at home to fall to 24–27 at the All-Star break. They were 5½ games behind Denver for the eighth spot in West.

Cheeks went with a starting lineup of Davis, Randolph, and Miles on the front line with Stoudamire and Anderson in the backcourt. Off the bench, Abdur-Rahim and Ratliff—greeted with long standing ovations by the home fans—made their mark. Shareef scored 20 points and grabbed 12 rebounds in 30 minutes. Theo had 14 points on 6-for-7 shooting (with four dunks), 10 boards, and four blocks in 28 minutes. But the trade offered a new set of problems.

Patterson, relegated to 19 minutes, wasn't happy.

"There are too many players here," he said after the game. "We can't share the minutes. How do you think I feel? How do you think Darius feels? It has been like this ever since I have been with the Blazers. I like to play. If they don't think it's good for me to play, then there will have to be some kind of changes. I'm hurting, for real."

Patterson even logged a few minutes at the two behind Anderson.

"I ain't no shooting guard," he said. "That ain't going to work. We have no one to back up Derek."

Randolph had only eight points against the Nuggets, making 2-of-7 shots from the field. Late in the game, he threw his headband and armband into the stands.

It was finally Stoudamire's team to run. Gone was his competition at the point, from Rod Strickland to Rick Brunson to Scottie Pippen to Antonio Daniels to Jeff McInnis. Damon was the last man standing from the nucleus Bob Whitsitt put together that lost to the Lakers in the seventh game of the 2000 West Finals.

"It seemed like there was no future at one point last season, but things changed," Stoudamire said. "I have been able to weather the storm."

And Stoudamire, 30, was looking for a contract extension with one year left on his deal.

"I want to be here," he said. "I have gone through so much to get where I am. Portland is my home. There is really no place I would rather play. I would love to stay here until I retire."

While with Vancouver and Atlanta, Abdur-Rahim had never been on a team that won more than 35 games in a season.

"When you get down to it, all that matters is winning," Abdur-Rahim said. "Look at those great teams Portland had in the early '90s. I couldn't tell you how many points Clyde Drexler or Terry Porter or Buck Williams or Jerome Kersey averaged. I just remember they were a great team and they were winners. That's why people remember them. That's why people love them.

"I have accomplished a lot of things in my career, but I have always wanted to win. The atmosphere here is different than any I've been in through my career. I don't mind whatever role Maurice wants me to play. Numbers aren't important. Playing time isn't important. I know I can help this team. That is the main thing I want to do."

And, said Abdur-Rahim, "This is Zach's team. I'm the one who has to adjust, not him."

Cheeks was informed of Abdur-Rahim's comments and smiled.

"That tells you what Shareef is all about," the coach said. "Hopefully, Zach and our other young guys will pick up on that and learn from that."

* * *

Unfortunately, the problems weren't over.

Over the All-Star break, Qyntel Woods was involved in a drug bust as a passenger in his car. The driver, Joseph Blake, was stopped by the California Highway Patrol driving Woods's BMW at 102 miles per hour near Fresno.

Blake told officers the marijuana in the car was his. The Blazers fined Woods $2,000.

Then, Randolph and Davis were fined for sleeping through a shootaround before the team's February 17 loss (89–86) to the Lakers at Staples Center.

But four days later, on February 21, the Blazers burst to 22–0 lead on the way to 105–84 rout of Boston at the Rose Garden.

Randolph was back in the swing of things with 27 points and 15 rebounds as the Blazers scored at will in transition, with high-flying dunks from Miles, Patterson, and Woods.

"We're becoming more of a team," Cheeks offered. "I think you can see the potential."

Two nights later, the Blazers opened a four-game road trip with an 89–81 win at Miami, using a 14–0 run to overhaul the Heat. It was the fourth straight win for the Blazers (28–28), pushing them to .500 for the first time since December 31, and moving them within three games of Denver for the eighth spot in the West.

Randolph totaled 22 points and 12 rebounds for his 32nd double-double of the season. Stoudamire scored 20 points and Ratliff, who finished with four points, seven rebounds, and two blocks, had a presence at the defensive end.

"Words can't explain what Theo does for us," Cheeks said. "He changes the outcome of every game we will play in. We have been down so long, but with the changes we have made with the trades, it has given us new life. The new guys have given us some energy, and they see that something special could happen."

After a 94–91 overtime win at Orlando to go to 29–28 on the season, the Blazers' five-game win streak ended with an 89–85 loss at Houston. Even so, Cheeks was in a good mood afterward.

"I was sitting on the sideline, and I told someone I love our team," he said. "I just love the way we compete. I love the way we play, the way we still go at it."

* * *

As the calendar turned to March, public enemy's No. 1 and 2 returned to the scene of the crime. Memphis, with Bonzi Wells, and Detroit, with Rasheed Wallace, visited for back-to-back games at the Rose Garden.

Greeted by boos from the crowd at every turn, Wells scored 28 points to lead the Grizzlies to a 97–88 win over his former team.

"The booing added incentive and gave me a little more pep in my step," Wells said afterward. "I hope they boo me for the rest of my career."

Later, he admitted, "The boos hurt a little. I know there are some people who love me here, and I know there are some people who may not like me. That's cool. That's how it is in some places."

The following night, a crowd of 20,243 was on hand, the third sellout of the season to "greet" Wallace back to Portland. Unfortunately for the Blazer partisans, Detroit won handily, 83–68. As Wallace was received by a mixture of boos and cheers during pregame introductions, he bowed his head and raised his right fist. He then went out and collected 13 points, nine rebounds, and three blocks in 34 minutes.

It was the lowest scoring output of the season for the Blazers, who shot .342 from the field. The Pistons won the rebound battle 51–35 to send the Blazers to their fourth straight loss, dropping them to 29–32 for the season.

"Whether it was their defense or our ineptitude, we had no offensive flow," Cheeks said.

The Blazers would rebound, winning 12 of their next 17 games, starting with an 81–70 win over Utah in which Ratliff would register seven blocked shots. But there was no getting around one problem. Randolph and Abdur-Rahim were both power forwards. They were two of the team's five best players, and Cheeks knew he needed production from both. He continued to bring Abdur-Rahim off the bench and, at times, play them together.

"Both of them need to be on the floor," Cheeks said. "Let's just say it all can't stay the same next season, that's for sure."

On March 9, Stoudamire took a drug test at the Blazers' practice facility, producing a urine sample for *The Oregonian*'s John Canzano. Before the season started, he had made a verbal agreement with Canzano that he could test him at any time. Moments before the test, Damon asked Cheeks to serve as a witness.

Stoudamire passed the test, testing negative for marijuana and five other drugs. The next day, the NBA Players Association said the Blazers were in violation of the collective-bargaining agreement when Cheeks witnessed it.

"I didn't see any harm in it," Cheeks said. "I didn't do it for any other reason than to be there for Damon."

On March 12, the Blazers pulled out a thrilling 83–81 win over Sacramento, knocking off the best team in the West. Stoudamire had 20 points as Portland (32–33) stayed in contention for a playoff spot. ESPN analyst Bill Walton, calling the game that night, offered plenty of opinions on the recent trade.

"It's a chance for the Blazers to work their way back to the top," Walton said. "Rasheed had destroyed so many of the tenets that make a franchise viable. The sun has come out from behind the clouds in Portland again. The Blazers have made the right moves to make the team and community feel they are in this together."

As for Wallace in Detroit, Walton added, "I would love to see him go on and achieve all the levels of greatness people have predicted for him forever. I would love to see him become a historical level player, model his life after Abraham Lincoln and Mother Teresa, give up his life for the sake of others and . . . should I hold my breath?"

As far as Abdur-Rahim and Randolph playing together, Walton said this: "They can definitely make it work. These are two good players. The 1986 Celtics didn't have a classic point guard. There have been great teams that hasn't had clearly defined small and power forwards. The key is to find a way. That is what great coaches do."

On March 16, Anderson and Miles each scored 20 points as Portland prevailed 100–99 at Milwaukee for its fourth straight win, going above .500 again at 34–33.

"They have the ultimate defender back there in Theo and some guys on the perimeter who can defend pretty well," said Bucks coach Terry Porter, the ex-Blazer great. "They have Zach Randolph, and a 20/10 guy coming off the bench in Shareef. Since the trade, they have blossomed into a team. Before, they were just a bunch of individuals."

But even with the change in players, they still couldn't shake the Jail Blazers image.

Three days later, Woods and Miles were involved in a brawl with at least three men at Exotica strip club in North Portland at 2:30 a.m. According to witnesses, the fight started when the three men jumped Woods after he pushed away a man who had blocked his path after words were exchanged in the parking lot. During the melee, the men loaded into a car and sped at Woods, attempting to pin him against another car. He avoided impact by hopping onto the car's hood.

The Blazers chose to take no action against the players.

"Their view of what went on is basically that they were attacked," Steve Patterson said. "I see no reason at this point to doubt that."

"We got into a situation that we couldn't get out of," Woods would say.

"I feel bad about the situation," Miles said. "It's a distraction to the team and a distraction to the Portland fans, who have been treating me so well since I got here. We are focusing on the playoffs, and I'm sorry we are talking about this right now."

On March 24, Stoudamire scored 20 of his season-high 32 points in the fourth quarter of a 91–85 comeback win over the Clippers. The Blazers, 36–35, were hanging on for dear life in their drive for the playoffs.

"By far, in terms of the pressure and what it meant to the team, this is the most important 32 points I've ever had in a game," Stoudamire said.

Three nights later, Stoudamire was sterling again, going for 23 points, eight assists, six rebounds, and three steals in 49 minutes of a 115–108 overtime win over Seattle. Randolph had 25 points and nine rebounds, Anderson contributed 22 points, seven assists, and four steals, and Ratliff collected 18 points, nine rebounds, and six blocks as the Blazers won for the seventh time in nine games.

After an excruciatingly tough 92–91 loss at New York to open a three-game road trip, Miles had his biggest game in a Portland uniform in a 105–98 victory at Boston. The small forward scored a career-high 31 points on 13-for-17 shooting.

Miles was growing in self-confidence that shifted into cockiness.

"I am the backbone of this team," he said. "All the way from the backbone to the wrist bone, if something ain't working, I got to keep it all together."

Miles would be a restricted free agent after the season, and the Blazers would be faced with a decision to extend his contract or match another team's qualifying offer.

"Darius has shown us a lot of things," Nash said. "He is long and hard to defend. He can take the ball in transition, take a defensive rebound, and be at the offensive end in short order. I like his ability to score around the basket. The areas in his game he needs to work on are perimeter shooting and turnovers. But we hope to be able to keep him for years to come."

* * *

April had arrived and, going into final two weeks of the regular season, Portland was battling Denver and Utah for the final playoff spot in the West. In an interview with the *Portland Tribune*, owner Paul Allen said he was happy because the Blazer fans were happy.

"The great thing for me is that feeling in the [Rose Garden] is very much changed from earlier in the season," Allen said. "That is heartening to see. When we began last summer, I told everybody we were going to make changes, that we would have different expectations of our players, and that the adjustment process issuing to take some time and we have going to have to be patient. It took a while, but I am convinced we are in a better place going forward."

The other goal going into the season was stemming the financial bath Allen had been taking with the club the past two years. After losing $100 million the previous season, the organization laid off more than 70 employees and began an austerity program that included a reduction in player payroll after leading the NBA at around $106 million in 2002–03. When the Blazers made the trade to unload Wallace, however, they took on an additional $25 million in player salaries for the following season.

"I had to make a substantial financial commitment for next year to have the kind of roster our basketball people want so we could have more flexibility in the near future," Allen said. "It was expensive, but it was the right thing to do. It puts the franchise talent level on a better footing for the future."

Allen said he was happy with the direction the Blazers had taken.

"I was talking with Shareef at our team photo session last week. He told me he hadn't played in a city where people really are excited about basketball and care about the team to this level. That is the thing that has always stood out about Portland in my mind. It is unique to Portland that people really want to get behind and care about the team. There are different expectations on player behavior than there are in, say, a major metropolitan area on the East Coast. And that's OK. We have addressed that. It's heartening to see the fans give their wholehearted support to what we have done."

On April 3, the Blazers suffered a crippling 94–81 setback to New Orleans at home. The Hornets were going without their injured stars Jamal Mashburn and Baron Davis, who were averaging 44 points between them. Portland shot a dismal .243 from the field, with Stoudamire and Anderson combining to make 3-of-25 shots.

On April 6, Portland shocked the Lakers 91–80 at Staples Center. Stoudamire scored 24 points on 10-for-17 shooting, Randolph had 22 points, nine rebounds, and five assists, and Anderson chipped in 17 points, nine boards, and eight assists. The Lakers (53–25), battling Sacramento and Minnesota for the best record in the West, were held to .397 shooting. Kobe Bryant had only 12 points on 5-for-23 shooting while Shaquille O'Neal had a manageable 17 points and 12 boards.

"We live for another day," Stoudamire said. "Every win we get from here on out saves our season."

The following night, the Blazers pulled out a come-from-behind 87–81 win over Golden State at home, improving to 41–37 and moving into a three-way tie with Utah and Denver for the eighth spot in the West. Miles had another stellar game with 21 points while Randolph added 20, but nobody was bigger than Ratliff, who hauled in 13 rebounds and eight blocked shots.

"I always want them coming at me because I know I'm one of the best defenders in the league," Ratliff said.

Cheeks was buoyed.

"We have four games left. We have to win and get some help. But I like my team. I feel like we are already playoff-tested."

It would be Portland's final win of the season.

After coming up short against San Antonio, 84–74, playoffs hopes were diminished two nights later in a 110–100 overtime defeat at Denver.

It was a demoralizing loss, and Cheeks had a rare meltdown near the end of regulation. With the score tied at 94–94, referee Jack Nies ruled Stoudamire was fouled before he attempted a shot with 2.3 seconds left in regulation. The Blazers weren't in the bonus, so they got the ball out of bounds. Damon then missed a desperation 3-point try, forcing overtime.

"That was a shooting foul," Stoudamire said afterward. "They got a gift. They didn't foul me on the floor. If they fouled me on the floor, how did I get a shot off?"

After regulation time ended, Cheeks flew into a tantrum. The coach had to be forcibly restrained by assistants from chasing Nies around the court. He fumed and pouted through the extra session, which the Nuggets dominated, 16–6.

Cheeks was hot afterward, stalking the halls and shouting at his assistants, "It's not right," as they tried to calm him down. The staff eventually let him be, and he drifted toward the referees' locker room before being stopped by Denver police.

As he met with media afterward, Cheeks still hadn't cooled down.

"It was a heck of a game . . . but for the game to end like that—like that?" he said.

Dwight Jaynes of the *Portland Tribune* placed plenty of blame on Cheeks for his team's loss.

"With a season on the line, it was unpardonable behavior from a man who is supposed to be the team leader," Jaynes wrote. "And that—as much as all the strategic mistakes he continues to make during games, as much as the lack of offense and defensive discipline his teams continue to show—is why there is no way he should be back next season. The race for the No. 8 playoff spot in the West was decided by coaching, not talent. A good coach would not have lost his composure in Denver with a playoff berth on the line."

The Blazers now had to win their final two games and hope that Denver and Utah lost their final two so that the team could continue a 21-year playoff run.

On April 12, San Antonio won its 10th straight game, shutting down Portland 78–66 at the Rose Garden, ending the Blazers' chances at the playoffs.

Portland shot .308 from the field and scored 25 points in the first half, one shy of the franchise low.

"I think the call, or non-call, in Denver took so much out of us," Cheeks said afterward. "We couldn't refocus."

The Blazers ended the season with a 105–104 double-overtime loss at home to the Lakers. Bryant, who finished with 37 points, knocked down a leaning 3-point shot as time expired to win the game, stunning the sellout crowd of 20,609.

Portland had taken a 104–102 lead when Stoudamire rebounded a miss by Bryant with 8.6 seconds left and raced the length of the court for a layup.

After a timeout, the Lakers inbounded the ball to Bryant. He lost control of the ball, but Miles was called for a foul, giving the Lakers the ball with 1.1 seconds left. Kobe took the next inbounds pass and launched a high-arching shot over Ratliff that tickled twine as time expired.

"I distinctly remember that play," Ratliff says now. "Kobe hit that 3-pointer over me from almost half court. It was like, 'You gotta be kidding me.'"

With the win, the Lakers (56–26) wrapped up the Pacific Division title. The Blazers finished at 41–41, their first non-winning season since 1988–89.

"It took a heck of a shot—two shots—by an extraordinary player for them to win that game," Cheeks said afterward. "But our guys competed, and that's really all you can ask for.

"Although we did not make the playoffs, I am very excited about this team. This is a team that is going to be successful for years to come. This team is going to get back in the playoffs and make a run in the next few years."

After the game, Stoudamire took the microphone and told the Rose Garden fans, "I promise you this won't be happening next season."

He was right, but not in the way he intended.

Chapter 10

RECOVERY

(2004–2005)

Actor Jay Ellis, who interned for the Trail Blazers while in college, appeared as a guest on *Jimmy Kimmel Live!* in 2017:

"It was probably the darkest years in NBA history. This was the Jail Blazers era. Maurice Cheeks was the head coach. I feel so sorry for this guy. He had Ruben Patterson, who called himself the Kobe-stopper, to which Kobe dropped 40 points every time he played them. He also had Bonzi Wells, who got suspended for a fight, Damon Stoudamire, Rasheed Wallace. . . . It was a crash course in learning what *not* to do in life. I was an intern in the PR department. You can feel my pain. So I learned how to write a lot of press releases. Every time the players would get in trouble, we'd have to spin some story about why they got in trouble, which usually was just an apology to the fans and the NBA. Only so many times can you say, 'No, it wasn't them. They weren't driving from Seattle with a bunch of weed in the car. We're so sorry. They'll never do it again—until next week.'"

Jimmy: "That's pretty crazy."

Ellis: "Yeah, it was amazing. It was a good time."

The Trail Blazers had made major strides in distancing themselves from the Jail Blazers era with a number of changes during the 2003–04 season, including the trades of Rasheed Wallace and Bonzi Wells.

In his first year-plus as team president, Steve Patterson had hired a general manager, traded the team's two most talented but enigmatic players, presided over a concerted effort to reconnect with the community in the face of plummeting ticket sales and a crumbled team image, and served as point man for Paul Allen's bankruptcy proceedings with Oregon Arena Corporation and the Rose Garden.

"Someday," Patterson said before the 2004–05 season, "the focus will be on basketball."

But remnants of the bad old times remained, with some bad new times ahead.

Basketball was indeed on the agenda of Patterson and GM John Nash, who opted to retain Maurice Cheeks for the final year of his contract—a surprise to some observers.

"We were still in the midst of trying to evaluate whether you could rehabilitate the team you had or blow it up," Patterson says today. "Initially, there was reluctance to [blow it up], but as the [2004–05] season went on, it became clear that was the path we'd go down. In retrospect, would it have been wiser to start that process earlier? Yeah, probably. When you're in the midst of it, that's a tough decision to make. It's going to be an ugly three- or four-year process."

Patterson hired ex-Blazer guard Darnell Valentine to succeed Jerome Kersey as the team's director of player programs. Kersey had been hired as an assistant coach on the Milwaukee Bucks, where Terry Porter was now head coach.

Valentine, who had served the previous 11 years as a regional representative to the NBA Players Association, lived in Portland and was familiar with the players. By this time, every team in the league had a director of player programs.

"The idea was for each team to have a foot soldier to be hands-on with working with the players, getting them toward their maturation, make them aware of being an NBA player," Valentine says today. "It was helping them be responsible financially and through whatever situations and image and awareness of maximizing their career."

The Blazers had some "old-school veterans," but they also had younger players who were "having difficulty transitioning to the Portland culture," as Valentine puts it.

"It was a mediocre team with a players' coach in Mo Cheeks and a reputation they couldn't escape," says Valentine, who would serve three seasons in his position with the Blazers. "The guys they were bringing in weren't as mature, and some guys were frustrated with the organization in some ways. All it took was one guy to step out of line, and the house of cards started collapsing. We were an organization and team trying to move out of that Jail Blazer reputation, but some guys didn't grasp onto that concept very well."

Darius Miles was one of them.

"Darius was an enigma," Valentine says. "He was a difficult guy to understand. He just didn't have the maturity. He was too young to process things as they were happening. He was overwhelmed and not emotionally stable enough to manage circumstances at that time."

Zach Randolph was another.

"Zach is a wonderful person, but he was from a different place," Valentine says. "He had a culture he surrounded himself with, and Portland was an outlier. It was a strange place for Zach, an environment he wasn't accustomed to."

The Blazers, however, did not have an entire roster of bad actors.

"The Derek Andersons, Shareef Abdur-Rahims—they were trying to do the right thing," Valentine says. "With all the incidents, though, they couldn't escape the exposure reaped from the other guys. Once people associate you with that type of thing, it keeps bubbling up. It only takes one or two bad guys to stain the whole organization. Steve Patterson had a difficult time managing that whole process, but he had no choice. The community demanded that it be addressed."

Marijuana use was at the root of some of the Blazers' problems. Today, Oregon is one of nine states where recreational use is legal.

"How radically has the acceptability of so many things changed, not just pot?" Valentine observes. "But back then, it was unacceptable. Now it's part of the landscape.

"The city of Portland probably was a little more conservative where the players' image was concerned than it is today. Things the players were doing then wouldn't be publicized now. But beginning about the time I started with the club, there was more thought given to the type of people they were bringing in. That changed dramatically with Brandon Roy, LaMarcus Aldridge, and Greg Oden coming in. Those guys were stellar personalities."

* * *

With the No. 13 pick in the 2004 NBA Draft, the Blazers chose New York City legend Sebastian Telfair. The 6-foot, 165-pound guard, the smallest high school player ever to jump directly to the NBA, was a childhood star. He began practicing his autograph in fourth grade, was named the nation's top sixth-grader by one magazine and, as an eighth-grader, became the youngest player ever to participate in the Adidas ABCD high school camp. Telfair came into the league with a six-year deal with Adidas worth as much as $15 million with incentives.

The Blazers passed on some players who carved out longer, more successful careers, including Al Jefferson, who went to Boston with the 15th pick, Josh Smith (Atlanta, 17), J. R. Smith (New Orleans, 18) Jameer Nelson (Orlando, 20), and Tony Allen (Boston, 25). Telfair would last 11 NBA seasons but was a full-time starter for only one season—in 2007–08 with Minnesota—and was out of the league by age 29. Jefferson, who played with Indiana in his 14th NBA season in 2017–18, averaged at least 16 points nine years in a row from 2006–2015.

"It was between Sebastian and Al Jefferson, a decision we went back and forth on until the moment we took him," Nash says today. "We took Telfair, who had a world of promise but didn't pan out. We all thought he was going to develop the shooting skills he never did in the NBA.

"Jefferson's people didn't see why we'd take him when we already had Zach Randolph. He wouldn't visit Portland. We finally got them to agree to allow us to watch a workout in Seattle. He got injured in that workout. We never really did get to watch him work out. We had lunch with him and talked to the young man. We gave him a psychological test. He was 4½ hours late for that. It was clear he didn't want to be in Portland. Even so, we debated until the final moment. I missed on that one."

Nash ran into a similar situation with the draft the following season. The Blazers owned the third pick and targeted Wake Forest point guard Chris Paul.

"Chris didn't want to play in Portland," Nash says. "He refused to come in and work out. I finally got his agent to agree to work him out at the Chicago pre-draft camp. He wouldn't visit Utah, either. [Jazz GM] Kevin O'Connor and our staffs were at Loyola of Chicago. He worked against one of our Portland scouts [Mike Born]. They played some one-on-one, and Chris tanked the workout.

"I asked him why he didn't want to come to Portland. He said, 'You already have a point guard in Telfair.' I said, 'That doesn't mean you can't win that job.' Players didn't want to come to Portland. That was a problem back then. In some cases, the veteran players didn't want to be associated with the Jail Blazers."

Portland wound up moving back in the draft, sending the No. 3 pick to Utah for the No. 6 and 27 selections. The Blazers chose Seattle high schooler Martell Webster at No. 6 and Lithuanian forward Linas Kleiza at No. 27. At No. 3, Utah took point guard Deron Williams of Illinois, and Paul went at No. 4 to New Orleans. Williams was a three-time All-Star and a starter in each of his dozen seasons in the league. Paul is a future Hall of Famer.

Webster played 10 NBA seasons, including five in Portland, but only two seasons as a starter. Kleiza would play seven seasons in the NBA, none for the Blazers, and none as a starter.

"I regret that those draft picks didn't work out," Nash says today. "We were reaching for the moon and taking high school kids."

* * *

Following the 2003–04 campaign, Patterson and Nash had a priority list that included re-signing Darius Miles, negotiating an extension for Randolph, and re-signing Ratliff.

In June, Miles was captured on video in his hometown of East St. Louis,

Illinois, as part of a police sweep of four city blocks in search of drug dealers. He wasn't arrested, but officers found marijuana on him and two other men who were riding with Miles in his SUV. One was charged with possession; the other tossed a gun under the parked vehicle and faced federal charges as a convicted felon in possession of a weapon. He had previously served time on drug charges.

The city's deputy police chief told the *St. Louis Post-Dispatch* that Miles was "uncooperative" and "combative" with officers, and that he should "carry himself in a more professional manner."

After watching the police video, Patterson defended Miles, saying the player was picking up a friend to go to a cousin's high school graduation and just happened to be in the area when the sweep occurred.

"He was being very cooperative [when confronted by police], and you could hear him say, 'You know me; I'm Darius Miles, I'm not a trouble-maker,'" Patterson said. "And you could hear the cop, who was holding a gun threatening to blow his head off with a dozen expletives. Darius is one of the few success stories to come out of East St. Louis, and he winds up with a cop's gun to his face."

Initially, the Blazers offered Miles, a restricted free agent who made $4.1 million in 2003–04, a four-year, $24-million contract. Miles wound up signing a six-year, $48-million pact. The Blazers didn't have to go nearly that high; they were basically bidding against themselves. Allen, evidently, was in love with Miles as a player and didn't want to take any chances on losing him.

"Paul really wanted to do that," Patterson says today. "When you work for somebody and the owner decides he wants to do something, that's his prerogative."

Miles was appreciative of the owner's generosity.

"It's more than I thought I could get when the season ended," Miles said at the time. "It's a whole lotta money."

Later in July, Abdur-Rahim's agent, Aaron Goodwin, said it wasn't going to work out in Portland for his client, who played the same position as Randolph.

"We are absolutely asking for a trade," Goodwin said.

Goodwin said Abdur-Rahim would not report to training camp on October 4. Nash would calm down the situation by assuring Abdur-Rahim he would get every opportunity to be a starter for the Blazers at small forward.

"I didn't want to disrupt things, but it seemed like there was no future for me there," Abdur-Rahim says today. "John didn't like the trade options, but it was a bad situation. My family stayed in Atlanta. They never came back to Portland with me. There was some dysfunction. It's tough to play in that situation."

A starter in each of his 7½ seasons before joining the Blazers, Abdur-Rahim had been excited to go to a team with a winning tradition when he arrived at mid-season the previous year. But he quickly learned that he was getting into an unforeseen situation.

"Portland was in a time of transition," says Abdur-Rahim, now the NBA's VP/basketball operations. "Theo [Ratliff] and I had come to the team, and Travis Outlaw, Zach Randolph, and Darius Miles were really young. We had a mixture of younger and older guys, some who had been there before. For an organization that had had a lot of stability, I caught it at a bad time.

"The community wasn't as engaged as it had historically been. I made some relationships that are still good to this day, but it wasn't a very stable time. My second year, especially, was a transition year for everyone."

Abdur-Rahim, a natural power forward, had Randolph for competition there, with Miles and Ruben Patterson at small forward.

"Early in my career, I had played small forward, but I was a power forward by then," Abdur-Rahim says today. "We had so many guys at both spots. On paper, it didn't make a lot of sense. It was a time where I had to figure out how to be productive, and to offer what I could to the younger guys.

"As a young player, I had guys who had shown me how to be professional and a good teammate. I wanted to offer that to Darius, Travis, Zach, and Sebastian. But it wasn't an ideal situation. There wasn't a clear-cut spot for me. I'd been used to playing a lot and having a lot of the offense revolve around me. This was a different experience. But it's how you handle things. I wanted to be professional and be a good teammate. I wasn't going to allow things being a little uncomfortable to define me.

"I had built up equity prior to being a Blazer. I believe I had a positive impact with the guys I played with there. To see Travis have success after I left, to see Zach become the professional he became, some of that was built in Portland—not necessarily from me, but from that time."

Abdur-Rahim felt for coach Maurice Cheeks.

"I loved Mo," he says. "He was in a tough spot, with all of the things happening. Whatever the strategy and direction the team was on wasn't what he was hired under. A lot of things changed after he came in. There was a lot of peripheral stuff going on beyond basketball that he had to manage. He had established veterans. Theo and I had been All-Stars. Damon [Stoudamire] was a really good player. You mix that with young guys who wanted to establish themselves. It was a lot to manage.

"I'm not sure how much support Mo got. But the thing I loved about him, when things were bad, the worst games we had, those were the times when he would come in and be honest and say, 'Tonight was F'ed up, but that's on me, and we're going to figure it out.' It wasn't always true. Sometimes it was on us. But that was always his approach. He was always positive, and he worked at it. My first year, it was good that way. We were competing and playing for something. The second year, with so many guys in flux coming into the season, from the very beginning it was not good at all."

Abdur-Rahim resented the Jail Blazers image.

"Folks coin phrases. From the outside looking in, you have a perspective of guys getting in a lot of trouble. Once I was there, being with those guys, I thought it was unfair. It wasn't a complete collection of bad guys. You had serious basketball players. You had some young guys. You had some guys who had gotten in trouble. But some of it was communal. I don't think Portland as a community has the appetite for guys having run-ins like New York would have. Values are different. When you get guys from different places, you get some of that."

On July 17, Qyntel Woods revealed he had spent a month at a substance treatment center in Atlanta as part of the NBA's anti-drug program, just as Stoudamire had done the previous summer. Woods voluntarily entered the program to deal with his marijuana use. He had not tested positive in the league's random drug-testing program but had several off-the-court incidents.

"A lot of people look at me as a thug, but that's not really the case," Woods said. "It's just the look, the braids, and all of that. But I'm a professional, and I need to start acting like one. I really think my career is in jeopardy, so it's time for me to make some changes."

Woods would play in the 2004 Rocky Mountain Revue summer league, but would never play another counting game for the Blazers. He played three games for Miami in 2004–05 and 49 games for New York in 2005–06, then would be out of the NBA at age 24. Woods went on to play professionally abroad for more than a decade.

In late July, the Blazers traded Dale Davis and guard Dan Dickau to Golden State for guard Nick Van Exel. Davis, 35, had a disappointing 2003–04 season, averaging career lows in scoring (4.4) and rebounds (5.1) while losing his starting job. Van Exel, 33, had suffered through an injury-plagued season and a half with the Warriors. Both Davis and Van Exel were on expiring contracts.

Van Exel did not arrive with a spotless record. In 1996, he had been involved in a nasty incident, shoving referee Ronnie Garretson into the scorer's table and earning a seven-game suspension. Asked afterward if he would apologize, Van Exel said, "No, I would expect an apology from him. If he apologizes to me, I'll apologize to him."

In 1998, when he was with the Lakers, Van Exel had been fined $10,000 for his part in a fight with San Antonio's Monty Williams, which ended with Van Exel flashing an obscene gesture to the crowd. Three times over the years, Van Exel had been fined for criticizing officials.

During his time with Denver from 1998–2002, Van Exel had played well, averaging between 16 and 18 points through 3½ seasons. He also turned down an opportunity to be team captain and missed two workouts without contacting team officials. In a nine-month stretch in 2000–01, Van Exel was fined $125,000 by the Nuggets or the league.

With Golden State the previous season, Van Exel had gone three weeks without talking to anyone in the organization. He verbally sparred with Coach Eric Musselman over his role and the team's style of play.

"Tell the fans: Don't worry," Van Exel said after the trade to Portland. "The good Nick will be there. There's a bad person in everybody and, in the NBA, losing brings out the bad in people. The reason I had problems at Golden State was because of my injury. I wasn't able to do what I had done in the past, and that got me into nasty mood swings."

* * *

As training camp opened, the Blazers signed Ratliff to a four-year, $46-million extension. Ratliff had registered six blocks or more 12 times in his 32 games with Portland the previous season. Almost as important, he was a quality human being.

"From the time he arrived in Portland, we identified with Theo's superior play on the floor and his lifestyle and character off the court as a member of the community," Nash said.

As the regular season opened, the Blazers signed Randolph to a six-year, $84-million contract extension.

Patterson and Nash were taking a leap of faith on the 23-year-old power forward, who led the Blazers in scoring (20.1 points) and rebounds (10.5) the previous season.

About that time, Jeff Benedict came out with a book entitled, *Out of Bounds: Inside the NBA's Culture of Rape, Violence, and Crime*. Of 35 players mentioned and their records explored, 12 were current or former Blazers—and Randolph wasn't even one of them. Included were Ruben Patterson, Damon Stoudamire, Bonzi Wells, Rasheed Wallace, Cliff Robinson, Gary Trent, Dontonio Wingfield, Qyntel Woods, Nick Van Exel, Erick Barkley, Scottie Pippen, and Gary Grant.

Benedict's original title was *We Smoked It All Up*. That was the infamous line Wallace was alleged to have said to officers when asked where the rest of the marijuana was during the bust of Wallace and Stoudamire in 2002.

It was another reminder to Blazer brass that player behavior mattered.

In mid-October, the Blazers indefinitely suspended Woods, who was suspected of fighting pit bulls, hosting such fights, and of abandoning his dog. Dogfighting is a felony in the US.

Clackamas County investigators searched his Lake Oswego home on October 11 and 15 following a television news report alleging he had abandoned his dog, "Hollywood." The station also reported that the pit bull had fresh puncture wounds, scars, and bruises on her chest, belly, and legs, ostensibly from dogfighting competition. The dog was found roaming loose in Northeast Portland.

Investigators found bloody paw prints in a room above Woods's garage. KATU-TV asked Woods about the dog. Initially, he denied ownership. KATU-TV quoted a witness as saying Woods was the owner and that he discarded the dog because it wouldn't fight.

After admitting he was the owner, Woods said he had never fought pit bulls and that, "I was going to breed it with my other dog [Sugar], but they didn't take, so I just decided to get rid of it."

Woods told KATU he had given the dog away.

"I know this guy and took my dog over there [to Northeast Portland]," he said. "He saw the dog and wanted it, so I gave it to him."

Investigators removed evidence and dug up disturbed areas in Woods's backyard looking for dog remains.

On October 30, the NBA would give Woods a five-game suspension for violation of the league's anti-drug program, which meant it was at least his second violation.

"All in all, he does not appear to be a candidate for the J. Walter Kennedy Citizenship Award," Dwight Jaynes wrote.

Cheeks went through the preseason with a deep group featuring Abdur-Rahim, Randolph, Ratliff, Anderson, and Stoudamire as starters, with Miles, Ruben Patterson, Van Exel, Telfair, and newly acquired center Joel Przybilla in the second unit.

"Ruben will be what he has always been during his career—a bench player," said Nash, an unusually harsh comment to come from a GM. "I don't see him getting many minutes."

On November 5, before the Blazers' home-opening win over the Clippers (94–81), owner Paul Allen made himself available to fans, shaking hands and signs autographs.

Allen's overture to fans was well-received, but he would not do it again. Reclusive by nature, he would make himself less and less available to the media. By the 2016–17 season, he would make no public appearances and offer no interview opportunities to reporters.

On November 7, a week after signing his $84-million contract extension, Randolph missed the team flight to Toronto to start the first prolonged road trip of the season. He was fined and held out of the starting lineup in the Blazers' 101–97 loss to the Raptors.

"Overslept," he told the media. "Set the alarm and everything. It happens to everybody."

Portland hovered around .500 for the first two months of the season. Ratliff, who had been so effective after being acquired in the mid-season trade the previous season, wouldn't be nearly as productive this season.

"Theo played his butt off for three months to get that contract," one team official says today. "Then, almost from the day he inked that contract, he shut it down. He was in and out and played whenever."

Ratliff missed 25 games with a sore back and started only 19, giving way to Przybilla.

"Cheeks would be running practice on one court, and Theo would be running up and down on the other," the official says. "He'd ask Theo, 'What percent do you think you are now?' Theo would say, 'I don't know, maybe 75 percent.' And Maurice would say, 'Your 75 percent is more than the 100 percent of guys we're using now.' And Theo still wouldn't play."

Today, Ratliff doesn't see it that way at all. He believes he gave his heart and soul to the Portland organization during a time it needed some help.

"Coming to the Blazers [during the 2003–04 season], I wanted to step up and help the team," he says. "I knew we were a fairly young team, but we had the potential to get to the playoffs. We just fell short. But I gave it my all both seasons in Portland. I got hurt the second season, but it wasn't for lack of trying and doing my best."

Ratliff cherishes the memory of the fans in Portland, "and how they embraced me. They have a tremendous fan base in Oregon. They're loyal no matter whether they're winning or losing. I enjoyed being a part of that.

"It was a change of atmosphere for the franchise," says Ratliff, who now lives in Atlanta working in a real estate partnership and heading the

Theo Ratliff Foundation. "It was the beginning of a period where they were trying to bring in a different type of person. They respected me as more than a basketball player, but also a guy who hadn't had legal troubles, and as a leader to help the guys on the team to change their attitude as far as how they approach things and being professional."

Ratliff spent time mentoring Randolph.

"We had several conversations about giving back to the community, about having people recognize him for things besides all the negativity with his crews and getting in trouble and having the law involved with his name," Ratliff says. "He had kids. I asked, 'Do you want to be the role model when it comes to your kids, or are they gonna grow up that way?' The idea was to change that to him doing positive things and having a positive image. He eventually did that, and that kept him around the league in a long-term situation."

Ratliff says he tried to be a role model for the Blazers' young players such as Randolph, Miles, and Telfair.

"They had a lot of young guys on the team who were enjoying themselves but doing some over-the-top things," Ratliff says. "The organization didn't want a bad influence for those kids. They wanted to bring in a different attitude. I was the catalyst of that."

Ratliff had played in Philadelphia when Cheeks had served as an assistant coach there.

"Cheeks was my man. Maurice Cheeks IS Philadelphia. I always respected who he was as a person more so than a coach. He was that consummate guy who was trying to bring it together like he did as a player as a point guard. He wasn't aggressive, hollering and screaming at guys, but he tried to bring his calmness and attitude about the game to coaching."

Ratliff says there is merit to the team's Jail Blazers image, though he felt only a few of his teammates fell under that category.

"I got to know all those guys personally. They just made bad decisions. They never were bad guys that I knew of. I was cool with all those guys before I got there. Many of them became coaches.

"Sometimes you let your decision making overrule what the decision should be just for the sake of your satisfaction. When you indulge in an illegal activity, the law is going to get involved. That happened to one, two, three guys, and then it kept going in that direction, and it became that stigma. Being hard-headed and arrogant about it and not accepting they were wrong and they shouldn't be doing what they're doing—that's wrong, too.

"Perception is reality. They had police calling every other week. That's where you build that reputation. That's not good for the NBA, let alone the Trail Blazers."

* * *

On December 10, the Blazers lost 92–87 in overtime at Utah to fall to 9–9. Cheeks blew a gasket during the extra session and roamed the court after the game, shouting expletives at the officiating crew of Jack Nies, Violet Palmer, and Tommy Nunez Jr. The coach directed most of his ire at Nies, who shouted back as Cheeks was escorted from the court by security. When he finally emerged from the locker room to meet with media, Cheeks was still upset and cursing.

On January 1, after a 97–88 win over Golden State, the Blazers were 14–14. They would lose 10 of their next 11 games. Eleven days later, Abdur-Rahim would undergo elbow surgery. Miles and Randolph also had injuries to take them out of action for a while.

Cheeks made Van Exel and Stoudamire the starting backcourt, and for a 10-game stretch, they averaged 43.7 points and 12.4 assists with .468 3-point shooting between them.

But the team continued to lose fans. Average paid attendance in the 19,980-capacity Rose Garden through January 11 was 9,843, down 13 percent from the 11,343 average at the same time the previous season. Portland ranked 28th in the NBA, ahead of only Atlanta and New Jersey.

On January 14, the Blazers couldn't win for losing. Stoudamire exploded for a franchise-record 54 points, but the Blazers lost 112–106 to the Hornets (5–30) to fall to 15–20 for the season. Over his previous 14 games, Damon had averaged 25.0 points and 6.4 assists.

A week later, the Blazers waived Woods, ending his tenure with the team after he pled guilty to first-degree misdemeanor animal abuse in Clackamas County Circuit Court. Woods was sentenced to 12 months' probation and 80 hours of community service. He had been under investigation for more serious charges relating to dogfighting and had been suspended indefinitely without pay since October.

On January 26, after a 95–88 home loss to Dallas, the Blazers' record dropped to 16–25. Afterward, Miles—who had a good game off the bench with 15 points, six assists, four rebounds, and two steals in 29 minutes—told a reporter that "changes need to be made." Asked about it again, he said, "I don't have any suggestions; I'm just a player. I'm not the coach."

While breaking down game video in a team meeting the next day, Cheeks offered some criticism at Miles, who told the coach to take his words elsewhere. The argument escalated to the point whether neither would back down. According to at least one source, Miles used the "N" word multiple times. Miles told Cheeks he didn't care what he said because he was going to be fired. Cheeks told him to leave the arena, and Miles said he'd have to call the police to make him leave. The argument continued as Cheeks headed for Nash's office.

"That's right," Miles said, "run to your daddy."

Ratliff says it was an uncomfortable moment for everyone in the room that day.

"Things got out of hand. Words were said, but Cheeks being the calm guy that he is, he didn't get out of hand himself. He addressed it to Darius, and Darius was the one who got out of control. You can't do that. That's not allowed. Management got involved, and then it was done."

Steve Patterson says today that Miles's comments were "fairly benign."

"Before practice the next day, the assistant coaches [Dan Panaggio, Jim Lynam, and John Loyer] got to Mo," Patterson says. "The coaches got him all jacked up about Darius being insubordinate.

"Mo's style of coaching was old-school. He instigated the foul language [in the verbal altercation with Miles]. That was not the way to talk to Darius. Certain writers took Mo's view of the incident because he had a history of leaking things to them. I'm not saying it was an argument I'd like to see involving my employees. But the way it was presented, it was solely Darius's fault. The fact of the matter was, by all accounts from everybody in the room, Mo instigated it, made it worse, and it's not something either one of them would say they're most proud of. But foul language in the broadest sense was not something uncommon in that locker room, though some of it may be culturally insensitive.

"Darius is a smart guy. He had opinions. In my view as part of a management team, people are entitled to that. My expectations of that are, express yourself and argue your position in the room. But once you go out of the room, everybody should be on the same page."

Cheeks sought a long suspension. Patterson and Nash suspended Miles for two games along with a $150,000 fine. Cheeks offered to resign, but Nash wouldn't accept it.

"The Miles incident took the legs out of Mo and undermined his authority," says Darnell Valentine, the team's director of player programs at the time. "He couldn't hold guys accountable anymore."

"That incident crushed Maurice," says a member of the Blazers' staff, who asked to remain unidentified. "Maurice stood up to Darius for what he thought was inappropriate behavior. All the guys in the locker room sided with Maurice on that one. Maurice was a stand-up guy. That really put a dagger into his heart. It made your heart sink. For Darius to use those kinds of words against Maurice was tough to hear.

"Darius had a lot of talent, but he just didn't understand how hard one had to work to maintain that level. If he really had put his work into it, he could have been anything he wanted. I'm not saying he didn't work, but if he worked hard like other guys did to get to a high level, the sky would have been the limit."

The day the suspension was announced, Miles read a public apology statement to the fans but did not mention Cheeks. Afterward, while answering questions from media, Miles said, "You're trying to make something that's really nothing into something. Me and Cheeks talked [about the incident]. We laughed; we joked. It was never really no problem. It was a situation that just happened. We're two grown men. We just disagreed on something."

The coach accepted partial blame, saying he had come on strong in his criticism.

"He went over the line," Cheeks said, "but I had a little part in it because something in my voice was antagonistic, which made him go that way."

Weeks later, there was a revelation of an unsigned document slipped to *The Oregonian*. The proposed settlement agreement would have the club reimburse Miles $150,000, plus interest, in turn for withdrawal of a grievance and a promise not to sue. Blazer management contended the document was drawn up by Miles's agent, Jeff Wechsler, and that the team had not agreed to its stipulations.

At the time, Patterson said his intention was to devise a plan by which Miles would agree to a high standard of deportment with the team and in the community over a period of time. The next incident would result in a five-game suspension; a third would draw 10 games. At some point, he would have the opportunity to clear his name and put his money toward a charitable cause, as Stoudamire had done two years prior.

> After Stoudamire's third marijuana arrest in the summer of 2003, the Blazers fined him $250,000. Damon underwent rehab and aftercare and agreed to regular urine tests. Management rescinded the fine with the promise he would donate $100,000 to Albina Head Start.

Today, Steve Patterson addresses the subject this way:

"Some members of the press didn't understand the collective-bargaining agreement and what has to happen with fine money. As a club, you don't get to keep it. You put it in an escrow account, and it has to go someplace. There's no benefit to the greater community if you take a fine from a millionaire and give it to a billionaire [i.e., Paul Allen]. Our plan was to contribute to a fund, so kids could go to games and there would be community education and involvement around that. And that's what happened to it. Darius didn't get to keep the money."

Miles would say as much in 2005, in the weeks after the incident with Cheeks.

"I haven't gotten my money back," he said. "My agent handles those things, but he never told me nothing like that. Far as I know, we paid it, and that's it."

Miles showed little remorse in an interview with the *Portland Tribune*.

"It probably shouldn't have even gotten to a suspension," he said. "I read where Ricky Davis got into it with [Boston coach] Doc Rivers, cussed him out in front of a bunch of kids, and he ain't been suspended. Larry Brown said his team needed to practice more and play harder, and Ben Wallace said, 'I'm tired of hearing that shit.' You ain't heard nothing else about it . . . nobody taking names on Ben Wallace and making it into something big."

The day after the Miles/Cheeks incident, the Blazers beat the Clippers 90–86 to improve to 17–25.

"It's been the hardest 42 games of my life," Cheeks said.

Ratliff says it took years for Cheeks's young players to appreciate their coach.

"To this day, Zach, Darius, and those guys always show love to Maurice for him and his understanding," Ratliff says. "There were a lot of things he could have gone to management about, but he handled them within the locker room to the best of his ability."

Looking back, Nash says it's just another example of the situation he inherited when he came to Portland. The Blazers unloaded some players for other players "who didn't always work out, either. They weren't necessarily the answer, and in some cases, the reason they were available is they were difficult with their prior team. Darius was one of those."

* * *

Miles scored eight points on 4-for-4 shooting while playing 21 minutes in a 91–83 loss to Minnesota on February 27, the team's sixth defeat in eight games.

"I look at it as a job," he said. "It ain't fun no more. It's work."

On March 1, Detroit handled Portland, 103–89, falling 11 games under .500 (22–33). Randolph threw a tantrum after being removed from the game in the third quarter after arguing a non-call on a missed shot, which prevented him from getting back on defense. He threw his headband, ripped off his wristband, and repeatedly asked Cheeks, "You taking me out because I missed a shot?"

Cheeks did not reply. After the game, he said, "I didn't pay attention to Zach's outburst. It meant nothing to me. If I was paying attention to what he said, then I wouldn't be coaching the game."

The next day, the Blazers fired Cheeks, ending his 3½-year run with the club. His regular-season record was 162–13, but with a playoff mark of 3–7.

Later, Cheeks told *The Oregonian* he knew he was gone after the first week of the season, the day after the team's opener at Golden State. The next day, he had an argument with Nash over lineups. "I got heated and almost walked out," he said.

After that, Cheeks said, the two rarely talked. Nash disagreed, though he said he was always the one to initiate any conversation.

By late November, Cheeks said, "they were itching to fire me."

Today, Nash says he had misgivings about Cheeks, who had played for Philadelphia during Nash's time there as general manager.

"He would not have been my choice [as Portland's head coach]," Nash says. "The greatest positive was his ability to deal with players on their level, having been a player himself. He talked their language. But I saw some of the flaws. I didn't think he was technically equipped to succeed at the level we wanted. That came to bear when he came back to Philadelphia and coached there.

"When we were both in Portland, we seemed to coexist OK, but he was always suspicious of both Steve and me. By the time we let Maurice go, things had come to a head. But neither one of us were on a campaign to get Maurice."

The Miles incident, Nash says, "may have accelerated his departure. Maurice was adamant that he wanted Miles suspended for a substantial time. It was the straw that broke the camel's back."

Director of player personnel Kevin Pritchard took over as interim head coach for the final 27 games of the season, of which the Blazers would win only five. The club cashed in on the season, using young players and tanking for the draft.

"The veterans were upset at throwing in the towel," Nash recalls. "We were trying to see if Travis [Outlaw] and [Sebastian] Telfair and the young guys were going to help us moving forward; then we would reassess at the end of the season. Damon was very much opposed to that at the time."

Ruben Patterson didn't care for the decision, either.

"We still had a chance [for the playoffs]," he said, "and they gave up on us."

Pritchard held a team meeting.

"We were only four or five games out of [the No. 8 spot in the Western Conference], but they made the decision to go young and go for a lottery pick," Bob Medina says today. "They told Derek and Ruben they could go home, they were going to play younger guys like Sebastian and Travis."

Pritchard decided Abdur-Rahim, Ratliff, and Stoudamire would continue to play.

"When Cheeks was fired, the secretary there called and told me what was going on and said Kevin wanted to meet with me," Abdur-Rahim says. "Several guys had meetings with Kevin. He thought it would be helpful to have me stay and continue playing. His thing to me was like, 'I'm taking over. I need help. It would be great if you were with me.'

"Some of the guys who didn't meet with Kevin were told, 'You're not going to play. If you want to go back to your hometown, go ahead. But we're going to do things a little different. You can stay and train and be around the team, but you're not going to play.'"

In the end, Pritchard sat Patterson, Van Exel, and Anderson. Patterson, under the guise of "knee tendinitis," went on the injured list and sat out 11 games, returning to Columbus, Ohio, to visit his children. Patterson eventually returned, played a few games, and then decided he'd sit out the final four contests in a postgame tirade after a loss to Dallas.

"It's obvious they want to play the young guys," Patterson said, "and I'm too good a player for that. They just need to trade me."

Van Exel didn't play a game after March 5.

"My knee is getting a little bit sore, so I think I'm going to sit down," he said at that point. "It would be better for the younger guys, anyway, to get more playing time for them."

Medina recalls Van Exel was disgruntled with the decision to tank on the season.

"I remember Nick saying, 'We're still in this; let's keep playing,'" Medina says now. "They told Nick, 'We don't want you to dress. Be kind of an assistant coach and help out.' Nick said, 'Screw that; I want to play.' But he saw the direction they were going."

When a couple of players suffered legitimate injuries, the Blazers began having trouble fielding a roster.

"[Management] had to ask the guys they told to leave to come back," Medina says. "I was there when they told Nick they wanted him to play. He was doing a leg press machine with all this weight stacked on. They came in sheepishly to talk to Nick, saying, 'We want you to start playing.' He was pressing 400 pounds and said, 'I can't. My knee hurts.'

"He was a competitor. He wanted to finish his career the right way. He didn't want to give up like that. That broke his spirit, when they said they were going to play the younger guys and give up on the season."

Today, Van Exel says he understood where management was coming from.

"Coming into the season, we had hopes to get to the playoffs," he says, an assistant coach with the Grizzlies during the 2017–18 season. "That didn't work. Once it started to unravel, things went downhill. A lot of things were going on in the inside, a lot of internal stuff, and we were never able to shake it.

"I don't think Mo Cheeks ever had the full support of management. Once they fired him, they wanted to go with the younger movement, which was understandable."

Van Exel said he got along well with Cheeks.

"I liked Mo. He just needed a veteran group. We had some young guys, and they are a little different. Mo was a laidback, even-tempered kind of coach. With a group of veterans who understood the NBA, it would have worked. He was really good with veteran guys, but it was a little bit tough on him with younger guys like Zach and Darius. And he didn't have the love from the front office."

At 33, Van Exel was just about shot physically.

"I wasn't the same player I was before. My knee was never the same after hurting it with Golden State the year before. Fortunately, I had a good brain to get me through things."

After Cheeks was fired, Van Exel says, "they just wanted to go with the younger guys, especially Sebastian. They gave us the choice to play or sit [and watch from the bench] in a suit. They sent Derek and Ruben home. With the rest of us, we got an option to play 10 minutes one night, maybe 20 the next night, maybe sit the third depending on how things were going, all in order to help the young guys develop.

"It wasn't hard at all. I couldn't play at the same level I wanted to. I was such a competitor, I wasn't about to keep playing on one leg and look terrible in front of the guys, especially Sebastian. I chose to try to help him develop as a player."

Abdur-Rahim appreciated a meeting he had with assistant coach Tim Grgurich, along with Ratliff and Stoudamire.

"Coach Grgurich pulled us into a room at the Rose Garden and starts telling us about the season and the stuff we had done for the young guys," Abdur-Rahim says. "I had known Coach Grgurich since I was in college. For him to tell how the things he felt like we were doing for the younger guys meant a lot. Damon continued to be good with Bassy [Telfair], to work with him and teach him what he could teach him. That was one of the really cool and special things even in that tough year, for him to take the time to say that to us."

Ratliff felt bad for the players who were told they would no longer play.

"Nick and Ruben knew they were better than the guys who were playing," he says today. "Any time it comes to that situation, it can get a little tense. They were just trying to tank games. They're trying to get young guys minutes, but you're like, 'OK, this guy should not be in the game right now.' That was what was going on with Portland that season. I could understand how those guys felt. You don't want people saying, 'You're quitting, you're not trying to play, you gave up on the team.'"

Anderson would miss most of the second half of the season with injuries that were reported as migraines, back spasms and, toward the end, a "toothache." The latter, Anderson says today, pissed him off.

"I had back spasms," he says, "but after Mo got fired, it was really because I was unhappy with my role. I got frustrated. I went [to Patterson and Nash] and talked to them. They told me to go home to Louisville. They said, 'Hang in there. We're going to make a trade.' So, I sat out for a while and [Patterson] told people I had a toothache. That was completely false. He was messing with me. He was messing everything up."

Anderson felt he was a scapegoat for the Blazers' shortcomings.

"That's not true at all," Steve Patterson says today. "I expected the guy to play. He wanted to be traded. We were working on that. Given that he was grossly overpaid for his production, that wasn't easy."

Anderson liked Cheeks as a person, but felt he was overmatched for the job.

"It was Coach Cheeks's first time as a head coach. He was figuring things out on the fly. That hindered a lot of us. Everyone was trying to figure their way through things. Some of the stuff you wish didn't happen. Things just went bad. It was just a rookie coach with a lot of veteran players. There was so much stuff he didn't know yet.

"It was hard for him to juggle all that talent. That's hard for any coach, especially a rookie coach. We needed an experienced guy coaching us. He didn't know how to give discipline. When he went to Detroit [in 2013–14], they fired him in a couple of weeks.[1] It was hard for him. He was a great player, but sometimes it's hard for great players to coach.

"There were so many things happening, and the dynamics of it were, everyone was frustrated from almost the first day. People were trying to figure out their roles. We just never did. At the end of games, who was getting the ball? We didn't know. But we had the talent. You can't say we didn't."

Anderson points to the time during the 2002–03 when Cheeks benched Damon Stoudamire.

---

1   He actually lasted 50 games, going 21–29.

"It changed the dynamics of the team. Damon was frustrated. I felt bad for the dude. He had been starting his whole career. It came at a time when so many people were caught up in a whirlwind of different roles."

Anderson thought the chemistry on those teams was fine.

"Most guys liked each other. I don't think that was a problem. It wasn't personal. But there were a lot of incidents off the court. You got tired of it coming from every side."

Was the Jail Blazers tag deserved?

"Every time you looked up, someone was being arrested. So, it was accurate. But I don't think you should call everyone on those teams a Jail Blazer. That characterizes a lot of people. That wasn't fair to some of the players. That wasn't fair to the people who worked there. It wasn't fair to Paul Allen."

Assistant coach John Loyer, who went down with the Cheeks ship, came away with respect for the owner.

"I was amazed at how much Paul Allen wanted to win," Loyer says today. "He was into giving you the resources to do that. It was my first job, and I just thought that's the way the NBA was. It's not that way everywhere. To have an owner like Paul Allen who supports his team that—I didn't realize how good it really was. It's special to have that. It was first class in every way."

Loyer, who had coached for Bob Huggins at the University of Cincinnati from 1999–2000 before joining the Blazers as a video coordinator and advance scout, isn't sure if the team had too much talent when he was there.

"That's the million-dollar question," Loyer says. "We had a collection of very professional guys. Some years they mesh; some years they don't entirely. But that was the most talented group I've ever been around. If we'd had the chemistry the way it should have been, we would have probably gone further."

* * *

On March 15, Randolph had knee surgery and called it a season. Anderson would come back to play for a few games in late March. From that point, it was Stoudamire, Abdur-Rahim, Ratliff, Miles, Przybilla, Patterson, and a summer-league crew.

On April 14, Miles had words with Pritchard after a 102–90 loss to Dallas. Miles had pulled himself out of the game in the fourth quarter because a sore neck was bothering him.

The next day, Miles accompanied the Blazers to Oakland but was not in uniform. Patterson decided to play and had 17 points, six rebounds, and four assists in 40 minutes in a 108–88 loss. "But I ain't taking my trade demand back," he said. "I want to go somewhere with cats who want to win and cats who care."

Three days later, with Miles's neck miraculously healed, he went for 47 points, 12 rebounds, and five blocks in a 119–115 loss at Denver in the season's penultimate game. Fans should YouTube the game. It's a look at the kind of talent Miles had, and the potential he possessed, still only 23 years old.[2]

"He was a talented guy who came straight from high school to the NBA and had no background in fundamentals," Loyer says today. "He would have had a longer NBA career if he hadn't gotten hurt."

Portland finished the 2004–05 campaign at 27–55, its worst record in thirty years (1973–74).

It was also the end of Stoudamire's 6½-year run with his hometown team. "Mighty Mouse" would sign a four-year, $17-million free-agent contract with Memphis. Anderson would move on to Houston.

"I hated to see Damon go," Medina says. "I love the person he is. I don't think he gets enough credit for the things he did. He was tremendous for our team. I saw him go through a lot of things in Portland. He was a star, and then there were times when he had to take a back seat. I saw him go from the top of the depth chart to the bottom.

"We'd be on the road and Damon wasn't playing, and we'd go to the

---

2   Miles would play only 74 more NBA games—40 for Portland in 2005–06, then 34 for Memphis in 2008–09 after the Blazers had medically retired him.

arena at 4 p.m. so he could get shots up. He was going to work his way back into it. You look at the marijuana busts. Young kids make bad decisions. But Damon tried to make everything right. He was a stand-up guy.

"With a lot of NBA guys, they deal with problems two ways. Either you pout if things don't go your way, or you quit. In college, pouting probably worked for them. Very few of them figured out a way to work it out. Damon was one who did."

At the end of the season, the Blazers would use their one-time amnesty clause to get rid of Anderson and his contract.

"Why would I get amnestied?" Anderson says today. "I never got in trouble with the organization. I never got in trouble with the law. I never got a technical foul. The only one I ever got in my career, I appealed and got it rescinded. I was always respectful to fans. I spoke to everyone. I was the scapegoat."

Anderson still has good thoughts about his four seasons in a Blazer uniform.

"I love it there," he says. "The city. The people. The stuff that happened on the business side of basketball wasn't all good, but the people there are just genuine.

"The fans deserve more than all the backlash and negative stuff they've had over so many years, including the Sam Bowie/Michael Jordan stuff. It's always something that keeps the city from giving those people what they deserve. They have what, one title in 50 years? They deserve more. It's like the Chicago Cubs with them. People in Portland will be so happy when the Blazers get that second title. And I'll be happy for them."

Cheeks is reluctant to talk about his time coaching in Portland, and a bit defensive about what went wrong under his watch.

"We had good teams," he says, now an assistant coach with Oklahoma City. "We had good ownership. Great fans. It was exciting for me, being my first head coaching experience. We had a few trials there but, overall, it was fun."

Cheeks, who would be inducted into the Naismith Hall of Fame in 2018 as a player, had never envisioned being a coach during his playing days.

"I didn't think my personality at the time was one where I would be coaching," he says now. "Once I started coaching, I found I enjoyed it. It was fun for me. You're teaching young people certain things about basketball, about life. It turns out to be very beneficial to me and to the guys I was working with.

"I thought I did a pretty good job there for my first time as a head coach. I don't know if you ever know you're ready until you get into the situation. I had good people around me. It helped me find my way and be the best coach I could be at that time."

Cheeks never felt he had too many players who deserved minutes.

"Any time you have guys who want to play, it's not a bad thing," he says. "That's a good thing. Nobody wants to just sit there and wait. Not everybody can play. But that doesn't stop players from wanting to play."

Asked if it became a problem in Portland, Cheeks decided the interview had reached an end.

"I'm not going down a negative road."

* * *

On July 6, 2005, Portland hired Nate McMillan as head coach. McMillan, who had coached Seattle for the previous 4½ seasons, was an old-school taskmaster—much the opposite of the laissez-faire Cheeks. Management hoped a disciplinarian could make some inroads with the roster led by the likes of Randolph, Miles, and Patterson.

McMillan had been in limbo in Seattle, even after going 52–30 and reaching the Western Conference Semifinals in 2004–05, his fifth season with the Sonics. He wasn't sure if he was going to get an extension.

Meanwhile, owner Paul Allen and president Steve Patterson got permission to speak with McMillan, who soon was signed to a five-year contract to coach the Blazers.

"I didn't know much when I signed on," says McMillan, now head coach of the Indiana Pacers. "It wasn't until I got there, when reporters and people started to talk about it, that the name Jail Blazers came up.

"But it was a part of why I did go down there, when I talked with Steve and Mr. Allen about coming to Portland. They wanted to rebuild the team. They wanted to be patient, to change the culture and build mainly through the draft. It was going to take some time.

"I knew how successful the organization had been, and that they had fallen on some hard times. With the Sonics not knowing which way they were going to go, it seemed like a good opportunity for me. I was in a sense beginning my coaching career anew."

The once-talented Portland roster had been depleted. The best players were Randolph and Miles—not exactly character guys.

"I'd heard some stories about some of the players," McMillan says today. "I didn't know Zach or Darius [Miles]. I didn't know what type of people they were. I was familiar with Ruben [who had played for McMillan in Seattle].

"Once I got down there, I just dealt with what I had. We had some guys who were going to challenge the coaching and everything that was going on. You just had to handle it."

McMillan quickly instituted rules, including no headbands and no cell phones in the locker room. Some of the players were fine with that. Others, such as Randolph, rebelled. Zach called McMillan "Sarge," and it wasn't a term of endearment.

"I took that as being OK," McMillan says. "I kind of liked it. I didn't look at myself like that, but I thought, 'At least he knows what I'm trying to do here. He knows who's in charge.'"

McMillan felt rules were necessary those first couple of seasons at the helm.

"That was when cell phones were starting to get popular," McMillan says. "Guys were carrying them around as if they were doctors on call. I just didn't think that was needed when you were at practice or on the bus. It was like your kids having dinner, and they're sitting there at the kitchen table staring into their phones. I didn't think it was appropriate at practice or on the bus. If you were on the plane, that was OK. It was business. But you want your guys communicating and talking and building chemistry with each other, and not on their cell phones talking to agents about me."

Several of the Portland players had taken to wearing headbands the previous year, and McMillan equated it to a rebellious attitude he felt the team didn't need.

"It was like it was all about them and not about the game. Zach had worn headbands. He gave in and didn't wear them for a while. Then I relented, and one time he came up the floor and threw the headband into the stands. I told the trainers, 'Don't order them anymore.'"

In those years, the Blazers held their training camp at Linfield College in McMinnville.

"I had to put out a fire every single day," McMillan says. "The first day, two guys were late for the bus to take us to McMinnville. They called [trainer] Jay Jensen and told him, 'We're on the highway, and will be there in 10 to 15 minutes.' That wasn't what we were going to be about. We left those players; they had to drive down there themselves."

McMillan assigned each player a roommate at the team hotel in McMinnville.

"A couple of the veterans complained with, 'I'm grown. I don't sleep with another man.'" I said, 'Well, you're not going to sleep with him, you're going to room together.' It was about developing chemistry."

Initially, two players checked out of their rooms, refusing to bunk with a teammate. They were sent back to their rooms and eventually complied.

"I felt like we had to get some discipline, to build a culture and try to create something where it was about the Blazers and that organization and not about us as individuals and brands. We eventually got there. Management did a good job of drafting players. Everything was on course to be successful until the injuries that crippled the organization."

McMillan's reference was to the injuries to Brandon Roy and Greg Oden as the Blazers were building to become a force led by Roy, LaMarcus Aldridge, and Oden in the late 2000s.

The first season under McMillan, though, was a lesson in humility. The Blazers started poorly and finished even worse, going into tank mode in March, losing 19 of their last 20 games to finish a league-worst record of 21–61.

In November, Patterson was placed on the inactive list and sent home in the middle of a six-game East Coast trip a day after he directed a verbal outburst at McMillan during a loss at New York and demanded a trade to GM John Nash in the locker room after the game.

"Ruben eventually apologized for that," McMillan says. "He was very emotional and very competitive. Things like that happen. You just hope you can control it out on the floor, then talk about it rationally in the locker room afterward."

In February, Nash would acquiesce, sending Patterson to Denver in a four-team trade that brought the Blazers forward Brian Skinner from Sacramento.

That month, Telfair was arrested after a loaded gun was found on the team's private jet at Boston's Logan Airport. He said the weapon, registered to his girlfriend, had been packed by accident. The Blazers fined him.

"He thought he could get it through by packing it in a pillow on his seat," a team official would say later. "We couldn't even board the plane after that game."

Randolph would carry the Jail Blazers flag for a while.

In June, police cited a member of Randolph's "Hoops Family" for street racing in downtown Portland at 3:15 a.m. Randolph, a passenger in his Dodge Magnum driven by Taquan Portis, was carrying two legally permitted semi-automatic handguns. Portis, 22, was cited for speed range, careless driving, failure to obey a traffic signal, and no front plate. He was estimated to be driving 50 to 60 in a 20-mph zone.

The same night, Randolph was accused of, but not charged with, sexual assault by a stripper in a downtown Portland hotel. The woman later filed a civil lawsuit that was settled out of court.

There were often reports from neighbors about gunfire coming from Randolph's home on Stafford Road, where his "Hoop Family" entourage would rendezvous. One summer, he had contracted Bell's Palsy, and a team official was asked to go out and check on him. It was a gated residence and, once inside, Randolph told the official, "Man, you gotta call before you come out here. We shoot people we don't know." The official wasn't sure if he was kidding.

Randolph always had pit bulls at his place. There were indications he'd had some of them participate in dogfights, as had good friend and teammate Qyntel Woods.

"From where those guys had come from—their worlds are different than ours," long-time TV analyst Mike Rice says today. "You have to have a pit bull attitude to survive."

Former New York sportswriter/sportscaster Peter Vecsey and his wife, Joan, are dog and animal rescuers.

"After the Portland incidents happened, Zach came to Madison Square Garden, and my wife was cursing him out during timeouts," Vecsey says. "She stood up and let him have it."

In March 2007, when the cousin of his then-girlfriend, Faune, was murdered, Blazer management granted Randolph "bereavement leave" to attend the funeral in Indiana, expecting him to leave town that day. The following night, as the Blazers were beating Washington 100–98 at home; Zach was at a north Portland topless club, Exotica, departing in the wee hours without paying his tab.

Two days later, assistant GM Kevin Pritchard—who would be named GM a week later—issued a prepared statement.

> We have made tremendous strides this season in developing a culture that values character, both on and off the court. We think we've made significant regard as a team and an organization, and our fans have responded with renewed enthusiasm and support. At the end of this season, we'll sit down with each of our players and review their performance, including their standing in the community. Character will be a key measuring tool for whether each of our players continues to be a part of the ongoing effort to build toward a championship-caliber club. When players make mistakes off the court, they are often private matters between the team and the player. We know our fans respect the need to handle certain matters internally. We will continue to hold our players to a very high standard and take appropriate action when necessary.

Loyer still holds Randolph in very high esteem.

"Zach is one of my top two or three all-time favorite NBA players," Loyer says. "He might be No. 1 or 2. I spent a lot of time with Zach. During the summer between his rookie and second year, I went back to his hometown to work with him, and I really got to know him. When Zach came into the league, he had no idea what the NBA was all about after only one year in college. He worked his tail off to become a great player."

All of the incidents Randolph was associated with don't faze Loyer.

"You never want those kind of things to happen, but Zach is a person I'd swear by," says Loyer, now a scout with the Clippers. "We all make mistakes. We've all done some things we regret. Both Zach and Rasheed Wallace are misunderstood. They're graded upon a few of their actions. If I were in a foxhole, I'd want the two of them in there with me, and I'd have a pretty good chance of getting out."

* * *

In his final game with the Blazers on March 29, 2007, Randolph scored a career-high 43 points and grabbed 17 rebounds in, ironically, a 96–92 loss to Memphis. He had hurt his right hand against Minnesota and played the next two games with a protective wrap.

After the game, Randolph underwent surgery for ligament damage in his thumb and missed the final 10 games. He finished the season averaging 23.6 points and 10.1 rebounds with 36 double-doubles on a team that ended with a 32–50 record.

Years later, Randolph was asked why he had experienced so many problems in Portland.

"I was 18, you know what I mean," said Zach, who was actually 20 as a rookie. "Just getting older, being more aware. It would have happened like that in Portland had I stayed."

Were Wallace and Wells bad influences?

"I don't think so," he said. "Actually, I learned a lot from those guys. I learned from a lot of the older guys during my years there. Scottie Pippen is a Hall of Famer. So is Arvydas Sabonis. Sheed should be one day. I learned so much from them. They're real people. That's what it's all about, man. Being real. All of these guys were great."

How did he feel about the Jail Blazers label?

"It didn't bother me."

Was it deserved?

"Ahhh . . . I don't know, man. Some people are so sensitive. I really don't know. I was young."

Did he change his ways as he got older?

"Not really. It was just a matter of people getting to know me. I was good in Portland, too."

Does he have regrets about any of his behavior during his time with the Blazers?

"No. No. No regrets. It was God's plan. I had a great career. I've been blessed, and I'm thankful. Coach Cheeks put me in the playoffs [in 2003]. I had my coming-out party. He helped me develop. Coming into the league, I'm thankful I had a coach like that."

Now 37, a 17-year veteran playing for the Sacramento Kings, Randolph is grateful for his six seasons in Portland.

"I have so much respect for Paul Allen and how he made that organization. It starts at the top. This was one of the best organizations I've been in. High standards. It was great. I learned a lot. Great city. The fan base is great. I loved it here. I grew up here."

But in another interview, Randolph would also make this remark about his former city: "They don't take well to young, black, urban kids coming out, having come from nothing. You come to Portland with braids, with cornrows—people can't relate to that. They peg you in a different way. If a guy's got braids, he's a thug."

Nash had received calls from Randolph's neighbors complaining of gunfire on his property.

"I saw a lot of quality in Zach as a person," Nash says today. "He was more a follower than a leader and a tad immature. He didn't get the opportunity to mature socially in college, and he didn't always surround himself with the best of friends. When I dealt with him one-on-one, though, I believed he was sincere. I would trust Zach with my grandkids as a babysitter, but I wouldn't want some of the people associated with him around."

After the 2005–06 season, Nash was fired. Patterson took over a dual role as president and GM before Pritchard would assume the GM position upon Patterson's resignation in March 2007.

"I enjoyed working with Steve and respected him," Nash says today. "When he let me go, he thanked me and said, 'You did a lot of the heavy lifting for us.' Well, that's what I was hired for. I would have liked to have stayed. I thought we were ready to turn the corner, but you always think that.

"When I went there, I knew it was going to be a tough assignment in that there was a mandate to change the culture of the team. But at the same time, nobody enjoys losing. Nobody truly understands that by changing the culture, it's likely when you're trading veteran players and going with younger players, you're going to take a step back.

"I thoroughly enjoyed the city of Portland and the people there. I made some great friendships. I enjoyed my association with the broadcasters. I loved the fans. I felt very badly when I left that I hadn't been able to deliver them a winning team."

* * *

After the 2006–07 season, Portland traded Randolph to the New York Knicks, along with guards Dan Dickau and Fred Jones, for Steve Francis and Channing Frye.

"We traded Zach Randolph to the Knicks, ending an era that none of us would miss," Paul Allen wrote in his autobiography, *Idea Man*. "The following season, we had the youngest team in the league and not a single arrest or suspension. The culture had changed."

Randolph would eventually become a respected member of the Memphis Grizzlies, with whom he was a finalist for the NBA's J. Walter Kennedy Citizenship Award in 2015.

"I always remember what Shareef Abdur-Rahim, one of the best guys ever, told me about Zach," says Jerry Reynolds, long-time executive and broadcaster with the Sacramento Kings. "Shareef said, 'He's not a bad guy. He's a follower, though.' In Memphis, he finally got to a place in his life and his career where he was a different person than he'd been in Portland. Probably a better one."

During his first couple of seasons in Portland, before he had established the culture he had in mind, McMillan saw himself as something of a father figure to many of his players.

"It was more than coaching with that group," he says today. "We had a majority of young black men on the team, and when I heard they were called the Jail Blazers, that bothered me. I told them during that first training camp, 'This is what they're saying about you. When you go out and do the things some of you guys are doing, people are going to say things about that.'

"I was really looking at those guys as young black men who I wanted to try to help mentor and to develop them as men. I was trying to shed some light on the opportunities they had, if they would only handle things in the right way."

Character mattered to McMillan.

"It still does. For me, it's the No. 1 thing; that you respect the game, the organization, your teammates, the fan base, and the NBA logo. You work your behind off to succeed, and you behave the right way. And if you take that approach, good things will happen to you."

Chapter 11

REFLECTIONS

"Scottie told me, 'They're hoochie mamas. They're here for us.'"

—Stephanie Smith-Leckness, flight attendant on "B-1," Paul Allen's private jet

Memories of the Jail Blazers era, from those who observed and/or took part

For nine years, Stephanie Smith-Leckness served as a flight attendant on Paul Allen's private jet, which flew the Trail Blazers to all their road games.

"I truly loved a lot of the people who were part of the Trail Blazer organization through those years—people like Brian Wheeler, Jeff Curtin, Geoff Clark, Bobby Medina, Mike Rice, Kim Anderson," says Smith-Leckness, who flew with the Blazers from 1997–2006. "The players would change, but a lot of the same people—trainers, coaches, TV and radio people—they remained. It was like a family, it really was."

The plane was a 38-seat Boeing 757, now owned by Donald Trump, who bought it for $100 million from Allen in 2011.[1]

"We called it B-1," says Smith-Leckness, who also flew the Seahawks and Mariners on "B-2," a bigger corporate jet also owned by Allen. "It was

---

1 The jet has Rolls Royce engines. The seat belts now, like everything else, are 24-carat gold-plated. There is a 57-inch television screen and the sound system of a top Hollywood screening room.

an unbelievably beautiful plane. When Paul would take B-1 to Hawaii at Christmas, the Blazers would use B-2."

Allen had his own private bedroom on the plane.

"The players weren't allowed in Paul's bedroom. A couple of times, a player was sick, and I'd let him go in there and lie down for a while."

Smith-Leckness—known as "Stebby" to everyone in those years—found her job both fun and challenging.

"It was a lot of really hard work. Providing safety and feeding a bunch of really young, way-too-rich kids was challenging at times. I was kind of like the mother hen."

Stephanie worked during the coaching eras of Mike Dunleavy, Maurice Cheeks, and Nate McMillan. She remembers Cheeks calling her over on one flight and gesturing to rookie guard Sebastian Telfair.

"Steph, go ask Sebastian why he thinks he needs to drive a Bentley while living in Tualatin," he said.

"I got a lot of respect from the players most of the time," Stephanie says. "If they acted up or yelled at a flight attendant, I'd talk to them. One time, I was told by Zach Randolph, 'You're not my mama.' I said, 'You would never talk to her the way you just talked to me.'"

Stephanie's first few years were during the Dunleavy years.

"Some of the players were horrible," she says. "J. R. Rider once had his finger in the face of [flight attendant] Donna Clark. It was something over tuna fish, if I remember right, and it happened right in the coaches' portion of the airplane. They sat in the back in the first-class seats. Not one coach even looked at him. No one stood up. I remember running back there and telling [Rider], 'Get your finger out of her face.' She was shaking and had tears in her eyes.

"I know the guy was crazy, but nobody did anything. It was really sad. The guy had a screw loose. He just wasn't well. I was appalled the coaches didn't say anything. No judgement. It was months later when I realized the guy was a really loose cannon."

During that time, Rider and a few other players were boning up on something other than game video.

"We'd be flying somewhere after a game, and they'd be watching 2 Live Crew videos," she says. "They were like soft porn—not appropriate for a team plane, in my view. I'd listen to the language—'cocksucker, motherfucker, nigger.' It was awful. The coaches wouldn't do anything about it. I remember running out and saying, 'Really? You think this is OK?'"

During the early years, several players kept marijuana on the airplane.

"I smelled it a few times. I went to who I thought put it there and told him, 'I'll pull it out the next time and show it to customs.' Never had that happen again."

During his second season, Dunleavy said Jermaine O'Neal had asked for her to come by and see his new house. Dunleavy went with her.

"Jermaine had a bunch of family members living there. They were all eating and watching TV and playing video games, and the house was a mess. He opened up the garage door. It stunk bad, and there was a load of stuffed-full trash bags in there. Mike said, 'Jermaine, it stinks.' He said, 'They told me to put it in the garage.' Mike said, 'You have to put it on the curb, and somebody will pick it up if you sign up for service.' His family members, who were mooching off of him, didn't know enough to say, 'Let's put the garbage out by the curb.'"

Once Rider departed after the 1998–99 season, Stephanie found herself growing closer to players such as Damon Stoudamire, Scottie Pippen, Greg Anthony, and Rasheed Wallace.

"I called them 'Shit birds,'" she says. "It was definitely a term of endearment. I loved those boys. They were just young and stupid."

During her later years with the Blazers, Smith-Lockness came up with the idea of mentoring players with their everyday lives.

"I remember talking with Nate [McMillan] about creating a job especially for me. I wanted to teach those guys how to write a check and pay a bill and take garbage to the curb. How to talk nicely to people and to put their hand out when they meet somebody. I told him, 'If we can make them winners off the court, we can do it on the court.' Nate was with me, and he asked Paul Allen about it, but there was no backing from the team."

Stephanie was Allen's personal flight attendant for nine years.

"He used my name one time. That was when I accidentally locked him in the bathroom. I hear this 'ding, ding, ding.' Then I heard him screaming, 'Stephanie!' I ran back and opened up the door. He said, 'You locked me in the bathroom.' That was the one time he used my name.

"But I knew what my role was. I didn't care if he liked or didn't like me. Paul is super gifted, super smart, just socially inept. I wish he could have felt more comfortable. He'd spent thousands of dollars catering food he may or may not like, and then he was nervous about asking, 'Do you think I could have pizza on the way home tonight?'

"Really, he was a very nice man. I wasn't there to be a friend of his. I wasn't there to crack his shell."

Smith-Lockness heard plenty of stories from the players. A lot of times, they weren't too worried about curfew, since there rarely was any.

"I'd ask them, 'Why do you go out until 4 in the morning and know you have to be shootaround at 10?' Once in New York, several of them had been at some famous strip club the night before the game. They all got back to the hotel at 6 or 7 (a.m.). Then they lost to the Knicks that night.

"But I liked those guys. They were good to me and the other girls. They weren't disrespectful to us. But what they were doing off the court was not going to make them winners on the court."

Smith-Lockness was privy to some stories about players with groupies, too.

"I'm naive and kind of a Pollyanna. We're checking into the Houston Galleria hotel at about 3 one morning, and I see a bunch of women in the lobby. I said to someone, 'I don't think there would be a wedding at this time of night.' Scottie told me, 'They're hoochie mamas. They're here for us.' And I said, 'But I don't understand. If you're going to do that, why are you married?' I just couldn't understand that aspect.

"Maurice Cheeks was really afraid to fly. If it was really bumpy and late at night, we'd sit together sometimes, and he'd explain to me why he is and will always be the way he is with women, even if he has the most beautiful girlfriend. He said it wasn't natural for him [to be with one woman]. I asked,

'What if she were the same way?' And he said, 'Well, it wouldn't work.' I never understood it."

Stephanie calls Wallace "one of my favorite men in the world."

"He was one of the few guys on those teams who never did anything like that," she says. "Rasheed gave me a card one time that said, 'Thank you so much for all you've done. I love you.' He was like a kindred spirit. Everyone thought he was really mean. He was wonderful in a lot of ways."

Stephanie had mixed emotions about Shawn Kemp.

"I adored the man. He was really troubled but a great guy. We were told at one point we couldn't have any desserts on the airplane. He needed to lose some weight and had an addictive personality. We couldn't have cookies and stuff out for the other guys. Everybody knew that he was addicted to drugs, alcohol, women, sugar. And the sugar was what they all focused on. I knew he was beyond that."

In the late '90s and early 2000s, "Tonk" was the players' card game of choice on the plane.

"Usually it was Scottie, Greg, Bonzi Wells, and Dale Davis—the same four guys. Everybody was getting off the airplane, and they'd have a heavy hand, and we'd be cleaning up around them. Finally, I'd have to say, 'Guys, it's 2 a.m., we still have to restock this airplane and fly to Seattle so we can get home to our families. Get off the airplane.' And they were like, 'Stebby, this is a $30,000 hand.' I'd say, 'Now you're really out of here.' They were betting hundreds of thousands of dollars sometimes. We're talking big dough."

The players would never leave a tip, though.

"But if those guys lost a C-note on the airplane, you'd have to tear the whole airplane upside down. They never left a penny. But they would have $30,000, $40,000, $50,000 hands. It was unbelievable."

Several times, Anthony would take a case of Evian water out of the compartment in which it was stowed and leave the plane. Once, Smith-Lockness confronted him.

"Every time you take one of those off the airplane, one of us girls has to restock it and carry it up the stairs."

"'But my wife really likes it,' he told me.

"Finally, Mike Dunleavy stood up for us and said, 'For Christ's sakes, Greg, they sell Evian in Portland, too.'"

The year before she left her job with Paul Allen, Stephanie and her husband built a house in Kirkland, Washington.

"One day I got a huge package at our door. It was a plethora of goodies from the Pottery Barn from Maurice Cheeks, with a loving note. It brought me to tears.

"There was a lot of love during my time [with the Blazers]. Even the shit birds. That was all part of the fun."

* * *

Steve Kerr played only one of his 15 NBA seasons in Portland, in 2001–02, the penultimate season of his career. He had come into his own as an off-the-bench contributor with the Chicago Bulls during their heyday in the 1990s and would win five NBA championships as a player—three with Chicago, two with San Antonio.

Kerr was in and out of the rotation during his one season with the Blazers, averaging 4.1 points in 65 games while shooting .470 from the field, .394 from 3-point range, and .975 from the foul line (that's right—39-for-40).

"I had a great time," says Kerr, who coaches Golden State and led the Warriors to NBA championships in 2014–15 and 2016–17. "I loved that season. I loved living in Portland. I enjoyed that team. There was some dysfunction and a perception of players that people have, but they were fun guys to be around. We had a good season with a disappointing finish."

In Maurice Cheeks's first year as coach, the Blazers had Rasheed Wallace, Bonzi Wells, Scottie Pippen, Damon Stoudamire, and Dale Davis as starters, with Ruben Patterson, Shawn Kemp, Derek Anderson, Kerr, Chris Dudley, and rookie Zach Randolph coming off the bench.

"We were loaded," Kerr says. "Rasheed, Bonzi, and Damon were in their prime. Scottie was still a hell of a player. We could have been better. We just couldn't quite get over the hump.

"What stands out the most is we enjoyed each other. We enjoyed being in that locker room together. We had fun together. We had a lot of talent and guys were pretty unselfish. We played hard and got along well."

After four years coaching the Warriors, Kerr has developed an appreciation for what it takes to become a champion.

"The roster makeup is important in this league. You want a nice blend of things. You want stars and role players. You want guys who are willing to accept their roles and other guys who are hungry to make their mark. You can definitely have an imbalance one way or the other, and that can hurt you."

Did the 2001–02 Blazers have that imbalance?

"Possibly. We had a lot of mouths to feed, for sure."

Kerr says he enjoyed playing for Cheeks.

"Mo is a pretty cool customer, but it was not an easy first job. We had some volatile, emotional people on that team. It was not an easy gig.

"When you're around a really good team, you can feel a sort of magic that exists. And the fans can see it. Fans fall in love with certain teams because they can see the camaraderie and the joy and the magic. We never quite got there in Portland. That team had promise that was unfulfilled, but it wasn't because we were bad guys. It wasn't because guys were selfish. The mix wasn't quite right. The leadership within the group wasn't quite right. We were a little wayward. We couldn't really create the magic that I'm talking about."

During that season, Kerr would react negatively to a *Sports Illustrated* article castigating the Blazer players for their on-court antics and off-court shenanigans.

"I remember resenting that article," Kerr says today. "They used a couple of photos of our guys huddled up away from the group of kids we were with, whatever the charitable outing was. It was totally misrepresentative of the situation. We had just spent an hour interacting with the kids. Give me a break. We didn't always do the exact right thing, and we did have a couple of guys who got into legal issues. But that was just wrong."

Kerr took on a big brother role with Randolph, often sitting with the rookie and Dudley on the team plane.

"I loved Zach. I love looking back at what he was and what he has become. Chris and I were trying to take him under our wing and teach him about the NBA. The stewardess on the team plane called him 'The Baby.' She would come back and ask, 'How is the baby doing?' He was a child. He didn't know anything about the NBA. But he was such a good kid; you could see the heart he had. I'm in awe of what he has made of his life and how much good he has done. He came from a pretty rough place. He needed to learn about the world. He needed to learn how to conduct himself. And he did all that."

There were some players around Randolph in Portland—Kerr and Dudley excluded—who weren't the ideal role models.

"It was a dangerous mix," Kerr concedes. "It's not like he was going to the Spurs to play with Tim Duncan and Tony Parker. He was in the midst of some dysfunction as a rookie."

Kerr never understood the Jail Blazers label.

"We had a few guys who had been in trouble. It was a catchy nickname more than anything. I don't know that we were that much different from most teams. We had our share of issues, but who doesn't?"

Nearly two decades later, Kerr has seen a lot of things go on with a lot of teams in the NBA.

"Everything is exposed these days. In the old days, only the athletes or the musicians or the actors were exposed. The perception was, 'These NBA guys are bad.' Now it's in the White House, people beating their spouses, and all kinds of issues.

"People have issues. It's not just athletes. We're human beings. We're all flawed. Nowadays, there is so much exposure, you realize people everywhere have problems whether wealthy or not, or in a place of power or not. People make mistakes. Stuff happens. I don't think our Portland team was that special in that regard."

* * *

Pete Simpson has been with the Portland Police Bureau for 25 years and is currently a sergeant assigned to the criminal intelligence unit. Through his career, Simpson has worked as a public information officer, a gang enforcement detective, and a hostage negotiator. From 1993–1996 he was a patrol sergeant, then worked the gang unit through the rest of the Jail Blazers era.

A Portland native, Simpson grew up a fan of the Trail Blazers. From 1985–1990, beginning with Jack Ramsay's last season as coach and ending when Rick Adelman's team reached the 1990 NBA Finals, Simpson was a ball boy during middle school and his high school years at Benson.

"I got to know the players during that period really well," Simpson says. "It was a really well-run organization, a family organization back then."

Things had changed by the time the mid-'90s arrived. By that time, Simpson was working the gang unit.

"We started seeing investigators coming across things that were troublesome with the Blazers. We had guys we were talking to who were intersecting with some of the players and their entourages. You started to see some bleed-over there. It seemed like some of the players were really active in hanging around the local criminal or gang crowd. Zach Randolph, Qyntel Woods, and Darius Miles were the three we saw a lot of, and we would hear about from people who were at a certain place and something would happen."

One player was involved in a shooting at the Exotica strip club in Northeast Portland.

"We had some informants in the gang world saying that a lot of the stuff that happened had to do with a player and some of his friends throwing money around, taking all the girls from the gangsters and criminals who were there, and they took exception to that. It was Zach and people he was hanging around with. It got to the point where we'd respond to a call and be convinced that one of the Blazers would be hit."

In the early- to mid-'90s, Randolph's "Hoop Family" kept police officers busy.

"Zach kept some interesting company, way more so than most guys do who come to Portland. They were real criminals he was hanging around with. Whether he knew it or not, or didn't care, I don't know. It was a concerning time. You'd see some of the cars registered to players in places they shouldn't be. It was a theme for a while."

Many of the Blazers were products of unstable backgrounds.

"A lot of guys came from the mean streets. They'd get to the NBA and make it, and sometimes people in any industry who come from a rough background and get to success, their toes still dip back to the rough upbringing that can be a problem for them."

Randolph was once featured in an episode of *MTV Cribs*, a show highlighting the homes of celebrities.

"I happened to be watching the show. In the middle of his pool table, the camera flashed on the star of David—for David Barksdale, who is one of the founders of the Gangster Disciples, very big in the Midwest. It seemed clear there was some affiliation there."

Simpson once received a photo of gold-plated 50-caliber handguns on stacks of cash in Randolph's house.

"You grow up in a neighborhood, you may be affiliated by virtue that you live there. Now that you're a millionaire, you have a custom-made pool table with a gang symbol on it, and the question has to be asked: Are you still affiliated? Being a gang member isn't a crime, but there were issues with his Hoop Family and some of the hangers-on who were around him.

"It was strange, seeing a lot of those guys. I knew them from the streets. They would talk as if they signed the contract for a million. It was always, 'We just got the big contract.' I'd look at these guys thinking, 'Where's the *we* in this?'"

In the early 2000s, Simpson's unit tracked a rumor that some Blazers were involved in a marijuana operation.

"The players were allegedly buying marijuana out here at $2,500 a pound and getting it back to the Midwest, where it would go for $8,000 to $10,000 a pound. We still see that today—not from the players. People from Minnesota and Illinois and the Dakotas will come here, buy 50 or 60 pounds of weed and go back home where it's not legal. And it's high-quality. Oregon makes very good marijuana."

Marijuana wasn't the investigators' chief concern.

"Our focus was with violent crime. If it didn't intersect with that, we probably weren't going to look at it real hard. The shooting things were really concerning. There was a gun culture. Several players got caught with guns during that time."

In recent years, members of the Portland Police Bureau have had an annual preseason meeting with the Blazers, talking about Oregon laws concerning guns.

"We want them to be aware," Simpson says.

One year in the mid-2000s, Blazers management had high-profile attorney Stephen Houze conduct a preseason briefing with the players.

"One of the things he told the players was, 'Don't roll your windows down. Don't consent to a search if you get stopped.'" This isn't fair to Stephen, but it's almost like you're bringing in a mob lawyer to tell these guys how not to get caught."

The newspapers picked up on it and ran stories on Houze's message.

"Later that day, we got three or four dozen donuts delivered to the precinct by 'Blaze' [the team mascot] with a note saying, 'You guys are our real friends.'" It was a strange time. They knew the article would rub the police the wrong way. It was a bit of a slap in the face."

Given his background, it was hard for Simpson not to take things personally.

"Having worked around the team for five years in a great era, seeing it shift so far was really disheartening. It's mind-blowing how a franchise can go from this great pillar of the community to a period where people were walking away from interest in the team. I didn't watch their games for several years, and I was a die-hard. How does that happen?"

* * *

Bobby Medina worked as the Blazers' strength and conditioning coach for 16 years, from 1997 to 2013. General manager Bob Whitsitt hired the Nevada-Las Vegas grad away from the Seattle SuperSonics, where he had worked in the same capacity for the previous five years.

"Bob told me, 'We have a lot of young players, including Jermaine

O'Neal, who is kind of what Shawn Kemp was when he got to Seattle,'" says Medina, now working under the title Assistant Athletic Director for Sports Performance at Santa Clara. "They were building a new practice facility in Portland. We'd just done that in Seattle. It was a perfect fit for me."

Medina had worked early in his career at UNLV, when Mark Warkentien and Tim Grgurich were on staff under Jerry Tarkanian. Whitsitt had hired both in Seattle and brought them down to Portland—Warkentien as director of scouting and assistant GM, Grgurich as an assistant on Mike Dunleavy's coaching staff—after he took over the Blazers' front office. The Sonics' head coach at the time was George Karl, whom Grgurich had recruited as a player many years earlier. Seattle assistant coach Bob Kloppenburg had been an assistant at UNLV for a year.

"People talk about the Jail Blazers and the renegades that they were," Medina says. "I didn't see it that way. We had guys like that at UNLV. I was there with Stacey Augmon and Larry Johnson. To me, that was nothing. We had some really good players who didn't always behave. We knew how to make it successful; you needed to manage them. That wasn't just during practice; it was also before and after practice.

"We did a good job doing that at UNLV, and we tried to replicate it as much as we could in Portland, but we couldn't manage [the players] all the time. You had a lot of young guys making bad decisions. When you're winning like we were for a while, fans will overlook it a little bit. But when you start to lose, then those things become magnified."

Medina defends Whitsitt as an excellent GM and basketball mind.

"I'm still shocked how he was able to trade J. R. Rider for Steve Smith. It's amazing anybody could pull that off. Also, that you could use a guy like Gary Trent in a trade and turn that into a Damon Stoudamire."

Medina grew close with such players as Rasheed Wallace, Bonzi Wells, and Ruben Patterson during his time with the team.

"When you talk about Rasheed and Bonzi and the guys in that Jail Blazers era and how bad they were? When you talk to my family and kids, they have nothing but positive things to say about them. All my interactions were good. I spent two summers with Bonzi in Indiana, helping him train.

He told me one time he was going to legally change his last name to Medina. I love Ruben. I know I could call Ruben today and he would do anything for me.

"I have a special place in my heart for those guys. I never had a problem with any of them. Being a strength coach in the NBA is a difficult job. It's hard to get guys to do something they don't always want to do. From the outside, you'd think that must be hard to deal with these guys, to get them to lift weights and condition. It wasn't that way for me with this group."

During his nearly 30-year career in strength and conditioning at the college and professional level, Medina rates three players above the rest in terms of being the best teammates.

"Larry Johnson would be No. 1. Rasheed would be second. How could I say that, with all the technicals and suspensions? Rasheed was all about fairness. Every time he got a technical, it was about him getting cheated, or his team getting cheated. When he wasn't in the game, he was cheering his teammates on. He wasn't unplugged or disconnected. He was waving the towel, cheering his teammates on."

Medina's third player is guard Nick Van Exel, who played one season [2004–05] with Portland at the end of the Jail Blazers period.

"Unbelievable teammate. He changed Joel Przybilla, encouraging him, giving him confidence, prodding him to play at a higher level. Nick was great with young guys, almost like a coach."

Asked for the hardest workers during his time with the Blazers, Medina mentions Jermaine O'Neal.

"He was so frustrated he wasn't playing, he would come in to the weight room and lift every day. It was the only positive thing he had going on. He'd go in there and start getting after the weights. When he came to us, he had no tattoos. He started getting bigger and got a tattoo on his arm that said, 'The Year of the Resurrection.' His body started blowing up.

"Brian Grant was a guy who fed off of what we were doing in the weight room. He was in there getting after it every day. He was the heart and soul of some of those teams. We went through some key losses in personnel that changed the whole thing. Brian leaving after the trade for Kemp was a killer. Shawn wasn't the Shawn he had been for us in Seattle. Brian was soon to be on his way down, too; the peak of his career was with the Blazers.

"Detlef Schrempf was always one of the hardest workers. Consummate pro. First guy to practice; last guy to leave. He took care of his body. Another guy is Scottie Pippen. Unbelievable from the day he got there. I learned so much from him about being a pro. He would get all the young guys and say, 'Practice starts at 11? We're all in here at 10.' He would be the guy rounding up the troops.

"The guys you wouldn't think would be compliant were great, guys like Bonzi Wells, Ruben Patterson, and Damon Stoudamire. Those guys loved [the weight room]. They believed in it."

During the Mike Dunleavy era [1997–2001], the Blazers' depth was the best in the league.

"The practices we had were some of the best I've ever seen in the NBA. Your second team was better than your first on some days, with [Greg] Anthony, [Stacey] Augmon, and O'Neal. They were super competitive. It reminded me of the way it was when I was at UNLV.

"Coach Dunleavy would play scrimmage games, best of three. If the second team won, the starters would say, 'Bullshit, we're playing again.' Coach Dunleavy would say, 'Practice is over.' They'd say, 'No, we're running again.'"

Medina enjoyed his relationship with both of the coaches he worked with during the Jail Blazers era—Dunleavy and Maurice Cheeks.

"Mike was a really good guy. One of the struggles with him was, he had been a GM as well as a head coach [with the Milwaukee Bucks]. When he got to Portland, he didn't have that control anymore. The players they brought in were Bob's guys. Bob was doing what he could to keep Jermaine happy. He hired George Glymph [O'Neal's high school coach]. Coach Dunleavy didn't like that. He never really accepted George as part of the staff."

When Dunleavy was hired, Medina says, one of the conditions laid down by Whitsitt was he had to bring O'Neal along as a player.

"Bob told Mike, 'I'm not telling you to start him, but play him,'" Medina says now. "Mike wouldn't do it. There was a big debate about putting Jermaine on the playoff roster after his second year. Mike left him off. He didn't think Jermaine could help us as much in the playoffs that year as some other guys."

Medina and Cheeks formed an instant relationship.

"He was awesome as a guy, and he had a funny side. I heard him tell Zach [Randolph], 'When I took this job, they told me I was going to be coaching No. 50. I thought I was going to get David Robinson, and I get you.'

"One time, Ruben was unhappy with his role. He was saying, 'If you don't play me, trade me,' before practice one day. Coach Cheeks said, 'Ruben, we've been trying to trade you. Nobody wants you. Find us someone who wants you, and we'll do it.' And Ruben was like, 'Man, that's fucked up, coach.'"

During Cheeks's first season, Wallace had gotten a technical foul.

During an ensuing timeout, "Coach Cheeks said, 'You can't be doing that kind of bullshit. We're losing this game because of that,'" Medina recalls. "He went after him. We ended up winning the game."

The next day before practice, Wallace approached Cheeks.

"I've played for a lot of coaches," Wallace said. "You're the first black coach I've had. Nobody's ever talked to me like that before."

"Hey, sorry, but those are things we need to do to win," Cheeks told him.

"Well, don't let that shit happen again," Wallace said.

"And Coach Cheeks is like, 'Is he serious? Wow.'" If Coach Cheeks would have had a more veteran staff and more veteran players, he could have won. But the younger guys followed Rasheed. They mistook kindness for weakness."

Medina saw something good in nearly every player he worked with in Portland.

"I tried to learn something from every guy we brought in. I did that with Steve Smith—what it was like in Atlanta, what it was like to play with the Olympic team. He was always a professional and a good businessman. He had bought some apartment buildings outside of Michigan State, then remodeled them as an investment. He decided to buy into a Domino's pizza franchise right next to it because he figured all those kids would need a place to eat. I remember telling Steve, 'I want to work for you one day.' He said, 'You'll never work for me; you'll work *with* me.' He realized the value of working together. That made him a good teammate in the NBA."

Enough craziness happened, though, that team employees became a bit jaded to any shenanigans.

"We were playing San Antonio in an NBC game, and the Spurs made a run. We called timeout. I was sitting right behind the bench, writing down the plus-minus numbers. Rasheed was pissed off about something and came over and kicked a chair. The chair flew by me. I looked up, and I just went back to writing. No shock. Any normal person would have jumped up, startled. You're subjected to things so much, you see things and they don't affect you. You're just used to it. It's like being in prison and seeing a fight.

"There were a lot of high-emotion guys. From the outside looking in, you'd think it would be a nightmare dealing with them. Those were some of my most fun times in the NBA. Sometimes, you had to protect them from themselves. But when it came to game time, we were going to do whatever it took to win. Those guys came in with that swagger. They didn't care who it was, they were going to go in and win."

* * *

Will Perdue played just one season with the Blazers and saw action for only 58 minutes in 13 games. It was the 2000–01 season, the last of a 13-year career in which he spent the rest of his time with two great franchises— the Chicago Bulls from 1988–1995 and 1999–2000, and the Spurs from 1995–1999. He won three NBA championships with the Bulls and one with the Spurs.

Perdue, now a studio analyst for NBC Sports Chicago, offers a unique perspective on the 2000–01 Blazers, who were swept in three games by the Los Angeles Lakers in the first round of the playoffs, a year after losing to the Lakers in seven games in the Western Conference Finals.

"We were the best team in the league for a good part of that season,"

Perdue says. "Then we ended up the No. 8 seed, having to play the top-seeded Lakers in the first round. You just saw it unravel. It was bizarre, to say the least. I thought I'd seen everything until I got to Portland. Then it totally opened my eyes to a different perspective. There was a lot of petty stuff that just snowballed."

Perdue thought Mike Dunleavy was a good coach and was surprised at the reception he got from some of the players.

"I didn't think there was the respect for Dunleavy there needed to be, and that bubbled over," Perdue says. "Eventually, he lost the team; it wasn't necessarily so much him, but the dynamics of the personalities we had. We had guys fighting in the huddle. I'd never experienced anything like that. I'm sure guys regret it."

Perdue had played seven seasons in Chicago with Scottie Pippen before they reunited in Portland.

"I felt sorry for Scottie. He tried to be a leader but, because he was injured a lot, the guys didn't listen to him. As much as a disaster as that season was, there was a positive that came out of it—the Scottie Pippen I saw then compared to the one I saw before.

"Scottie wanted to be the man. He wasn't ready for it in Chicago. He didn't have the same skill set [in Portland], but he did try to be a leader, to try to talk to these guys, to use the experience he had in winning championships to help those guys. The guys just shut him out. That was unfortunate, but I saw a much more mature, adult version of Scottie Pippen than when I played with him in Chicago."

The midseason additions of Rod Strickland and Detlef Schrempf didn't work, Perdue says.

"Detlef and I would go to lunch a lot and he'd be like, 'What the hell did I get myself into?' When you bring guys in like that, players start questioning themselves. You think, 'What, they don't like me? I'm not playing well enough? They don't respect me?' You get defensive.

"The personalities on that team were so across the board. If you would get them on an individual basis, they were all good guys. But once you got them together as a group, it was a herd mentality. Somebody would make an outlandish statement, and the other guys would all be like, 'Yeah.' But it also had something to do with guys looking out for their own agenda."

Dunleavy wound up sacrificing his principles, Perdue says.

"As a coach, you take one of two paths. You either take the path of least resistance—which he ultimately ended up doing—or you go the path where, 'If I'm going to get fired, I'll do it my way.' Mike saw those guys weren't going to do it his way. It got to the point where guys weren't listening to him. They got defensive when he'd talk to them about mistakes they made. There were arguments in the huddles.

"His approach with this group of guys didn't mesh. The personalities just didn't work. That was unfortunate for him. He took the 'Let's all be friends, kumbaya' approach. It worked for a while that season. We had the best record in the league. Then it started to go south, and he tried to implement a little discipline, and it didn't work."

Perdue was in Portland for the last of Dunleavy's four years as head coach.

"Most of those guys had already been there. I came in on the back end. I don't know what had developed from years' past, what type of relationship those guys had. As long as we were winning, things were fine. When you don't, and you have to try to make some changes, that didn't go over well."

Perdue has mixed emotions about Rasheed Wallace.

"Rasheed was one of the most talented guys in the league. He was an All-Star. Guys were used to his explosions at referees. You expected it. The distraction aspect of it was, you just didn't know when it was going to happen. It was very unpredictable. But off the court, outside of competition, he was one of the nicest guys I've ever dealt with."

Perdue recalls a home game in which Wallace had been ejected. After the game, Perdue's girlfriend at the time told him about a scene in the team's "family room," where spouses and children and girlfriends congregated. After Rasheed had gone to the locker room and showered, he came into the family room, got down on all fours, and played basketball with everybody's kids.

"This was after he got kicked out in a violent rage, and we had to restrain him and push him off the floor. She said it was like he had just finished grocery shopping and came in and joined a playgroup. It was the oddest thing."

Perdue says each of the organizations for whom he played was different.

"With the Bulls, when the game was over, we went 12 or 13 different directions. I would occasionally do things with John Paxson or Bill Cartwright, but we rarely had a team-oriented event. I wouldn't say we were a tight-knit group off the court. But when we stepped on the floor, we played for one another.

"The Spurs were a family oriented organization. We did stuff together all the time. There was a good chance 90 to 100 percent of the guys would show up and do things after a game. A lot of that had to do with Pop [coach Gregg Popovich] and Avery Johnson. That was their M.O.

"Then I get to Portland, and I remember thinking, 'This isn't like anything I've experienced before.' There were serious cliques. Guys would constantly argue in practice. Guys would go at each other during games. It was a weird dynamic. I can't think of one guy on that team where you would think, 'That guy is an asshole. He's a jerk. He doesn't give a shit.' It was like if you take all those individual personalities and keep them separated, you're OK. Together, it was a very volatile situation. It wasn't like that in the beginning of the season, when we were winning games. You could always sense the team was on the edge, that there was some tension. And it just blew up when we started losing."

Has there ever been a team like it, before or since?

"Not that I was ever a part of, and not that I know of."

Rasheed Wallace did not answer interview requests for this book but, in January 2017, on Kevin Garnett's "Area 21" show on TNT, Garnett addressed the Jail Blazers issue. He began with the Game 7 loss to the Los Angeles Lakers in the 2000 Western Conference Finals.

"We weren't a league darling. I was going through my technical things and the media. Going against the Hall of Fame franchise . . . we had this game. I remember looking at their bench. They had guys looking in the stands. Phil [Jackson] was sitting down. He wasn't paying attention. We were on a roll. We had the ball. Our coach [Mike Dunleavy] called a timeout when we were running with the ball. Nobody was tired; we were all geeked. Six minutes and we're on to playing the Pacers in the championship, and he called a timeout . . . that's what gave them their spark. [Brian Shaw] threw up a last-second bank shot that went in [at the end of the third quarter], and it was downhill from there. We missed 13 straight shots."

Talk turned to the team's reputation.

"Unfortunately, it was some mishaps in there. Guys might have gotten speeding tickets or some DUIs . . ."

Garnett: And they blew it up like it was all over the top.

Wallace: They were going to do that in Portland because we were the only professional sports show in town, at the time, between Seattle and LA.

[Well, there was Golden State and Sacramento.]

"We were small as far as our marketing. The only things that could blow up or make local writers big is if they would try to report everything that was happening—speeding tickets, or if you parked in a handicapped spot—they would report anything. We knew it was all about us. We had to stick together and fight through it. We did, no matter what they labeled us."

The season he was traded to the Pistons, everything fell into place. Wallace wound up winning the NBA championship he had always craved.

"When I ended up in Detroit, I kinda sorta felt the same way, except we didn't have the Jail Blazer name. We had a bunch of misfits. Chauncey [Billups] and Rip [Hamilton] had been on a few teams. We were all coming from different spots and different teams. When it all came together, it just clicked."

Mike Dunleavy took over the Blazers in 1997, inheriting a roster he felt he could win with immediately. Dunleavy did, with four straight winning seasons and a 190–106 record (a .641 winning percentage). But he never got the Blazers to the NBA Finals, and was let go after the 2000–01 campaign.

"It was just a great time," says Dunleavy, now head coach at Tulane University. "I really enjoyed it. It was a process. When I came in, we were trying to get the right players to have a winning team. There was some real talent there. I just don't think the chemistry was totally there. We had some guys who weren't always on the same page."

Surprisingly, Dunleavy's biggest disappointment wasn't the Game 7 loss to the Lakers in the 2000 Western Conference Finals.

"It was that we broke up that team after the season. We came so close to beating the Lakers. They were the champs. We should have kept that team together another year. We had new pieces. We had younger guys that we could do it with."

Dunleavy didn't agree with general manager Bob Whitsitt's decision to trade Brian Grant and Jermaine O'Neal.

"I wasn't on board with it. Part of the excuse I was given [by Whitsitt] was, 'Well, you're forcing me to trade Jermaine because you're not playing him.' He was 21 years old, and he had just signed a new deal. Just because his agent was yelling at you, there was no need to trade him."

Dunleavy's argument to Whitsitt was this: "We have [Arvydas] Sabonis, Grant, and Wallace up front, and I'm expected to win every game. You're not telling me to lower the number of wins I get. I've got a job to do, and I have to manage it the way I manage it. A year from now, Jermaine will be playing 40 minutes a game. Sabonis is going to be dropping off at some point."

Dunleavy wishes he'd had more say in personnel matters.

"A lot of times, Bob had deals already done when he came to me. The only deals I took a stand on and said absolutely not were trading Jermaine and Brian for Dale Davis and Shawn Kemp. Shawn was 325 pounds and wasn't anywhere near the player we needed him to be.

"During [the 2000–01 season], Bob came to my office in February. We're still fighting for the best record in the West, and he said he thought Shawn should be playing more minutes, that we should be trying to develop the guy, that we need to get him sharp. I'm doing all I can playing him 16 minutes a night. This is torture for me. He said, 'We like you, but this is a fireable offense.' I said, 'How about we send him away to a fat farm to show me he's committed?' Bob wanted me to play him 28 minutes. If I did that, I'd lose my players. They know who should be playing. The only time I take a stand against management is if it's going to put your credibility with your players in question."

Dunleavy has many thoughts about Game 7 of the Lakers series, in which the Blazers led by 17 points late in the third quarter, only to lose 89–84.

"It could have been one of the worst moments of my coaching career, except for one thing. I've heard a lot of people say, 'Your players choked.' My definition of 'choke' isn't that. If somebody chokes, he walks to the free-throw line with a chance to win it, a great free throw shooter who doesn't make it. You can say that's a choke. If somebody starts pressuring you, you turn the ball all over the place, maybe you choke. If you take bad, rushed shots, I agree.

"But in the fourth quarter of that game, we had one turnover, one missed defensive rotation, and no bad shots. The issue was, we missed 13 shots in a row. Of those, 11 were great shots, and two of them were just good. Four by Rasheed and four by Steve Smith. Rasheed had 30 points and Smith 18 in the game. We had the right guys shooting the ball. Bonzi [Wells] had a couple of in-and-outs."

Critics say Dunleavy shouldn't have taken Wallace out of the game for 2:36 late in the third and early in the fourth quarter. He vehemently disagrees.

"That's one decision I made that I would never be able to live with if I hadn't—do I give Rasheed his rest or try to play him through it? I gave him his rest and put him back in the game, and we were still up double figures. If I'd left him in that game and we went on that streak [of missing shots], I'd have thought, 'He was tired,' and you beat yourself up over that. But we'd given him his rest and got him back in when we were still up 10 or 11."[2]

Dunleavy points out the fouls went against the Blazers down the stretch, including two against Sabonis that fouled him out in the closing minutes.

"The biggest play came when we were down by four inside the final minute. Smith goes down the middle and gets planted. No question it was a foul. And he's a 90-percent free throw shooter, so we'd have been down two. If the foul gets called, it's a totally different game."

In 11 regular-season and postseason games that year, the Lakers outscored the Blazers by a total of five points. "The minutes Sabonis was on the floor," Dunleavy says, "we won.

"I was proud that we were down 3–1 in the series and forced a seventh

---

2   Portland's lead was actually 75–60 when Wallace returned with 10:28 remaining.

game. That team showed grit and determination to fight back the way we did. Even though I was on the wrong side of it, it was a great series."

On March 5, the 2000–01 Blazers were 42–18—the best record in the NBA. About that time, Whitsitt added veterans Detlef Schrempf and Rod Strickland to an already crowded roster. Many believe that caused the Blazers to implode.

"At that point, I had the all-time winningest percentage of any coach in Portland history. Something did happen. I'm not going to go into that. It totally changed our whole mindset. The last 25 games, we were 7–18."

But Dunleavy felt he had a "great" relationship with Whitsitt.

"Bob was really smart. He was good about putting deals together. Some of the time he would ask me questions, and he'd be trying to steer me in the direction he wanted me to go. He probably already had the deal done. It's kind of like a hidden card trick. But if you gave me the option of having more or less talent, even if that talent is tainted, I'm going with more, and I think I can manage it."

Dunleavy says he was well aware of the egos on his Portland teams.

"I didn't care about contracts or status; I played the guys who gave us a best chance to win. But I wasn't dumb, either. I knew guys wanted their chances to score. I'd go into the arena the next game and ask, 'Who got offended last game? Who didn't get their shots?' I'd run the first two plays for them, to let them know I loved them. You had to play that game."

Dunleavy offers insight into the incident late in the regular season against the Lakers, when Wallace threw a towel in Sabonis's face during a timeout. Afterward, there was a confrontation between Dunleavy and Wallace in the locker room.

"When it happened, I went up to Sabonis and said to him, 'Sabas, you want me to take care of this now or after the game?' He said, 'Coach, whatever you want to do.' I thought, 'It's a one-point game. Let's try to win this game.' We lost the game, anyway.

"I go into the locker room, and with everybody there, I said, 'Rasheed, you owe Sabas an apology.' He said, 'I don't owe anybody an apology. He knocked my tooth out.' I said, 'Sheed, he's your teammate. He didn't do it on purpose.' He said, 'I ain't giving no apology.' I said, 'OK, I'm going to suspend you, and it will cost you $50 grand.'

"He said, 'Fuck you, Mike. Suck my dick. I ain't doing that.' I'd thought about it. I knew exactly what I was doing. I baited him. I said, 'No, motherfucker, you can suck my dick and pay me $50 grand.' He charges me. The guys stop him. I said, 'Let that big motherfucker go. I've been here four years, I haven't seen him hit anybody yet.'

"If he'd come after me, I was going to tackle him and do what I could to keep him off me, but I wasn't going to suspend or fine him. He turned around and said, 'All right, Michael, I'm not falling for any of that Brooklyn shit.'"

Today, Dunleavy says there are no hard feelings.

"I loved Rasheed as a player. He was a great teammate. At times we cracked heads a little bit because I made him play inside. I thought it was best for the team. Never in practice did he complain one bit. He always practiced hard."

During his first two years in Portland, Dunleavy coached J. R. Rider.

"I called him 'The Sun,' because everything revolved around him," Dunleavy says. "He was a very charismatic guy. I actually loved his game. He could score, post up, pick and roll. But he had a wild tick about him. One year, I fined him a total of $450,000 for being late and different suspensions. We talked about it. I said 'J. R., you have two years left on your deal, and then you can make $50 or $60 million. All you have to do is show up for practice on time and have the right attitude.'

"For some reason, he did it on purpose. He'd be on time and sit there in the parking lot until he was late. I said, 'You can't get religion in the last year of your deal. You have to trick them for two years. There are people who have questions about you and everything that goes with it.' But it didn't get any better. It's too bad."

His last three seasons with the Blazers, Dunleavy coached Bonzi Wells.

"I loved 'Bonz Eye,'" he said. "Loved his game. I got the best out of him. We posted him, we iso'd him, we worked on his shooting. His shot got better. He had a little bit of a wild hair at times, but it was no big deal."

The Blazers acquired Damon Stoudamire midway through Dunleavy's first season.

"Damon was a really talented player, particularly at the offensive end of the floor. We had conflicts. Not that we butted heads, but I'm sure he was disappointed that I used Greg Anthony to close games at times. Greg was a much better defender and could hit a standstill 3, so he didn't hurt you on offense. A lot of times, I'm playing as a defensive coach. We're in position to win a game. All we have to do is tighten up the defensive end. Damon was disappointed he didn't finish games."

Dunleavy had Kemp for his last season with the Blazers.

"The hard part was, Shawn was a really nice guy. He was just too heavy. He went from being one of the best athletic bodies and runners/jumpers in the history of the game to 325 pounds. He still knew how to play somewhat, he had some skill, and he was never a bad teammate in any way."

Dunleavy wishes it had turned out different for Jermaine O'Neal in Portland.

"Jermaine was just a kid. He had a lot of athletic ability, and he was growing and learning the game. All players want to play. There was nothing wrong that he complained to Bob to try get him more playing time. Jermaine could have fit in, but he wasn't there yet. No doubt in my mind he would get there."

O'Neal had a high-powered agent in Arn Tellem.

"That didn't matter. They had no leverage. He was under contract. I just never understood the deal. When they fired me, I said to Bob, 'I'll move on, but I don't understand how you made that fucked-up move. You bring us [Kemp's] $100 million contract with a guy who can't play dead, and I'm the one who gets fired.'"

Dunleavy felt the Jail Blazers label was "harsh."

"But there were some guys on those teams who didn't have the best character. The first time I came in and talked to Bob about the team, I said, 'There are a lot of great athletes, but I'm not sure about the chemistry and character.' I was on a winning team every year I played, and you win with character. Over 82 games, there are a lot of ups and downs. You have to have the right guys in the trenches with you. I told Bob, 'I understand your plight, and I'll do the best I can with these guys, but just don't fall back in love with them.'"

Dunleavy wishes he'd had more time in Portland.

"I loved living there. I loved the people. We had a great run. We had a real shot at winning a title. I would have liked to keep that team together. The same thing happened in Philadelphia when we lost to Portland in the 1977 Finals. They moved some pieces around there, too. I'm like, 'Why not give it another try?'"

* * *

Antonio Harvey is in a unique position to evaluate the Jail Blazers. A reserve forward/center for the Portland teams from 1999–2001, he would go on to serve 11 seasons as the team's radio analyst.

Harvey says the 1999–2000 team that lost to the Lakers in Game 7 of the Western Conference Finals was an extremely tight-knit group.

"We went to dinners together," he says. "We hung out. It was not uncommon to see Scottie Pippen in the same place as Damon Stoudamire and Bonzi Wells and the rest of the group. That helped forge a bond to get us as far as we did. It speaks to how tight a group we were and how much we enjoyed being around each other."

Rod Strickland's addition, Harvey says, caused friction at the point guard position.

"It made guys uneasy," he says. "Damon and Greg had been there almost a whole season. Neither of them knew what their minutes were going to be like. Rod's addition disrupted the chemistry.

"Same thing when they added Detlef Schrempf. No knock on Det, but Stacey was killing it. Then Stacey's minutes go down. You could see the chemistry had been disrupted."

Harvey was toward the end of an eight-year career as an NBA journeyman during his time in Portland.

"They were the best two years of my NBA career, even though I didn't play much. I had hurt my knee the summer after I left Portland. If I had been able to maintain my health, I'd have been a different player after facing guys like Rasheed Wallace and Arvydas Sabonis and Pippen every single day in practice. They were All-Stars, some of them Hall of Famers. When you faced those dudes on a daily basis, it's almost osmosis. I got better being around them. I became a smarter player.

"The two guys on that roster with the highest basketball IQ were Scottie and Rasheed. Watching those guys play defense changed everything I thought I knew about defense at the NBA level. Steve Smith was one of the craftiest players you'll ever see. He'd lost some athleticism, but he could still create opportunities for himself. I went to Europe after that and absolutely killed."

Harvey calls Dunleavy "the smartest X's and O's coach I've seen in my life."

"The only reason I made the team [in 1999–2000] was because, of the guys trying out, I was the only one who could really understand all the plays. That's how thick the playbook was. If you didn't go home at the end of practice and study the playbook, there was a possibility you'd get lost the next day."

Wallace, Harvey says, "was one of the best teammates I ever had."

Were the rash of technical fouls a distraction to his teammates?

"No," Harvey says, applying this logic: "If he'd gotten one every blue moon, it would have been. But he got so many technicals, it became the norm. It got to the point where him not getting a technical was a story."

Harvey doesn't appreciate the Jail Blazers label being applied to his team.

"It's totally unfair. You could use the arrest records from the two seasons before I got there, and the three seasons after I left—OK. But not our seasons."

Even with players such as Wallace, Bonzi Wells, and Shawn Kemp on the roster making news?

"There are 15 guys on the roster, and you named only three guys. If you take 15 US citizens, you'd find the same ratio of trouble. It wasn't the Jail Blazers, it was a few Trail Blazers who got themselves into trouble.

"The trouble some of them got themselves into was so egregious at times, it was on every front page. I'm not defending what they did. Those guys were dumbasses. But the stereotype was wrong, at least during the time I played. Dale Davis, Sabonis, Steve Smith—those guys get lumped in with the Jail Blazers, and it's unfortunate."

Harvey spent seven seasons in the NBA.

"The two [seasons] in Portland were the best of my career. It was a fun group of guys to be around, and it created a home for me beyond the game of basketball."

* * *

Like Maurice Cheeks, Dan Panaggio had never coached in the NBA when he was hired as an assistant coach with the Blazers in 2001. Panaggio had been a head coach in the CBA for nine years, though, winning a pair of championships with the Quad City Thunder. Dan's father, Mauro, was a CBA coaching legend, owning the most victories of anyone in the minor league's history.

Cheeks had spent a year on the bench as an assistant for the junior Panaggio when he won his first CBA title in 1993–94. When Cheeks got the Portland job seven years later, he returned the favor, asking Panaggio to be a member of his staff. He would stay until Cheeks's firing after 3½ seasons.

"I have really good memories of my time in Portland," says Panaggio, who now runs a sports academy in Daytona Beach, Florida. "Maurice and I were close. We went in with great anticipation. There was some really good talent. It was a strange mix of characters, a mixture of young and old."

Panaggio would later spend four years with the Los Angeles Lakers' organization, notably as head coach of the D-League LA D-Fenders.

"Leadership roles with the Lakers were real clear. There were no ifs, ands, or buts about who the leaders were—Dr. [Jerry] Buss, the owner; [coach] Phil Jackson, [GM] Mitch Kupchak, and [players] Kobe Bryant and Derek Fisher. They worked well together. In that organization, everyone fell in line. There was strong leadership all across the board."

It wasn't that way, Panaggio says, with the Blazers.

"In Portland, it was craziness. It was competing agendas. It was volatile players. It was undisciplined lives. You had quite a division between management and the team. It was a tough job from the beginning and, in hindsight, a sure recipe for disaster. It was a great opportunity for Maurice to be a head coach, but one in which his chances for success were slim from the beginning."

The Jail Blazers' era was already about five years in the making when Panaggio came on board. Fans had tired of the behavior, on and off the court, of some of the players. And they were beginning to sour on GM Bob Whitsitt.

"Before we walked into the doors, the franchise was already irreparably damaged with the community. From Day One, fans were clamoring for the good old days, when they could respect the people involved in the franchise. That went from players right up through management.

"We wanted that thing to work. We were doomed from the beginning. We replaced Mike Dunleavy, a really good coach. But he, too, had his hands full."

Panaggio didn't get to know Whitsitt well but felt he had a good read on him as a general manager.

"There's no question he did it wrong. He was thinking, 'I'm the GM. I'll throw together as much talent as I can. Then I'll let the coaches sort it all out.' He didn't carefully craft the pieces. He may not have been capable of that.

"He wasn't a basketball guy at heart. He was a smart guy, but he was an absentee GM. He was living in Seattle, also doing football plus some of Paul Allen's other related businesses. He had his hands full with too many responsibilities. He was a back-and-forth [Seattle to Portland] guy. You can't stomp out all the little things that need to get stomped out and water the things that need to be watered if you're working long distance. You can't do that unless you are there on a daily basis."

Panaggio was not among those who appreciated Rasheed Wallace, at least in the context of him being a veteran and one of the team's most talented players.

"Everybody liked Rasheed. Coaches liked him. Players liked him. But he was high-maintenance.

"Rasheed was never a leader. He would report to training camp and wasn't in condition. He would play his way into shape. When your best players are guys who set a great example and lead, you know you're in good shape as a team. Let's compare that with the guys in San Antonio, Tim Duncan, and David Robinson. That franchise had great leadership from their best players. Rasheed would be the first to admit he wasn't a leader and didn't want to be a leader."

Panaggio did not feel that Wallace was a good role model for Bonzi Wells.

"Bonzi was talented—what a defensive rebounder, scorer, post-up player. But culturally, not good. Too young, too undisciplined. You can have some of those types of guys. The Bulls had Dennis Rodman, but they had such a strong culture around him, they could keep him in check. But in Portland, there was too much of that—way too much."

Wallace and Wells were two players who showed Zach Randolph the ropes during his first three seasons with the Blazers.

"Zach was a likeable guy and a talented player, but he was a kid when he came to us. He needed good, strong people around him until he got to a certain level of maturity. There were growing pains with him."

In late January of 2005, Cheeks and forward Darius Miles had an ugly postgame incident, which resulted in a two-game suspension for the player but also eroding confidence in the coach. Miles had been acquired in a mid-season trade the previous year.

"Maurice was already doomed at that point. He was doomed probably when there was a change in management. They were committed to changing out all of the pieces."

John Nash had replaced Whitsitt as GM before the season.

"Even though John was a Philly guy and wanted to give Maurice a fair shake, a new GM wants to have his own guy." The Miles incident "was probably the straw that broke the camel's back. Maurice's days were numbered. They were going to get rid of him. That was an incident that hastened things.

"Maurice was not the guilty party there. That was Darius Miles losing all professionalism, all self-control. Darius is a guy who never should have been put on our plate. Come on—that's like you're struggling to swim, and I throw you a bowling ball. They were going crazy in Cleveland with him, so it's, 'OK, we'll take him.' You kidding me?"

Little more than a month later, Cheeks and his staff were fired.

"We were all disappointed we couldn't have done better with the whole deal. But overall, crazy as it was, those are good memories for me."

* * *

Elston Turner worked four seasons as an assistant coach with the Blazers, the first under P. J. Carlesimo (1996–97), the last three under Mike Dunleavy (1997–2000). Portland was his first stop as an NBA assistant. He now has 22 years as an assistant in the league, with stops in Houston, Phoenix, Memphis, and Sacramento, where he is currently employed.

Turner broke into the NBA during the final year of Carlesimo's run in Portland.

"P. J. was a teacher," Turner says. "He would challenge guys to make sure they'd perform to the best of their abilities. With some of his challenging, he used to get up into [the players]. That's missing a little bit in coaching today. He was a disciplinarian. He didn't hold back on his comments. He'd pick and choose. It wasn't always that way, but whatever he wanted to say, he'd say it. From where I sat, it went over well. You're either going to perform or sit down. When the practice lights came on and game lights came on, boom, he was ready to make you perform for him. After that, totally different. We must have gone out to eat every night. He loved to eat out. He was fun to be around. Comical. I enjoyed my time with him tremendously. A good human being."

Dunleavy retained Turner when he took over in 1997.

"Mike was a big-time teacher, a little more mild-mannered than P. J. [Carlesimo] had been. Mike was similar in terms of demanding production. When he came to the Blazers, we had a roster built for winning a championship. He got us in the position to bring it home. We were loaded. One of the things that stood out was our practices. It wasn't a clear-cut victory for the first team. They got their butt kicked plenty of times.

"I can't recall chemistry being a problem. We didn't have a bunch of choirboys on that team, no. When they left the arena and went on their personal journey, that was sometimes out of my control. There were some bar fights, an arrest of two. But when the lights came on and it was time to hoop, they could do that. That's what brought them to Portland. They could really play basketball. It was fun to watch and fun to coach. I just wish we hadn't fallen short of bringing a championship to the city."

Turner spent a lot of time with J. R. Rider. Turner played professionally for 14 years, eight of them in the NBA, and had ended his playing career only a year before he joined Carlesimo's staff.

"I was trying to build a relationship with J. R. and let him know we could talk about anything going on, on or off the court. We had our flare-ups. We argued. There were some locker-room skirmishes—not between me and him. Things happen. You chalk most of it up to guys being competitive. Some things don't go their way, and they don't handle it well.

"J. R. was a challenge. He was set in his ways. But he had extraordinary talent. He was strong for his height and position. He could shoot it. He was athletic. And we had a good relationship."

Turner felt the same way about Rasheed Wallace.

"Rasheed was great to work with. I mean great. My coach in Denver was Doug Moe. When the lights came on, he was a yeller and screamer, foaming at the mouth. That was totally different than the way he was away from the court, playing cards, laughing and joking, and going out to eat.

"That was Rasheed to me. My wife [Louise] and I have been to his house at functions. What you saw when the lights came on between him and the referees, that was not him. He's a good dude. The referee stuff, you had to settle him down and reason with him and use some strategy and psychology. You didn't want his outbursts to get the team in a bad way. He had in his mind that a lot of referees had a vendetta against him."

Turner came to Portland during Jermaine O'Neal's rookie year. They would spend four years together, honing the youngster's budding game.

"He was one of my primary projects. A hell of a talent. He was young, but mature basketball-wise. Guys tried to welcome him to the league in his rookie year. He stood up to it pretty good. They were trying to intimidate it, and he wouldn't have it.

"Unfortunately for him, he had veterans in front of him in Portland. He had to wait his turn. I had conversations with him. With the Lakers, Kobe Bryant [who was in O'Neal's draft class] got extensive minutes his second year and became a starter his third year. Jermaine spent a few years sitting and watching but learning in practice because he had to go against Rasheed and Brian Grant and Arvydas Sabonis. He was honing his skills. It wasn't easy for him, either. He wanted to play. He finally got the chance when he went to Indianapolis and became [a six-time] All-Star. I was happy for him."

* * *

Walt Williams was included in the trade that brought Damon Stoudamire to Portland in 1998. Williams spent a season and a half with the Blazers, mostly as a reserve small forward with 3-point shooting range. He was in the middle of an 11-year NBA career in which he averaged 11.8 points and shot .379 from beyond the arc.

"It was a great time," says Williams, now working as a financial advisor in Brookeville, Maryland. "We won a lot of games. We were a pretty close team, on and off the court. The Rose Garden was the loudest arena I ever played in. It was deafening in there when things were going good."

Williams had been a starter through most of his career when he arrived in Portland to a team featuring Rasheed Wallace at small forward and J. R. Rider and Stacey Augmon at shooting guard.

"We were stacked, but I knew I would play consistent minutes," Williams says. "We could go three-deep at every position and get a bona fide, legitimate guy you could argue was a starter on any other team. I understood the situation I was in. I just tried to maximize what I could do and try to help the team win. I knew I was around a host of talent on both ends of the court.

"Nobody was satisfied with sitting on the bench. Everybody wanted to play 30-plus minutes. In a normal situation, there would have been some unrest, some friction about playing time. But we all understood that we were very talented, and each of us had to maximize time when we got out there."

Williams felt a camaraderie with the players.

"Those guys were like my brothers. Most of us were in the middle range of our careers. We had a genuine enthusiasm for each other, a kinship. We worked hard and competed in practice.

"We would do things off the court. It was six, seven, eight guys hanging out together on a consistent basis. We'd go play paintball and other activities. We had a real brotherhood going on. That was lost in translation with all the other things that went on with that team. But we had a love for each other. It carried out on the court."

Williams says Mike Dunleavy was "a passive coach."

"He wasn't real boisterous. We had an aggressive team. We could have benefitted from a more disciplined environment, but he did a good job of managing playing time and getting everybody an opportunity. He was fair in that respect. But his personality was in contrast to the players."

Williams had a strong respect for Rider.

"J. R. was a dog out there, a beast. He was fearless, a guy who you knew was a terror to other teams. I could do many things, but the thing I was known for was shooting the 3 and spacing the floor. Most nights, J. R. was going to get doubled. I used to salivate over the opportunity to get an open shot playing alongside him. It was amazing to play with a guy like him. He reminded me of my neighborhood friends, guys I grew up with."

Williams learned to accept Rider's frequent transgressions.

"We all knew J. R. Sometimes he would be late. Because of that, coach [Dunleavy] wouldn't want to show preferential treatment, so he'd get suspended. It was just the way J. R. went about his business. But when he stepped on the court, he did his thing on a consistent basis. He was also a very genuine person, had a good spirit about him. He wasn't a bad person at all."

Williams also had an appreciation for Wallace.

"Being his teammate, you got an opportunity to see one of the greatest to play the game. I think his career was underrated. You have to have a little selfishness about you to take it to the highest level. Rasheed wasn't like that. He would pass the ball on a consistent basis. It was great as a teammate because he was so unselfish.

"He was a bona fide scorer on the block and one of the best 3-point shooters on the team. He could guard wings or on the post. He could play one-on-one. He was cerebral at the game—a very intelligent man. So, it wasn't all about arguing with the referees with him. He talked to us a lot as teammates, talking about situations, about making sure everybody was in the right place on the court. He was a fantastic teammate and a guy with a great spirit about him."

As far as the technical fouls and the wars with the referees . . .

"Even in practice, he talked a lot. We were used to that. The bad thing is that techs give up points. You tried to calm him down in that instance. But we were used to it. We didn't let things like that bother it. We just went out and played the game."

Williams says the Jail Blazers label was "unfair."

"You resent things like that. Coming from the neighborhoods we came from, [the player transgressions] were nothing. So we laughed that off. We didn't let that bother us at all."

Williams was sent to Houston as part of the six-for-one trade that brought Scottie Pippen to the Blazers in 1999. Williams wishes GM Bob Whitsitt would have kept the group together.

"The trades they made that year and in the next couple of years, even though they brought in some fantastic talent, they got older. The window of opportunity shrunk. The squad we had together had a good mixture of three- to eight-year range.

"I wish we'd had time to jell together and build something. I always think about that. I wish we'd have been together longer. We didn't have an opportunity to get familiar with each other's games. We didn't get it done, but I felt like I was on a championship-caliber team. Had we stayed together for a few more years, we'd have shown that."

* * *

Mike Rice earned legendary status while serving 26 years as the Trail Blazers' television analyst. Everybody's favorite eccentric uncle made viewers laugh but also to reflect on his wisdom after a decade as a Division I head coach at Duquesne and Youngstown State.

"You didn't know what to expect from day to day," Rice says of the Jail Blazer era. "Bob Whitsitt and Mark Warkentien always said chemistry didn't matter. I agree that you want the best players, but somewhere along the line, you have to blend it all together."

The Blazers made the playoffs through most of those seasons.

"It was exciting to watch them even in practice," Rice says. "The 1999 and 2000 teams were capable of winning an NBA championship. But it was just as exciting to see what they would do off the court."

For a while, Rice says, "it really didn't matter what the players did off the court, because they won.

"It got pretty chaotic, and they had to try to fix it. They had plenty of talent; they just didn't have enough leadership. You had Brian Grant and Steve Smith and Steve Kerr and Scottie Pippen. But it seemed they had way too many Sheeds and Bonzis, guys who could really play but, oh, the antics.

"You just never knew what would happen with J. R. Rider. He'd be great in a playoff game, and you'd go, 'Wow.' But you'd wonder how he could play like that when he's enjoying life as much as he does off the court. You had Cliff Robinson and Bonzi Wells, guys who could take over a game one night, but only half their body shows up the next game."

Rice empathized with such as P. J. Carlesimo, Mike Dunleavy, Maurice Cheeks, and Nate McMillan.

"After seeing what the coaches went through to try to control the players, I would never want to go through that. I don't care how strong you are mentally, some of those groups just wore you down."

Rice recalls the plane rides that flight attendant Stephanie Smith-Leckness worked in the late '90s and early 2000s.

"The late '90s teams had too many guys living life to the fullest. If you went on the back of the plane, if you inhaled too much . . . I won't go any further. I never saw anybody [smoke pot or use drugs], but they were a wild group. Rider was the one you had to watch the most. Some guys had more than just winning basketball games on their mind."

Rice would often be asleep late at night on the plane when he would awaken to the sound of a movie playing on the big screen of "B-1." It wouldn't be the *Sound of Music* playing.

"You were never sure who put on what movie, but sometimes it was pretty racy. Finally, the flight attendants would go in and get them to change it."

Rice was also privy to the high-stakes card games on the flights.

"When Scottie came to the team, the games got really interesting. There were stacks of money on the table. You never knew how much, but I know there were a lot of $100 bills. It got to the point where later, they started putting chips on the table, and finally they cut out the card playing altogether.

"Some of the games would get real heated—probably real close to a fight. Sometimes we'd be de-planing and getting ready to board a bus, and you'd have to wait because somebody was losing a lot of money and he didn't want the game to end."

Rice has interesting takes on the Blazers' head coaches, and some of their stars, among them:

- P. J. Carlesimo: "A funny guy. He was great about getting everyone together and going to restaurants and having a good time as a team. He knew basketball, but when he first came in from Seton Hall, he didn't understand the difference between a college and pro player. It took him a long time to understand the difference in how you had to deal with guys in college and guys in the NBA. I think that hurt him in Portland."
- Mike Dunleavy: "He was kind of a con man. Maybe he had to be, with the group of players he worked with. He tried to stay one step ahead of them. He knew what he was doing, but he never knew if things were going to explode because it was so hard to bring those players together. He had some good winning years, and that solves a lot of problems. When you start losing, they show you the door."
- Maurice Cheeks: "Maurice wasn't interested in coaching as much

as Carlesimo or Dunleavy. He understood the game, though. He knew the players hated to practice. As a coach, he probably hated to practice, too. He thought if you got a couple of stars, he'd make sure they got the shots. He didn't concentrate enough on what the team could do differently each night to win a game. If the opponents had more talent, he wasn't going to win that night. Really, he acted like one of the players. The rules were too lax. It was like, do what you do, but don't get caught, and show up for the games."

- J. R. Rider: "He was a coach's nightmare, the typical star who had way too much talent for how he behaved. He was so talented, he could do anything, and they'd let him get away with it."
- Rasheed Wallace: "Sheed was into winning. He was an emotional guy who had talent. He was a team guy more than you'd think. He was an easy guy to get to know and like. He'd call you by name. A lot of guys, like LaMarcus Aldridge, didn't even know what you did for the team after six or seven years. Sheed would kid with you. He had a lot of freedom, and he got away with a lot of stuff. He was a lot like [Golden State's] Draymond Green, who gets so emotional with referees. They both needed more control."

Rice chuckles at how the Jail Blazers would have fared into today's wired world.

"Those teams could never exist with today's social media. It would be the most fun in the history of sports to see what would happen, with the way social media is. It would be the greatest thing ever. It would just be wild."

* * *

Dale Davis was in the maelstrom of the Jail Blazers era, a dirty-work center from 2000–2004. Davis, who was 31 when he came to Portland, arrived in the trade that sent Jermaine O'Neal to Indiana. An All-Star with the Pacers the season before he arrived, he was a useful player for the Blazers, starting for the first 3½ of his four seasons.

But it would be a poor trade for Portland; O'Neal would go on to become a six-time All-Star for the Pacers and one of the best-ever players in Indiana franchise history.

"The thing I remember most was the camaraderie of the players and the excitement of the fans in Portland," says Davis, who now works in sports management in Atlanta. "During my time, we had a couple of good teams, a couple of great teams. We had some of the best basketball players and minds. It's unfortunate we didn't win a championship."

Davis felt confident the Blazers would win the title in 2001 before the late-season additions of Detlef Schrempf and Rod Strickland.

"They were great players. Normally, you would love to bring those guys on board. But it threw our chemistry off. "

Was there too much talent, then?

"That could be a part of it. But I felt guys made sacrifices based on the situation. It just didn't blossom at the right time. There was a lot of off-the-court stuff that went on. But we were talented enough and still competing at a high level. One break here or there, and it could have gone the other way. We could be talking about an NBA championship today."

Davis played for Mike Dunleavy his first season in Portland, then for Maurice Cheeks his final three years.

"I liked Mike. He did a good job. He was pretty fair. He tried to make sure everybody got their minutes. He did a pretty good job managing the overall situation.

"Cheeks was a straight players' coach. Knowledgeable. He did a good job teaching the younger players. He let us play within our capabilities. He was a relationships guy. Maybe it was because he had been a point guard. It worked out pretty well but, sometimes, the clock runs out. We didn't get to where we thought we'd be."

Davis lays the Blazers' issues in part to "immaturity."

"To a degree, we were victims of circumstance. But everybody has to be accountable. We all make mistakes. We made some. But we stayed together no matter what it was. We had each other's backs."

* * *

Herb Brown is the older brother of Hall of Fame coach Larry Brown, five years Larry's senior. Herb, who had a half-season as head coach of the Detroit Pistons, spent more than five decades coaching at nearly every level. He was an NBA assistant for 16 years with eight organizations, including two seasons (2001–2003) in Portland.

Cheeks and Brown came into a Portland roster flush with veteran talent.

"Trader Bob felt if you had great ability, it was the answer, rather than great chemistry," Brown says. "When I coached the Pistons, we had 10 or 12 guys who could all play. They were all at each other's throats. It wasn't that they didn't like each other, but they were jealous of each other's contracts and minutes. I played them all off each other and got away with it, but it was really difficult."

Brown, who has chosen to make Portland his home after retirement, says the off-court issues of the Jail Blazers years did not fit Portland.

"Come on," he says. "That's the wrong city. This city takes pride in its players. We had our problem guys, for sure. But we had character on those teams, like Steve Kerr and Chris Dudley. Scottie Pippen was great. Arvydas Sabonis was great. Dale Davis was salt of the earth. We had some great kids, too."

Brown is a Rasheed Wallace fan. Herb was an assistant coach on brother Larry's staff in Detroit in 2003–04 when the Pistons acquired Wallace at mid-season. Wallace's contribution helped them win the NBA championship.

"I'd go to war with Rasheed any day of the year. He was a great defender, a team defender. It wasn't important to him to be the high scorer or best rebounder. He really wanted to win. After we traded for him in Detroit, the culture changed. He gave us an edge.

"I'm not condoning, by any stretch of the imagination, Rasheed getting technicals. He's a proud guy. He wants everything to be done right. He felt the officials should do it a certain way. Whether he was right or wrong, it doesn't make him right to behave like that. I never addressed the technicals with him. I was told to leave him alone. During the summers, I wanted to work with Rasheed. I was told no."

Brown says Pippen told him Wallace was a "victim" because of the way the team handled his relationship with officials.

"Nobody sat him down and said he has to do it this way, because the chemistry wasn't important to them. What was important was winning games. If Rasheed gets technicals, it's the organization's responsibility to take care of the problem. Rasheed is a very bright person.

"One time at practice, I told him something, and he threw the ball from one end to the other. I said, 'You're recalcitrant.' He said, 'What does that mean?' I said, 'Look it up.' The next day, he came in and said, 'Coach, I'm not stubborn.'

"You have to hold the players accountable. If they don't do what you want them to do, you have to do something, whether it means sitting them down or whatever. It was done to a degree in Portland, but I don't know that it was done enough."

Wallace could be stubborn. He liked to do things his way. Once, former *Oregonian* sportswriter Wayne Thompson—a fellow North Carolina Tar Heel—was writing a piece about ex-UNC coach Dean Smith. Wallace refused comment, and Thompson figured that was that.

"The next day, Rasheed brought a written statement, a couple of pages, on what he thought about Dean Smith and gave it to Wayne," says Brown, a close friend of Thompson.

Brown offers excellent perspective on Cheeks.

"Mo was in his first two years as a head coach. That's kind of tough, dealing with those kinds of teams. Mo was a very good game coach. He understood what was going on in the game and he could see it two or three plays ahead of time. I've sat with a lot of guys on the bench over the years. He knew what was going on in the game.

"He was not a very good practice coach. He never expected to be a head coach, so he hadn't spent a lot of time preparing for that. Maybe if I'd been with him longer, I'd have seen more involvement or interest in practice but, when I was there, it wasn't there. Mo would get there at 10 or 10:30 for an 11 a.m. practice. I don't think his thing was practice. He was such a great player and was on a team with great players that maybe he didn't value practice as much as he should have."

Did Cheeks get too close to the players?

"He still had a little player in him. After practice, he'd get into shooting games with them. But those groups handled it well. We could coach them in practice and talk to them in film sessions and meetings, and they were terrific."

In 2002–03, before a game at Seattle, the Blazers bussed to owner Paul Allen's mansion in Bellevue, Washington, to practice on his personal court. The next night, after a 92–77 win over the Sonics, Ruben Patterson caught an attitude in the locker room.

"He said some shit, and I went right at him," Brown says. "I'd been coaching for a lot of years. I had plenty of international experience and in the minor leagues as a head coach. There were certain things I'd tolerate and certain things I wouldn't. I think I shocked him and everybody else.

"We did not need Ruben Patterson. He was good but not a great player. He thought he was a better player than he really was."

Brown felt Pippen was the team's on-court leader.

"Scottie's skills were diminishing, and I'm not sure he realized it. It bothered him that he couldn't do some things he did before, but he was not a destructive force by any means. He worked his butt off in practice. He tried to do everything the coaches wanted. He was a true pro. He was a great teammate. Scottie and Kerr were terrific."

Brown wishes the Blazers could have gone further but is proud of the success they had during his two seasons.

"We won 99 games. Good for Mo. There aren't many coaches who win almost 100 games in their first two seasons. We had talent, but not the chemistry that was necessary to make a title run."

* * *

Eddie Doucette worked as a broadcaster for the Blazers from 1992–1999, serving as the play-by-play man on the television side for five of those seven seasons. Before coming to Portland, Doucette had been the original voice of the Milwaukee Bucks, working there for 16 years, including during their championship season in 1970–71. In 2013, he was honored as recipient of the Curt Gowdy Media Award at the Naismith Basketball Hall of Fame ceremony.

During his seven years in Portland, the Blazers made the playoffs every year.

"But honestly, I was very disappointed," says Doucette, now retired and living in San Diego. "I felt when I was hired, there was a chance to win a championship. Otherwise, I might not have ventured there.

"But I loved my time there. I loved the people, the community. I enjoyed the Northwest. I've always had a special fondness for my time in Portland, other than the way things ended for me with Bob Whitsitt and [Blazers executive vice president] Harry Hutt. It was an altogether different experience at the end than in the beginning."

Doucette arrived the year after the Blazers, led by Clyde Drexler, had reached the NBA Finals for the second time in three seasons. When general manager Geoff Petrie and coach Rick Adelman left after the 1993–94 season, Whitsitt succeeded Petrie running the basketball side of the organization.

"I was enamored of Bob when he came in. He had some good ideas. I thought he was going to do a good job. But he had a dictatorial demeanor about him."

Doucette questions whether Whitsitt made the right moves in many of his player acquisitions.

"People in the league will say you never have enough talent, but you need to understand what your needs are before you make a deal," Doucette says today. "Then go out and get the right pieces, like what San Antonio has done for years. Some of the pieces Whitsitt brought in were contrary to that and, while they were talents, they didn't fit."

In 1996, Whitsitt brought on J. R. Rider and Rasheed Wallace.

"J. R. was a kid with a whole lot of natural ability, but you never knew who was going to show up from night to night. I always made sure I'd get to the game early to watch the guys warm up, to see what kind of mood they were in, where their heads were. With him, you could tell going through the warmup lines. If he came by and he made some comment, you could tell he was up for the game. If he was running around with his lips on the floor, you knew you weren't going to get much out of him that night.

"There were nights he could put a team on his shoulders. He was like an unharnessed bulldog. He had all the game you could want a guy to have. I could see why a GM felt like he could take that 100 pounds of clay and reshape it. But I can also see when that clay would fall apart. That's not the kind of person you want on your team when you're trying to build cohesiveness."

Doucette felt much the same way about Wallace.

"I got the feeling he was an angry young man. He did things as a player that were terrific. He made himself into a good talent in the league. I didn't think he was a real fun guy to be around. The things he did were sometimes disrespectful to the game, to his team."

Doucette says the player he most enjoyed watching during his time in Portland was Arvydas Sabonis.

"I saw most of the great ones," says Doucette, who called Kareem Abdul-Jabbar's games in Milwaukee. "Arvydas was one of the top five big men I ever saw play the game. If he'd been healthy when he got to Portland, he'd have been in the top three. Aside from Bill Walton, he was the best-passing big man I ever saw."

Whitsitt brought in Hutt, who would become the team's executive VP/ marketing operations and oversee the broadcasting department.

"They didn't want you to say anything bad on air about the players they brought in," which didn't sit well with Doucette or his broadcasting partner, Steve "Snapper" Jones.

During Doucette's last season, 1998–99, the Blazers lost a playoff game at Utah.

"Snapper was a guy who would say whatever he wanted to say and be objective as possible. He was very professional. I wasn't going to sugarcoat anything, either. The game was televised by TNT, as well by our broadcast going back to Oregon.

"I got a call the next morning from Harry, purportedly delivering a message from Whitsitt. He said, 'What are you doing? You're all over me. They didn't say those kind of things on TNT.' He was reading me the riot act. They took offense to anything that would shed a negative light on things they had done to try to make the team better.

"I guess in some ways I can understand that—we were paid employees of the club—but as broadcasters, we have to be somewhat objective. Your local viewers don't want to hear a lot of negative things about their team. But if things are bad and you're saying it's good, your credibility is on the line, too."

Doucette was already unhappy with the way things were going on the job.

"That was like the last straw. After we lost [in the Western Conference Finals] to San Antonio, I'd made up my mind I was going to quit. I sat down in the hotel and wrote a letter. I put it in my briefcase. They wanted a mouthpiece. That wasn't going to be me."

When he returned to Portland, Doucette set up a meeting with Hutt. He waited eight hours outside Hutt's office.

"Then his assistant came out and said, 'You'll have to come back in the morning.'" I came in for four hours the next morning, and he still didn't have time for me. I never had my meeting. That was the beginning of the end for me. I've never been around a guy who treated people so poorly. He was disrespectful and demeaning."

Doucette, who resigned after that season, believes the Jail Blazers' label was warranted.

"I don't know who came up with that term, but I think it was pretty appropriate. That said, I would never want that to besmirch the reputation of the franchise and the people in that community. Working in Portland was truly one of the high spots of my career."

* * *

There are those who believe Brian Grant was the best free-agent signee in Trail Blazer history. He didn't come cheap. Bob Whitsitt signed the 6-foot-9,

250-pound power forward to a seven-year, $63-million contract in 1997, though he would opt out of that deal three years later.

Grant had averaged only 10.5 points and 5.9 rebounds while playing 24 games following knee surgery the previous season in Sacramento. But he was 25, tough-minded, and physical, with his best basketball ahead of him. He would have three productive seasons with the Blazers, winning the 1998 J. Walter Kennedy Citizenship Award and becoming one of the most popular players in club history.

Grant joined a personnel group that featured J. R. Rider, Rasheed Wallace, Arvydas Sabonis, Gary Trent, and rookie Jermaine O'Neal. Damon Stoudamire would come on at midseason during his first year.

"We had really solid talent," Grant says. "Everybody was carefree, and I don't mean that in a bad way. I like when people are themselves. They don't do things to impress somebody. That's the way it was with our group."

Grant started his first season with the team at power forward, Wallace swinging to small forward.

"It was a little awkward at first. We were both natural fours. We'd battled against each other the year before. We had a mutual respect. I knew I couldn't play the 3, and it gave him a shot to show his outside game. He could also take you inside. He could run. He was long, had that turnaround jumper, and was a great defender. Unselfish. He was out there to win. We were always in it for each other."

Grant never understood why Wallace had such a thing for the referees.

"A ref makes one bad call, [Wallace] is going to ride you the whole night," Grant says today. "You're just waiting for the next one. It was like he was thinking, 'I can't wait for somebody to foul me and they don't call it. I'm going to go get on the ref.' From time to time, I'd go over and say, 'C'mon Sheed, we need you, calm down.' He'd say, 'Cheater.'"

Grant played his first two seasons in Portland with Rider.

"I loved J. R. because he was such a competitor. I'd look at him and think, 'Man, you could be so much more than what you are.' So much talent. So ready to go. When he brought it, he was really good. When he did, it was like, 'I can't believe he just did that.'

"But he had his problems. Everybody was waiting for him to break out of it and realize it's a short window as a professional athlete. When you're done, you're done. That's what happened to him. He fell back on the idea, 'I'm too good to be kicked out. There's always somebody who will take me.' Well, there's always somebody ready to take over for you. That's the way it really is. There's no reason why he shouldn't have been a perennial All-Star, and our team would have been much better."

Shortly after he signed with Portland, Grant started hearing "Jail Blazers" for the first time.

"I knew there were individuals on the team with problems. A lot happened to me, too; just nobody put me out there. I never felt embarrassed about it at all."

Once in Atlanta, Todd Shaw—a rapper who went by "Too Short"—approached Grant before a game.

"My heart is always going to be in Oakland," Shaw told Grant, "but y'all's my team."

"What do you mean?" Grant asked.

"We don't want the clean type of teams. We want the rebels. That's how most black America is looking at it."

Were the Blazers black America's team then?

"According to Too Short," Grant says with a smile.

Grant played with Wells during the swing man's first two years in the league.

"Bonzi was a young fella but a damn good player. His shot was a knuckleball, but it was deadly at times. We had John Crotty on the team. He was one of those old-school veterans who went hard. You were going to earn it with him. Bonzi didn't like that. They ended up getting into it one day. I told Bonzi, 'Hey man, grow up. You don't have to do it with fists. Do your thing on the court, not here.' The next day, Bonzi crushed him in practice."

Grant enjoyed playing for Mike Dunleavy.

"He doesn't get his due credit. You don't know what he was dealing with. Forget all the craziness off the court. Just having one through 12 who could be starting somewhere . . . Jermaine O'Neal never got off the bench.

"Dunleavy was a dude who, when you put it down for him, he trusted you. He was going to go with you no matter what. With all the personalities we had, it was hard for him to juggle that. But don't test him because he will bite you. I saw him on a couple of occasions when dudes were in his face, and he said, 'Let's go.'"

During the strike-shortened 1999 season, Grant averaged 11.5 points and 9.8 rebounds as Portland's starting power forward. The Blazers would beat Utah in the Western Conference Semifinals, then get swept by San Antonio in the Conference Finals.

"Winning the Utah series was probably the worst thing that could have happened to us. We exhaled, and it was like, 'We got this.' We were playing damn good ball going into the Conference Finals. We should have won Game 1 against the Spurs. Then Sean Elliott hit the miracle in Game 2. If we win that first game, that lights something in us. We'd have needed three more wins to get to the Finals."

After the season, Grant had microfracture surgery.

"Recovery is supposed to take nine months. I got back in 5½ months, but I wasn't the same player that next season."

Grant went to a bench role, backing up Wallace and Sabonis at the four and five spots on the Portland team that blew a 15-point lead late in the third quarter and lost to the Lakers in Game 7 of the Conference Finals.

"Even through that fourth quarter, I still thought we were going to pull it out. All of a sudden, we couldn't hit anything. There were some foul calls missed. That sounds like sour grapes now, but there were some questionable calls.

"We should have won that game. It shouldn't have come down to the last minutes. Once they started coming back, we started playing not to lose instead of playing to win. It's the No. 1 biggest disappointment in my career."

After the 1999–2000 season, Grant wound up in a three-way deal with Miami and Cleveland, going to the Heat while signing a near-max seven-year, $86-million contract.

"I visited New York. They rolled out the red carpet. My agent [Mark Bartelstein] called Whitsitt and said, 'Brian wants to go to New York.' He said, 'Nope, not doing that deal.' Then I'm in Ohio on my way to visit Miami, and Mark tells me that Jim Paxson [the Cleveland GM] wants to fly in and talk to me and [my wife] Gina in Cincinnati. He flew in and said, 'We'll give a max contract. I've always liked you.' Gina said, 'Let's take the deal.' I said, 'Oh man, I don't know if I can live here.' All my family was in Ohio. It would have been hard. Then at first, I didn't think I could play for Pat Riley [in Miami]. But I was really impressed during our meeting. He said, 'We have the $2.5 exception for a year, but we can talk after that.' I couldn't go back to Portland by then.

"Whitsitt came back with an offer, but I had made my decision to go to Miami. The next day, people were saying I was stupid to turn down the $91 million in Cleveland to take the $2.5 million in Miami. I couldn't sign for 30 days. Riley called and said, 'You sure you don't want to stay in Portland?' I said, 'I gave you my word.' The next day, he said, 'Call Mark. I think you'll like what I did.' I called Mark, and he said, 'Riley worked an almost impossible trade, and it went through. You're going to get your contract.' He wanted to reward me."

Grant remembers his flight back to Portland after news broke of his trade. He was stopped by dozens of disappointed Blazer fans.

"It took an hour to get through the airport from the gate to baggage claim. This little old lady was crying and said, 'You're such a positive role model for my grandson.' It was emotional."

Grant made a connection to the community by being a part of it. He was a regular visitor to Doernbecher Children's Hospital. He would choose to make Portland his home after retirement.

"I always tried to do the right thing. That don't mean I always did. There was so much love, it was like, 'Wait a minute, I'm human, too.' I tried to keep myself out of trouble. I liked being grounded. Going to Doernbecher grounded the heck out of me. It also let me feel like when I was going through things, it was nothing like what those families were going through."

* * *

Mark Warkentien was Bob Whitsitt's trusted second-in-command, beginning with three years working for him as a scout in Seattle from 1991–1994. Warkentien had been an assistant coach at Nevada-Las Vegas from 1980–1991, on the bench when Jerry Tarkanian coached the Runnin' Rebels to the 1989–90 NCAA title and then to a 34–1 record and the Final Four the following year. When Whitsitt came to Portland in 1994, he took Warkentien with him and served as Portland's director of scouting from 1994–1997. When assistant GM Jim Paxson left Cleveland, Warkentien took over the title and held both positions from 1997–2003. He would stay on one more year after Whitsitt's firing, working as director of scouting under John Nash in 2003–04 before moving on to work with Paxson in Cleveland.

"I had a great relationship with Bob," says Warkentien, who lives in Portland but has been director of pro player personnel for the Knicks since 2011. "He was an outstanding general manager. We went to the playoffs every year we were in Portland. Not once in a while—every year. We won 50 games a year. We went to the playoffs for a decade. We had record attendance. We made two trips to the Conference Finals.

"One thing that is lost is, the championship window had closed when Bob took over. We got under the salary cap, built up the roster, and became a contender again. We went back into a championship window without visiting the lottery. Try to think of other teams that have done that. The Celtics [had to rebuild]. They went to the lottery. The Lakers went to the lottery. Usually, you have to be bad before getting good again."

Warkentien was the chief architect of the draft for the Blazers, a shrewd talent evaluator who orchestrated picks of Jermaine O'Neal [No. 17 in 1996] and Zach Randolph [No. 19 in 2001], and a trade that landed rookie Bonzi Wells for the No. 27 pick in the 1999 draft.

"Zach and Jermaine both became All-Stars and max-contract players with non-lottery assets," Warkentien says. "Trading [No. 27] for Bonzi—that's pretty good."

During Warkentien's time in Portland, the Blazers were coached by P. J. Carlesimo, Mike Dunleavy, and Maurice Cheeks.

- On Carlesimo: "P. J. is the best guy ever. If I were running a cancer society fundraiser, I'd want him to be my spokesperson."
- On Dunleavy: "Coach of the Year [in 1998–99]. He was a good coach."
- On Cheeks: "Mo might be the best person on the planet. He was really good for some of our guys. He was tremendous for [the development of] Travis Outlaw. It might not have been a great fit with a veteran team."

All three coaches were eventually fired, as happens with most.

"Coaching changes are not referendums on whether the guy is a good coach or not. I look at it like Major League Baseball. You take [Dodgers pitcher] Clayton Kershaw out of the game and make a pitching change. Does that mean that Kershaw can't pitch? He's a great pitcher. Situations change.

"One of the thoughts on Mo at that time, we needed Rasheed Wallace to become that great player. Who can do that? Mo was a Philly guy. Rasheed grew up idolizing Mo. Maybe Mo can get to him. We liked Mo. He wasn't in it for the paycheck. With a lot of coaches, it's about how much they can make. They're 401K guys. Mo's first job was as an assistant in the CBA. He was a guy who needed to be in the gym. We were hopeful he could get Sheed to the next level."

Was he able to do that?

"No, although he helped Sheed. He left here and became a champion in Detroit. He put a ring on [the Pistons'] fingers. I really like him. Doting father, fabulous teammate, good defensive player. They got mad at him because he didn't post up, which I thought was an interesting thing. If Sheed were from Paris rather than Philadelphia, they'd be saying, 'Rasheed is so skilled.' Because he was an American player, he should be dunking all the time. I thought he was unfairly critiqued. He was an All-Star. For us, he was a net-positive."

Why did the Blazers not get to the NBA Finals, or win a title, during the Whitsitt/Warkentien era?

"I'll give you two answers—Kobe and Shaq. We almost got them [in 1999–2000], though they weren't quite Kobe and Shaq yet.[3]

"The problem was we didn't have a truly great all-time player. Who has won a title without one? Closest would be the 2004 Detroit team, with Sheed, Ben Wallace, Richard Hamilton, and Chauncey Billups. Our teams were strength in numbers. We didn't have a guy who was a top-50 all-time player or a generational player. The Lakers had two. Great beats good."

Did the Blazers have too much talent through those years?

"I don't like the question. I hear all the theories. The worst one is the law of not enough guys."

Is that fair?

"No. Our teams had winning records on the road all of those years. You can't win on the road without character. Citizenship and character are two different things."[4]

Then what about citizenship?

"What about it?"

Was it a problem with that group?

"I never had to get anybody out of jail. The Jail Blazers? I don't remember a trip to jail. It was a cute phrase because it rhymed with 'Trail.'"

How did Warkentien feel about J. R. Rider?

"I don't remember him missing a lot of practices. We went to the conference finals with him, didn't we? I liked him."

Bonzi Wells?

"He was a net-positive. I'm a big [New England Patriots head coach] Bill Belichick guy. You are what your record says you are. We were 50 wins a year, making the playoffs every year. No one ever attended Blazer games

---

3   The Lakers won the Western Conference title four of five times from 1999–2004. The Spurs beat the Blazers in the 1999 Conference Finals.

4   Portland road records during Warkentien's time: 18–23 in 1994–95 and 1995–96, 20–21 in 1996–97 and 1997–98, 13–12 in 1999, 29–12 in 1999–2000, 22–19 in 2000–01, 19–22 in 2001–02, 23–18 in 2002–03, and 16–25 in 2003–04.

more than they did during that period. We just couldn't get through Kobe and Shaq."[5]

Was deportment an issue with the players through the Whitsitt era?

"Obviously. You want everybody to be an All-NBA Player and a Boy Scout, but that isn't what you get."

Warkentien has always had an affinity for Randolph, even after the Marion, Indiana, native was linked with Qyntel Woods to illegally fighting their pit bulls, leading to Woods's departure from the team in 2004.

"Dogfighting in Portland," Warkentien says, "is a bigger deal here than it is in Marion, Indiana."

* * *

The Trail Blazers, led by Rasheed Wallace, waged war with officials through most of the Bob Whitsitt era. Three referees during that period conducted interviews for this book—two who asked for anonymity, and Joey Crawford, who now works as an evaluator of officials in the NBA office.

Crawford refereed in the NBA from 1977 until his retirement after the 2015–16 season, tying Dick Bavetta for the longest tenure in league history—39 years. With what mindset did he go into a game during the Jail Blazers era?

"It was just like any other team," Crawford says. "With the other referees in your morning meeting and before the game, you talk about who the players are and what you're going to be dealing with that night. [The Blazers] were aggressive guys. As a ref, you know what you're presented with. There are no secrets.

"When you do your homework as an NBA referee, you know the personalities of the players. If somebody's coming at you every call, you try to defuse it. You try to get the coaches to do it. If they don't, depending on the

---

5   The Blazers had strong attendance figures through much of the Whitsitt era, but it began to dip in 2001–02, when Portland's home attendance averaged an announced 19,044, with 12 sellouts in 41 games. It continued a downward trend for several years after that.

personality of that ref that night, he might take care of it. Some refs are more aggressive than others."

Crawford was more aggressive than most. He handled players with a stern hand but understood that players weren't going to accept every call.

"You call a foul on a guy, he's not going to clap for you. There's going to be some pushback. Some guys give you more pushback than others. Some of the players on those Portland teams were aggressive, and then you had to figure things out. My motto was, 'If we're going to do this thing tonight, let's set the tone early. Don't wait until the last two minutes. If you can quell the situations early, you do it.'"

Did he have any particular problems with any Portland players of that era?

"Yes. They were more aggressive than most other teams. And to be perfectly frank, a lot of that could be the coach. Sometimes the coach doesn't accept the responsibility of controlling the players—like 'knock it off, we don't need you to get a T, we don't want you to get you ejected.' In that case, in essence, it was up to the refs to do it."

Wallace is No. 3 on the NBA's career technicals list. Crawford called his share on him. How did he feel about "Mr. T"?

"You're not going to believe this. He was one of my all-time favorite guys, I guess because we were both Philly guys. I get asked all the time about Rasheed. With him, you knew what you were going to get. As soon as you called a foul and he didn't think he did something, it was very easy. You just took care of it.

"And to be honest, he respected you when you had strength. He was one of the smartest players I ever reffed. The only guy smarter than him was Kareem Abdul-Jabbar. They knew the different facets of the game. They knew them inside and out. A lot of times, Rasheed wasn't wrong. You might have screwed up a play. He just took it a little farther than most guys did. If you're going to be a good ref, you have to understand when you make mistakes. Rasheed was correct some nights, but that doesn't allow him to take it as far as he did sometimes."

Wallace received a seven-game suspension for an incident with referee

Tim Donaghy in 2003. Donaghy later served a 15-month prison term for betting on games in which he officiated.

"I wish Rasheed would have beat him up," Crawford says. "It wasn't the fact he disrespected my profession. I'm talking about Donaghy being what he was. It may not make sense to your readers, but it makes sense to all of us [referees]. What Donaghy did was against everything a ref ever stood for. I wish Rasheed would have beat the hell out of him."

Do players who complain a lot get a break from officials, because they can't call technicals on everything? Can they wear a referee down?

"That's a fallacy. A lot of coaches and players believe it. But, in reality, you just deal with it. One of the great refs, Joe Gushue, told me, 'If the guy is screwing up your concentration, just get rid of him. Eject him. Get him out of the game.' I took that approach. A lot of times, I was very frank with players, saying, 'Listen, you're getting me off what I do, so leave me alone.' If a player didn't, I'd hit him with a tech. If he didn't stop at that point, I'd toss him.

"It wasn't carte blanche. You do that, you're going to be criticized. You're going to get a phone call from your employer, asking, 'Could you have handled that a little differently, Joe?' At the end of my career, I was better with it. I don't know if it was age or maturity or seeking guidance from outside sources. I was more patient at the end of my career than I was at the beginning."

Near the end of his tenure in the league, Crawford regularly met with a sports psychologist, Joel Fish.

"I still call the guy. I'm proud I went to him."

Crawford has an anecdote involving the Blazers he offers to share.

"It was a playoff game [in 2003]. Mo Cheeks was coaching. Bonzi Wells was averaging about 15 points a game. Usually, when a player gets his second foul in the first six minutes, he goes to the bench. I called this horrible second foul on Bonzi. I had lost my concentration. That wasn't me. I always prided myself on that. But I lost it, and I was standing in front of Mo.

"He says 'Joe, he's averaging 15 points a game, and you just put him on the bench.' I stopped, and I said, 'I apologize, Mo. I lost my concentration.'

To this day, I tell that story at every clinic I go to. I tell the referees, 'There are ramifications to every one of your whistles, and you must keep your concentration up for every minute you're out there.' That was my 'aha' moment. I thought, 'God almighty, what did I do?' I put this kid to the bench.

"You never want to do anything to put a team in a bad situation. It impacted my officiating the rest of my career. I remember that like it was yesterday. It impacted the hell out of me. I always said to myself, 'No wonder Mo Cheeks hates my guts.'"

Two other officials, both retired, had somewhat different views.

"When you worked a Portland game during those years, you knew you had to be good," one says. "That's the best way I can put it. You had to be really good that night. If you didn't, they would come at you hard. You had to be prepared when you went out there. They made you mentally tough. When you worked other games, a lot of times it was like a night off. With them, you couldn't afford to have an off night and open it up for negative dialogues on their part."

Wallace was a special case.

"Some nights, Rasheed was fine, like any other player," the referee says. "Other nights, you could call nine plays in his favor, and you'd miss one or one he thought you were wrong on, and all hell would break loose. At those times, he was just unreasonable with referees."

Was there anybody like that ever in the league?

"Not that I can think of," he says. "Draymond Green is different. He settles down quicker. Allen Iverson got a lot of technicals, but he was different. It happened less frequently with him. Dennis Rodman was different. He upset opponents more than referees. He wasn't that hard to referee. He got a lot of T's, but he was a good guy on the floor with us."

The second official came into a Portland game with a different mindset than with other teams, especially for a game at the Rose Garden.

"Going to the arena was much more on your mind, working with that environment," the referee says. "You dealt with it if you had to. There were some nasty fans. They were just brutal. There was this lady who used to sit on the free-throw line. She was so into her tan, and she was young. She was wild and profane. One night I turned around and said, 'Hey Leatherface, what is your problem? What are you so pissed off all the time about?' After that, she hated me even more."

Even on the road, a Portland game was a handful.

"I call those games 'the root canal zone,'" the referee says. "You know you have to go to the dentist. You know it's going to suck, but you have to do it. You have no choice. Get it over as soon as possible. And that's what it was like. Do it with as little damage as possible and get on to the next game. I've never seen a team where, so many times, one through five were fucking nuts."

The second referee disagrees with Crawford in terms of cumulative effect of complaints to the officials.

"Sometimes, they do wear you down. It's like at some point they get sort of a free pass. The guy has gotten himself a little more room. And now there's the rule where they're suspended for a game with the 16th technical [of the season]. That builds a certain pressure. If a player nears that threshold, you better make sure it's right on, that it's justifiable with the league office."

Wallace, of course, was a special case.

"Rasheed was nasty to referees. There was no dealing with him. He was so unreasonable. He was belligerent from the get-go. Usually, it was just yelling at you. If you answered a question that he asked, he just yelled at you more. You were told you were fucking wrong and that was fucking BS."

The season after Wallace set the NBA single-season record with 41 technicals (2000–01), commissioner David Stern asked referees to have a "gentler approach."

"The very first game in the preseason, I have Portland at Sacramento," the referee says. "Rasheed starts right in the first quarter. Halfway through the third quarter, during a free throw, he's ragging on me. The whole arena is quiet, and I'm at the end of my rope. I lose it and say, 'You motherfucker, shut your mouth.' I saw Mike Dunleavy's face drop. I knew I was in trouble. I got fined for unprofessional behavior.

"It just seemed like Mike had trouble controlling that team. And if a coach can't control his team, no one else will do it."

* * *

If asked to name the only former Trail Blazer ever to run for governor and you guessed Billy Ray Bates, you missed it by a mile. It's Chris Dudley, who as the Republican candidate was beaten by John Kitzhaber—he lost by about 5,000 votes—in the 2010 Oregon election.

Dudley served two terms with the Blazers, from 1993–1997 and again from 2001–2003. He joined the team as the Jail Blazer era was beginning and left it when ownership and management were ready to turn the corner to a new time in the franchise's history.

Dudley lasted 16 seasons in the NBA as a hard-nosed rebounder and defender, and one of the worst free-throw shooters in league history (career percentage .458). When the Yale graduate arrived in Portland at age 28 in 1993, Geoff Petrie was general manager and Rick Adelman was head coach. Dudley played for Adelman and P. J. Carlesimo during his first stint and for Maurice Cheeks during his second stint.

"I played with great guys on both sides," says Dudley, now a financial analyst living in San Diego. "There were also a cast of characters, but I enjoyed my time with those guys. And I loved the Portland community. I met my wife [Chris] there. I got married there. Everybody from the team came to my wedding. It was a real family environment. That's what you remember more than the wins and losses."

Bob Whitsitt was the GM through most of Dudley's time in Portland.

"Whitsitt was very smart, and he knew how to get talent," Dudley says. "Sometimes with the great players, you have to figure out the chemistry, too. That does matter."

Dudley is uncomfortable with the Jail Blazers tag.

"It was unfair as a whole. I never felt like I fell into that category, but I felt bad for the team. It was a tough time for the organization. I felt bad for the people who spent years building that sense of community and connection with the team.

"There was so much goodwill built up when I first came in, starting with people like Harry Glickman and Geoff and Rick. There were some years thereafter that where it felt like that tie to the community frayed. That was the bummer of it. I felt like some bad incidents were magnified, but stuff did happen. The way management handled it was sometimes not the right course of action. It frayed that relationship between the fans and the team, which took the team a while to recover. That was real unfortunate."

Dudley enjoyed playing for both Carlesimo and Cheeks.

"P. J. was a great guy and a good basketball mind. It was his first crack at the NBA, and maybe he wasn't fully prepared, but we won a lot of games on his watch.

"I think highly of Maurice. He was a players' coach. His main deal was to come in and clean up the environment after what had happened during the 2000–01 season, when the team imploded down the stretch of the regular season. They brought in [Detlef Schrempf and Rod Strickland] late in the season, and it messed up the chemistry. You could feel the team's psyche had been damaged with what happened in losing that series with LA. Maurice was relaxed. He brought back joy to the game. He gave guys confidence. It was a looser team. It worked for us."

Dudley's favorite teammates in Portland included Steve Kerr and Scottie Pippen.

"We had responsible veterans during that period. I'd sit in the back of the plane and have great conversations with Z-Bo [Zach Randolph] and Steve, the three of us just hanging out. It was the right tone and mix on that team. I heard after I left it got more relaxed, and it didn't work as well. You need to have responsible players. You need to have grownups.

"I really enjoyed Scottie, both on and off the court. [My wife] Chris and I became friends with him and his family. I'd go golfing with him and his brother in the offseason. He was just a good guy and a great teammate. He was all about winning. I was at the end of my career, and his was, too. He was not physically the same, but he was still a dominant player on the floor. He still could lock people up with his defense and make a difference."

If there was a frustration for Dudley during his time in Portland, it was in not being able to reach Rasheed Wallace.

"Rasheed was a great teammate. He had everybody's back. It was frustrating in that everybody would tell him he couldn't let the refs get to him, which got worse as he went through his time in Portland.

"His downfall, if you want to call it that, is that he really wanted to be one of the guys. He didn't want to be the superstar, the No. 1 guy. He wanted to be just one of the guys who helped win a championship. He was unselfish almost to a fault. And he sometimes had a chip on his shoulder. You just wanted to say, 'You can't let that stuff throw you off your game.'"

* * *

Coach P. J. Carlesimo labeled him "The Kid," or "T.K.," and it stuck, at least during his Portland years. Jermaine O'Neal, who spent his first four seasons with the Blazers, would go on to a sensational 18-year career in which he was a six-time All-Star.

O'Neal, now retired and a businessman and entrepreneur living in Dallas, looks back at his four years in Portland with fondness. He met his wife and the mother of his two children, the former Lamesha Roper, in the City of Roses.

"I wasn't fully prepared as a 17-year-old teenager from Columbia, South Carolina, coming to a wonderful city," he says. "I had no idea what it was to be a professional, to be an athlete at the highest level. I look at that as two different parts—the professional part of it, and then the athletic part of it. I was more ready for the athletic part, but not totally ready for that, either, at least at first.

"My four years there were very memorable. The city of Portland was perfect. It was the best place for me out of high school. Not to mention an organization that was fully prepared and ready for a 17-year-old kid who had all the things available. I had good leadership from my teammates, people to help me with transition, people to understand what kind of a change it was in my life."

In Portland, O'Neal learned there was a whole new world out there.

"I saw a different culture. Everything was so much more open. I saw interracial dating for the first time. I didn't understand that until I got to Portland. I was able to grow. It was a different type of life out there for me. Those great people out there in Portland, they're phenomenal. It was a perfect scenario for a kid who wasn't mentally or physically ready for that challenge. I had the talent, but you don't know about that until you get into the fire. I was with a great group of people, teammates, organization, and community."

O'Neal never regretted coming straight to the NBA out of high school.

"I was able to learn my craft. Not very many players get the opportunity I got, to have so many different teammates. I got to play with some iconic names. There was no college in America that could have helped get me ready for the NBA than the Portland Trail Blazers and all my teammates. I know there's a perception about guys like Rasheed Wallace, Gary Trent, J. R. Rider, Cliff Robinson, but those guys helped me understand what pro basketball was about.

"I couldn't have been in a better place to get me ready for life. At that age, you're teaching a young kid how to be a man. It was the best—between my experience with the community and the fans—how they chanted for me and rooted for me every single night, to Mr. [Paul] Allen and his mom being super supportive of me, to just the city in general."

O'Neal never became a starter in Portland, playing behind the likes of Robinson, Wallace, Brian Grant, and Arvydas Sabonis at the center and power forward spots.

"No university in the country would have prepared me like going against those guys every day in practice. It was pretty incredible. The only thing that was a negative was, at least the last two years, I was ready to play, and I don't think Coach Dunleavy was ready for me to play. He was going to go with the veterans. I understand it now but, at the time, I didn't like it."

The coach for O'Neal's rookie year was Carlesimo.

"P. J. was a very aggressive coach. He was what I thought coaches would be. I knew he had to be from a major city [New York] because he cursed all the time. I think he believed in me. He knew I needed some work, to get stronger, understand the game. But he and [assistant coach] Rick Carlisle always communicated with me. It was a great situation for me, coming out of high school with that kind of coach."

Dunleavy was O'Neal's coach during his final three seasons with the Blazers.

"I think he was pressured to win now. When you have a young kid and the pressure of veteran players and the organization around you, sometimes the kid doesn't fit into that scenario. I felt ready to contribute the first two years, but by the third and fourth years, I knew I was ready. I could never break into the lineup. I was disappointed about that."

O'Neal learned from role models, both good and bad, during his time with the Blazers.

"I learned a lot of the business side from Kenny Anderson. I learned basketball and handling business from guys like Rasheed, Brian, Greg Anthony, Scottie Pippen, and Steve Smith. I was able to take all the good stuff they were giving me and put it into a system that worked for me. And then I was able to watch some of the bad things that I was able to push aside. I knew that was the area I didn't want to go to. I was prepared for Indiana based on what I learned through four years in Portland, and I'm grateful for that."

O'Neal felt a kinship with J. R. Rider based on similar backgrounds.

"J. R. was different, but he was still a good dude. A lot of professional athletes come from backgrounds where we are missing things. We don't have the traditional storybook upbringing. We don't have the supporting cast other people have. Sometimes you have to figure it out on your own. That can be a very stressful thing.

"With J. R., his reaction to things was never basketball-related. As a kid who struggled with not meeting my dad until I was 30, I could relate. We carry a different type of burden. Sometimes we don't handle it well. J. R. was one of the most gifted athletes I played with, but he couldn't put it together completely, and it ended up costing him his career."

During his second year in Portland, the Blazers brought on O'Neal's high school coach, George Glymph, to serve as a mentor and help him with the process of becoming a professional.

"George Glymph helped save my life. The environment I was raised in, not having a father, not even knowing him—Coach Glymph became my father. He helped me understand how to make it in life. You can put him in that group of people who had huge impacts on my life."

O'Neal counts Wallace as one of them, too.

"Rasheed is one of the most misunderstood people I've come across. I dressed across from Sheed every day for four years. He was a family-driven guy. Talk to him away from sports, you wouldn't know that's the same guy getting all those technicals on the court. We've all made decisions we weren't proud of. When you're in the pro basketball limelight, everything is magnified by the thousands. On the court, he was an out-of-control person. Off the court, he was everything but that."

O'Neal will always be grateful for the way the veterans showed him the ropes when he came in as a young rookie.

"I was initiated into the club. I couldn't do very much with them, because I was underage—way underage. Those guys would bring video games and sit in the room and play them and take me out to dinner. That's pretty impactful. It would have been easy for them to say, 'Look, I'm going to go out and do my thing.' They always made sure I had something to do. For a 17-year-old kid given millions of dollars out of high school, they were acting like big brothers. They were protective of me and made sure I had somebody to talk to."

Does O'Neal ever think what could have happened if he'd stayed with the Blazers through your career?

"I do think about that. 'What ifs' keep you wondering. I'm more of a reality person. We don't know how that thing would have turned out. I would have been happy to stay in Portland my entire career. It could have meant great things. But what it did was position me to have a great run in Indiana. I took what I learned my days in Portland and transitioned seamlessly to Indiana."

* * *

Steve Patterson arrived in Portland in 2003 to clean up the mess left by his predecessor as the Blazers' president and general manager, Bob Whitsitt. Patterson had NBA experience on the basketball side (GM of the Houston Rockets) but was being asked to focus on taking care of the financial side in Portland.

"We had at that point the second-highest payroll and the second-highest luxury tax payment in the league," Patterson says today. "They hadn't made the playoffs and had lost north of $100 million the year before. There were a lot of people who were justifiably unhappy with what was going on off the floor with the players."

Patterson had been on the job two months when the Blazers and the affiliate Oregon Arena Corporation laid off about one-third of the club's employees—more than 100 in all. The office staff would be cut from 293 to under 200. Erin Hubert would take the bullet for the moves, but Patterson was the one blamed by the public and media for the layoffs.

"The evaluation plan had been in place for six or eight months before I got there," says Patterson, now president of the NHL Phoenix Coyotes. "It finally got to the point where you have to execute on it. A handful of Paul Allen's companies had been shut down, from the high-definition truck to Charter Cable to the WNBA team to pursuit of an NHL team."

A month after the pare-down, the Blazers announced reduced season ticket prices and a 25-point mission statement that would include a player code of conduct as part of any contract offered by the club.

"It came about by working with the entirety of the staff. It identified those issues that needed to be worked on and corrected. That's what we focused on. That's what we fixed. Those things don't happen overnight, particularly when you have to move as many contracts as we did. Paul was clear that was the commitment he wanted to make at that time, and [the Blazers] have stuck with that to this day."

To the public, it seemed as if one of the earliest missions for Patterson and his general manager, John Nash, was to make trading Rasheed Wallace and Bonzi Wells a priority. Both were gone before the end of the first season of the Patterson/Nash regime.

"I wouldn't say that," Patterson says now. "In fairness to those guys, everybody matures at a different rate. The guy who appears difficult or who makes mistakes when he's 21 can be a pretty charming individual by the time he is 30, 40, 50. At the same time, we all do knuckleheaded stuff when we're 21.

"Rasheed was great in Detroit after leaving our team. But to try to put him in the role of a leader of a team that was going to get younger, that's not a role he wanted. He had the talent, but Portland wasn't going to be the right place for a guy who was older. He wanted to play on a team that was winning, and he didn't want to be the guy, a mentor. That's not who he was. And in the right environment, he flourished.

"Bonzi was never able to capitalize on his skills or maximize his potential. When guys don't succeed, that's sad, because you work hard to get to a place and you're trying to take advantage of the gifts you have.

"Fans, and to a certain extent the media, can afford that luxury of just cleaning house. If you're trying to operate a franchise where you have to be responsible for those decisions, that's a very different role to be in. You must maximize your assets. It's a delicate balance."

Patterson resigned in March 2007.

"My contract was about to expire. I met with Paul and told him, 'If you want me to work here, great. If not, let me know. I'll go do something else.' At that time, he said he wanted to make a change. I said, 'OK, let's make a change.'"

* * *

Dan Dickau was the third Portland-area native to wear Trail Blazer togs, following Steve "Snapper" Jones (1975–76) and Damon Stoudamire (1998–2005). Dickau was born in Portland and lived in the Vancouver, Washington, area, across the Columbia River, after second grade.

"I grew up understanding what it meant to be a Portland Trail Blazers fan," says Dickau, who now lives in Spokane, Washington. "I'd get a pair of Blazer tickets as a Christmas present every year. I understood more than anybody—except Damon—how important the Blazers were to the area."

Dickau, a guard who had been among the first of a line of outstanding

Portland-area guards to thrive at Gonzaga, managed to carve out a six-year NBA career, including an excellent 2004–05 campaign with New Orleans in which he averaged 13.2 points in 67 games. Mostly, though, he was a low-end reserve who put in two stints with the Blazers—for 20 games in 2004 and for 50 games during the 2006–07 season at the end of the Jail Blazers era.

Dickau was part of the trade that sent Rasheed Wallace to Atlanta in 2004.

"To be traded to Portland was a dream come true," Dickau says today. "It was eye-opening as well. Things were going sideways there, and some guys were making some off-court noise that fans weren't appreciating. The crowds weren't as rabid as I had remembered as a kid. You still had your diehards, but I could sense they had lost some of the support, because the Portland fans expect better than what they were getting."

When Dickau arrived in 2004, the Blazers had a decent amount of talent, including Zach Randolph, Derek Anderson, Damon Stoudamire, Ruben Patterson, and Dale Davis.

"And Shareef [Abdur-Rahim] and Theo [Ratliff] came over with me from Atlanta. Theo didn't do much in Atlanta because he wasn't healthy and fully engaged. But in Portland, he was a completely different player and became the most exciting player Portland had seen for a while. He was blocking shots and dunking off lobs. We had a talented team, but it took a little too long a time to gel and mesh."

Dickau had a good relationship with Maurice Cheeks.

"I liked Coach Cheeks. He was a very nice guy and had a really good staff. Jimmy Lynam, with all his experience, was phenomenal. He was a big help to me, talking the game. John Loyer was an unbelievable coach and was willing to spend time in the gym with me."

Cheeks never settled on a backup point guard behind Stoudamire, giving opportunities at times to Dickau, Omar Cook, and Eddie Gill.

"He never chose one of us. I'd play two games, play real well, and then I wouldn't play for three games. Then I'd get another shot, play five games and not play for the next two. It was a difficult stretch, knowing I had put my best foot forward, wanting it to work out more than anybody in that entire locker room."

Steve Blake is the only Trail Blazer to serve three stints as a player with the club. Dickau is the only person to put in two stints as a player and a third as a coach—during the 2008–09 season, the year after he retired as a player at age 29.

"It was an unbelievable chance for a kid from the area to fulfill a dream. But nobody understands just how different that dream can be when you get there. I was appreciative and loved every second of it, but did I want it to turn out differently? Of course."

Paul Knauls didn't play a second, but he was synonymous with Trail Blazers basketball through the years.

Knauls, who operated a nightclub and a beauty salon in Northeast Portland for many years, held season tickets beginning with the inaugural 1970–71 season until the late '90s, during the height of the Jail Blazers' reign.

"I kept going to games during that era, but my wife wouldn't go," says Knauls, now 87 and still working at the salon, Geneva's. "She said, 'They have to behave better.' She hated all the off-the-court stuff. She stopped going for five or six years. Wouldn't even go to the playoff games. She said, 'They ain't going to take my money.' But it was still her money, because I was going."

When Knauls would travel, he would introduce himself to people as "Paul Knauls from Portland, Oregon."

"The reaction would usually be the same. They would say, 'Ah, Jail Blazers.' It was a sad time for Portland fans, the ones who were hard-core like I was."

---

* * *

Jon Spoelstra worked for 12 seasons in the Trail Blazers' front office from 1979–1990, first as VP/marketing and then as senior VP/general manager for three years, focusing on the business side.

Spoelstra, father of Miami Heat head coach Erik Spoelstra, also spent five years in management with the New Jersey Nets, served as president/CEO of Mandalay Baseball Properties, and he has owned seven minor league baseball teams. He has kept a residence in Portland all through the years and looks askance at the Jail Blazers era.

"It was terrible," he says. "I traveled a lot at that time. It became where I was embarrassed to say I came from Portland. What is unique about Portland—and it's true to this day—is the fans here consider the players an extension of their family. This isn't true in other markets. Here in this nice community, we were bringing in quasi-criminals. That was a mistake by the Blazers."

Spoelstra was not a fan of the general manager during that era, Bob Whitsitt.

"He specialized in picking the low-hanging fruit. A lot of those guys he brought in were really good players, but easily acquired because of their [poor] reputation and attitude. He brought in some quality guys, too—Steve Smith, Detlef Schrempf. You can get away with a problem guy, if it's one guy per team. Dennis Rodman wasn't a sweetheart in Chicago, but Michael [Jordan] and Scottie [Pippen] kept him under control. But if you have seven Dennis Rodmans, you're in trouble."

For a while, fans put up with Wallace's on-court antics and those of his teammates off the court.

"Winning can mask a lot of things. When they lost to the Lakers [in the 2000 Western Conference Finals], that was the turning point. Who knows what happens if they win that series and go on to win a world championship? Then you'd be writing a book about the victors."

After Paul Allen purchased the Trail Blazers in 1988, Spoelstra worked there for two years before moving to New Jersey.

"Paul let the Portland market down. When I was there, there was some disagreement in the philosophy of the organization. [Former director player of personnel] Stu Inman considered character as a skill. He looked at players with their talent, but also put character in there as an important attribute. In the 1980s, we had a lot of high-character guys, guys you really enjoyed being with. You could hold a conversation with them on a lot of different subjects. I didn't know any of the Jail Blazers personally, but I'm just not sure that is the case with a lot of them."

ACKNOWLEDGMENTS

When Jason Katzman of Skyhorse Publishing in New York City reached out about the possibility of working together on a book about the Jail Blazers, my immediate thought was "I don't think so."

After all, that era of Trail Blazers basketball—from the mid-1990s to the mid-2000s—isn't what most Blazer faithful would choose as the happiest period in franchise history.

In pitching the idea, Mr. Katzman offered a national perspective—the collection of extraordinary personalities and the successes and failures, both individual and team-wide, make it an important story to tell—that I hadn't fully digested during those years.

It didn't take me long to come around that the project was a worthwhile one, one that needed to be told, and one in which I wanted to take part.

Over a period of nearly a year, I dug through the archives and reacquainted myself with the goings-on during the Bob Whitsitt era, when P. J. Carlesimo, Mike Dunleavy, and Maurice Cheeks served as head coaches. And during the much shorter Steve Patterson/John Nash era, in which Cheeks and Nate McMillan ran the club and owner Paul Allen did what he could to make good with the Portland community for what had gone wrong in years previous.

I conducted interviews with about seventy coaches, players, executives, broadcasters, club employees, and referees. Also with a flight attendant on the Blazers' team plane during that period and a Portland police officer who worked the crime beat through those years. As well as with John Lucas, who runs a rehab center in Houston and has worked with several of the Blazers throughout the years.

I interviewed all of the head coaches, most of the assistant coaches, and twenty-seven players, some of whom played for opposing teams during that period. Their quotes are sprinkled throughout the book, as the story is told in chronological order from the early 1990s to the late 2000s. Others were gathered as a "reflections" package in the final chapter.

I was unable to interview several subjects I felt worthy, including owner Paul Allen, who, through a public relations representative, turned down the opportunity to contribute to the book. Bob Whitsitt, Rasheed Wallace, and J. R. Rider did not return phone calls. Among others who declined interview requests were Scottie Pippen, Bonzi Wells, and Steve Smith.

Damon Stoudamire—whom I've known since his sophomore year in high school, when he helped Wilson to the Oregon 3A state championship in 1989—returned my call, and we spoke for 15 minutes. He respectfully told me he wasn't going to speak on the record for the book, because he and a few former players, including Wallace and Wells, were putting together a documentary film. "We want to put it in our own words," said Stoudamire, who said he had been working on the project for "more than a year."

Damon, unfortunately, holds some resentment toward the city in which he grew up. He feels the "Jail Blazers" got a bum deal and suffered from an unfair reputation during their time in Portland. It's something I'm not sure he'll ever get past, which is a shame.

"I'll always be a Northeast Portland kid," Stoudamire, now head coach at the University of the Pacific, told me. "That's not going to change. But I'm on the outside looking in now."

I received valuable input from the sources who were willing to speak for the book. And I was able to piece together a fairly comprehensive picture of what went on with the Blazers during those crazy years of winning basketball and perpetual naughtiness.

I have many people to thank, beginning with the book's editor, Jason Katzman, whose patience through our journey together cannot be understated. His knowledge of the subject—for a New Yorker, at that—was both useful and appreciated.

Thanks to the coaches who spoke to me for the book: Head coaches P. J. Carlesimo, Mike Dunleavy, Maurice Cheeks, and Nate McMillan. Assistant coaches Herb Brown, Tony Brown, Johnny Davis, Jim Eyen, John Loyer, John Lucas, Neal Meyer, Dan Panaggio, and Elston Turner. And especially to head coaches Mike D'Antoni of Houston (a former Blazer assistant), Steve Kerr of Golden State (an ex-Blazer player), and Scotty Brooks of Washington, who all made time for me in their hectic schedules during the latter stages of the 2017–18 regular season.

Thanks to the players: Shareef Abdur-Rahim, Derek Anderson, Kenny Anderson, Rick Brunson, Jamal Crawford, Dale Davis, Dan Dickau, Clyde Drexler, Chris Dudley, Sean Elliott, Brian Grant, Antonio Harvey, Hersey Hawkins, Joe Kleine, Jermaine O'Neal, Will Perdue, Zach Randolph, Theo Ratliff, Cliff Robinson, Rod Strickland, Gary Trent, Nick Van Exel, Buck Williams, and Walt Williams.

Thanks to the executives: Harry Glickman, Erin Hubert, John Nash, Steve Patterson, Jim Paxson, Jon Spoelstra, and Mark Warkentien. And team employees Mark Cashman, Jay Jensen, and Bobby Medina. And broadcasters Mike Barrett, Bob Costas, Eddie Doucette, Jerry Reynolds, Mike Rice, and Peter Vecsey. Thanks, also, to referee Joey Crawford, police officer Pete Simpson, and flight attendant Stephanie Smith-Leckness. As well as fans Harvey Platt and Paul Knauls.

Thanks to Chuck Charnquist, PR director emeritus for the Trail Blazers, for providing information on Game 7 of the 2000 Western Conference Finals, which changed the course of the franchise.

Thanks to Steve Brandon, my sports editor for the *Portland Tribune*, for understanding I had two jobs for a 12-month period. And to former

ACKNOWLEDGMENTS

colleague Dwight Jaynes, for taking a thorough once-over look at the manuscript before submission.

And special thanks to photographers Steve DiPaola and Tom Treick, who provided the visual evidence that the Jail Blazers era really did exist.

—Kerry Eggers

INDEX